The Twentieth Century
READINGS IN GLOBAL HISTORY

The Twentieth Century

READINGS IN GLOBAL HISTORY

WALTER MOSS

JANICE TERRY

JIU-HWA UPSHUR

•

Eastern Michigan University

McGraw-Hill
College

Boston   Burr Ridge, IL   Dubuque, IA   Madison, WI
New York   San Francisco   St. Louis
Bangkok   Bogotá   Caracas   Lisbon   London   Madrid   Mexico City
Milan   New Delhi   Seoul   Singapore   Sydney   Taipei   Toronto

McGraw-Hill College

A Division of The **McGraw·Hill** Companies

THE TWENTIETH CENTURY: READINGS IN GLOBAL HISTORY

This book is printed on acid-free paper.

2 3 4 5 6 7 8 9 0 DOC/DOC 9 3 2 1 0 9

ISBN 0-07-289324-9

Vice president and editorial director: *Thalia Dorwick*
Editorial director: *Jane E. Vaicunas*
Senior sponsoring editor: *Lyn Uhl*
Developmental editor: *Donata Dettbarn*
Senior marketing manager: *Suzanne Daghlian*
Project manager: *Mary Lee Harms*
Production supervisor: *Laura Fuller*
Coordinator of freelance design: *Michelle D. Whitaker*
Senior photo research coordinator: *Carrie K. Burger*
Compositor: *Carlisle Communications, Ltd.*
Typeface: *10/12 Times Roman*
Printer: *R. R. Donnelley & Sons Company/Crawfordsville, IN*

Freelance cover designer: *Kristyn A. Kalnes*
Cover image: © *Steve Edson/Photonica*

Library of Congress Cataloging-in-Publication Data

Moss, Walter.
    The twentieth century : readings in global history / Walter Moss,
Janice Terry, Jiu-Hwa Upshur. — 1st ed.
        p.   cm.
    ISBN 0-07-289324-9
    1. History, Modern—20th century.   I.   Terry, Janice J.
II.   Upshur, Jiu-Hwa Lo, 1937- .   III.   Title.
D421.M63   1999
909.82—dc21   98-41745
                                                        CIP

www.mhhe.com

ABOUT
THE AUTHORS

Walter Moss is Professor of History at Eastern Michigan University, where he has taught history since 1970. He attended Xavier University in Cincinnati and received his Ph.D. from Georgetown University. He is the author of *A History of Russia,* 2 vols. (McGraw-Hill, 1997). He also coauthored *Growing Old* and edited *Humanistic Perspectives on Aging.* He has written numerous book reviews and several articles on Russian history, literature, and philosophy and has traveled on many occasions to Russia, the former Soviet Union, and other parts of Europe.

Janice Terry is Professor of History at Eastern Michigan University. She received her Ph.D. in modern Middle East history from the School of Oriental and African Studies, University of London. She is the author of many publications in anthologies and journals and of *The Wafd, 1919–1952: Cornerstone of Egyptian Political Power* and *Mistaken Identity: Arab Stereotypes in Popular Writing.* She is also a coeditor and contributor to a forthcoming book on the Arab-Israeli conflict: *1967 War after Three Decades.* Dr. Terry has lived and traveled extensively throughout the Middle East and Africa. She is a coauthor of another college textbook, *World History.*

Jiu-Hwa Upshur is Professor of History at Eastern Michigan University. She received her B.A. from the University of Sydney and her Ph.D. in Chinese history from the University of Michigan, where she was a Rackham Prize Fellow. She is the author of articles and book reviews on Chinese history and two catalogs on Chinese art. She is coauthor of a college textbook, *World History,* and coeditor of *Lives and Times: Readings in World History.* She chairs the World History Committee of the College Board.

Walter Moss, Janice Terry, and Jiu-Hwa Upshur, along with Richard Goff, also coauthored *The Twentieth Century: A Brief Global History,* 5th ed. (McGraw-Hill, 1998).

TABLE OF CONTENTS

PREFACE

This book of readings (*TCRGH*) is intended to supplement the primary text for a course on twentieth century **global** history. Its organization makes it especially useful as a supplement to Richard Goff, et al., *The Twentieth Century: A Brief Global History,* 5th ed. (McGraw-Hill College, 1998), which the three of us coauthored. However, we selected readings that would also fit well with other twentieth century texts, allowing instructors to tailor *TCRGH* to their own needs. The readings should prove especially helpful to those instructors wishing to encourage their students to analyze and discuss historical materials. A discussion question appears at the end of each chapter for this purpose, but instructors may wish to create their own questions to guide their students' reading.

In choosing selections, we were guided by several principles. We wanted readable, primary sources dealing with the most important topics of twentieth century history—for example, scientific/technological developments, nationalism and self-determination, imperialism, decolonialization, militarism and warfare, feminism, the Cold War, communism, fascism, modernization, globalization, consumerism, Third World concerns, and cultural conflict. We also wanted to include readings dealing with social life as well as politics, reflecting the fact that history is about ordinary people as well as leaders. Thus, many selections are autobiographical and deal with a wide range of people from different occupations and from different parts of the world. Even experienced instructors have not seen many of the readings before. Several on China, for example, have been translated into English for the first time.

To aid students, each reading (or occasionally several shorter selections grouped together) is prefaced by an introduction that provides context and basic facts. The readings are divided into 21 chapters, and each chapter provides an overview of the topic or topics illustrated by the selections. Finally, the book is divided into three chronological periods, with an introduction to each period.

ACKNOWLEDGMENTS

We are grateful for the support provided by the staff of McGraw-Hill Higher Education, particularly our editors Leslye Jackson and Lyn Uhl, their assistants Amy Mack and Donata Dettbarn, and project manager Mary Lee Harms. We would also like to thank the reviewers of the original manuscript for their helpful suggestions. These include: Lynda S. Bell, University of California, Riverside; Louis Haas, Duquesne University; Laird M. Easton, California State University–Chico; Eric Dorn Brose, Drexel University; John Livingston, University of Denver; Robert Patch, University of California, Riverside; and Marla Stone, Occidental College.

We are also indebted to the following colleagues at Eastern Michigan University for their suggestions and assistance: George Cassar, Robert Citino, Richard Goff, and Michael Homel. Gersham Nelson provided both suggestions and administrative support. As with most of our projects, we are once again grateful to Nancy Snyder and her secretarial staff, especially Gayle Wuttke, who provided extra support as a student assistant on the project, and Kiersten King.

Walter Moss

Janice Terry

Jiu-Hwa Upshur

The Twentieth Century

READINGS IN GLOBAL HISTORY

PART ONE

The Era of Western Domination

Nationalism, imperialism, militarism, and industrialism were some major movements at the beginning of the twentieth century. They remained strong trends as the century drew to a close. These and other themes, including the quest for women's emancipation, social justice, and economic betterment will be discussed through original writings of men and women from all parts of the world and walks of life throughout the three parts of this book.

The modern nation state—an area whose people share customs, history, identity, loyalty, and frequently language—first developed in Europe. By the late nineteenth century, nationalism had also become a pervading sentiment in two highly successful emerging powers outside Europe, the United States and Japan. The twentieth century would see the spread of nationalism globally, where it remains an important force.

Nationalistic competition among European states extended to overseas enterprises and contributed to the growth of imperialism. Because of Europe's superiority in the sciences and technology, European states plus the United States and Japan dominated the world at the turn of the twentieth century. There were other factors besides nationalistic pride that motivated the successful states to conquer overseas empires. One is economic, to obtain raw materials and markets. Another is strategic, to secure geographically important locations and to deny them to one's rivals. Reading 3.2, the British conquest of the Sudan, is an example of strategic imperialism, to secure the source of the Nile River for British-controlled Egypt and to deny possession of the Sudan to France, Great Britain's imperial rival in Africa. Feelings of racial, cultural, or national superiority also contributed to imperialism. It is reflected in Japan's quest to denationalize Koreans and turn them into docile Japanese subjects (Reading 3.1A).

The resistance to foreign domination and the development of nationalistic feelings among threatened or dominated national groups is evident in several readings throughout this book. In Reading 2.3, we see the leaders of the newly organized government in Meiji Japan adopting conscription for its military and mandating patriotic education in schools, because they realized that a military modelled on Western lines and modern schools would be keys to Japan's emergence as a powerful modern state. Japan alone among non-Western states successfully overcame conservative traditions and became a powerful modern state.

In both Readings 3.1 and 3.2, we see examples of the emergence of strong nationalistic feelings among the dominated peoples. This is demonstrated in Reading 3.2A by a Korean woman, Louise Yim, who describes how teenage students in an American missionary-run school in Korea showed defiance to Japanese rule by secretly learning about their country's history, a subject banned by the Japanese colonial masters. Yim's story also demonstrates the role of Western schools in fostering nationalism in the colonized lands. Readings in Parts 2 and 3 will show that many nationalist heroes of the twentieth century, including M. K. Gandhi, Jawaharlal Nehru, Sun Yat-sen, Ho Chi Minh, Julius Nyerere, and the Chinese students of the May 4th Movement were all products of modern Western schools.

The foundation of Western power at the turn of the twentieth century was its scientific and technological superiority. This is because the scientific and industrial revolutions had begun in Great Britain and then had spread to other parts of Europe and the United States. Only Japan outside the Western world had succeeded in mastering Western sciences and technology by the beginning of the twentieth century. Thus, Japan alone among Asian countries emerged as a modern imperialist power.

Reading 1.1, from a biography of aviation pioneers Wilbur and Orville Wright, indicates the spirit of experimentation and adventure that contributed to scientific and technological progress. While these advances brought many blessings to humanity, progress always took a toll on people and environment. Leo Tolstoy, a Russian aristocrat, great writer, and philosopher, was a forerunner among twentieth-century critics of what many considered progress: the ecological harm technological advances often produced, the haphazard urbanization that would spread across the world, and the moral effects of an ever-expanding production and consumption of new products (see Reading 1.3). Mohandas Gandhi was a Tolstoy disciple; he, too, opposed industrialization. (Some of Gandhi's ideas are explored in Part 2, Chapter 10).

The industrial revolution introduced large numbers of women to jobs outside the home, but up to World War I no country outside Australasia had granted women the right to vote in national elections. By the turn of the century, however, a feminist movement had emerged in Great Britain to spearhead what would become universal demands for women's suffrage. Reading 2.2 highlights the crusade of British suffragette leader Emmeline Pankhurst to win political equality for women. After World War I, women in Great Britain, Germany, the United States, several other Western countries, and India achieved equal voting rights with men. The quest for gender equality would spread globally. It will be the subject of readings in Parts 2 and 3.

The technological advances brought about by the scientific and industrial revolutions in the West and Japan were readily translated into superior armaments and weapons, used to conquer and subjugate the rest of the world. The British conquest of the Sudan in Africa (Reading 3.1) is a dramatic demonstration of the superiority of British gunnery and the hopelessness of the bravery of the poorly armed Sudanese who opposed the British. The unequal contest resulted in Great Britain conquering the Sudan and ruling it for half a century.

In Asia, Korea fell victim to Japanese imperialism because its leaders failed to modernize. Japan's spectacular and conclusive defeat of China (1895) and Russia (1905) also demonstrated to the rest of the world its readiness to go to war to control Korea, which it annexed in 1910. The plight of the weak in an age of imperialism is demonstrated in the poignant memorandum of Korean nationalists to the U.S. delegation at the Washington Conference in 1921. Korean arguments fell on deaf ears, and the Korean demand of independence was ignored at Washington (Reading 3.2B).

Many other "isms" played important roles in the twentieth century, including several schools of socialism. Socialist theories, among them Marxism, advocated the creation of organizations to advance workers' causes and to right the inequities created by the early industrial revolution. Reading 2.1 focuses on ideals shared by many socialists working for better working conditions for laborers through collective bargaining and strikes. It also indicates the suspicion many socialists shared concerning the strong militaristic tendencies of many industrial powers. However, the attainment of universal or near universal male suffrage in most Western states prior to 1914 produced widespread social and economic reforms, which undercut Marxist calls for the overthrow of existing governments. It was World War I that caused the Communist revolution to occur in barely industrialized Russia in 1917, which will be discussed in Chapter 7.

Competition among the great world powers popularized militarism and fostered an arms race. Newly unified Germany especially gloried in militarism and in the spectacular German military successes in several wars fought in the 1860s. Germany, however, was dissatisfied with its comparatively small overseas empire and its world status. Thus, German leaders who glorified war and demanded continued military buildup received respectful attention. Reading 4.1, by German general Friedrich von Bernhardi, reflects the militarist view, which was shared by the general staffs of other great European powers and Japan as well (which had modelled its army on that of Germany).

Because the wars among European nations during the second half of the nineteenth century and the one fought between Russia and Japan between 1904 and 1905 had been short, leaders believed that similarly short future wars could settle pending issues between nations. Thus, the belligerents who declared war in August 1914 confidently believed that their soldiers would be home before the year ended. None could have foreseen the horrors and massive bloodletting that continued for over four years. Reading 4.2 by a German soldier describes the hell that he lived through at the Second Battle of Ypres during the stalemated trench warfare along the western front.

The twentieth century has been one of bloody warfare unparalleled in human annals, yet voices have been raised against war. Pacifism had not been a widespread movement before the outbreak of World War I. Patriotic feelings ran high in all the belligerent nations when war began. Most people put aside their ideological differences to support the war effort. However a minority persisted in voicing their pacifism throughout the war. One of them was an English journalist, whose antiwar writing is included in Reading 4.3.

CHAPTER ONE

Modernization: Science and Technology Challenge Tradition

In 1900 few people could have predicted or even have imagined the vast changes in science and technology that would occur during the twentieth century. Major discoveries—for example, knowledge of the dynamics of electricity—and innovations—including the electric lightbulb, the phonograph, motion pictures, and automobiles—accelerated the processes of industrialization and urbanization around the world.

Between 1880 and 1913, the production of manufactured goods increased at three times the rate of global population increase, which itself was rapid. Among the new and improved products, many had military applications, such as explosives, improved artillery, submarine torpedoes, and machine guns, all designed to kill more people more efficiently. By the beginning of World War I in 1914, there was over 100 times as much manufactured metal, much used for military applications, available in Europe as there had been a century earlier. Thus, during World War I at the third Battle of Ypres, the British were able to fire more than 4 million shells in nineteen days.

These global transformations contributed to changing lifestyles that frequently conflicted with traditional mores and religious practices. During this period and throughout the century, scientific and technological inventions prolonged life, lowered infant mortality, and made day-to-day living easier and healthier for large portions of the population worldwide. Inventions in communication and transportation facilitated travel, trade, and the diffusion of cultures. Exploration into space, the seas, the earth, and atomic structures added to human understanding of the dynamics of the universe. Although the possibilities for scientific and technological invention seemed rapid and limitless, many worried that, because human needs and social interactions changed at a far slower pace, inventions in medicine, armaments, and a host of other fields might well outpace human abilities to adapt, with catastrophic ecological, political, or military consequences.

The selections in this chapter focus on this dichotomy. The first two (1.1 and 1.2) highlight the drive for exploration and invention. The first describes the Wright brothers' work in the new field of aviation, and the second provides a glimpse into Henry Ford's work in the growing automotive industry. In the third reading (1.3), Leo Tolstoy, a noted Russian author and thinker, criticizes many aspects of modernization. In many ways, the Wright brothers and Ford stand in marked contrast to Tolstoy. The Wright brothers were eager explorers into the mysteries of flight, while Ford's manufacturing innovations contributed to mass-produced automobiles that were in the buying range of many Western consumers. Like most of their contemporaries in the West, the Wrights and Ford exuded optimism over the potential of new technology. In contrast, Tolstoy was far more cautious, believing that many technological developments harmed human societies more than they helped. Contradictory visions regarding the benefits and applications of technology would continue throughout the twentieth century. Thus, the tension and conflicts between the forces of modernization and tradition remain unresolved.

READING 1.1

The Wright Brothers' First Flights

Wilbur (1867–1912) and Orville (1871–1948) Wright were pioneers of the new field of aviation. The Wright brothers knew that they were competing with others in the United States and Europe to be the first to fly successfully in a power-driven airplane. They were also aware of the enormous potential for fame and fortune that being first could bring.

They began by building various machines in their bicycle shop in Ohio. Then, they began testing gliders and other power-driven vehicles at Kitty Hawk, North Carolina, where the wind currents were favorable for airflights. In his biography, *Wilbur and Orville: Biography of the Wright Brothers,* author Fred Howard describes their love affair with aviation and their struggles to build and fly early aircraft. The following reading from Howard's biography details Wilbur and Orville's test flights in the blustery weather of December 1903. After some initial failures, Wilbur made the longest flight—lasting almost one minute at over 800 feet—and, with photographic evidence, thereby entered the record books.

The Wright brothers' successes ushered in a new age of air travel and led to further developments in the field of aviation. From the outset, the Wrights recognized the military potential of the airplane, as well as its commercial aspects. As the twentieth century progressed, air transport would become a major form of travel around the globe. In addition to its civilian applications, air transport was to be used by militaries for reconnaissance, bombing missions, transport, and attacks with machine guns and cannons. Aviation later led to the development of rockets and space travel. The Wright brothers typified the explorers, scientists, and inventors who conceived and contributed to major innovations in a host of scientific and technological fields during the twentieth century.

During the early morning hours of Thursday, December 17, the wind rose. By dawn the puddles and ponds left in the hollows around the camp by the recent rains were encrusted with ice. After breakfast, Wilbur and Orville went outside and measured the wind with their hand-held anemometer. It was not quite gale strength, a cold, gusty north wind of from 22 to 27 miles per hour. They went back indoors to wait for the wind to slacken, but at no time that morning did it drop below 20 miles per hour. With their minds set on being home by Christmas, they decided to go ahead. At 10 A.M. they hung out the signal for the men in the lifesaving station. . . .

It was Orville's whack now. He lay down with his hips in the padded cradle and the toes of his shoes hooked over the small supporting rack on the trailing edge of the wing. He did not don automobile goggles like Charles Manly before his first precipitous plunge into the Potomac on Langley's Aerodrome, nor did he have an aneroid barometer sewed into his trouser leg for indicating altitude. Both he and Wilbur that morning wore their usual business suits, starched collars, neckties, and caps.

Howard, Fred. *Wilbur and Orville: Biography of the Wright Brothers.* New York: Alfred A. Knopf, 1987, pp. 135–40.

At 10:35 Orville slipped the rope restraining the Flyer. It started slowly down the track, Wilbur holding the right wingtip to balance it on the rail. On Monday, Orville had been unable to keep up with Wilbur's headlong dash down the slope of Big Hill. On Thursday, Wilbur had no trouble keeping up with Orville as the Flyer rolled down the track against a wind of more than 20 miles an hour. The Flyer's speed through the air when it reached the end of the track was close to 30 miles per hour, but its speed over the ground was only about 7 miles per hour, making it possible to record the start of the flight on one of the slow photographic plates of 1903, even though the sky was overcast. Orville had set the camera on its tripod before the flight, focusing the center of the ground glass on a point just short of the end of the track. Before taking his place on the Flyer he had inserted a plate holder in the back of the camera, withdrawn the black slide, and entrusted the rubber bulb that activated the shutter to the large hand of John Daniels, after instructing the surfman to squeeze the bulb as the Flyer neared the end of the track.

Daniels did exactly that. As the clattering machine lifted into the air and the wooden truck under its skids dropped away in the sand, the camera shutter clicked open and for a fraction of a second light poured through the lens, impressing its pat-

Orville and Wilbur Wright carefully documented the world's first successful airplane flight in 1903. Here, Orville pilots the plane while Wilbur watches from the ground. The short flight of 120 feet took about twelve seconds. Archive Photos/Percy T. Jones

tern of bright and dark on the four-by-five-inch glass plate. Then the shutter snapped shut, trapping inside the black bellows of the camera one of the great moments of this century. It would be several days before the first print made from the small glass-plate negative would emerge from its bath of developer in the red-lit darkroom behind the house on Hawthorn Street in Dayton. When it did, it would reveal a photograph of accidental excellence, but Orville was too busy that December morning to worry whether Daniels had snapped the shutter at the right moment or not. Like Wilbur on December 14, he was finding that the big two-surfaced front rudder, turned sharply upward at the moment of takeoff, was difficult to manipulate. It was balanced so near the center that the slightest movement of the control lever started it moving upward or downward of its own accord, with the result that the Flyer would rise until it was about ten feet in the air and then, when the direction of the rudder was reversed, dart suddenly for the ground. One of these downward darts ended the first flight about 100 feet from the end of the starting track, or about 120 feet from the point where it had risen from the rail. The impact cracked one of the skids and set the stopwatch on the flight-recording instrument back to zero. Wilbur in the excitement of the moment forgot to stop the stopwatch in his hand, so the time of the flight had to be estimated. They made it 12 seconds.

The true import of those few seconds in the air, as compared to all other flights made by man before 10:35 A.M., December 17, 1903, has nowhere been expressed as accurately and concisely as in Orville's 1913 *Flying* article, where he described the flight as

> the first in the history of the world in which a machine carrying a man had raised itself by its own power into the air in full flight, had sailed forward without reduction of speed, and had finally landed at a point as high as that from which it started.

The witnesses of the flight helped Wilbur and Orville carry the machine back to the starting track, where repairs were made to the cracked skid. Then all six men and Johnny Moore went inside the camp building to warm up. . . .

Half an hour later, Orville made the third flight. They had decided to make all flights as close to the ground as possible. While safer, this made it difficult to maneuver in gusty winds. Both brothers were gratified, however, to find that the response of the warping mechanism was so much more prompt and effective in fast powered flight than in slow glides. Orville was prepared now for the peculiar behavior of the sensitive front rudder and made more careful adjustments, so his flight was steadier and longer than Wilbur's—a little over 200 feet in 15 seconds. It ended when a side gust lifted the Flyer from twelve to fifteen feet in the air, after which the wind, in Orville's words, "sidled the machine off to the side in a lively manner." Wilbur took a picture of the machine from the rear just before it landed, with the right wing almost touching the ground. It is not a photograph to go down in history, but it was the only one taken of the 1903 Flyer in the air beyond the end of the starting rail.

At noon Wilbur made the fourth and longest flight of the day. By the time he had covered 300 feet he was more familiar with the feel of the front rudder. His progress was less undulating, and the Flyer ambled along on a more or less even keel, its motor popping confidently, the large propellers biting the cold wind, the transmission chains clanking in their metal-tube guides. There is no telling how much farther Wilbur might have flown across the sandy plain if he had not turned up the front rudder to clear a small hummock about 800 feet from the starting point and, when he turned the rudder down again, turned it down too far, so that the Flyer plowed into the sand. Its speed over the ground against the strong wind had never been more than 10 miles an hour, so Wilbur was not thrown from the machine, but the front rudder frame was badly smashed.

The times and distances of the first three flights had only been estimated. The fourth flight was carefully measured—852 feet in 59 seconds. Two photographs were taken of the Flyer after it landed. One, taken from the camp, showed the starting rail so that the relatively small size of the Flyer would serve as pictorial proof of its distance from the end of the track. The other, taken at the landing site, showed the damage to the front rudder. When the picture taking was over, the station men helped the Wrights carry the machine back to the camp and set it down outside the shed. As they stood a few feet away, talking over the last, long flight, a powerful gust of wind got under the wings of the Flyer and flipped it over.

The men rushed to hold it down. Wilbur grabbed the uprights in front, but the wind threatened to carry his slight frame away with the machine and he let the wooden struts slip through his fingers. Orville and John Daniels grabbed the rear uprights. Orville had to let go, but Daniels retained his grip and was carried along inside the Flyer, entangled in the rigging wires. As Orville described it later, the large surfman was shaken about like a rattle in a box until the Flyer finally came to a stop and he rolled out on the sand, scared but sound. The others considered it a miracle that he had escaped with only a few painful bruises and scratches.

The damage to the Flyer was more serious. Almost all the ribs of both wings were broken beyond the rear spars. One spar and a number of uprights were splintered. The legs of the engine frame had all snapped off, and the chain guides were badly bent. There would be no more flights in the 1903 Flyer. After their helpers returned to the lifesaving station, Wilbur and Orville had lunch. Then they washed the dishes and set off on the windy four-mile walk to Kitty Hawk to send the wire countermanding Wilbur's cryptic injunction to his father in Tuesday's telegram ("success assured keep quiet").

Joseph Dosher was still manning the telegraph key at the Weather Bureau station on the beach. He tapped out Orville's telegram to Bishop Wright on the afternoon of December 17 while in another corner of the room the brothers examined the wind velocities for the day on the bureau's wind-recording instrument.

That their Flyer had gotten off the ground was no longer news in Kitty Hawk. Captain S. J. Payne of the Kitty Hawk lifesaving station just down the beach must have been informed by phone of the impending flights by Bob Westcott at the Kill Devil station, for he claimed to have seen at least one of the flights through a spyglass. The plain between Kitty Hawk and Kill Devil Hills was as bare of vegetation as a desert, so the captain's line of sight would have been unobstructed, but even with the most powerful glass, it is doubtful that he could have made out much of what was going on at the Wright camp from his three-story perch above the beach—four miles away.

Whether Joseph Dosher, Captain Payne, or anyone else in Kitty Hawk realized the sensational nature of the events of that day is something else again, but somebody at the Norfolk end of the Weather Bureau wire evidently did. Before James Gray, the Norfolk operator, had a chance to relay Orville's message to Western Union for transmittal to

Dayton, he was back on the wire with a question for Dosher in Kitty Hawk. Would it be all right to give the news to a reporter friend?

Wilbur and Orville's answer was an unequivocal no. Orville had already spelled out a plan of action for the release of the news in a letter to his father and sister four weeks before: "If we should succeed in making a flight, and telegraph, we will expect Lorin as our press agent (!) to notify the papers and the Associated Press." Orville's exclamation point was significant. The Wright brothers were not shunning publicity, they were actually courting it—but on their own terms and in their own good time.

READING 1.2

The Tin Lizzie

The following reading from *U.S.A.*, a massive trilogy by novelist John Dos Passos (1896–1970) vividly describes Henry Ford's contributions to the transformation of industrial production. By adopting mass production with assembly lines, standardized parts, and efficiency, Ford plants were able to turn out thousands of assembly line–produced automobiles at reasonable costs. Ford's first assembly line went into production prior to World War I and in the postwar era turned out thousands and then hundreds of thousands of Model T motor cars. In the process, Ford became the largest automobile producer in the world and a multimillionaire.

An ardent commentator on social conditions in the United States, Dos Passos was often deeply pessimistic about many aspects of American life; however, his narrative is generally historically accurate. As Dos Passos emphasizes, Ford initially opposed World War I and U.S. involvement in it, but he also prospered from the manufacturing of armaments. Dos Passos also stresses Ford's manifold impact on the lives of everyday Americans. The push for standardization and cheap consumer goods accelerated the process toward homogeneity and mass production. Although jobs on assembly lines in industrial plants often paid higher wages than in other fields, the constant repetition was mind-numbing, while demands for ever higher productivity and speed-ups produced stress and dissatisfaction among the labor force.

In the 1920s, Ford was known for paying high wages, but he expected his workers to adhere to stringent moral standards and social behavior. By the 1930s, wages in the Ford plants had fallen behind those paid by other automotive companies, and Ford plants were hit by a series of union-led strikes and demonstrations. An outspoken opponent of unionization, Ford hired men to harass union sympathizers, and, as the excerpt by Dos Passos describes, these men used force and violence against the demonstrators. Although many opposed Ford's social stances, none could deny his major contributions to twentieth-century industrial production.

He was forty years old before the Ford Motor Company was started and production began to move.

Dos Passos, John. *U.S.A.* New York: The Modern Library, 1930, 1937, pp. 49–55.

Speed was the first thing the early automobile manufacturers went after. Races advertised the makes of cars.

Henry Ford himself hung up several records at the track at Grosse Pointe and on the ice on Lake St. Clair. In his 999 he did the mile in thirtynine and fourfifths seconds.

But it had always been his custom to hire others to do the heavy work. The speed he was busy with was speed in production, the records in efficient output. He hired Barney Oldfield, a stunt bicyclerider from Salt Lake City, to do the racing for him.

Henry Ford had ideas about other things than the designing of motors, carburetors, magnetos, jigs and fixtures, punches and dies; he had ideas about sales, that the big money was in economical quantity production, quick turnover, cheap interchangeable easilyreplaced standardized parts; it wasn't until 1909, after years of arguing with his partners, that Ford put out the first Model T.

Henry Ford was right.

That season he sold more than ten thousand tin lizzies, ten years later he was selling almost a million a year.

In these years the Taylor Plan was stirring up plantmanagers and manufacturers all over the country. Efficiency was the word. The same ingenuity that went into improving the performance of a machine could go into improving the performance of the workmen producing the machine.

By 1913 the Ford Motor Company was turning out thousands of Model Ts; 12,000 workers at the Highland Park plant in Michigan built all the cars seen here in only one day. From the collections of Henry Ford Museum & Greenfield Village Research Center.

In 1913 they established the assemblyline at Ford's. That season the profits were something like twentyfive million dollars, but they had trouble in keeping the men on the job, machinists didn't seem to like it at Ford's.

Henry Ford had ideas about other things than production.

He was the largest automobile manufacturer in the world; he paid high wages; maybe if the steady workers thought they were getting a cut (a very small cut) in the profits, it would give trained men an inducement to stick to their jobs, wellpaid workers might save enough money to buy a tin lizzie; the first day Ford's announced that cleancut properlymarried American workers who wanted jobs had a chance to make five bucks a day (of course it turned out that there were strings to it; always there were strings to it) such an enormous crowd waited outside the Highland Park plant all through the zero January night that there was a riot when the gates were opened; cops broke heads, jobhunters threw bricks; property, Henry Ford's own property, was destroyed. The company dicks had to turn on the firehose to beat back the crowd.

The American Plan; automotive prosperity seeping down from above; it turned out there were strings to it.

But that five dollars a day paid to good, clean American workmen who didn't drink or smoke cigarettes or read or think, and who didn't commit adultery and whose wives didn't take in boarders, made America once more the Yukon of the sweated workers of the world; made all the tin lizzies and the automotive age, and incidentally, made Henry Ford the automobileer, the admirer of Edison, the birdlover, the great American of his time.

But Henry Ford had ideas about other things besides assemblylines and the livinghabits of his employees. He was full of ideas. Instead of going to the city to make his fortune, here was a country boy who'd made his fortune by bringing the city out to the farm. The precepts he's learned out of McGuffey's Reader, his mother's prejudices and preconceptions, he had preserved clean and unworn as freshprinted bills in the safe in a bank.

He wanted people to know about his ideas, so he bought the *Dearborn Independent* and started a campaign against cigarettesmoking.

When war broke out in Europe, he had ideas about that too. (Suspicion of armymen and soldiering were part of the midwest farm tradition, like thrift, stickativeness, temperance and sharp practice in money matters.) Any intelligent American mechanic could see that if the Europeans hadn't been a lot of ignorant underpaid foreigners who drank, smoked, were loose about women and wasteful in their methods of production, the war could never have happened.

When Rosika Schwimmer broke through the stockade of secretaries and servicemen who surrounded Henry Ford and suggested to him that he could stop the war, he said sure they'd hire a ship and go over and get the boys out of the trenches by Christmas.

He hired a steamboat, the *Oscar II,* and filled it up with pacifists and socialworkers, to go over to explain to the princelings of Europe that what they were doing was vicious and silly.

It wasn't his fault that Poor Richard's commonsense no longer rules the world and that most of the pacifists were nuts, goofy with headlines.

When William Jennings Bryan [U.S. Secretary of State and famous orator] went over to Hoboken to see him off, somebody handed William Jennings Bryan a squirrel in a cage; William Jennings Bryan made a speech with the squirrel under his arm. Henry Ford threw American Beauty roses to the crowd. The band played *I Didn't Raise My Boy to Be a Soldier.* Practical jokers let loose more squirrels. An eloping couple was married by a platoon of ministers in the saloon, and Mr. Zero, the flophouse humanitarian, who reached the dock too late to sail, dove into the North River and swam after the boat.

The *Oscar II* was described as a floating Chautauqua [a summertime, educational resort for adults]; Henry Ford said it felt like a middlewestern village, but by the time they reached Christiansand in Norway, the reporters had kidded him so that he had gotten cold feet and gone to bed. The world was too crazy outside of Wayne County, Michigan. Mrs. Ford and the management sent an Episcopal dean after him who brought him home under wraps, and the pacifists had to speechify without him.

Two years later Ford's was manufacturing munitions, Eagle boats; Henry Ford was planning oneman tanks, and oneman submarines like the one tried out in the Revolutionary War. He announced to the press that he'd turn over his war profits to the government, but there's no record that he ever did. . . .

In 1918 he had borrowed on notes to buy out his minority stockholders for the picayune sum of seventyfive million dollars.

In February 1920, he needed cash to pay off some of these notes that were coming due. A banker is supposed to have called on him and offered him every facility if the bankers' representative could be made a member of the board of directors. Henry Ford handed the banker his hat, and went about raising the money in his own way: he shipped every car and part he had in his plant to his dealers and demanded immediate cash payment. Let the other fellow do the borrowing had always been a cardinal principle. He shut down production and canceled all orders from the supplyfirms. Many dealers were ruined, many supplyfirms failed, but when he reopened his plant, he owned it absolutely, the way a man owns an unmortgaged farm with the taxes paid up.

In 1922 there started the Ford boom for President (high wages, waterpower, industry scattered to the small towns) that was skillfully pricked behind the scenes by another crackerbarrel philosopher, Calvin Coolidge; but in 1922 Henry Ford sold one million three hundred and thirtytwo thousand two hundred and nine tin lizzies; he was the richest man in the world.

Good roads had followed the narrow ruts made in the mud by the Model T. The great automotive boom was on. As Ford's production was improving all the time; less waste, more spotters, strawbosses, stoolpigeons (fifteen minutes for lunch, three minutes to go to the toilet, the Taylorized speedup everywhere, reach under, adjust washer, screw down bolt, shove in cotterpin, reachunder adjustwasher, screwdown bolt, reachunderadjustscrewdownreachunderadjust until every ounce of life was sucked off into production and at night the workmen went home grey shaking husks).

Ford owned every detail of the process from the ore in the hills until the car rolled off the end of the assemblyline under its own power, the plants were rationalized to the last tenthousandth of an inch as measured by the Johansen scale; in 1926 the production cycle was reduced to eightyone hours from the ore in the mine to the finished salable car proceeding under its own power, but the Model T was obsolete.

READING 1.3

Leo Tolstoy's Criticism of Modern Technology and Progress

Although many lauded the seemingly limitless progress of scientific and technological innovations, others, including the great Russian writer Leo Tolstoy (1828–1910), thought that such "progress" was in many ways harmful. Tolstoy thought that true progress came only with the overall improvement of human life. As early as 1862, he faulted many of his contemporaries for equating progress primarily with technological developments. Tolstoy believed that technological "progress" hurt the masses much more than it helped them and that "progress on one side is always paid back by retrogression on the other side of human life." He criticized such developments as railroads, the telegraph, and the growth of newspapers and urbanization.

Tolstoy was especially critical of most modern innovations in transportation. For example, he denounced railroads for bringing peasants closer to the "city temptations," for destroying forests, and for helping farm laborers migrate into the cities. In 1857, he wrote that "the railway is to traveling what the brothel is to love—just as convenient, but just as inhumanely mechanical and deadly monotonous." Tolstoy thought that trains, along with many other technological developments, helped destroy the common people's simplicity and moderation.

Tolstoy came from an aristocratic landowning family (he later depicted some of his ancestors in his great novel *War and Peace*), and he was always more at home in the countryside than in the city. In the 1870s he experienced a spiritual crisis and came out of it more convinced than ever of the essential goodness of the Russian peasant.

In the last three decades of his life, Tolstoy developed his own religious-political philosophy. He considered himself a Christian, but he rejected many traditional Christian teachings. The political philosophy he evolved was a form of nonviolent anarchism that preached the need to bring an end to centralized governments, which he thought protected upper-class interests at the expense of the masses. To realize his utopia, he suggested that people refuse to pay taxes or to serve in the military or other types of government service. Tolstoy's ideas on nonviolent resistance later influenced Gandhi (see Reading 10.1), with whom he corresponded.

In the following selection, which is taken from a work Tolstoy wrote about a rebellion in Russia in 1905, he criticized not only "the production of the most unnecessary, stupid, depraving products," but also those who encouraged such expanding production. Thus, Tolstoy was in direct opposition to Ford and the proponents of mass production. Tolstoy held the upper classes and their governments primarily responsible for these problems. Tolstoy's criticism challenged conventional thinking and stimulated rethinking such old ideas as the following: What is progress? Can technological developments (for example, new armaments) sometimes cause more harm than good? Did the representative governments of Tolstoy's time represent primarily upper-class interests? Although some of Tolstoy's ideas may seem dated, others are not (see, for example, Reading 14.2, in which a contemporary author echoes some of Tolstoy's criticism of "overconsumption").

Under representative Governments, instead of one or a few centres of depravity, we get a large number of such centres—that is to say, there springs up a large class of people living idly on others' labour, the class called the "bourgeois," i.e. people who, being protected by violence, arrange for themselves easy and comfortable lives, free from hard work.

But as, when arranging an easy and pleasant life not only for a Monarch and his Court, but for thousands of little kinglets, many things are needed to embellish and to amuse this idle life, it results that whenever power passes from a despotic to a representative Government, inventions appear, facilitating the supply of objects that add to the pleasure and safety of the lives of the wealthy classes.

To produce all these objects, an ever-increasing number of working men are drawn away from agriculture, and have their capacities directed to the production of pleasing trifles used by the rich, or even to some extent by the workers themselves. So there springs up a class of town workers so situated as to be in complete dependence on the wealthy classes. The number of these people grows and grows the longer the power of representative Government endures, and their condition becomes worse and worse. In the United States, out of a population of seventy millions, ten millions are proletarians, and the relation between the well-to-do and the proletariat classes is the same in England, Belgium and France. The number of men exchanging the labour of producing objects of primary necessity for the labour of producing objects of luxury is ever increasing in those countries. It clearly follows that the result of such a trend of affairs must be the ever greater overburdening of that diminishing number which has to support the luxurious lives of the ever-increasing number of idle people. Evidently, such a way of life cannot continue. . . .

And this corruption, with all its accompanying phenomena—the desire to avoid hard work and to benefit by comforts and pleasures provided by others; interests and cares, inaccessible to a man engaged in work, concerning the general business of the State; the spread of a lying and inflammatory press; and, above all, animosity between nation and nation, class and class, man and man—has grown and grown, till it has reached such dimensions that the struggle of all men against their fellows has become so habitual a state of things, that Science (the Science that is engaged in condoning all the nastiness done by men) has decided that the struggle and enmity of all against all is a necessary, unavoidable and beneficent condition of human life [Tolstoy alludes here to Darwinian ideas.]. . .

Nor is this all. The chief result of this participation of all men in power is, that men being more and more drawn away from direct work on the land, and more and more involved in diverse ways of exploiting the labour of others, have lost their independence and are forced by the position they live in to lead immoral lives. Having neither the desire nor the habit of living by tilling their own land, the Western nations were forced to obtain their means of subsistence from other countries. They could do this only in two ways: by fraud, that is, by exchanging things for the most part unnecessary or depraving, such as alcohol, opium, weapons, for the foodstuffs indispensable to them; or by violence, that is, robbing the people of Asia and Africa wherever they saw an opportunity of doing this with impunity.

Tolstoy, Leo. *The Russian Revolution.* Trans. Louise and Aylmer Maude. Christchurch, Hants, Eng.: Free Age Press, 1906, pp. 11–17.

Such is the position of Germany, Austria, Italy, France, the United States, and especially Great Britain, which is held up as an example for the imitation and envy of other nations. Almost all the people of these nations, having become conscious participators in deeds of violence, devote their strength and attention to the activities of Government, and to industry and to commerce, which aim chiefly at satisfying the demands of the rich for luxuries; and they subjugate (partly by direct force, partly by money) the agricultural people both of their own and of foreign countries, who have to provide them with the necessaries of life.

Such people form a majority in some nations; in others they are as yet only a minority; but the percentage of men living on the labour of others grows uncontrollably and very rapidly, to the detriment of those who still do reasonable, agricultural work. So that a majority of the people of Western Europe are already in the condition (the United States are not so yet, but are being irresistibly drawn towards it) of not being able to subsist by their own labour on their own land. They are obliged in one way or another, by force or fraud, to take the necessaries of life from other people who still do their own labour. And they get these necessaries either by defrauding foreign nations, or by gross violence.

From this it necessarily results that trade, aiming chiefly at satisfying the demands of the rich, and of the richest of the rich (that is, the Government) directs its chief powers, not to improving the means of tilling the soil, but to making it possible by the aid of machines to somehow till large tracts of land (of which the people have been deprived), to manufacturing finery for women, building luxurious palaces, producing sweetmeats, toys, motor-cars, tobacco, wines, delicacies, medicines, enormous quantities of printed matter, guns, rifles, powder, unnecessary railways, and so forth.

And as there is no end to the caprices of men when they are met not by their own labour but by that of others, industry is more and more diverted to the production of the most unnecessary, stupid, depraving products, and draws people more and more from reasonable work; and no end can be foreseen to these inventions and preparations for the amusement of idle people, especially as the stupider and more depraving an invention is—such as the use of motors in place of animals or of one's own legs, railways to go up mountains, or armoured automobiles armed with quick-firing guns—the more pleased and proud of them are both their inventors and their possessors.

VII.

The longer representative Government lasted and the more it extended, the more did the Western nations abandon agriculture and devote their mental and physical powers to manufacturing and trading in order to supply luxuries to the wealthy classes, to enable the nations to fight one another, and to deprave the undepraved. Thus, in England, which has had representative Government longest, less than one-seventh of the adult male population are now employed in agriculture, in Germany 0.45 of the population, in France one-half, and a similar number in other States. So that at the present time the position of these States is such, that even if they could free themselves from the calamity of proletarianism, they could not support themselves independently of other countries. All these nations are unable to subsist by their own toil; and, just as the proletariat are dependent on the well-to-do classes, so are they completely dependent on countries that support themselves and are able to sell them their surplus: such as India, Russia or Australia. England supports from its own land less than a fifth of its population; and Germany less than half, as is the case with France and with other countries; and the condition of these nations becomes year by year more dependent on the food supplied from abroad.

In order to exist, these nations must have recourse to the deceptions and violence called in their language "acquiring markets" and "Colonial policy;" and they act accordingly, striving to throw their nets of enslavement farther and farther to all ends of the earth, to catch those who are still leading rational lives. Vying with one another, they increase their armaments more and more, and more and more cunningly, under various pretexts, seize the land of those who still live rational lives, and force these people to feed them.

Till now they have been able to do this. But the limit to the acquirement of markets, to the deception of buyers, to the sale of unnecessary and injurious articles, and to the enslavement of distant nations, is already apparent. The peoples of distant lands are themselves becoming depraved: are learning to make for themselves all those articles which the Western nations supplied them with, and are, above all, learning the not very cunning science of arming themselves, and of being as cruel as their teachers.

So that the end of such immoral existence is already in sight. The people of the Western nations see this coming, and feeling unable to stop in their career, comfort themselves (as people half aware that they are ruining their lives always do) by self-deception and blind faith; and such blind faith is spreading more and more widely among the majority of Western nations. This faith is a belief that those inventions and improvements for increasing the comforts of the wealthy classes and for fighting (that is, slaughtering men) which the enslaved masses for several generations have been forced to produce, are something very important and almost holy, called, in the language of those who uphold such a mode of life, "culture," or even more grandly, "civilisation."

DISCUSSION QUESTION

Using the readings as a basis for your discussion, what arguments would be made by those favoring innovation and exploration into all aspects of the universe, as opposed to the arguments of those who support the continuation of traditional culture? What, if any, syntheses have been made between these two conflicting positions?

CHAPTER TWO

Demands for Political and Social Changes in Europe and Japan Prior to World War I

Prior to World War I, western European nations and Japan had emerged as among the most powerful on earth. Western Europe, Japan, and the United States had all experienced rapid industrialization and urbanization. As a consequence, their citizens enjoyed the highest standards of living in the world. However, while the upper and middle classes had generally prospered from industrialization and increased commercial activity, many among the working class and farmers remained impoverished. In the West, as unions and working-class movements gained popularity and support, they demanded increased pay and better working conditions. When owners rejected or ignored demands, workers retaliated with strikes and political action. Many also joined various socialist political parties to demand a complete transformation of the political and capitalist economic systems.

The first reading (2.1) in this chapter is an example of a socialist resolution calling for sweeping reforms. In this instance, the socialists were especially concerned about the increased militarism in industrial states. Some years before World War I started, socialists and others were already fearful that the stockpiling of armaments and mounting rivalries over imperial acquisitions among European nations might lead to a disastrous conflagration.

Although the political systems in most Western nations had gradually become more liberal, many people, particularly women, were prevented by law from voting or otherwise participating in politics. With industrialization, some women had become fulltime workers in jobs outside the home. With increased economic freedoms, women also began to demand fuller political and social rights. Early feminists, or suffragists, demanded votes for women and adopted a wide variety of tactics, including demonstrations, parades, rock throwing, and hunger strikes to draw attention to their cause. Reading 2.2 is from the autobiography of Emmeline Pankhurst (1858–1928), one of the leading feminists in Great Britain. However, demands for increased rights for women were not limited to Western nations; women in cities as far flung as Cairo, Istanbul, and Shanghai also organized to demand greater rights during the first decades of the twentieth century. Although women obtained the right to vote in most Western nations during the 1920s and 1930s, these rights were not extended to most African and Asian women until much later. Even as the century draws to a close, women around the world continue to fight for their rights (see Readings 14.1, 18.3, 21.1A, and 21.1B).

The last reading in this chapter (2.3) includes excerpts from three documents issued after the Meiji Restoration in Japan (1868). Although these reforms were instituted prior to 1900, their impact was not fully realized until the twentieth century. These excerpts focus on the sweeping changes the Japanese government initiated in its major institutions. The Japanese successfully combined Western technology and institutions, while maintaining their own unique and vibrant culture. In the process, Japan became one of the major world powers in the twentieth century.

READING 2.1

Socialist Parties Oppose Capitalism and Militarism

Prior to World War I, the struggle between conservative and revolutionary political forces was a major source of conflict in most European nations. In Europe, socialist parties supported, to various degrees, the theories of Karl Marx (1818–1883), who believed that society was split between the "haves," or owners of the means of production, and the "have nots," or the workers, who were forced to sell their labor to the haves. According to Marx, the ongoing conflict, or dialectic, between these two classes would inevitably result in violent revolutions, leading to the overthrow of the capitalist system and the gradual disappearance of the state. Workers would subsequently establish a "golden era" of a classless society in which the means of production would be owned equally and the profits of production shared among those who worked. Socialists also asserted that the capitalist drive for increased industrial production inevitably contributed to the growth of munitions industries that led to mounting militarism and the danger of all-out war.

However, the socialists were deeply divided by internal divisions and differed over how to achieve the goal of a classless society and the destruction of the capitalist domination of economies and governments. Although supporters of capitalism and liberal or conservative political parties feared that the existing systems might be overthrown, the socialists failed to overthrow any European government prior to 1914.

As the following reading indicates, the socialists had identified some inherent dangers in the growing militarism and armament races among the European nations. This resolution, issued by the International Socialist Congress (a gathering of various socialist political parties) held in Germany in 1907, called for working classes to oppose war and advocated the creation of volunteer militias organized along democratic lines to counter the growing power of military forces in Europe and Western empires. The socialists also urged workers to demand a speedy end to armed conflict should war break out. However, when World War I started, nationalism proved to be a far stronger force than internationalism or socialism, and most working peoples of all belligerent nations rallied behind their country's war efforts.

The Congress ratifies the resolutions against militarism and imperialism adopted by previous international congresses and declares once more that the struggle against militarism cannot be separated from the socialist class struggle in general.

Wars between capitalist states, generally, result from their competitive struggle for world markets, for each state strives not only to assure for itself the markets it already possesses, but also to conquer new ones; in this the subjugation of foreign peoples and countries comes to play a leading role. Furthermore, these wars are caused by the incessant competition in armaments that characterizes militarism, the chief instrument of bourgeois class rule and of the economic and political subjugation of the working class.

"On Militarism and International Conflict (Resolution of the International Socialist Congress at Stuttgart), August 18–24, 1907, in Stephen Fisher-Galati, Ed., *Twentieth Century Europe: A Documentary History.* Philadelphia: J. B. Lippincott Co., 1967, pp. 16–18; reprinted from Olga Hess Gankin and H. H. Fisher, *The Bolsheviks and the World War.* Stanford: Stanford University Press, 1940, pp. 57–59.

Wars are promoted by national prejudices which are systematically cultivated among civilized peoples in the interest of the ruling classes for the purpose of diverting the proletarian masses from their own class problems as well as from their duties of international class solidarity.

Hence, wars are part of the very nature of capitalism; they will cease only when the capitalist economic order is abolished or when the number of sacrifices in men and money, required by the advance in military technique, and the indignation provoked by armaments drive the peoples to abolish this order.

For this reason, the working class, which provides most of the soldiers and makes most of the material sacrifices, is a natural opponent of war, for war contradicts its aim—the creation of an economic order on a socialist basis for the purpose of bringing about the solidarity of all peoples.

The Congress therefore considers it the duty of the working class, and especially of its representatives in the parliaments, to combat with all their power naval and military armaments and to refuse the means for these armaments by pointing out the class nature of bourgeois society and the motive for maintaining national antagonisms. It is also their duty to see to it that the proletarian youth is educated in the spirit of the brotherhood of peoples and of socialism and is imbued with class consciousness.

The Congress sees in the democratic organization of the army, in the substitution of the militia for the standing army, an essential guaranty that offensive wars will be rendered impossible and the overcoming of national antagonisms facilitated.

The International is not able to mold into rigid forms the antimilitarist actions of the working class because these actions inevitably vary with differences in national conditions, time, and place. But it is its duty to co-ordinate and strengthen to the utmost the endeavors of the working class to prevent war.

Actually, since the International Congress at Brussels, the proletariat, while struggling indefatigably against militarism by refusing all means for naval and military armaments and by endeavoring to democratize military organization, has resorted with increasing emphasis and success to the most diverse forms of action so as to prevent the outbreak of wars or to put a stop to them, as well as to utilize the disturbances of society caused by war for the emancipation of the working class.

This was evidenced by the agreement concluded after the Fashoda incident by the English and French trade unions for the maintenance of peace and for the restoration of friendly relations between England and France; by the conduct of the Social Democratic parties in the German and French parliaments during the Moroccan crisis; by the demonstrations conducted by the French and German socialists for the same purpose; by the joint action of the socialists of Austria and Italy, who met in Trieste for the purpose of thwarting a conflict between these two countries; further, by the emphatic intervention of the socialist workers of Sweden for the purpose of preventing an attack upon Norway; and, finally, by the heroic, self-sacrificing struggle of the socialist workers and peasants of Russia and Poland waged against the war unleased by Tsarism and then for its early termination, and also for the purpose of utilizing the national crisis for the liberation of the working class.

All these endeavors are evidence of the proletariat's growing power and increasing strength to render secure the maintenance of peace by means of resolute intervention.

This action of the working class will be all the more successful if its spirit is prepared by similar actions and the workers' parties of the various countries are spurred on and consolidated by the International.

The Congress is convinced that, under pressure exerted by the proletariat and by a serious use of courts of arbitration instead of the pitiful measures adopted by the governments, the benefit derived from disarmament can be assured to all nations and will enable them to employ for cultural purposes the enormous expenditures of money and energy, which now are swallowed up by military armaments and wars.

If a war threatens to break out, it is the duty of the working class and of its parliamentary representatives in the countries involved, supported by the consolidating activity of the International (Socialist) Bureau to exert every effort to prevent the outbreak of war by means they consider most effective, which naturally vary according to the accentuation of the class struggle and of the general political situation.

Should war break out none the less, it is their duty to intervene in favor of its speedy termination and to do all in their power to utilize the economic and political crisis caused by the war to rouse the peoples and thereby to hasten the abolition of capitalist class rule.

READING 2.2

Women Struggle for Equal Rights

The following reading, by Emmeline Pankhurst, describes the struggle to achieve full suffrage—voting rights—for women in Great Britain. Emmeline Goulden Pankhurst and her husband, Richard Pankhurst, a lawyer, were both outspoken advocates for women's rights. A leader of several women's organizations, Pankhurst concluded, after peaceful negotiations had failed to achieve results, that violent tactics should be adopted in order to force changes. Her autobiography, *My Own Story,* vividly describes early suffragist demonstrations outside Parliament and the rock throwing at windows at Number 10 Downing Street, the official residence of the British prime minister, and at other locations in London.

The government retaliated by arresting, trying, and imprisoning hundreds of those women, popularly called Suffragettes. Pankhurst and the others remained undeterred and began life-threatening hunger strikes while in prison. Fearful that the hunger strikers might die and become martyrs to the cause, the government approved the forced feeding of the strikers—a brutal process that led to further outrage. When the women were released from prison, they resumed their demonstrations, in a "cat and mouse" game of confrontation between the suffragists and their opponents. During the 1920s, similar feminist movements emerged around the world.

All three of Pankhurst's daughters became ardent feminists, supporting women's rights in Canada, the United States, and Australia. One daughter also became active in pacifist, antiwar movements, supported socialist causes, and, toward the end of her life, championed the independence of Ethiopia against Fascist aggression in the 1930s. In addition to their struggle for equality of opportunity and greater political, social, and economic rights, many women's organizations were also in the vanguard of antiwar movements.

The early feminist movements, led by Pankhurst and others, paved the way for the continuation of struggles for equal rights between the sexes throughout the century; the suffrage movement was also part of ongoing struggles for human rights among those of differing genders, ethnicities, religions, age levels, and nationalities around the world.

The King's speech, when Parliament met in February 1912, alluded to the franchise question in very general terms. Proposals, it was stated, would be brought forward for the amendment of the law with respect to the franchise and the registration of electors. . . . We saw that the only course to take was to offer determined opposition to any measure of suffrage that did not include as an integral part, equal suffrage for men and women.

On February 16th we held a large meeting of welcome to a number of released prisoners who had served two and three months for the window breaking demonstration that had taken place in the previous November. At this meeting we candidly surveyed the situation and agreed on a course of action which we believed would be sufficiently strong to prevent the Government from advancing their threatened franchise bill. . . .

Our demonstration, so mild by comparison with English men's political agitation, was announced for March 4th, and the announcement created much public alarm. Sir William Byles gave notice that he would "ask the Secretary of State for the Home Department whether his attention had been drawn to a speech by Mrs. Pankhurst last Friday night, openly and emphatically inciting her hearers to violent outrage and the destruction of property, and threatening the use of firearms if stones did not prove sufficiently effective; and what steps he proposes to take to protect Society from this outbreak of lawlessness."

The question was duly asked, and the Home Secretary replied that his attention had been called to the speech, but that it would not be desirable in the public interest to say more than this at present.

Whatever preparations the police department were making to prevent the demonstration, they failed because, while as usual, we were able to calculate exactly what the police department were going to do, they were utterly unable to calculate what we were going to do. We had planned a demonstration for March 4th, and this one we announced. We planned another demonstration for March 1st, but this one we did not announce. Late in the afternoon of Friday, March 1st, I drove in a taxicab, accompanied by the Hon. Secretary of the Union, Mrs. Tuke and another of our members, to No. 10 Downing Street, the official residence of the Prime Minister. It was exactly half past five when we alighted from the cab and threw our stones, four of them, through the window panes. As we expected we were promptly arrested and taken to Cannon Row police station. The hour that followed will long be remembered in London. At intervals of fifteen minutes relays of women who had volunteered for the demonstration did their work. The first smashing of glass occurred in the Haymarket and Piccadilly, and greatly startled and alarmed both pedestrians and police. A large number of the women were arrested, and

Pankhurst, Emmeline. *My Own Story.* London: Eveleigh Nash, 1914, pp. 211–19.

everybody thought that this ended the affair. But before the excited populace and the frustrated shop owners' first exclamation had died down, before the police had reached the station with their prisoners, the ominous crashing and splintering of plate glass began again, this time along both sides of Regent Street and the Strand. A furious rush of police and people towards the second scene of action ensued. While their attention was being taken up with occurrences in this quarter, the third relay of women began breaking the windows in Oxford Circus and Bond Street. The demonstration ended for the day at half past six with the breaking of many windows in the Strand. . . .

The demonstration had taken place in the morning, when a hundred or more women walked quietly into Knightsbridge and walking singly along the streets demolished nearly every pane of glass they passed. Taken by surprise the police arrested as many as they could reach, but most of the women escaped.

For that two days' work something like two hundred suffragettes were taken to the various police stations, and for days the long procession of women streamed through the courts. The dismayed magistrates found themselves facing, not only former rebels, but many new ones, in some cases, women whose names, like that of Dr. Ethel Smyth, the composer, were famous throughout Europe. These women, when arraigned, made clear and lucid statements of their positions and their motives, but magistrates are not schooled to examine motives. They are trained to think only of laws and mostly of laws

Suffragists used a wide variety of means, including demonstrations, hunger strikes, and pickets in order to gain votes for women. Here a suffragist, under arrest, is being taken to jail during a demonstration for women's rights in Scotland. Popperfoto/Archive Photos

protecting property. Their ears are not tuned to listen to words like those spoken by one of the prisoners, who said: "We have tried every means—processions and meetings—which were of no avail. We have tried demonstrations, and now at last we have to break windows. I wish I had broken more. I am not in the least repentant. Our women are working in far worse condition than the striking miners. I have seen widows struggling to bring up their children. Only two out of every five are fit to be soldiers. What is the good of a country like ours? England is absolutely on the wane. You only have one point of view, and that is the men's, and while men have done the best they could, they cannot go far without the women and the women's views. We believe the whole is in a muddle too horrible to think of."

The coal miners were at that time engaging in a terrible strike, and the Government, instead of arresting the leaders, were trying to come to terms of peace with them. I reminded the magistrate of this fact, and I told him that what the women had done was but a fleabite by comparison with the miners' violence. I said further: "I hope our demonstration will be enough to show the Government that the women's agitation is going on. If not, if you send me to prison, I will go further to show that women who have to help pay the salaries of Cabinet Ministers, and your salary too, sir, are going to have some voice in the making of the laws they have to obey."

I was sentenced to two months' imprisonment. Others received sentences ranging from one week to two months, while those who were accused of breaking glass above five pounds in value, were committed for trial in higher courts. They were sent to prison on remand, and when the last of us were behind the grim gates, not only Holloway but three other women's prisons were taxed to provide for so many extra inmates.

It was a stormy imprisonment for most of us. A great many of the women had received, in addition to their sentences, "hard labour," and this meant that the privileges at that time accorded to Suffragettes, as political offenders, were withheld. The women adopted the hunger strike as a protest, but as the hint was conveyed to me that the privileges would be restored, I advised a cessation of the strike. The remand prisoners demanded that I be allowed to exercise with them, and when this was not answered they broke the windows of their cells. The other suffrage prisoners, hearing the sound of shattered glass, and the singing of the Marseillaise, immediately broke their windows. The time had long gone by when the Suffragettes submitted meekly to prison discipline. And so passed the first days of my imprisonment.

READING 2.3

The Foundations of Modern Japanese Power

Japan remained the most traditional major state in Asia, untouched by modern trends and unscathed by Western imperialism up to 1853. In that year, Japan was forcibly opened up by the United States, whose example was followed by other Western powers. They compelled Japan to sign unequal treaties that gave Western nations numerous concessions. In 1868 a revolution in the name of the young emperor, Meiji, overthrew the ineffective shogunal government that had been in power since 1600 and was widely blamed for Japan's humiliations. The event, called the Meiji Restoration, returned the hitherto figurehead emperor to power.

The principal goal of the Meiji leaders was to "enrich the nation and strengthen its arms": to build a modern economy so that Japan could support a powerful military and gain equality with Western powers. With the support of the people, in a success story unmatched before or since, Japan was able to rise from semicolonial to great-power status in one generation.

The Meiji leaders made the world their schoolhouse by learning from every successful Western nation, yet they never abandoned the basic ideals that were the foundations of Japan's society. Three of the most important reforms inaugurated during the Meiji Restoration were (1) the Military Conscription Ordinance of 1872, (2) the Imperial Precepts to Soldiers and Sailors of 1882, and (3) the Imperial Rescript on Education of 1890. The Military Conscription Ordinance obligated all men to serve; it was promulgated one year after imperial Germany's conscript army resoundingly defeated the selectively drafted army of France in the Franco-German War. Until 1872 the Japanese military had been a hereditary elite, while the rest of the population was forbidden to bear arms. The Imperial Precepts to Soldiers and Sailors gave moral guidance to the conscripts of its modernized armed forces. Finally, the Imperial Rescript on Education became the basis of mandatory courses on moral instruction for all students in the newly established modern schools, which provided universal education for boys and girls. These three late-nineteenth-century documents are quoted in part or in their entirety in this reading because they were the key to Japan's success in the first part of the twentieth century.

Although the Meiji leaders were ready to try new methods to strengthen Japan, these three documents make clear their strong adherence to traditional ideals and virtues to provide a framework for order and discipline. They remind the people of the glories of Japan's early history, appeal to Japanese pride in its past, and invoke nationalism to encourage sacrifice in order to fulfill Japan's destiny. However, they instill ideals that would become a pervasive cult of emperor veneration, which were later directed toward imperialism and militarism.

MILITARY CONSCRIPTION ORDINANCE, 1872

In the system in effect in our country in the ancient past everyone was a soldier. In an emergency the emperor became the Marshal, mobilizing the able-bodied youth for military service and thereby suppressing rebellion. When the campaign was over the men returned to their homes and their occupations, whether that of farmer, artisan, or merchant. They differed from the soldiers of a later period who carried two swords and called themselves warriors, living presumptuously without working, and in extreme instances cutting down people in cold blood while officials turned their faces. . . .

As a result of the Meiji Restoration, all are now equally the people of the empire, and there is no distinction between them in their obligations to the State.

No one in the world is exempt from taxation with which the state defrays its expenditures. In this way, everyone should endeavor to repay one's country. The Occidentals

De Bary, Wm. Theodore. Ed. *Sources of Japanese Tradition*, vol. II. New York: Columbia University Press, 1958, pp. 139–40, 197, 199–200.

call military obligation "blood tax," for it is one's repayment in life-blood to one's country. When the State suffers disaster, the people cannot escape being affected. Thus, the people can ward off disaster to themselves by striving to ward off disaster to the State. And where there is a state, there is military defense; and if there is military defense there must be military service. It follows, therefore, that the law providing for a militia is the law of nature and not an accidental, man-made law. As for the system itself, it should be made after a survey of the past and the present, and adapted to the time and circumstance. The Occidental countries established their military systems after several hundred years of study and experience. Thus, their regulations are exact and detailed. However, the difference in geography rules out their wholesale adoption here. We should now select only what is good in them, use them to supplement our traditional military system, establish an army and a navy, require all males who attain the age of twenty—irrespective of class—to register for military service, and have them in readiness for all emergencies. Heads of communities and chiefs of villages should keep this aim in mind and they should instruct the people so that they will understand the fundamental principle of national defense.

IMPERIAL PRECEPTS TO SOLDIERS AND SAILORS, 1882

Soldiers and Sailors, We are your supreme Commander-in-Chief. Our relations with you will be most intimate when We rely upon you as Our limbs and you look up to Us as your head. Whether We are able to guard the Empire, and so prove Ourself worthy of Heaven's blessings and repay the benevolence of Our Ancestors, depends upon the faithful discharge of your duties as soldiers and sailors. If the majesty and power of Our Empire be impaired, do you share with Us the sorrow; if the glory of Our arms shine resplendent, We will share with you the honor. If you all do your duty, and being one with Us in spirit do your utmost for the protection of the state, Our people will long enjoy the blessings of peace, and the might and dignity of Our Empire will shine in the world. As We thus expect much of you, Soldiers and Sailors, We give you the following precepts:

1. The soldier and sailor should consider loyalty their essential duty. Who that is born in this land can be wanting in the spirit of grateful service to it? No soldier or sailor, especially, can be considered efficient unless this spirit be strong within him. . . . Remember that, as the protection of the state and the maintenance of its power depend upon the strength of its arms, the growth or decline of this strength must affect the nation's destiny for good or for evil; therefore neither be led astray by current opinions nor meddle in politics, but with single heart fulfil your essential duty of loyalty, and bear in mind that duty is weightier than a mountain, while death is lighter than a feather. Never by failing in moral principle fall into disgrace and bring dishonor upon your name.

The second article concerns the respect due to superiors and consideration to be shown inferiors.

3. The soldier and the sailor should esteem valor. . . . To be incited by mere impetuosity to violent action cannot be called true valor. The soldier and the sailor should have sound discrimination of right and wrong, cultivate self-possession, and form their plans with deliberation. Never to despise an inferior enemy or fear a superior, but to do one's duty as soldier or sailor—this is true valor. Those who thus appreciate true valor should in their daily intercourse set gentleness first and aim to win the love and esteem of others. If you affect valor and act with violence, the world will in the end detest you and look upon you as wild beasts. Of this you should take heed.

— Dont aBuse

THE IMPERIAL RESCRIPT ON EDUCATION

Know ye, Our subjects:

Our Imperial Ancestors have founded Our Empire on a basis broad and everlasting, and have deeply and firmly implanted virtue; Our subjects ever united in loyalty and filial piety have from generation to generation illustrated the beauty thereof. This is the glory of the fundamental character of Our Empire, and herein also lies the source of Our education. Ye, Our subjects, be filial to your parents, affectionate to your brothers and sisters; as husbands and wives be harmonious, as friends true; bear yourselves in modesty and moderation; extend your benevolence to all; pursue learning and cultivate arts, and thereby develop intellectual faculties and perfect moral powers; furthermore, advance public good and promote common interests; always respect the Constitution and observe the laws; should emergency arise, offer yourselves courageously to the State; and thus guard and maintain the prosperity of Our Imperial Throne coeval with heaven and earth. So shall ye not only be Our good and faithful subjects, but render illustrious the best traditions of your forefathers.

The Way here set forth is indeed the teaching bequeathed by Our Imperial Ancestors, to be observed alike by Their Descendants and the subjects, infallible for all ages and true in all places. It is Our wish to lay it to heart in all reverence, in common with you, Our subjects, that we may all attain to the same virtue.

— Big STreSS on AncesTor Laying fore/NoaiT.on   October 30, 1890

DISCUSSION QUESTION

Discuss the programs and tactics adopted by various movements—political, feminist, social—in Europe and Japan prior to World War I.

THREE

Regions Under Imperial Domination

Several great European powers, the United States, and Japan dominated the world in the early twentieth century. Advanced in the sciences and technology, industrialized, and militarily powerful, Great Britain, France, Germany, the United States, and Japan carved out huge empires and exercised informal dominion in weak though nominally independent states. Most of the African continent came under European rule. Most Asians were ruled directly or indirectly by European powers, the United States, and Japan. The readings in this chapter demonstrate the failure of the Sudanese to resist British military power in Africa, and Koreans' struggle to be free from Japanese rule.

The British empire was the largest in the world; it also held more land in Africa than any other empire. European powers had partitioned Africa through mutual agreements without major military showdowns during the last decades of the nineteenth century. In acquiring and consolidating its African empire, Great Britain fought minor wars against Africans and recalcitrant Boers (Dutch-descended settlers in South Africa), as well as a major campaign against a powerful Muslim state in the Sudan. Reading 3.1 is an account by a British newspaper correspondent on the Battle of Omdurman, the climax of the British-led campaign to reconquer the Sudan. It describes the enormous courage of the Sudanese warriors who fought for their religious leader, the Khalifa; with their antiquated weapons, they were doomed to defeat, and the Sudan came under British domination.

By the turn of the century, the once great Ottoman empire had lost most of its European and North African territories (except for nominal sovereignty over Egypt), India had become a British possession, and the Chinese empire had been stripped of its dependencies and carved into spheres of influence by several great European powers and Japan. Only Japan among Asian nations had become modernized and industrialized, catching up with the advanced Western nations within one short generation. Japan demonstrated its new great power status by humbling China and Russia and then annexing Taiwan and Korea.

In a policy similar to that of Russia in its Polish territories and the Ottoman Turks toward their Arab subjects, the Japanese rulers attempted to strip Koreans of their national identity by prohibiting the teaching of the Korean language and history in the schools. Reading 3.2A is an account of how a young Korean girl resisted the Japanese authorities. Korean patriots tried to present their country's case against Japanese imperialism before the meeting of the International Court of Justice at the Hague in the Netherlands before annexation and failed. They tried again at the Paris Peace Conference in 1919 and were not granted a hearing. They persisted by pressing their brief against Japan in 1921 at the Naval Disarmament Conference in Washington, D.C. Again their pleas were ignored. Part of that document is excerpted in Reading 3.2B. Korea finally regained its independence after Japan's defeat in World War II.

READING 3.1

British Conquest of the Sudan

Most of Africa was partitioned by European imperialist powers during the late nineteenth century. Most African societies were unable to offer effective armed resistance. Sudan was an exception. Situated along the upper Nile River, Sudan was nominally an Egyptian dependency. A province of the Ottoman Empire, Egypt was in reality a British protectorate. In 1882 the Mahdi, a Sudanese Muslim religious leader, led a successful revolt against the Egyptians. His followers, called dervishes by westerners, captured the capital city of Khartoum in 1885 and massacred the small British force stationed there. Although the Mahdi died in 1885, the momentum of his movement continued under his successor, the Khalifa Abdullah.

Great Britain decided to reconquer the Sudan, motivated in part by imperialist rivalry with France, which was interested in expanding its empire into the Nile valley, and by a desire to secure the Nile's water supply for Egypt's needs. General Lord Herbert Kitchener commanded the expeditionary army of British, Egyptian, and Sudanese troops that reconquered the Sudan between 1896 and 1898. Kitchener proceeded with great caution, building a railroad as he advanced southward from Egypt. The decisive defeat of the Khalifa's forces at the battle of Omdurman on September 2, 1898, secured the Sudan for Great Britain. The Khalifa fled Khartoum but was killed in 1899. After negotiations and a convention that ended France's involvement in the Nile valley, the Sudan came under British control as the Anglo-Egyptian Sudan.

This reading is from a book titled *The Downfall of the Dervishes* by Ernest N. Bennett, an Oxford University professor, who covered the expedition as a special correspondent for *The Westminster Gazette,* a British newspaper. It describes the Battle of Omdurman, the climax of the largest colonial war fought by Great Britain in the nineteenth century. His description of British military and technological superiority also provides insights into the reasons Western powers succeeded in gaining control over Africa.

Few of the twenty-three thousand men who passed that night within the zeriba [enclosure] are likely to forget it. We felt certain of a battle on the morrow, for all doubts as to whether the Khalifa would stand and fight, or flee away into the uttermost parts of the Sudan, were now set at rest. The two armies actually lay encamped within five miles of each other on an almost dead level! . . .

[Next morning] on either side of Gebel Surgham, and then on towards the western slopes of Kerreri, line upon line of Dervish infantry and cavalry appeared. Gigantic banners fluttered aloft, borne on lofty flagstaffs. The rising sun glinted on sword blades and spearheads innumerable, and as the mighty host drew nearer, black heads and arms became visible amongst the white of the massed *gibbehs*. And now, too, a dense volume

Bennett, Ernest N. *The Downfall of the Dervishes or Avenging of Gordon, Being a Personal Narrative of the Final Soudan Campaign of 1898.* London: Methuen and Co., 1898, pp. 152, 162–63, 165–67, 171–73, 190, 195–96, 230–31.

of sound came rolling over the desert as the fanatical Arabs raised continuous shouts of defiance, mingled with chants to Allah and the Prophet—their final battle-cry before the inevitable death awaiting them—the veritable requiem song of Mahdism! In the clear morning air the pageant was truly magnificent, a splendid panorama of some forty thousand barbarians moving forward all undismayed to do battle with the largest army which Great Britain has placed in the field for forty years. So marvellous a picture—once seen, never to be seen again—must surely have impressed itself indelibly upon the memory of all who witnessed it!

Our men stood unmoved within the zeriba. Suddenly a cloud of white smoke massed itself along the enemy's front, and one realised that the Dervishes had opened fire on us. The Khalifa's forces possessed eighteen thousand Martinis and a still larger number of Remingtons [types of rifles]. . . . But as none of the Dervishes understood the sighting of their rifles, and many of them had actually knocked off the back-sights as a useless encumbrance, their opening volleys at over two thousand yards, being fired point blank, were useless. They simply wasted ammunition; for most of the bullets of course struck the sand hundreds of yards in front of us, and comparatively few got as far as the zeriba. No response came from our silent ranks for another five minutes. Then at 6.20 a roar came from the batteries on the left, and a shell shrieked through the air and burst about twenty yards in front of the formidable line advancing against the southern face of the zeriba. Almost simultaneously the other batteries opened fire on the dense masses of the enemy advancing round the western slopes of Surgham, and still farther away towards the ridge of Kerreri.

The battle had now commenced in dire earnest. As the enemy rapidly advanced, bullets of all sizes and shapes soon began to whistle over the zeriba from the Martinis, Remingtons, and nondescript weapons of the enemy. A battery, too, which they had placed on the western slope of Surgham, fired at the portion of our line held by the Camerons and Seaforths. More than forty rounds were fired from these Dervish field guns, but the shells did little, if any, damage, as, although the fuses were beautifully timed and the projectiles burst at an excellent height above the ground, the range was too long, and they all fell short. . . .

Our own artillery had very soon found the range accurately. The British fifteen-pounders and the short Maxim-Nordenfeldts of the Egyptian gunners were admirably worked, and the precision of the shell fire was marvellous. Scores of shrapnel burst just over the advancing line, and other shells struck the ground under their feet, tearing huge gaps in the ranks and throwing up clouds of earth and stones. The division of the enemy nearest to the zeriba was advancing over the ridge between Surgham and the river, and with a good field glass I could see the fearful havoc played by the fire of our guns. . . .

Thousands upon thousands of Dervish infantry and cavalry advanced all along the line in a rough semicircle, with frenzied shouts and a continuous but irregular fire upon the western face of the zeriba. Towards the left centre the Khalifa's black ensign stood out above the white *gibbehs* and red sashes of his bodyguard—that heroic and devoted band who rallied to the last round their leader's flag, and died to a man in its defence! . . .

After his decisive defeat at the Battle of Omdurman, the Khalifa, leader of the Sudanese, was killed, and his movement collapsed, with the result that Great Britain would rule the Sudan for the next half century. The Board of Trustees of the National Museums and Galleries on Merseyside, Walker Art Gallery.

About seven o'clock a marvellous attempt to break our lines was made by the enemy. The Dervish leader in the centre—perhaps Yakub, the Khalifa's brother—actually dispatched a body of about one hundred and fifty cavalry against the British position. That any sane man could be guilty of such criminal folly is almost incredible. The devoted band galloped towards the zeriba over the open desert in the very teeth of Maxims and Lee-Metford volleys! Needless to say, not one of these brave fellows got within five hundred yards of our lines. The Maxims and rifles rained bullets upon them, the murderous sheet of lead mowed them down, and they simply vanished from sight. One heroic leader struggled on in front of his comrades, until he too, with his beautiful Arab charger, went down like the rest, and lay there, a silent witness to the magnificent valour of the Khalifa's followers. Not one man in twenty returned from this wild charge, which, for the utter recklessness of its bravery, must be almost unexampled in military history.

The interchange of shots continued until about 8.30, by which time the Dervish forces had been practically annihilated, with the exception of two or three large masses, which had retreated in excellent order behind the hills on the south-west and north-west. . . .

As the Sirdar [commander-in-chief General Kitchener] appeared to think that all danger from Dervish attack was now past and over, the entire army received orders to leave the zeriba and march in *échelon* straight on Omdurman. . . .

In places, as we marched along, the ground was strewn thickly with bodies, as the fire had struck the enemy down in little heaps. In one spot I saw a ring of nine men and three horses, all evidently slain by the explosion of a single shell. . . .

As we marched on through the apparently interminable suburbs of the city, the regimental drums and fifes and the Highlanders' bagpipes struck up some lively tunes. The effect of music at such a time was simply marvellous: it put fresh heart and vigour into all of us. All along the broad street which runs through Omdurman to the central square we were greeted by bands of women, who stood in clusters at the doors, and welcomed us with curious trilling cries of joy.

The Khalifa had escaped from the southern end of the town about an hour before our foremost troops arrived, and had been followed by a panic-stricken mob of men, women, and children, with camels and donkeys. . . .

On 4th September, at 9.15 A.M., four gunboats conveyed the Sirdar and various detachments of troops, with most of the correspondents, across the Nile to Khartoum. . . .

At ten o'clock the Union Jack was run up from one of the flagstaffs which surmounted the ruined façade of the palace, and almost immediately afterwards the Crescent flag of Egypt was unfurled.

READING 3.2

Koreans Resist Japanese Imperialism

Korea has an ancient heritage and proud traditions. It has strong cultural links with China that date back to the dawn of its history, accepting from China Confucian ideology, a bureaucratic government, and Buddhism. Although Korea had its own king and government, it was a Chinese vassal state until 1895. In the late nineteenth century, Korea became the target of both Russian and Japanese imperialism. Defeated by Japan, China was forced to renounce its overlordship over Korea in 1895. After losing the Russo-Japanese War in 1905, Russia, too, conceded Korea as a Japanese sphere of influence. Japan annexed Korea in 1910 and ruled it harshly until its defeat in World War II in 1945.

Modern Korean nationalism developed after 1895. It was centered among the educated young in Korea's traditional and modern schools, including those established by Japanese colonial authorities with the hope of producing docile, assimilated Japanese subjects. In this respect, Japanese imperial authorities failed, just as those of Britain and France failed when they established modern schools in their colonies. Christian missionaries, especially Protestant missionaries from the United States, were a second source of modern Korean nationalism. Missionaries founded the first schools for Korean women, and missionary teachers often sympathized with Korean nationalism and made their pupils aware of modern Western ideals.

In March 1919, responding to U.S. President Woodrow Wilson's doctrine of national self-determination at the Paris Peace Conference, Korean students led more than a million people in peaceful demonstrations against Japanese rule and for independence. They were put down brutally by Japanese forces, who killed or injured more than 20,000 demonstrators and jailed 19,000.

Reading 3.2A is from the autobiography of Louise Yim, a lifelong fighter against Japanese control of her country. Here she recounts her first acts of defiance against Japan when she was a student in an American missionary school.

Reading 3.2B is excerpted from "Korea's Appeal to the American Delegation to the Conference on Limitation of Armament" held in Washington, D.C., in 1921. A delegation of Korean nationalists, led by Syngman Rhee, another lifelong fighter against Japanese imperialism, attempted but failed to rouse international action to support Korea's cause at the conference. Rhee became the first president of independent South Korea after World War II.

READING 3.2A: SCHOOL GIRLS DEFY JAPANESE AUTHORITIES

One day we demanded that our teachers give us courses in Korean history. When they refused, I called three of my closest friends. "Let us find a Korean history book and each night copy a few pages. It will be slow work, but in time we each will have in our possession the treasured story of our nation."

I went alone to Pastor Kim's house and told him what I wanted to do. He looked at me for a few minutes and then smiled.

"You are really determined to save Korea, aren't you? I will take a chance. But remember, you are taking a chance too. If the Japanese should ever find you with this book in your possession, they will chop off your head."

I told him I was not frightened, but I was, and he knew it. Nevertheless, he went to a secret hiding place and took out a beautiful leather-bound book on which were written the words *Dongkook Yuksa*. Translated literally, this means "Oriental History." But the book was the work of Korean historians writing mainly about our country. He handed the book to me, saying, "Here is your heritage. Love it. Cherish it. Protect it."

I wrapped the book in the folds of my *sigachima* and returned to school. That night, my friends and I began our laborious task. We could light no lamps and we had to keep our candles carefully shaded. At times our eyes felt as though they were going blind.

But we kept on working, month after month. As soon as we finished a copy, we smuggled it out of the school grounds and Pastor Kim helped us get it into the hands of patriotic young men and spiritual leaders who were forming secret study circles that would someday become centers of the resistance movement.

One morning, Miss Golden and a few of the teachers came to our class. Their faces were white. Miss Golden spoke, but she did not look at us.

"Girls, something is happening here that is not good for the school or for any of us. If I do not tell the Japanese police about it and they find out by themselves, this school will be closed and all of you will be jailed, possibly beaten, perhaps even killed. You all know to what I am referring" [reading and copying banned books]. . .

We discussed a new rule that had been made in school which forced us to sing the Japanese national anthem each morning and to bow down before a photograph of the Japanese Emperor. We decided neither to sing nor to bow.

Yim, Louise. *My Forty Year Fight for Korea.* New York, A. A. Wyn, Inc., 1951, pp. 60–61, 66–68, 78.

We refused to yield and after a few mornings of helpless rage the Japanese teachers surrendered to reality. The morning routine of bowing and singing became a mere memory. . . .

One day we became bolder. Pictures of the Japanese Emperor hung in every classroom. Before class began, a few of us slipped through the rooms with sharpened pencils and punctured the eyes in all the pictures.

This time the Jap teachers were not to be quieted. With anger in their hearts, they burst into Miss Golden's office. Just a corner behind them I followed until, when the door slammed shut, my ear was at the keyhole.

"Now you must find the trouble maker!"

Miss Golden's reply came in a fluttery voice. "Er . . . I will do all I can. After all, we can't *force* the girls to speak."

"For such a crime, the Japanese police know how to force an answer . . . even from little girls!"

I ran away before they came out and reported what I had heard to my classmates. Soon after, Miss Golden walked into our classroom. The two Japanese teachers trailed behind her like monkeys.

"Girls, you must help me. The latest incident—the insult to the Japanese Emperor—was really too much. If you are honest Christian girls, believers in the truth, then the one among you who is responsible will speak up."

We all stood up. We all cried out, "I did it! I did it! I did it!" Each tried to shriek louder than the other.

Miss Golden rapped her ruler on the desk.

"Order! Order! Order! Now I'm going to leave this classroom. No one will be permitted to walk out—for any reason—until the guilty party confesses."

She left and locked the door. Luncheon hour passed. We sat perfectly quiet in the classroom. No one even whispered. No one even smiled. The sun set and it became dark.

Hourly Miss Golden poked her head through the door, asking, "Which one of you committed the crime?"

The response was always the same—a host of "I dids." And then the door would slam shut and we would resume our silence. Finally the supper hour passed and Miss Golden came in—a beaten woman. She had thought she knew all about Koreans. Now she learned another fact, one which many others have since learned: We are a very stubborn people. . . .

Times were changing. During my two years at [school in] Chunju, I had not been fully aware of it. But returning this summer in 1916 I could see what this tenth year of the Japanese occupation meant. Everywhere one could see the ugly little islanders in their ill-fitting uniforms. Many Japanese civilians were coming over from the "homeland" and settling in Korean homes. Where a Japanese now resided, a Korean family once lived. The side streets were beginning to show signs of these evictions, as families encamped temporarily in rude shacks near the homes they once owned. Many were dazed. Their new rulers kept saying they were there to "help" them. But what strange ways they had of doing good!

- WONDERING How OLD, REFERED TO as LITTE GirlS
- EVERYONE IN Class MUST HAVE FELT SAME WAY
  - STANGE IF CONDITIONS WERE So BAD

READING 3.2B: KOREA'S APPEAL AT THE WASHINGTON CONFERENCE

GENTLEMEN: We have been delegated by the people of Korea to present their cause to you and to the Conference on Limitation of Armament.

The Korean question is one of the vital far eastern questions. As such it should be considered by the conference. Korea should not be held up merely as an object lesson to illustrate the possibilities of ruthless and aggressive oppression. Her wrongs should not simply be commiserated. They should be righted if the objects of the conference are to be attained. Twenty million people, clamoring for restored independence and freedom and craving the justice to which they are beyond all question entitled, can not be denied a hearing without a reflection upon the worthy objects which you are appointed to secure.

. . . The Korean problem is very simple. Japan holds military possession of, and forces its sovereignty upon Korea, without her consent, in violation of the terms of her treaty of alliance with Korea, and in direct conflict with other treaties that were made by her at different times with that nation. This military possession and enforced sovereignty without consent is due to the fact that neither the United States nor any of the great powers invited to participate in the coming conference used their "good offices" to prevent it, as by several of their treaty covenants with Korea they solemnly engaged themselves to do.

. . . In 1904 Japan and Korea, just prior to the Russo-Japanese war, entered into the treaty of alliance . . . and that by virtue of such treaty Japan was permitted to occupy Korea with her military forces and to use Korea as a military base in her operations against Siberian Russia.

The compensating clause to Korea in that treaty of alliance was Japan's guaranty of her territorial integrity and independence. It was negotiated at the instance of Japan. Yet she has never recognized the sanctity of that clause. . . .

With the conclusion of the Russo-Japanese War Japan, instead of removing her troops and armed forces from Korea, as the treaty contemplated, established permanent military bases at Seoul, the capital, at Peng Yang in the northwest, at Nannam in the northeast, and at Taiku in the southeast, with naval bases at Fusan on the southern coast and Wonsan on the eastern, notwithstanding her naval base at Darien and Port Arthur. . . .

Thus the temporary military possession of Korea, which Japan obtained by reason of the treaty of alliance, has been perpetuated. . . .

The people of Korea vigorously challenge the assertion that they or their Government ever acquiesced in or consented to the assumption of the sovereignty of Japan over Korea. . . .

Following this assumed sovereignty under military coercion there has been much oppression. The people are taxed without representation and have absolutely no voice in their own government. They are oppressed economically and have no redress. Their courts are presided over by Japanese judges and clerks. Japanese teachers installed in

67th Congress, Second Session, Senate Document no 109. *Korea's Appeal to the Conference on Limitation of Armament.* Presented by Mr. Spencer, December 21, 1921. Washington, D.C.: U.S. Government Printing Office, 1922, pp. 8–10.

their schools compel their children to learn a foreign language. Immoral practices are imposed upon them that they abhor. Intellectually they are being strangled and are being reduced to the position of ignorant serfs and slaves. The people and the country are being exploited for the sole benefit of a foreign power and a foreign people. . . .

Japan justifies her conduct by contending that her occupation of Korea has conferred a material boon upon Koreans. But investigation demonstrates that harbors have been deepened and improved for war vessels and that railways and roads have been extended and improved with special reference to military and not for economic uses. Afforestation is claimed, but the facts are that the 101,000 acres afforested are belittled by the 5,391,000 acres of virgin timber cut over. In terms of dollars and cents, there has been $168,000,000 spent in Korea by Japan for improvements, and $418,000,000 has been taken out of Korea by Japan through increased taxes over normal Korean taxes and increase of the Korean national debt. Japan has taken out of Korea $250,000,000 to assist in the support of her military machine.

— apparently treaties meant nothing because nobody ever listened to them anyway

DISCUSSION QUESTION

How did the Korean and Sudanese nationalists feel about the foreign countries that dominated them? Based on these readings, do you see differences in their methods of resistance?

CHAPTER FOUR

Militarism and World War I

Along with nationalism, imperialism, and other causes, militarism helped propel Europe into World War I. Its adherents glorified war or at least thought it inevitable or preferable to refraining from war. Many militarists, many of whom were also nationalists and imperialists, attempted to apply Charles Darwin's ideas about the "struggle for existence" and "survival of the fittest" to international relations. Writer Leo Tolstoy was thinking of such ideas in 1906, when he objected that science "has decided that the struggle and enmity of all against all is a necessary, unavoidable, and beneficent condition of human life" (review Reading 1.3).

Reading 4.1, by German general Friedrich von Bernhardi reflects well the militarist view, a view by no means limited to generals or Germans—for example, Theodore Roosevelt, the U.S. president throughout most of the first decade of the century, frequently made statements such as, "No triumph of peace is quite as great as the sublime triumphs of war."

Militarists such as Bernhardi, however, failed to foresee or to mention how horrific war could be, and later generations can only wonder if countries would have entered World War I if they had realized how widespread the resulting slaughter would be. Would French leaders and the population in general have supported war, for example, if they had realized that three out of every ten Frenchmen ages eighteen to twenty-eight would be killed in the war?

One battle site that symbolized the tremendous suffering of World War I was the area around the Belgian city of Ypres, where three major battles were fought. Reading 4.2, by a German soldier in the trenches, deals with the second of these three battles. The selection not only captures some of the horrors of trench warfare but also indicates Great Britain's widespread use of colonial troops—"black, brown, yellow, red, a whole conglomeration of nations." From India, for example, the British sent more than 600,000 troops to take part in overseas conflicts during World War I.

Before the war, socialists were not the only people opposed to militarism (review Reading 2.1); nonsocialist pacifists also challenged the militarists. Many women were active pacifists, including Austrian baroness Bertha von Suttner, a tireless advocate of peace conferences, who in 1905 received the Nobel Peace Prize. Once the war began, pacifism became less popular, and most women, like most men, supported their own country's war effort. However, some women continued to oppose the war. One such woman was English journalist, pacifist, and feminist Helena M. Swanwick. She expresses her views on the war in Reading 4.3. Especially interesting is what she has to say about the relationship between women and war. Her words not only are relevant to World War I but also raise the larger question of possible gender differences in regard to attitudes toward war, as well as other political issues.

READING 4.1

German General Friedrich von Bernhardi on War

In 1909, General Friedrich von Bernhardi (1849–1930) took over command of Germany's Seventh Army Corps. He became most known, however, for his military writings, especially *Germany and the Next War,* part of which is reprinted here. The book was published in numerous editions after he completed it in 1911. It received wide attention abroad, as well as in Germany. Although Bernhardi was writing as an individual and not as a government spokesman, historian Fritz Fischer has argued convincingly that many of Bernhardi's ideas were widely shared by German nationalists and to some extent the German government. Indeed, many Germans shared Bernhardi's belief that Germany was a great scientific, industrial, and cultural force in the world and that it had a right to exercise more authority in Europe and beyond than other world powers were willing to allow.

War is a biological necessity of the first importance, a regulative element in the life of mankind which cannot be dispensed with, since without it an unhealthy development will follow, which excludes every advancement of the race, and therefore all real civilization. "War is the father of all things."* The sages of antiquity long before Darwin recognized this.

The struggle for existence is, in the life of Nature, the basis of all healthy development. All existing things show themselves to be the result of contesting forces. So in the life of man the struggle is not merely the destructive, but the life-giving principle. "To supplant or to be supplanted is the essence of life," says Goethe, and the strong life gains the upper hand. The law of the stronger holds good everywhere. Those forms survive which are able to procure themselves the most favourable conditions of life, and to assert themselves in the universal economy of Nature. The weaker succumb. This struggle is regulated and restrained by the unconscious sway of biological laws and by the interplay of opposite forces. In the plant world and the animal world this process is worked out in unconscious tragedy. In the human race it is consciously carried out, and regulated by social ordinances. The man of strong will and strong intellect tries by every means to assert himself, the ambitious strive to rise, and in this effort the individual is far from being guided merely by the consciousness of right. The life-work and the life-struggle of many men are determined, doubtless, by unselfish and ideal motives, but to a far greater extent the less noble passions—craving for possessions, enjoyment and honour, envy and the thirst for revenge—determine men's actions. Still more often, perhaps, it is the need to live which brings down even natures of a higher mould into the universal struggle for existence and enjoyment.

There can be no doubt on this point. The nation is made up of individuals, the State of communities. The motive which influences each member is prominent in the whole

---

*πόλεμος πατήρ πάντων (Heraclitus of Ephesus).

von Bernhardi, Friedrich. *Germany and the Next War.* Trans. Allen H. Powles. New York: Longmans, Green and Co., 1914, pp. 18–22, 26–27, 105–8.

body. It is a persistent struggle for possessions, power, and sovereignty, which primarily governs the relations of one nation to another, and right is respected so far only as it is compatible with advantage. So long as there are men who have human feelings and aspirations, so long as there are nations who strive for an enlarged sphere of activity, so long will conflicting interests come into being and occasions for making war arise.

"The natural law, to which all laws of Nature can be reduced, is the law of struggle. All intrasocial property, all thoughts, inventions, and institutions, as, indeed, the social system itself, are a result of the intrasocial struggle, in which one survives and another is cast out. The extrasocial, the supersocial struggle which guides the external development of societies, nations, and races, is war. The internal development, the intrasocial struggle, is man's daily work—the struggle of thoughts, feelings, wishes, sciences, activities. The outward development, the supersocial struggle, is the sanguinary struggle of nations—war. In what does the creative power of this struggle consist? In growth and decay, in the victory of the one factor and in the defeat of the other! This struggle is a creator, since it eliminates."[†]

That social system in which the most efficient personalities possess the greatest influence will show the greatest vitality in the intrasocial struggle. In the extrasocial struggle, in war, that nation will conquer which can throw into the scale the greatest physical, mental, moral, material, and political power, and is therefore the best able to defend itself. War will furnish such a nation with favourable vital conditions, enlarged possibilities of expansion and widened influence, and thus promote the progress of mankind; for it is clear that those intellectual and moral factors which insure superiority in war are also those which render possible a general progressive development. They confer victory because the elements of progress are latent in them. Without war, inferior or decaying races would easily choke the growth of healthy budding elements, and a universal decadence would follow. "War," says A. W. von Schlegel, "is as necessary as the struggle of the elements in Nature." . . .

Struggle is, therefore, a universal law of Nature, and the instinct of self-preservation which leads to struggle is acknowledged to be a natural condition of existence. "Man is a fighter." Self-sacrifice is a renunciation of life, whether in the existence of the individual or in the life of States, which are agglomerations of individuals. The first and paramount law is the assertion of one's own independent existence. By self-assertion alone can the State maintain the conditions of life for its citizens, and insure them the legal protection which each man is entitled to claim from it. This duty of self-assertion is by no means satisfied by the mere repulse of hostile attacks; it includes the obligation to assure the possibility of life and development to the whole body of the nation embraced by the State.

Strong, healthy, and flourishing nations increase in numbers. From a given moment they require a continual expansion of their frontiers, they require new territory for the accommodation of their surplus population. Since almost every part of the globe is inhabited, new territory must, as a rule, be obtained at the cost of its possessors—that is to say, by conquest, which thus becomes a law of necessity.

[†]Clauss Wagner, "Der Krieg als schaffendes Weltprinzip."

The right of conquest is universally acknowledged. At first the procedure is pacific. Over-populated countries pour a stream of emigrants into other States and territories. These submit to the legislature of the new country, but try to obtain favourable conditions of existence for themselves at the cost of the original inhabitants, with whom they compete. This amounts to conquest.

The right of colonization is also recognized. Vast territories inhabited by uncivilized masses are occupied by more highly civilized States, and made subject to their rule. Higher civilization and the correspondingly greater power are the foundations of the right to annexation. This right is, it is true, a very indefinite one, and it is impossible to determine what degree of civilization justifies annexation and subjugation. The impossibility of finding a legitimate limit to these international relations has been the cause of many wars. The subjugated nation does not recognize this right of subjugation, and the more powerful civilized nation refuses to admit the claim of the subjugated to independence. This situation becomes peculiarly critical when the conditions of civilization have changed in the course of time. The subject nation has, perhaps, adopted higher methods and conceptions of life, and the difference in civilization has consequently lessened. Such a state of things is growing ripe in British India.

Lastly, in all times the right of conquest by war has been admitted. It may be that a growing people cannot win colonies from uncivilized races, and yet the State wishes to retain the surplus population which the mother-country can no longer feed. Then the only course left is to acquire the necessary territory by war. Thus the instinct of self-preservation leads inevitably to war, and the conquest of foreign soil. It is not the possessor, but the victor, who then has the right. . . .

War, from this standpoint, will be regarded as a moral necessity, if it is waged to protect the highest and most valuable interests of a nation. As human life is now constituted, it is political idealism which calls for war, while materialism—in theory, at least—repudiates it.

If we grasp the conception of the State from this higher aspect, we shall soon see that it cannot attain its great moral ends unless its political power increases. The higher object at which it aims is closely correlated to the advancement of its material interests. It is only the State which strives after an enlarged sphere of influence that creates the conditions under which mankind develops into the most splendid perfection. The development of all the best human capabilities and qualities can only find scope on the great stage of action which power creates. But when the State renounces all extension of power, and recoils from every war which is necessary for its expansion; when it is content to exist, and no longer wishes to grow; when "at peace on sluggard's couch it lies," then its citizens become stunted. The efforts of each individual are cramped, and the broad aspect of things is lost. This is sufficiently exemplified by the pitiable existence of all small States, and every great Power that mistrusts itself falls victim to the same curse.

All petty and personal interests force their way to the front during a long period of peace. Selfishness and intrigue run riot, and luxury obliterates idealism. Money acquires an excessive and unjustifiable power, and character does not obtain due respect:

"Man is stunted by peaceful days,
In idle repose his courage decays.
Law is the weakling's game,
Law makes the world the same.
But in war man's strength is seen,
War ennobles all that is mean;
Even the coward belies his name."
      SCHILLER: *Braut v. Messina.*

"Wars are terrible, but necessary, for they save the State from social petrifaction and stagnation. It is well that the transitoriness of the goods of this world is not only preached, but is learnt by experience. War alone teaches this lesson."[*]

War, in opposition to peace, does more to arouse national life and to expand national power than any other means known to history. It certainly brings much material and mental distress in its train, but at the same time it evokes the noblest activities of the human nature. This is especially so under present-day conditions, when it can be regarded not merely as the affair of Sovereigns and Governments, but as the expression of the united will of a whole nation.

All petty private interests shrink into insignificance before the grave decision which a war involves. The common danger unites all in a common effort, and the man who shirks this duty to the community is deservedly spurned. This union contains a liberating power which produces happy and permanent results in the national life. We need only recall the uniting power of the War of Liberation or the Franco-German War and their historical consequences. The brutal incidents inseparable from every war vanish completely before the idealism of the main result. All the sham reputations which a long spell of peace undoubtedly fosters are unmasked. Great personalities take their proper place; strength, truth, and honour come to the front and are put into play. "A thousand touching traits testify to the sacred power of the love which a righteous war awakes in noble nations."[†] . . .

In the first place, our political position would be considerably consolidated if we could finally get rid of the standing danger that France will attack us on a favourable occasion, so soon as we find ourselves involved in complications elsewhere. In one way or another *we must square our account with France* if we wish for a free hand in our international policy. This is the first and foremost condition of a sound German policy, and since the hostility of France once and for all cannot be removed by peaceful overtures, the matter must be settled by force of arms. France must be so completely crushed that she can never again come across our path.

Further, we must contrive every means of strengthening the political power of our allies. We have already followed such a policy in the case of Austria when we declared our readiness to protect, if necessary with armed intervention, the final annexation of Bosnia and Herzegovina by our ally on the Danube. Our policy towards Italy must follow the same lines, especially if in any Franco-German war an opportunity should be

---

[*]Kuno Fischer, "Hegel," i., p. 737.

[†]Treitschke, "Deutsche Geschichte," i., p. 482.

presented of doing her a really valuable service. It is equally good policy in every way to support Turkey, whose importance for Germany and the Triple Alliance has already been discussed. . . .

. . . Finally, as regards our own position in Europe, we can only effect an extension of our own political influence, in my opinion, by awakening in our weaker neighbours, through the integrity and firmness of our policy, the conviction that their independence and their interests are bound up with Germany, and are best secured under the protection of the German arms. This conviction might eventually lead to an enlargement of the Triple Alliance into a Central European Federation. Our military strength in Central Europe would by this means be considerably increased, and the extraordinarily unfavourable geographical configuration of our dominions would be essentially improved in case of war. Such a federation would be the expression of a natural community of interests, which is founded on the geographical and natural conditions, and would insure the durability of the political community based on it.

We must employ other means also for the widening of our colonial territory, so that it may be able to receive the overflow of our population. . . .

A part of our surplus population, indeed—so far as present conditions point—will always be driven to seek a livelihood outside the borders of the German Empire. Measures must be taken to the extent at least of providing that the German element is not split up in the world, but remains united in compact blocks, and thus forms, even in foreign countries, political centres of gravity in our favour, markets for our exports, and centres for the diffusion of German culture.

An intensive colonial policy is for us especially an absolute necessity.

READING 4.2

A German Soldier's View of the Second Battle of Ypres

In the first battle of Ypres (October 30–November 24, 1914) the Germans attempted to penetrate British lines near Ypres in order to reach the English Channel. A year earlier, many of these German soldiers had been students, and the German losses were great, as were those of the original British Expeditionary Force sent to this part of Belgium Flanders. But the British and other Allied troops held, and, for the next three years, despite millions of casualties, neither side was able to advance its trench line in Belgium and France more than about ten miles. The second battle of Ypres occurred April 22–May 25, 1915. Part of this battle is described by an anonymous German soldier in this reading, which was originally printed in the German press not long after the events he describes. He fails to mention, however, that the German success was partly because of its gas attack, the first major use of poison gas in the war. Nevertheless, the German success proved short-lived, and Ypres itself remained under British control.

One of the conditions alluded to by the German soldier is the water that so often plagued the soldiers in the trenches. During the third battle of Ypres (July 31–November 10, 1917), British general Douglas Haig ordered a preparatory bombard-

Ruins of St. Martin's church in Ypres, Belgium, the site of three major battles in World War I.
Archival Research International/Double Delta Industries, Inc.

ment of more than 4 million shells (which would take 55,000 workers a year to produce). It, plus exceptionally heavy rains that summer and autumn, turned the normally damp area and its drainage dikes into a muddy bog, a bog across which the
British soldiers were supposed to advance and kill or rout the entrenched Germans.
The total casualties (dead and wounded) for both sides exceeded 500,000 men. For
their efforts, the British advanced their line only about five miles. One of the German participants in the battle was a young corporal who would later become
famous—Adolf Hitler. About a year later, in October 1918, Hitler would again be
dug in near Ypres, when he was temporarily blinded by a British gas attack.

The long expected and eagerly longed for day has at last arrived—at last our heart's desire has been granted. We have crossed the Yser Canal and taken up positions on the opposite bank at a sufficient distance from the water way, which in the course of the past
few months has often well-nigh brought us to despair. The monotonous view of the Canal
has at last disappeared and we are thankful at no longer hearing the gurgling of the yellow brown waves, which even with a moderate wind so often honoured us with a visit in
the trenches, drenching us to the skin! How often did we pray for this, when on cold winter or stormy early spring nights we kept watch in the trenches, shivering with cold and
our teeth chattering. And now it is really a fact, we have got across, have fairly dry ground
under our feet, and the principal—have given the Allies a sound and thorough thrashing.

War-Chronicle. Berlin: M. Berg, May 1915, pp. 60–62.

It all happened so suddenly that it seems almost incomprehensible now, although for days before we could all see that something was in preparation. Conjectures and assumptions were exchanged, watchwords flew hither and thither, still nobody believed in the seriousness of the situation. Already for days past, we could hear incessant cannonading to our right, which was so violent that we supposed an extensive battle was in progress. In our section perfect calm prevailed, only the pioneers were more active than usual. Pontons were brought up, beams and planks piled up in our vicinity, while the pioneer officers passed by with mysterious glances. What was going on? But we soon learned what was in the wind, and I must say the news was received with such enthusiasm that it made us forget all the dreadfulness in store. Preparations were eagerly inaugurated for the great venture, and all of us could scarcely await the hour, which was to bring us victory or death.

This time, our artillery worked wonders, the whole enemy position had the appearance of a large Lake of fire. Incessantly our shells burst in and above the English trenches, working havoc and destruction. I cannot actually remember how long this bombardment lasted, whether long or short. None of us in the front trenches looked at our watches, our eyes were riveted on the gruesome, but magnificent spectacle before us. We suffered from the biting smoke which came over to our position in dense clouds and caused a choking sensation in our throats, so that we were hardly able to stand it, although we got but a fraction of what was sent to the enemy trenches. And yet no one left his place. We all stood and stared. When suddenly, as if at a given signal, our guns ceased fire and an almost solemn stillness reigned, many a one felt his head which was throbbing as a result of the fearful din, looked at his comrade and silently pointed over beyond, where the thick columns of smoke still darkened the sky. Was it a dream, or was it reality? . . .

But when the command came to advance, this entire depression disappeared. The company climbed up as one man from the trenches, their rifles firm in their hands, storming forwards, until—dashed—the Canal! We had quite forgotten it and could not get across. Still, wonders never cease. A regular bridge had been laid. Dozens of boats were standing ready, and in the water hundreds of swimmers could be seen who with a rifle in one hand swam across with the other. Our pioneers are splendid fellows—above all praise. Under cover of the artillery fire, they had brought up all their material without us having noticed anything, and now all we had to do was to march over or to enter one of the boats without fearing even getting our feet wet, if we did not prefer to swim across for a change.

In a few minutes we had all reached the opposite bank—and it did not take us long to lie flat and open fire. The English were not taken by surprise and those who had not been injured by the artillery fire, shot like mad. Mines, hand-grenades, and bombs flew hither and thither. We jumped up and were soon in the enemy entrenchments, where frightful hand to hand fighting ensued. Fresh supports were continually sent to us across the canal and in this way we continued to press forward, proceeding across the first, second and third lines of entrenchments. Now we have come to the main position! Hurrah, there are even guns! Who would have thought that we were to capture guns to-day! For we took them, nine in number, quite new English guns! We had not paid any attention to the machine guns and mine throwers in the first captured trenches—we had to press forward and had no time to bother about such trifles. The principal thing was that they were captured, by whom, did not matter in the least. But these guns—that was another thing—they were ours by right—and our slightly wounded, who kept guard, took good care that we got our rights. We had expected much greater resistance from the enemy and saw to our joy that we had suffered comparatively slight losses. Our artillery had done its work too well, the French and English had been well tamed down.

The sights in the captured positions were dreadful. Our heavy shells had made enormous tunnels in the ground, destroying the dug-outs and cover, and all around the slashed bodies and limbs of the English and French were to be seen. But it was not only Europeans that lay there stiff and dead—black, brown, yellow, red, a whole conglomeration of nations, where Death had reaped its reward. They all lay there dumb and stiff, most of them cruelly mutilated—proofs of England's brutal sentiments, that had sent them to certain death. Among the prisoners we made (which was quite a large number), were also many coloured, especially Canadians, who were apparently happy to have got off with their lives and be taken prisoners by the Germans. We were surprised, as we had thought that we only had English opposite us, and now we saw to our astonishment that we had been fighting against so many various races.

We had been victorious and the much longed for enemy positions were in our hands. Let them come and repeat our attack, we shall be ready for them.

READING 4.3

A British Feminist and Pacifist Opposes the War in 1915

After serving as a journalist for the prestigious newspaper *Manchester Guardian,* Helena M. Swanwick (1864–1939) for several years edited *The Common Cause,* a woman's suffrage journal. During World War I, she lectured and wrote opposing the war and was one of the leaders of the Union of Democratic Control, an organization which worked to establish a more democratic basis for international affairs. Swanwick's article reprinted here was first published by that organization in 1915. Despite considerable British hostility toward pacifism in the war years, Swanwick and organizations such as the No-Conscription Fellowship (NCF) continued to oppose the war. At its high point, the NCF's weekly journal sold 10,000 copies. In the United States, which did not enter the war until 1917, the American social work pioneer Jane Addams, like Swanwick, also emphasized women's special role as nurturers and protectors of human life. In 1915, Addams also helped found the Women's Peace Party and the Women's International League for Peace and Freedom.

One of Swanwick's long-held goals was finally accomplished in 1918, when British women age thirty and over gained the vote. Some historians, however, have attributed the gaining of this right, at least in part, to efforts opposed by Swanwick— women's support for the British war effort. Women's war efforts, including their work in munition factories, led a number of previous opponents of the suffragettes to change their position and support the granting of the vote.

Unlike the other major European powers, until 1916 the British relied on volunteers to serve in the military. Although this poster reflected government efforts to encourage enlistment, most British women, unlike Helena Swanwick, did support the war. Imperial War Museum, London.

WOMEN'S SHARE

"We do not war upon women and children!" This is a commonplace of British rhetoric at the present moment. But it is not true. War is waged by men only, but it is not possible to wage it upon men only. All wars are and must be waged upon women and children as well as upon men. When aviators drop bombs, when guns bombard fortified towns, it is not possible to avoid the women and children who may chance to be in the way. Women have to make good the economic disasters of war; they go short, they work double tides, they pay war taxes and war prices, like men, and out of smaller incomes.

There are in this country seven millions of "gainfully occupied" women and girls, and yet it is curious how officialism generally overlooks this large body of wage and salary earners and assumes that all is well if there is not extensive unemployment of men. The sea and land forces draw off a million men and thus a shortage of male labour is created and (what we are very apt to forget) a shortage of the useful things which that male labour would have created for the benefit of the country; but men and women so largely still do different work that this withdrawal of men does not create any considerable demand for female labour, and the curtailment of men's work often causes the dismissal of the women whose labour dovetails with men's. To take only

Swanwick, Helena M. *Women and War.* Pamphlet no. 11. London: The Union of Democratic Control, 1915, pp. 1–6, 10–11.

the clerks and typists, we have seen how the reduction of business by the withdrawal of men has hit the women. Again, the effect of war upon all the luxury trades, in which so many women are employed, is sudden and disastrous, throwing out thousands of dressmakers, milliners, embroidresses, and so forth, while teachers, artists, and many classes of professional women suffer terribly also. One half of these earning women have relatives dependent on them, making the strain and the suffering heavier. And, if we take the other half of the working women of the country—those who are humorously reckoned as not being "employed persons," the working housewives—it does not take much imagination to realise what a rise in the prices of necessaries amounting to 25 per cent, means of pinching and penury to the woman who is trying to housekeep on a sum which is round about a pound a week in the towns and far less in the rural districts.

But, far more heavy than the burden which they share with men, is the burden more particularly their own, which war lays upon women. Two pieces of work for the human family are peculiarly the work of women: they are the life-givers and the home-makers. War kills or maims the children born of woman and tended by her; war destroys "woman's place"—the home. Every man killed or mangled in war has been carried for months in his mother's body and has been tended and nourished for years of his life by women. He is the work of women: they have rights in him and in what he does with the life they have given and sustained. . . .

And the homes of the women? Within the zone of war, what is left to the women? The best that can be done for them is to round them up with the children, like cattle, sick and old, the nursing mothers and the women with child, and turn them into concentration camps, to rot and go mad and die. And the worst—Ask Belgium and East Prussia and Serbia.

These are notorious facts, which no rhetoric can abolish. Another obvious fact is that a constant state of preparedness for war requires a tremendous yearly sacrifice of the fruits of toil; wealth, which might be used to nourish and enlarge and make beautiful the life which is women's charge, is wasted in the competitive increase of armaments, yearly scrapped and replaced by fresh inventions of destruction. Men cannot afford to protect motherhood adequately and to start their children well in life, because they must expend so much wealth in making engines to destroy the children of foreign nations. Again, homicidal wars tend greatly to reduce the proportion of young men to young women, and this disproportion must result either in polygamy or in the establishment of a very large class of celibate women, or of a combination of both, such as we are at present familiar with. There are, besides, all the deep injuries to women created by the barrack system and the corrupting effect of the breaking up of homes. Moreover, when men are called upon to waste their lives in war, women are called upon to spend (and frequently to give up) their lives in child-bearing to make good the waste; the greater the waste of life the greater the waste of women in repairing life. Militarist states always tend to degrade women to the position of breeders and slaves.

In all these ways the possibility of war, the preparation for war, the militarist basis of States (whether "civilised" or "uncivilised") affect the position of women and affect it altogether evilly.

WHEN MIGHT IS RIGHT

There are, however, other less-obvious ways in which women, and through women the causes of civilisation and democracy, suffer from militarism. The fact that so many people do not clearly apprehend these injuries makes them particularly insidious. They are, however, the inevitable result of a barbarous conception of the foundations of government. In militarist states, women must always, to a greater or less degree, be deprived of liberty, security, scope, and initiative. For militarism is the enthronement of physical force as the arbiter of nations, and under such an arbitrament women must always go under. Women, whose physical force is specialised for the giving and nurture of life, will never be able to oppose men with destructive force. If destructive force is to continue to dominate the world, then man must continue to dominate woman, to his and her lasting injury. The sanction of brute force by which a strong nation "hacks its way" through a weak one is precisely the same as that by which the stronger male dictates to the weaker female. Not till the idea of public right has been accepted by the great nations will there be freedom and security for small nations; not till the idea of moral law has been accepted by the majority of men will there be freedom and security for women. . . .

People who desire the enfranchisement of women will only be effective workers if they work for pacifism, or the control of physical by moral force. Pacifists will only be effective if they admit that woman's claim to freedom is based on the same principle as the claim of small nations. The anti-suffragist's major premise of force as the basis of political power is not argument; it is man's knock-out blow. We have no right to assume that what has been always will be; that men are incapable of development; that they must always worship the god of brute force. There is no reason whatever why men should not gradually learn that they get no good, but much evil, from the uncontrolled domination of force. They have shown already in countless ways that they are learning the lesson. They will learn it much faster when women have studied the causes of war and set themselves against them; when women cease to idealise pugnacity in men and see it in its true light as fretful egotism; when, finally, women who demand citizenship join with democratic men and thus show that they understand the very foundation of their own claim and can teach men to understand better the democratic creed which they profess.

Women will then be more effective peace-makers than, with all their good will, they have been in the past. On the whole, no one can doubt that they have been more opposed to war than men, because they have had nothing to gain and all to lose in war. But they have been subjected, ignorant, inarticulate, disorganised. Those who have kept them so should be the last to blame them. British women are rapidly emerging from subjection and are catching up with men in respect of knowledge, power of organisation, and expression. . . .

ARE WOMEN PACIFISTS?

There remain the people who venture to doubt whether women's influence or vote would really be for peace. They will tell you that they have heard more bloodthirsty and violent talk from women than from men. These comparisons are always very difficult to check, but it would seem natural that, in militarist circles, the women should be more violent in speech than the men, because they can only relieve their feelings by words, whereas the men can go and fight. Professors and journalists and other sedentary men are notoriously more bloodthirsty in their language than the fighting men. But it does not follow that even these women would be anxious to go to war, and we must further remember that it is the conversation of such women which sticks in the memory; the millions of heart-sore women are, for the most part, silent. They have a deep sense of loyalty to their men and are acutely aware of their sufferings and sacrifices. Not for the world will they say anything which would seem to undervalue these, or suggest that they are offered for a wrong or a mistaken cause. So that, in backing their men in the war in which they are actually engaged, many women seem to be backing warfare itself, although in their hearts they abhor it.

There are, again, among suffragist women, two groups which hold aloof from widely different causes. One says she will take no part in "men's politics" until men have enfranchised her: the other fears that, by adopting a definitely pacifist attitude, women would "antagonise" militarist men. We may think both these views wrong, but men, at least, should be tolerant of a state of mind created by their own neglect to do justice. They cannot have it all ways, and the unfree will not all have all the virtues of the free. Women have learned by bitter experience that, unless they concentrate upon winning their own liberty, they are very apt to be made merely the catspaws of political parties, and that, when the party for which they have worked is triumphant, it pushes aside the women's claim with more or less polite circumlocution. But to work for a right foundation of government; to endeavour to establish public right in control of physical force, is not to work merely for a party victory; it is to work for the very foundation of a free and secure existence for women. Every suffrage society ought to be a pacifist society and realise that pacifist propaganda is an integral part of suffrage propaganda. If there are some suffragists who do not yet see this, they are matched by some pacifists who do not see that their creed removes the only real obstacle to the enfranchisement of women.

The difficulty in seeing these connections is due to mere muddle-headedness, but there is something a little contemptible about the fear of antagonising the militarist men. No one ought to wish to get the vote on false pretences. The timid may, however, be recommended to consider this: these men who would not give women the vote if they believed women would vote pacifist are the men who would not give women the vote at any price; these are the relics of barbarism; these are the men with whom it is no use reasoning at all. It is the civilised men who are going to enfranchise women, and it is with such men that women should ally themselves.

DISCUSSION QUESTION

According to Bernhardi, why is war necessary and what favorable developments can result from war? In what ways do the battles of Ypres and the views of Helena Swanwick suggest a view of war contrary to Bernhardi's?

PART TWO

From Revolutions to the End of World War II

The period from World War I until the end of World War II was characterized by revolution, nationalism, the rise of dictators, continuing scientific and technological advances, a global depression, and finally a war that was much more global and destructive than World War I had been.

While World War I was being waged in Europe, revolutionary movements were already underway in Mexico (see Chapter 5) and China (see Reading 10.2), and the war helped ignite a revolution in Russia that brought a communist government to power by the end of 1917 (see Reading 7.1). Although the revolutionary programs of Pancho Villa, Sun Yat-sen, and Vladimir Lenin differed greatly, all three men spoke against imperialistic foreign influences and for a greater egalitarianism to reduce the vast gap between rich and poor. After World War I, the new communist regime in Russia won a civil war, and communist influences spread to other parts of the world—for example, to China and Indochina, where Mao Zedong and Ho Chi Minh helped establish communist parties (see Reading 10.3A).

Geographical boundaries changed in Europe not only as a result of World War I, but also because of the nationalist forces it unleashed that insisted upon self-determination. Chapter 6 discusses how nationalism affected the postwar settlements, including the arrangement finally arrived at in 1921 between Great Britain and Irish nationalists. Readings 12.2 and 13.1 indicate that in Germany, in the 1930s, nationalism under Adolf Hitler could become terribly destructive when mixed with racism and aggression.

Outside of Europe, nationalism and the quest for self-determination were also major forces, as Chapters 10 and 11 make clear. Despite considerable anticolonial opposition, however, as in India under Gandhi (see Reading 10.1), non-Europeans achieved few interwar successes in obtaining independence. And many non-Europeans soon shared the sentiment of Ho Chi Minh, who believed that U.S. President Woodrow Wilson's doctrine of self-determination was a "big fraud" (see Reading 10.3B). Many non-Europeans accused white Americans and Europeans of racism and perceived a link between it, continuing colonialism, and the imperialistic powers' refusal to grant self-determination. Within the United States, racism continued to deny African Americans equal rights (see Reading 8.1).

When Woodrow Wilson asked the U.S. Congress to approve going to war against Germany in 1917, he proclaimed the need to make "the world . . . safe for democracy." Among others, Mexican revolutionaries, Sun Yat-sen, and Lenin also proclaimed their support for democracy, though they all defined it differently, and many Europeans were enthusiastic about it immediately after World War I. By the beginning of World War II, however, dictators or authoritarian nondemocratic governments ruled over most of Europe and Japan. The two most powerful dictators were Stalin and Hitler (see Chapter 12), and, despite championing very different ideologies, they had much in common.

Already before World War I, the United States was in the forefront of creating a culture of consumption, and this tendency escalated rapidly in the 1920s and beyond into present times (see Reading 14.2). Mass production techniques popularized by Henry Ford (review Reading 1.2) and labor efficiency studies pioneered by Frederick Taylor dramatically increased the production of goods. In 1925, Ford's assembly lines were rolling out 9,000 cars per day. Along with Ford and other automobile producers, other mass producers and distributors included such companies as Sears, Roebuck, whose millions of distributed mail-order catalogs were often used as learning aids for math, reading, and other subjects in rural schoolrooms. In the late 1920s, the average U.S. middle-class family owned not only an automobile but also a radio, telephone, phonograph, sewing machine, washing machine, and vacuum cleaner.

Like television later in the century, the radio's impact on everyday life was huge, particularly in the United States and Europe. Dictators such as Hitler and democrats such as Franklin Roosevelt used it effectively (see Reading 9.1A), both in peacetime and wartime, and later in the century it was an important instrument of propaganda during the Cold War (see Chapter 15). In the United States, radio helped popularize sports stars, entertainers, and other celebrities, and it covered such important events as the Scopes Trial (see Reading 8.2).

The radio was only part of the new mass media, a term first used in the 1920s, including newspapers and other print media, as well as films. Although newspaper circulation increased significantly, especially in the West, in Great Britain in the late 1930s two persons bought a movie ticket for every one who purchased a daily paper. Global tendencies such as increasing population, urbanization, literacy, and mindfulness of the masses helped stimulate the growth of the mass media, as well as mass production generally. In some societies, rising elite awareness of the masses led to increasing democratization, including the granting of suffrage to women; in other societies, such as Nazi Germany, it led to heightened efforts to influence and propagandize the masses. One of the most influential U.S. leftist periodicals of the years 1914 to 1917 was called *The Masses;* John Reed (see Readings 5.2 and 7.1) was one of its editors until it was banned by the U.S. government after the United States entered World War I in 1917. Some observers, such as elitist Spanish thinker Jose Ortega y Gasset in his *Revolt of the Masses*

(1930), decried the increasing influence of the masses, equating it with the vulgarization of cultural taste.

The increasing productivity and consumption of the 1920s—U.S. industrial production almost doubled during the decade—meant that after a while it became increasingly difficult to sell all of the new products being turned out. Even before the U.S. stock market crashed in October 1929, unemployment was increasing as the inventory of unsold goods increased. The "crash" helped turn a recession into a depression, and the Great Depression struck not just the United States but most of the rest of the world as well (see Chapter 9).

The effects of the depression helped subvert democracy in Germany and Japan and contributed to World War II, in which those two nations were the chief aggressors. Advances in military technology, including the development of bombers and the atomic bomb, were one of the main reasons that World War II was much more destructive than World War I.

Although media developments such as the radio and expanding film and print industries ensured that political leaders were not the only people who received media coverage, the impact of events on most ordinary people received little attention. Yet, as many of the readings which follow indicate, the effect of political and economic developments on common people was often great. In Reading 6.2, Irishman Thomas Hales describes how he was arrested by British officers outside a farm house in 1920 and subsequently beaten and tortured. Readings 7.2 and 12.1 describe the great suffering that many Soviet citizens experienced under Stalin. Readings in Chapter 9 relate some of the Great Depression hardships of ordinary people in the United States and Germany, and readings in Chapter 10 provide perspectives from Asians, including the area's leading political figures. The four selections in Reading 12.2 indicate the impact of Nazi racial and genetic policies on minorities, especially Germany's Jews. Finally, Readings 13.2 and 13.3 testify to the effect of World War II on average people—a young Chinese soldier and a female U.S. worker in an aircraft factory.

In the cultural realm, more modern ideas continued to challenge traditional beliefs (see, for example, Reading 10.2D, in which a Chinese woman recounts her opposition to some of the traditional ways of her culture). In the United States, the Scopes Trial (see Reading 8.2) indicated that many Protestant Fundamentalists were opposed to certain aspects of modern thinking. On this occasion, traditionalists opposed the teaching of Darwinian evolutionary ideas in the classroom, an opposition that has not completely died out three-quarters of a century later.

CHAPTER FIVE

Revolution in Latin America

In the beginning of the twentieth century, the diverse peoples in Latin America faced a variety of economic and social problems. In most of the region, strong-man dictators, often supported by the rich, landowning ruling class and the United States, dominated political life. As the economic powerhouse of the Western Hemisphere, the United States dominated the region economically and often intervened politically or militarily whenever its interests were threatened.

During the first decades of the century, middle classes, indigenous Amerindian groups, and peasants challenged the local ruling order and foreign domination in many Latin and South American nations. These challenges were particularly violent and far-reaching in Mexico. Práxedis Guerrero and the Flores Magón brothers, among others, helped to lay the intellectual foundations for the revolution of 1910 that overthrew dictator Porfirio Díaz, who had held power for thirty-five years. In Reading 5.1, Guerrero addresses both the abuses of tyrannical rule and the threat posed by North American domination to Mexican political and economic independence. Guerrero spoke out against the economic imperialism of the United States, just as socialists in Europe condemned Western capitalism (review Reading 2.1) during the same era.

When the Mexican revolution began in 1910, peasants in the southern provinces supported Francisco Madero and Emiliano Zapata, who demanded both the return of the land to the peasants and sweeping social reforms. Cowboys and farmers in northern Mexico rallied behind Francisco "Pancho" Villa to oust foreign landowners and investors. Pancho Villa was one of the most flamboyant of the Mexican revolutionaries. Reading 5.2 is taken from American journalist John Reed's vivid account, *Insurgent Mexico*. Here Reed describes Pancho Villa's commitment to social change, particularly improved education for Mexican children, and his relationship with

Venustiano Carranza, a Mexican politician who proved to be far more conservative than Villa. Villa's calls for education would be echoed by other Asian and African leaders, including the Tanzanian leader Julius Nyerere (see Reading 19.2A).

In 1917, after protracted warfare, Mexico adopted a new constitution, one of the most radical of the age; it provided for a powerful executive and a bicameral legislature, and it stripped the Catholic church in Mexico of much of its former power. The new constitution also called for political and social changes in Mexico, including a labor code and a declaration that Mexico's mineral, petroleum, and water resources belonged to the entire nation; however, the constitution was never fully implemented and often bore little relationship to the social and political realities of the country. Ultimately, a single party, the Party of the Mexican Revolution, later called the Party of the Revolutionary Institutions (PRI) emerged; the PRI dominated the political scene in Mexico well into the 1990s.

READING 5.1

Mexico's Romantic Revolutionary

At the beginning of the twentieth century, the dictatorship of Porfirio Díaz seemed firmly entrenched in Mexico. Díaz enjoyed the support of both the Mexican Catholic church and the upper classes; favoring the wealthy classes, Díaz had granted tax and land concessions to foreign capitalists, had encouraged the construction of railroads, and had supported the development of mines and industries. These policies had resulted in the forging of close economic ties between Mexico and the United States, which had provided massive foreign capital for Mexico's development. These policies had the effect of widening the divisions among the Europeanized upper-class Mexicans, the impoverished indigenous population, and the mestizos, or people of mixed ethnic origin. In widening the gap among these social classes, Díaz unconsciously laid the foundation for the revolution.

Because he combined writing with action, Práxedis Guerrero (1882–1910) is called Mexico's poet-revolutionary. Most of his works, written while on the run, show the influence of anarchism (an ideology that advocates the overthrow of all governments). Guerrero also wrote eloquently against the exploitation of the downtrodden by both the Díaz dictatorship and foreign economic interests.

Guerrero was known as a "haciendado-peon" because he abandoned the comfortable life of a landowner, which he had been born into, for a harsh life in copper and coal mines in the American Southwest. Operating on both sides of the U.S.-Mexican border, his activities brought him in contact with many Mexican Americans. In inspiring them to defend their rights, Guerrero became a player in Mexican-American history. As a result of his activities on both sides of the border, both governments declared Guerrero a wanted man. Guerrero's romantic image in Mexican folklore was enhanced by his early death, "on his feet," in 1910 in Chihuahua, Mexico. The following reading combines parts of two articles written by Guerrero shortly before his death.

"Why, if you want freedom, do you not kill the tyrant and thus avoid the horrors of a major fratricidal war? Why do you not murder the despot who oppresses people and who has put a price on your head?"—I have been asked many times. Because I am not an enemy of the tyrant, I have replied; because if I were to kill the man, tyranny would still be left standing, and it is the latter I combat; because if I were to blindly hurl myself against him, I would be doing what a dog does, when it bites a rock, hurting itself, but not knowing nor understanding where the pain comes from.

Tyranny is the logical result of a social disease, whose present remedy is the Revolution, since the pacific resistance of the doctrine of Tolstoy would only produce in these times the annihilation of the few who might ever have understood or practiced its simplicity . . . .

Tyrants do not just appear in nations through a phenomenon of self-generation. The universal law of determinism lifts them on the backs of the people. The same law,

Albro, Ward S. *To Die on Your Feet: The Life, Times, and Writings of Práxedis Guerrero.* Fort Worth, TX: Christian University Press, 1996, pp. 143, 145, 150–51.

manifested in the powerful revolutionary transformation, will make them fall forever, asphyxiated, like a fish deprived of its liquid environment.

Revolution is a fully conscious act, it is not the spasm of a primitive bestiality. There is no lack of just inference between the guiding idea and the action set upon. . . .

The threat of the North, the North American danger, has been, and is for many people the biggest patriotic reason to oppose the revolution. The fear of absorption by the Yankees, exploited by the Dictatorship and exploited by certain elements of the platonic opposition and of the "compromising" apostolate, has made the Mexican people forget, in part, the real danger into which the Government dealers have placed them.

During the violent Porfirian peace, both the larger and the smaller interests of Mexico have fallen into the threatening current of Yankee capitalism: natural resources, mines, forests, land, fisheries; and quickly the dependency on the financiers of the United States has been national reality in the political and the economic order. The will of the Yankee multimillionaires is, at the present time, the most powerful factor in the Mexican status quo. This is known by the Mexicans and also known by the foreigners. Peace in Mexico, as it stands today, constitutes the most favorable atmosphere for its complete absorption by the ambitious tendencies of the imperialism of the North, which works to preserve the peace, as it is understood that, if a Revolution does not completely snatch the prey from its hands, it will at least diminish the preponderant position of the United States, and the probabilities of absolute domination that it now holds for the future of Mexico.

People are saying, some with bad intentions and others out of ignorance, that the United States is waiting for a revolutionary movement in Mexico to intervene, to send its squads and troops and to declare the annexation by any means. And they advise us to preserve the peace at any cost, even the very cost of slavery, in order not to give the powerful and almighty Government of Washington a chance to declare us a Yankee province.

This is a childish argument, as childish as is the advice. The Government of the United States, which is both an instrument and servant of capitalism, is not waiting for, nor wants a revolution in Mexico; on the contrary, they fear it. All their actions have clearly demonstrated it. In violation of even the most trivial principles of justice, the Yankee government has been working toward the annihilation of the Mexican revolutionaries, launching against them a fury unprecedented in their history, which is filled with acts of different compliance toward all the revolutionaries who have sought refuge in their territory and who have organized from within it many movements, successful and failed. This persecution has had incidents that reveal the particular interest that Yankee capitalism places in not allowing the present peace to be disturbed, an interest that is far from being the simple wish of draining to the last drop the meaning of international treaties in order to preserve the power of a despot friend, but rather, of the desperate effort of someone who fights his own enemies, of someone who feels they are trying to take away from him a treasure of which he thought he was the undisputed owner. Otherwise, the Government of Washington would not have knocked so often and so audaciously on the doors of discredit, nor would it have raised, with its violence and abuses, that great movement of indignation that triggered the investigation now being carried out in the Congress for the illumination of the crimes committed against the Mexican Liberals in the United States. . . .

The United States does not want a revolution in Mexico; that has been plainly demonstrated by their conduct. The danger of absorption and conquest is not a future threat when the Mexican people may want to obtain their freedom by the only practical means, by means of a revolution. It is rather a present danger; it is the current that drags us and from which we will not come out by being passive; we are within it and we must swim, swim vigorously toward the bank, even if Filogonio yells at us, telling us we are going to die of exhaustion if we do.

Flocks of sheep do not command respect from anyone, only Don Quixote could see in them a squadron of combatants.

A passive people is slavery, it is honey on the corn flakes for the ambitious exploiters. A people who are revolutionary for their liberty and rights become feared by the conquerors.

Let's leave Filogonio and the prudent ones to argue about the dangers of exhaustion. Let us swim, in order to come out of the current.

READING 5.2

Pancho Villa's Economic and Social Programs

As a young American journalist, John Reed (1887–1920) covered Mexico during some of its most turbulent times. His accounts of the revolution were published in his first book, *Insurgent Mexico*. Reed personally identified with Mexico's revolutionary causes and wrote with an extremely sympathetic eye. Later he reported from Europe during World War I and opposed the entry of the United States into the war.

A committed socialist, Reed covered the revolutionary events in Petrograd during 1917 and wrote a moving rendition of the Russian revolution in *Ten Days That Shook the World* (see Reading 7.1). During Reed's travels in Mexico during 1913, he joined the forces of Pancho Villa, sending back firsthand accounts of Villa's followers' struggles. An ardent supporter of the revolution, Reed tended to romanticize its leaders, particularly Villa. The following reading describes Villa's support for education; like many revolutionary leaders, Villa realized that illiteracy condemned most peasants to a life of poverty.

In 1914, there was a brief moment of reconciliation between Mexico's various insurgent forces, during which time Pancho Villa and Zapata, two charismatic revolutionaries, met. However, differences soon reemerged. Although the United States had originally watched the revolution from the safety of the northern border, fearing that the revolution would take directions contrary to U.S. political and economic interests, the United States ultimately intervened militarily.

At the time Reed traveled in Mexico, Villa and Carranza, an established Mexican politician, were allies, and Reed describes their close relationship. But Carranza, who opposed meaningful land reform, outmaneuvered Villa and other Mexican revolutionaries to be elected president in 1917. A new constitution was enacted in 1917, when the more radical elements who had demanded that the land be redistributed to the peasants were on the defensive. Carranza was killed in a coup d'etat in 1920, and Villa was assassinated in 1923.

Pancho Villa and, to his right, Emilio Zapata, with his trademark sombrero, share a brief moment of comraderie during the Mexican civil war; the hoped for alliance between the two charismatic leaders never materialized. Special Collections, University of Texas at El Paso.

In the 1930s, President Lázaro Cárdenas extended land reform and implemented legislation similar to the New Deal program President Franklin Delano Roosevelt had championed in the United States. Much to the dismay of the United States, Cárdenas also nationalized the Mexican petroleum industry, in which British and American capital had considerable investments. Revenues from petroleum were then used for domestic development programs. Although limited reforms did undercut the power of the landowners in the southern provinces, Cárdenas's economic program emphasized commerce and industry at the expense of the agricultural sector, thereby perpetuating the gap between the wealthy and the poor peasantry. In addition, over half the land remained in the hands of large landowners, and most peasants remained desperately poor. The issues of unequal wealth distribution and landownership remain two of the most daunting problems in the Western Hemisphere and are important factors in the continued social unrest in most of the region.

Villa's great passion was schools. He believed that land for the people and schools would settle every question of civilization. Schools were an obsession with him. Often I have heard him say: "When I passed such and such a street this morning I saw a lot of kids. Let's put a school there." Chihuahua has a population of under 40,000 people. At different times Villa established over fifty schools there. The great dream of his life has been to send his son to school in the United States, but at the opening of the term in February he had to abandon it because he didn't have money enough to pay for a half year's tuition.

No sooner had he taken over the government of Chihuahua than he put his army to work running the electric light plant, the street railways, the telephone, the water works and the Terrazzas flour mill. He delegated soldiers to administer the great haciendas which he had confiscated. He manned the slaughter-house with soldiers, and sold Terrazzas's beef to the people for the government. A thousand of them he put in the streets of the city as civil police, prohibiting on pain of death stealing, or the sale of liquor to the army. A soldier who got drunk was shot. He even tried to run the brewery with soldiers, but failed because he couldn't find an expert maltster. "The only thing to do with soldiers in time of peace," said Villa, "is to put them to work. An idle soldier is always thinking of war."

In the matter of the political enemies of the Revolution he was just as simple, just as effective. Two hours after he entered the Governor's palace the foreign consuls came in a body to ask his protection for 200 Federal soldiers who had been left as a police force at the request of the foreigners. Before answering them, Villa said suddenly: "Which is the Spanish consul?" Scobell, the British vice-consul, said: "I represent the Spaniards." "All right!" snapped Villa. "Tell them to begin to pack. Any Spaniard caught within the boundaries of this State after five days will be escorted to the nearest wall by a firing squad."

The consuls gave a gasp of horror. Scobell began a violent protest, but Villa cut him short.

"This is not a sudden determination on my part," he said; "I have been thinking about this since 1910. The Spaniards must go."

Letcher, the American consul, said: "General, I don't question your motives, but I think you are making a grave political mistake in expelling the Spaniards. The government at Washington will hesitate a long time before becoming friendly to a party which makes use of such barbarous measures."

"Señor Consul," answered Villa, "we Mexicans have had three hundred years of the Spaniards. They have not changed in character since the *Conquistadores*. They disrupted the Indian empire and enslaved the people. We did not ask them to mingle their blood with ours. Twice we drove them out of Mexico and allowed them to return with the same rights as Mexicans, and they used these rights to steal away our land, to make the people slaves,

Reed, John. *Insurgent Mexico.* New York: D. Appleton & Co., 1914, pp. 127–30; reprinted Westport, CT: Greenwood Press, 1969.

and to take up arms against the cause of liberty. They supported Porfirio Díaz. They were perniciously active in politics. It was the Spaniards who framed the plot that put Huerta in the palace. When Madero was murdered the Spaniards in every State in the Republic held banquets of rejoicing. They thrust on us the greatest superstition the world has ever known—the Catholic Church. They ought to be killed for that alone. I consider we are being very generous with them."

Scobell insisted vehemently that five days was too short a time, that he couldn't possibly reach all the Spaniards in the State by that time; so Villa extended the time to ten days.

The rich Mexicans who had oppressed the people and opposed the Revolution, he expelled promptly from the State and confiscated their vast holdings. By a simple stroke of the pen the 17,000,000 acres and innumerable business enterprises of the Terrazzas family became the property of the Constitutionalist government, as well as the great lands of the Creel family and the magnificent palaces which were their town houses. Remembering, however, how the Terrazzas exiles had once financed the Orozco Revolution, he imprisoned Don Luis Terrazzas, Jr., as a hostage in his own house in Chihuahua. Some particularly obnoxious political enemies were promptly executed in the penitentiary. The Revolution possesses a black book in which are set down the names, offenses, and property of those who have oppressed and robbed the people. The Germans, who had been particularly active politically, the Englishmen and Americans, he does not yet dare to molest. Their pages in the black book will be opened when the Constitutionalist government is established in Mexico City; and there, too, he will settle the account of the Mexican people with the Catholic Church.

DISCUSSION QUESTION

Describe the activities of the key Mexican revolutionaries, with particular emphasis on their conflicting social and economic programs.

CHAPTER SIX

Postwar Settlements and Self-Determination

At the Paris Peace Conference of 1919, the political leaders of the victorious powers had different primary goals in mind. French Prime Minister Georges Clemenceau, for example, wanted to ensure that Germany would never again threaten French security, while U.S. President Woodrow Wilson stressed the importance of creating a League of Nations. In general, the treaties hammered out at the conference did what most previous treaties did after a war—punish the vanquished and reward the victors. Although this was hardly surprising, some observers had expected more balanced results, partly because of the idealistic utterances of President Wilson. However, the victors were not the only gainers. Some of the former subject nationalities of eastern Europe such as the Poles gained their independence.

One of the principles that Wilson emphasized both before and after the end of World War I was self-determination. As he said in a speech to Congress in February 1918, "National aspirations must be respected; peoples must be dominated or governed only by their own consent. 'Self-determination' is not a mere phrase. It is an imperative principle of action, which statesmen will ignore at their peril. . . . Every territorial settlement involved in this war must be made in the interest and for the benefit of the populations concerned and not as a part of any mere adjustment or compromise of claims amongst rival states." Although the term eluded exact definition, self-determination suggested to many that each nationality (for example, the Poles) was to have the right to live under a government of its own choosing and that, where feasible, European geographic boundaries were to reflect major national or ethnographic divisions (see Reading 6.1).

Five years before Wilson enunciated his principle, future Soviet leader Vladimir Lenin had written that Marxists were duty bound to defend the *right* of nations to self-determination. Moreover, in one of his government's first acts after coming to power in

November 1917, it put forth the Declaration of the Rights of the Peoples of Russia, which proclaimed "the right of the peoples of Russia to free self-determination, even to the point of separation and the formation of an independent state."

However, neither Wilson nor Lenin intended the principle of self-determination to apply universally. Wilson, and even more so the other Allied leaders at the Paris Peace Conference, were against allowing its implementation by the peoples of the still intact colonial empires of the European victors or in general by the non-Turkish peoples of the defeated Ottoman Turkish Empire (see Chapter 11). Instead, the major victorious powers implemented it or allowed its implementation almost exclusively in some of the other former lands of the defeated powers, primarily Germany and Austria-Hungary, and in some former territories of the now defunct Russian empire—at the time of the Paris Peace Conference, Russia was in the midst of a civil war and was not represented.

In some cases, the leaders at the Paris Peace Conference did little more than give their blessing to the creation of new nation states that local nationalisms had created amid the ashes of war in central and eastern Europe. The Allied leaders, however, were especially eager to encourage the creation of noncommunist states along the western borders of the new communist state of Russia. These leaders viewed such countries as Estonia, Latvia, Lithuania, and Poland as part of a *cordon sanitaire* that would help keep communism from spreading westward. Lenin's advocacy of self-determination was even more hedged with limitations and qualifications than was that of Wilson. It was primarily a political weapon to help break up monarchical and capitalist empires; where the Soviet government was able to prevent secession from Russia, such as in Ukraine and the Caucasus, it generally did so.

In their different ways, however, both Wilson and Lenin helped popularize a concept that has continued ever since to be a rallying slogan for peoples who believe that such a principle entitles them to create their own independent state, as more than 100 nations have done since the days of Lenin and Wilson. At the very time that the Paris Peace Conference was held in early 1919, one people, the Irish, were already proclaiming their right to self-determination, and before the year was out the battle for Irish independence became a bloody conflict between British forces and Irish rebels (see Reading 6.2). When the United Nations was created at the end of World War II, its charter stated that one of the purposes of the UN was to "develop friendly relations among nations based on respect for the principle of equal rights and self-determination." When the Soviet Union dissolved into fifteen separate countries at the end of 1991 and Yugoslavia was torn apart by ethnic rivalries in the early 1990s, self-determination was often again the rallying cry.

From the very beginning, however, the principle was easier to proclaim than to implement. One of the central problems was that many territories contained a mixture of nationalities and that even the definition of some nations or nationalities was not easy. The Catholic Irish might insist that the whole island of Ireland should be part of an independent Ireland dominated by them, but what then was to be the fate of the Protestants in Northern Ireland, many of them descendants of earlier Protestant immigrants from Scotland and other Protestant parts of Great Britain? In Yugoslavia, created in 1918 as the Kingdom of Serbs, Croats, and Slovenes, there were (as of 1981) six "leading nations" and eighteen other nationalities, often intermingled in such a manner that dividing them into separate ethnic territories would have been virtually impossible. There were also three major languages (four if Serbo-Croat is not considered one language) and three major religious groups—Catholic, Orthodox, and Muslim. The Muslims in Bosnia were for the most part Slavic, their ancestors once considered Serbs or Croats until they converted to Islam while under Turkish control.

In the interwar period in Europe, some nationalities such as the Ukrainians—who in 1991 proclaimed an independent Ukraine, with territory and a population about the size of France—did not win the right to self-determination. Instead, they were a minority population in other countries, especially Poland and the USSR (where *in theory* but not in practice they possessed their own union republic with the right to secede). In Czechoslovakia, newly created in 1918 and split into two countries in 1993, more than one out of every five persons in the 1920s was German. In Rumania there was a sizable Hungarian (Magyar) minority.

The problem of national minorities along with homage to the principle of self-determination led to numerous conflicts in the years after the Paris Peace Conference. Even before the conference started, Wilson's own secretary of state expressed his fears in his diary: "When the President talks of 'self-determination,' what unit has he in mind? Does he mean a race, a territorial area or a community? Without a definite unit, which is practical, application of this principle is dangerous to peace and stability."[1] In September 1938, in the midst of the Munich crisis, Hitler stated, "Now at last, almost twenty years after the statements of President Wilson, the right of self-determination for these 3,500,000 [Germans in Czechoslovakia] must come into force." In 1939, Hitler, not for the first time, insisted that the people of Danzig, overwhelmingly German, also had the right to self-determination and that what they wished was to once again be part of Germany—between the wars, Danzig was under the League of Nations' jurisdiction, so that Poland could exercise certain rights there. Poland, backed by France and Great Britain, refused to give way, however, and before the year was out Hitler seized Danzig, as well as most of Poland, beginning World War II in Europe.

[1]Quoted in Daniel Patrick Moynihan, *Pandaemonium: Ethnicity in International Politics* (Oxford: Oxford University Press, 1994), p. 82.

READING 6.1

U.S. Delegates' Accounts of Self-Determination at the Paris Peace Conference

On January 18, 1919, the Paris Peace Conference opened. Although twenty-seven victorious nations were represented, the important decisions at the conference were made by a Supreme Council made up of the heads of state and foreign ministers of the United States, Great Britain, France, Italy, and Japan. U.S. President Woodrow Wilson, British Prime Minister David Lloyd George, and French Prime Minister Georges Clemenceau were the dominant figures at the conference. By the beginning of the summer of 1919, the Allied leaders had decided the fate of Germany, which had little choice but to accede to it in the Treaty of Versailles. Austria, Hungary, Bulgaria, and Turkey later signed separate treaties imposed upon them.

In 1920, Colonel Edward House, Wilson's chief adviser at the Paris Peace Conference, arranged for a series of fifteen public talks in Philadelphia, which began that December, in order to explain to the U.S. public what had happened at the Paris Peace Conference. In 1921, these talks along with some supplemental materials were published in book form, and it is from this book that the two portions of Reading 6.1 are taken. The first (6.1A) is by Charles Seymour, and the second (6.1B) by Edward House.

READING 6.1A: NATIONALITIES IN EASTERN AND CENTRAL EUROPE

When the peace conference opened, therefore, the empire of Austria-Hungary was a thing of the past. One journalistic critic complains that the conference angrily broke up Austria into jigsaw bits; but the accusation betrays a wealth of ignorance and shows how much easier it is to be critical than correct. The United States and Great Britain would have been glad to create a federation of the Danubian nationalities which, without the vices that had led to the fall of the Hapsburgs, might have accomplished the economic integration and preserved the political order so essential to the tranquillity and prosperity of southeastern Europe. The suggestion would have been no more effective than a tenor solo in a boiler-shop. The nationalities would have none of it. They had freed themselves, they were instinct with the sense of their own capacity, bursting with nationalistic ambitions, suspicious of any federation as likely to revive the tyranny under which they had so long suffered. The Conference lacked the right, as well as the power, to impose union upon them. By virtue of the principle of self-determination it was for the nationalities to determine their own destiny, and if they preferred disunion no one could deny them. The independent sovereignty of the Czechs had been recognized; the union of the Poles of Galicia with the mass of the nationality in Russia and Germany was generally admitted; the right of Rumania to Transylvania had been acknowledged; and there were few inclined to dispute the union of the Serbs, Croats, and Slovenes of southern Hungary, Austria, and Bosnia, with their kinsmen in Serbia and Montenegro, although the prospect was not hailed with enthusiasm by Italy. . . .

Seymour, Charles. "The End of Empire," in *What Really Happened at Paris.* Eds. Edward Mandell House and Charles Seymour. New York: Charles Scribner's Sons, 1921, pp. 89–90, 91, 101–2, 103.

The Peace Conference was, accordingly, placed in the position of executor of the Hapsburg estate. The heirs were generally recognized—Czecho-Slovakia, Poland, Rumania, Jugo-Slavia, the new lesser Austria, lesser Hungary, and Italy. The duty of the Conference was to determine the character of the division. Even this had already been fixed in its broad lines, so that much of the task of the peacemakers consisted simply in the determination of detailed frontiers. The task, however, was not one which could be easily and satisfactorily accomplished. . . .

With certain exceptions, the boundaries finally approved conform roughly to the distribution of the several peoples, although in all matters of doubt the balance turns slightly against the former dominant nationalities—the Germans and Magyars. One of the exceptions to be noted is the case of the Austrian Tyrol, where the demands of the Italians for annexation of the Tyrol as far north as the Brenner Pass were granted. . . .

A second exception to the general rule that the political boundary should conform roughly to the linguistic is to be found in the case of Czecho-Slovakia. The Czechs demanded not merely union with their Slovak cousins of northern Hungary, a development which in view of their services in the war was inevitable and probably wise, but also that their boundaries should be so arranged as to include a large number of Germans and Magyars. The northern rim of Bohemia is almost exclusively German and a strict application of the principle of nationality in this region, and in Moravia and Silesia, would have given something more than 3,000,000 Germans to Austria and Germany (for the creation of a separate German-Bohemian state was hardly within the realm of practical possibility). But the Czechs argued that to rob Bohemia of its geographic and historic boundary would be to lay it open to the attack of Germany from the north. Furthermore, it would deal a mortal blow at the economic life of the new state by taking away districts essential to Bohemia's industrial prosperity. The districts in question, even though inhabited by Germans, were closely bound in the economic sense to the Czech districts, and naturally separated from Germany; the inhabitants themselves would suffer from any arrangement which cut them off. Such arguments, particularly those which emphasized the economic factors, seemed valid.

READING 6.1B: BOUNDARIES AND SELF-DETERMINATION

In the matter of boundaries the Paris Conference was confronted with almost its most difficult problem. There was no good way out, and any decision was certain to displease, and in many instances to do injustice.

It was easier to give nationality to races bulking large in numbers than it was to make an equitable adjustment of territory between two or more contiguous states, where it was difficult to decide whether the racial status or the natural boundaries should determine. Italy, in demanding a natural or strategic frontier to the north, has included two hundred odd thousand Tyrolese, who will not be reconciled to the change except through centuries of kindly treatment and good government.

House, Edward Mandell. "The Versailles Peace," in *What Really Happened at Paris.* Eds. Edward Mandell House and Charles Seymour. New York: Charles Scribner's Sons, 1921, pp. 429–31, 432.

An even more uncertain determination of justice, reached after the United States had practically withdrawn from the Conference, was the shifting of boundaries between Bulgaria, Roumania, and Jugo-Slavia, the result of which has left much dissatisfaction. It is doubtful whether any adjustment could have been made in this region which would not have left seeds of another war. Those who were present to advocate their claims succeeded in expanding their boundaries to an astonishing degree, but almost wholly at the expense of their defeated neighbors. It requires but little prescience to see that it will take a strong and vigilant League of Nations to hold these turbulent Balkan States in leash.

But in spite of unfortunate mistakes in details, it remains true that for the first time in history Europe enjoys a natural political map or, at least, a fair approximation to it, a map drawn in accordance with the unforced aspirations and the spontaneous affiliations of the peoples themselves. The map of Europe drawn by the Congress of Vienna and changed by later congresses, knew no such principle. Peoples were handed from sovereignty to sovereignty like chattels, the determining factors being the ambitions, the power, and the cunning of sovereigns and their foreign ministers. As they sowed so, indeed, did they reap, for most of the wars of the nineteenth century after 1815 had their roots in efforts on the part of oppressed groups and peoples to throw off alien rule and join congenial political units. Therefore, it was not unnatural that the Paris Peace Conference should have been carried away by the popular demand for self-determination. It was a slogan which stirred into action the dormant dreams of many ancient peoples.

When the great empires east of the Rhine began to totter, fulfillment of the cherished hopes of centuries sprang at once to the fore in the hearts of oppressed races. Some communities did not wait for Paris to act, but, with a courage born of strong desire, severed the political ties which had bound them for centuries and established governments for themselves in which their several racial entities dominated. It was the gladdest and yet, in some ways, the maddest movement in history. In the endeavor to be free everything else was overlooked. No tribal entity was too small to have ambitions for self-determination. Social and economic considerations were unreckoned with, and the only thought for the moment was to reach back to the centuries when they were nomads and were masters of their own fortunes and desires. The sufferings and hardships of the war seemed to fall from them in this hour of joy, and nothing appeared to matter if once again they might escape from the domination of their overlords.

During the winter and spring of 1918–1919 Paris was the Mecca for the oppressed not alone of Europe but of the earth. Pilgrims came in countless numbers to lay their hopes and grievances at the feet of those in the seats of the mighty. Many were in native costumes, some charming and some otherwise, but all picturesque and lending an air of interest to the great modern Babylon.

There was much that was pathetic in it all. Delegations would appear overnight, and then, after many weary weeks of waiting, would disappear and would be replaced by others. On the other hand, some coming from the ends of the world lingered through the greater part of the life of the conference. Nearly all had hearings, but these were of necessity of a perfunctory nature, and were given less to obtain real information than to be courteous to some sponsor among the Powers. Arguments would at times be made in the native language, which had to be first translated into French and then into English. When boundaries were described at great length it is doubtful whether any of those upon whom the final decision rested would have known if the speaker, sensing the irony of it all, had taken them a thousand miles afield, and had followed a line in no way pertinent to that which he was supposed to prove. . . .

While many failed to realize their aspirations, yet enough succeeded to change the map of Europe as it has never been changed within the memory of living man. And now that the theory of self-determination has been so largely put into practice, the question is, what will the outcome be? Some are already eager to expand beyond the limits of safety, and others are evincing an unreasonably selfish policy toward their neighbors. There is one thing that seems essential, and that is some understanding regarding customs, postal service, and the monetary unit. Without such an understanding, it is difficult to see how these small states can live in comfort and happiness. Many of them are landlocked, and some that touch the sea have no ports adequate to move their commerce. Few, if any, are self-supporting, and a free interchange of commodities is necessary in order to maintain a normal economic life. If a common monetary unit is adopted and there is no barrier to trade, it will probably not be long before some sort of federation will here and there come about. Then, and not until then, will those small states assume a position of importance and wield an influence commensurate with their aspirations.

READING 6.2

The Irish Fight for Self-Determination

For centuries the English had dominated Ireland, and the Act of Union of 1801 tightened British controls by ending the separate existence of the Irish Parliament and making Ireland part of a United Kingdom of Great Britain and Ireland. In the late nineteenth century, however, Irish agitation increased for the right to run their own internal affairs (Home Rule). In April 1916, in the midst of World War I, Irish rebels rose in revolt, seized some buildings in Dublin and other places, and proclaimed an Irish republic. The British government soon put down this rebellion and executed fourteen ringleaders.

In December 1918, however, the nationalistic Sinn Fein party won a sweeping victory in the election of Irish members to Parliament in London. The next month, they organized an Irish Parliament of their own and declared their independence from Great Britain. The British responded by attempting to forcefully crush the rebels. A vicious cycle of terror and counterterror followed, marked by bombs, arson, and torture. Finally, in December 1921, the British government and rebel leaders signed a treaty that recognized the Irish Free State, a self-governing dominion comprising most of Ireland. However, much of Ulster in the north, where the Protestants were dominant, remained a part of Great Britain, a provision that helped lead some Irish nationalists, including the Irish Republican Army (I.R.A.), to reject the treaty and fight an unsuccessful civil war that lasted until 1923. Not until 1949 did the Republic of Ireland declare its complete independence, but Northern Ireland, with its Protestant majority, continued to be united with Great Britain. In subsequent decades, the outlawed I.R.A. engaged in sporadic assassinations and bombings in order to end British control over Northern Ireland. In April 1998, British, Irish, and Northern Irish political leaders, both Protestant and Catholic, agreed to a tentative accord that would allow more autonomy to Northern Ireland, along with more Catholic Irish participation in decision making.

The following reading is taken from testimony and affidavits presented in January 1921 by Donal O'Callaghan, the lord mayor of the Irish city of Cork, to the American Commission on Conditions in Ireland. This commission came into being as a result of the initiative of the editors of *The Nation* magazine and contained 150 members, including public officials and private citizens and "representing [in the words of the commission report] a broad diversity of racial stocks and political and religious beliefs." Although the following excerpt presents the Irish nationalist view of the conflict and the influence of the concept of self-determination, it also indicates the frustration and hatred engendered in British soldiers by what they considered the terroristic activities of Irish rebels.

BARBAROUS TORTURE OF IRISH PRISONERS

There have been a number of cases where ill-treatment after arrest has been alleged. But as that has been a more or less recent development, and as the men in whose cases it has been alleged are still nearly all in jail, it has not been possible to get the particulars in a number of cases. Fortunately, in one case, and I think it is a most glaring as well as a most cruel case, we have got the deposition, although the man in this particular case is still in prison. The man concerned is Thomas Hales, one of the Hales family from Knocknacurra, near Bandon, County Cork. It is a family who are famous as athletes. His brother represents the Irish Republic as consular agent there. I had the pleasure of meeting him last July when I was there. I will read the deposition of Thomas Hales:

Affidavit of Thomas Hales

"On the 27th July, 1920, at about 5 P.M., I was standing outside a farmhouse at Laragh, about two and three-quarter miles from Bandon,—Mr. Hurley is the proprietor of the house. Some police and soldiers came and surrounded the house and took me and Harte. I was brought inside the house, and there saw Captain Kelly with other military officers."

The Witness [O'Callaghan]: Captain Kelly, I might explain, is one of the intelligence officers attached to the British Military Headquarters at Cork.

"I had no coat on at the time. They then took me into an outhouse, and took all my other clothes off me and searched them for documents. They found some documents on me, and on searching my coat, which was hanging up, they split out of it some cartridges. I had no cartridges in my possession, and I'm of the opinion that these were placed there by the military. Captain Kelly and Lieutenant Keogh took all my clothes off me. . . . When I was undressed they

American Commission on Conditions in Ireland. *Evidence on Conditions in Ireland.* Washington, D.C.: 1921, pp. 780–83, 848–51.

strapped my hands behind my back with leather straps, and put them around my neck and mouth. Harte was also strapped in a similar position. I was not in a position to defend myself, and Lieutenant Keogh hit me several times in the face and on the body. Kelly said, 'You have some documents from the Adjutant General per Michael Collins [one of the leaders of the Irish rebellion].' He apparently assumed that M. C. stood for Michael Collins. They dressed me again, tied my hands behind my back with leather straps, and also dressed Harte. Kelly said, 'You will be shot.' They put straps around my legs as well as round Harte's legs. They made me stand up, and made Harte stand behind me. They discovered a slab of gun-cotton in the farm. I do not know whether it was brought in by the military or not. They placed the gun-cotton on Harte's back, strapped it there, and Kelly said, 'Be prepared for a shock.' They looked round for a detonator, but could not find one. They then took the gun-cotton off Harte's back, and while my hands were strapped behind my back, and Harte's hands were also strapped behind his back, Lieutenant Keogh hit me and Harte in the face several times. He hit me very hard, and he had in his hand, I believe, the butt end of a revolver.

"They then tied my right leg to Harte's left leg, and marched us off to a lorry about 200 yards away. I was prodded by a bayonet, and I was hit in the nose by the butt end of a gun. I was very weak, and it was difficult to walk in a three-legged fashion. . . .

"On reaching the lorry, they were not able to throw us both in together, so they separated Harte from me, and they threw us into the lorry. I was nearly blind, as blood was running down my face from the injuries I had received. We were taken to Bandon into the Military Barracks yard, and were lined up to be shot. The soldiers were howling for our death, and were anxious to shoot us. We had our backs to the wall, and Harte was on my left-hand side. Keogh said, 'Do you want to be blindfolded?' We said, 'No.' I asked to see a chaplain. Keogh said, 'Damn it, why do you want to see a chaplain?' I said, 'All right, go ahead.'

"We were still tied with our hands behind our backs, and the soldiers hit us with their fists. My sight was getting very dim, owing to the blood that I was losing, and I felt very weak. Kelly paced out twelve to fifteen paces from us, and then put five or six men with rifles at the end of the fifteen paces. Harte was then very weak and could hardly see. He stuck a flag into Harte's hand, and made him hold his hand up. I recognized that the flag Harte was holding up was the Union Jack [the British flag], but Harte himself was too far gone to recognize it. A man came with a camera and took a snapshot. Kelly then said, 'We must get some information first before we shoot them.' We were then taken across the Barracks yard into a room in the Barracks. The soldiers were furious at not being allowed to shoot us, and they punched us and pummelled us the whole way across the yard.

"They locked us into a room. It was getting dark by this time. About midnight I was led out by the guard, and taken to an upper room. There were, I believe, six officers in this room, including Captain Kelly of the enemy Military Intelligence Department, stationed at Cork City . . . . They were sitting down as if they were going to try me. There were no soldiers, only officers in the room.

"Kelly opened the proceedings by saying,'We are going to try you.' My hands were still tied behind my back, and the strap was fastened round my neck and face. Kelly took up a book which he said was a Bible, and opened it and placed it in my hands behind my back. He told me to repeat the oath which he was going to say. I said, 'For what purpose?' He said, 'We want your name, and for you to answer other questions on oath. . . .'

"I said, 'I have no objection to giving my name.' They let my trousers and pants round my feet, my hands still being behind my back. 'Now,' said Kelly, 'repeat the following words after me.' He then started saying some form of oath and included in it the name of the Blessed Virgin. I did not repeat the name of the Blessed Virgin, and two of the officers took their canes and beat me on my bare legs for about five minutes. I was powerless to do anything. Kelly

Armored car and other vehicles used in the making of the film *Michael Collins* (1996), which dealt with the Irish Rebellion following World War I. Janice Terry

then asked my name. I said, 'Tom Hales.' He said, 'You are Commander of a Brigade.' I said I was one time. He asked me who was the man next in command to me. I said I refused to tell him. I said, 'You are foreigners to me, but I appeal to you, if you are gentlemen, to go ahead and get on with the shooting part of it. I am quite ready.'

"Kelly then told one of the officers to go out and get the pliers. He then said, 'You are an anarchist and a murderer. You have organized all the murder and attacks on barracks in this part of the country.' He said, 'Where were you on Sunday? Were you at mass, and at what mass?' I said, 'I was at mass at Rossmore.' He then asked me was I not responsible for raising the training camp at Glandore last year. I refused to answer. The two officers then gave me about forty cuts each on my bare legs. Kelly then said, 'Will you refuse to tell me was Professor Gerald Sullivan Commander of the camp?' I told him I did not know such a man. He said, 'You are a damned liar.' The two officers then gave me vicious blows on the leg, and the blood was flowing down my legs from several wounds in them. (Dr. Shannon, civilian doctor of Cork Prison, saw the scars that were on my legs.) The scars were visible for three weeks after this night's event.

"Kelly said, 'There was one of your dispatches intercepted connected with the camp and signed by you. Be sure we know more about you than you think.' Then he said, 'Where did you sleep last Sunday night?' I said, 'I was at home.' 'That is a dammed lie,' said Kelly. I said, 'I generally sleep at home. I hardly ever sleep in anybody else's house. The hay shed is good enough for me.' Kelly said, 'You organized and were in the attack on Farnivane Police Barracks.' I said, 'You may have been told that.' He asked me what rank did John Buckley of Bandon hold in the Irish Republican Volunteers. I said, 'He is a builder, and a good Sinn Feiner at that.' I was again viciously whipped for the statement. He said, 'What position does your brother John hold and where is he staying?' I said, 'I refuse to give you any information about him.' He then turned to the officer whom he had sent for the pliers, and he started bending and twisting and pinching my fingers at the back. He gripped them at the back, placing one portion of the pinchers against one side of my nail and the other portion of the pinchers against the other. He brought the blood to the tops of several of my fingers, and for some time afterwards my fingers were black on the tops, owing to congealed blood there. I was feeling extremely weak, almost fainting, and the blood was dropping down my legs. I was asked several questions about other individuals and about military matters, but I refused to give any information.

"Kelly also put the pinchers on my thighs, but my senses were becoming quite numb. After that, and finding I would answer no questions, he told me I would be shot at dawn. He said, 'You are a Commander of a Brigade and know all about these murders. If you do not know, you should know, or you can have no control over your men.' I said, 'If that is so that I have no control over my men, there are other people besides me that have no control over their men.'

"Keogh then untied my hands and told me to pull up my trousers. I did so, and my trousers were sopping wet with blood. Kelly said, 'The Court is closed for the finding.' He said, 'Stand up,' as my knees were somewhat bending, 'and we will see what a Tommy can do to you.' Keogh then landed me a terrific punch in the face. I said I would not defend myself; I would not give them an excuse to say I had hit them. Keogh hit me several times in various parts of the body, but especially in the face, and he broke the four teeth in my upper jaw. He then knocked me down on the ground. I was absolutely exhausted and nearly fainted, and my senses were beginning to go. He hit me on several occasions while I was on the ground. After a few minutes one of the officers said, 'That's enough.' I was then dragged up and led out of the room. My hands had not been retied since they had been undone in order to lift up my trousers. When I got outside my hands were tied up again and the straps fastened round my neck and face. Five or six soldiers hit me while I was going to the room where Harte was.

"After I had been placed in this room, bleeding and exhausted, Harte was taken upstairs. He was treated in a very similar fashion, and it has, unfortunately, had a detrimental effect upon his brain, and he is now practically mentally incapacitated.

"In the morning, at daybreak, the 28th July, the sergeant came in and loosened the straps that tied my arms. About half an hour afterwards Captain Kelly came in with a squad of men and took me out of the room. He noticed the straps were not tight. He said, 'Who in the hell loosened your straps?' He had them immediately tightened. I went into another room and had to kneel down. Harte was also brought in and told to kneel down; and we were left kneeling for about five minutes. We were then told to get up, and were taken into the barrack yard. They put me up against a wall. I said, 'Will you let me see a chaplain?' 'No,' said Kelly, 'I will not.' I said to Kelly, 'Your life will only be a short one, the same as mine.'

"He immediately drew out an automatic pistol and placed it against my temple and said, 'One question, and on the answer of this question depends your life. Give me the names of the six battalions.' I said, 'Even if I knew the names of the six battalions, I would not tell you.' Kelly said, 'I will give you another chance, and if you don't tell me the battalion names, I will shoot you dead.' I said, 'Go on. I won't tell you the names.'

"He then took down the revolver and walked over to where some of the officers were, and said something to them. I then heard him say, 'We will take him off, and we will give him some more torture.' They threw me into a motor lorry. Harte was also thrown into the same motor lorry, and we were brought to the Military Hospital in Cork. I was attended to by the doctor in the hospital, and my treatment and Harte's treatment in the hospital was satisfactory. We were given newspapers and were not in any way molested or struck, and our injuries were attended to.

"We were placed, though, in a ward where there were twelve wounded policemen, and they were all day and all night long talking at us and crying for our blood. This had a very detrimental effect upon Harte, who in consequence is now in a very weak mental state.

"On Tuesday, the 19th August, we were told by the military officer that we would be tried by court-martial sharp at ten o'clock. On August 20th, at quarter to ten, we were taken to the place where the court-martial was to take place. After waiting for half an hour, the sergeant was told to take us back, as the court-martial was postponed. At twelve o'clock we were taken again to the same place, and again, after waiting half an hour, the court-martial was postponed and we were taken back. At 2:30 we were taken again to the court-martial, and the court-martial took place. I refused to recognize the court, and I refused to cross examine, but I stated that I had no munition on me. The president asked me did I want to cross examine Captain Kelly. I said, 'No.' We were sentenced to two years' hard labor."

The Witness [O'Callaghan]: Well, that, gentlemen, is one of the most glaring cases I know of. . . .

MAYOR O'CALLAGHAN'S CONCLUDING REMARKS

I have just a few remarks in the nature of a summing up of the evidence generally. I think, gentlemen, that it would be well that, having come here and having testified as to conditions obtaining in Ireland, that that be supplemented by giving you what is Ireland's view at the moment: first of all, of her own position; and secondly, what she thinks she has a right to expect from the other free nations of the world, and especially from America; and finally, her position in the event of that help being refused. It will not take very long.

Ireland Seeks Right of Self-Determination

Ireland has declared a desire to be free in every legitimate way in which an oppressed country could do it, through the ballot box. She has elected her Republican parliament, her Republican councils, who function to carry on the administration of the country. The men engaged in that movement have not been dreamers, as has often been alleged. They are men who are at least as keen, and probably much more so, about the importance of commercial advancement and commercial progress than any recent generation, at all events in Ireland. These men have worked along these lines, even under the difficulties of the state of unrest which obtains in the country; and their efforts, in spite of these difficulties, have been to a large extent crowned with success,—a success which is only an indication of the state of things that would obtain were they free to work entirely on different lines, and to devote their energies and their abilities solely to that purpose.

I have described for you how the people are suffering, what their record is, what their daily life in Ireland is at present; and I put it to you, gentlemen, and through you to the American people, that that suffering is being entailed and is being endured by the Irish people because of their determination to seek the right to decide for themselves their own form of government.

In Ireland the term "Republican" is used, as it is used here in referring to Ireland, in order to convey a definite and a concrete conception of liberty, not definitely that a Republican, as such, or any other particular form of government has been decided on for the country, or is being insisted on for the country. The Republican parliament and the

Republican party ask merely for, and will be perfectly satisfied if they secure, the right of self-determination. They will be satisfied if that question is allowed to be decided by the people of Ireland themselves, be their verdict what it may, be the form of government which they decide on for themselves what it may.

Unanimity of Irish People for Freedom

In Ireland there is at least as much if not more unanimity on this question of freedom than there is in any other country in the world, or than there was in any other country in the world which struggled to be free. Obviously, clearly at no time in history was it possible to secure, never will it be possible to secure, and it is a good thing that it is so, a nation where every individual of that nation has his thoughts and has his mind running along the same lines as every other individual in that nation. Never, obviously, will a nation be found where there is absolute, thorough, and complete unanimity from the north and south, east and west. The most that one can expect is that a large majority of the people of the country are unanimous. That state of affairs obtains in Ireland, obtains to a very large extent. The fact that there are a very small number of people in one corner of Ireland does not in any way imply that the country, spoken of as a country and as a nation, is not unanimous in seeking freedom.

The New National Consciousness

The people in Ireland have also, during recent years while the struggle for freedom has been going on, awakened to the fact that their culture, their mentality, just as their race characteristics, are entirely different from those in England, and that is the aspect of the case which I put to you gentlemen. Parliament has awakened to the fact that through a very, very clever system of education, so-called, the Irish had been brought to the point, very recently, where they had almost lost all sense of race consciousness, where all that was best, inasmuch as all that was distinctive of them as a race, had been submerged, and where they were being modeled into a poor imitation of English men and women. All that is being changed, and contemporaneously with the fight for freedom there is the effort for reconstruction of the Irish idealism of our race. The Irish language, which, with all else that typified our individuality, had been crushed, is now more generally spoken throughout Ireland than for generations past. Every school in Ireland, practically without exception, teaches the Irish language. The children in Ireland today know their own language and are proud of their own language. They realize exactly what it is that makes that language so important and so dear to them.

England's False Pretense of Self-Determination

During the war England, and not only England but all the other nations that fought in that war, including America, were very, very loud in their declarations that the war was being waged for the right of self-determination. That principle awakened hopes in every country where freedom was being denied. It certainly awakened hopes in Ireland,

and the Irish people looked forward to freedom without much delay. The war ended, and England now very clearly shows by her conduct in Ireland that that pretense of self-determination, that pretense of fighting for the rights of small nations, was the merest humbug, the merest camouflage.

Were America's War Aims Also Insincere?

Before leaving you today, gentlemen, I do not think it is in any way out of place or in any way improper, even though it may perhaps seem harsh, if I ask you, and through you the American people, whether we in Ireland have got to take it that England was not alone in that respect; whether Ireland has got to take it that every other nation which entered the war ostensibly for that same reason, and which was equally responsible for awakening these hopes in Ireland and other subjugated countries, whether the position is the same in all of them, and whether it is equally admitted all around that that plea was the merest smoke screen and humbug?

Ireland Will Fight to Annihilation for Right of Self-Determination

Even should that be so, even if it should apply to America, which itself suffered somewhat along the lines of our sufferings such as I have been describing for you, and which itself fought the same fight that we are waging, and fought it against the same enemy; if it be true that America also refuses to stand by her declarations, and if Ireland is forced back on herself, forced to realize that no help is to come to her from any nation, Ireland is placed with a situation, on the one hand, which will show her as making a fight, after all the noisy pretenses of the great and free powers of the world, as making the fight alone, on her own small island, with her four and a half millions of people, against this great and powerful Empire, making their fight for self-determination, which it was alleged was being made on the battlefields of France and Belgium. While that is so, she will also be faced with a fight which would seem to lead almost with certainty to annihilation.

Ireland's Right to Aid From Free Nations

What I wish to put before you, gentlemen, and before the American people, is that we have a perfect right to expect help from every free nation of the world, not only because of the justice of our cause, but also because no nation, especially a nation which has been gifted in the past with ability and genius, can give of its best to the world, to the advancement and progress of the world and of civilization generally, while enslaved. For that reason, so that Irish culture might be developed freely and in an unhindered manner, and that Ireland might give of her best for the advancement of the world; for that, as well as for the reason of the absolute justice of the fight for her freedom,—if despite all these reasons we are told in Ireland that neither America nor any other nation is going to raise a hand to prevent our people being bled to death; if despite all that we say to them, through you, sirs, and the other powerful peoples who made the pretense of making this fight for self-determination, you now admit, when faced with a concrete case, that it was humbug, then we will make the fight, and in our case it will not be humbug. We will continue the fight, be the result what it may.

DISCUSSION QUESTION

To what extent were various nationalities able to realize self-determination after World War I? Did its application in Europe contribute to greater stability or instability? Explain.

CHAPTER SEVEN

Russia's Revolutions

In early 1917, dissatisfaction in Russia was extensive. World War I had already brought about millions of Russian casualties, Germany occupied western portions of the country, and food and fuel shortages existed in major cities. Many people blamed Russia's poor wartime showing on Tsar Nicholas II and his German-born wife, Alexandra. This discontentment helped lead to two revolutions before the year was out, one in March and one in November (February and October, according to the old Russian calendar).

The first revolution overthrew Nicholas II and established in his place a Provisional (temporary) Government. The second revolution, led by Vladimir Lenin and Leon Trotsky, overthrew the Provisional Government, which attempted to continue fighting World War I, and brought the Bolsheviks (called communists after March 1918) to power. Civil war and the intervention of foreign forces, including U.S. troops, soon followed, but the communist government survived. In 1921 it instituted a New Economic Policy (NEP), which helped stabilize the country by allowing some limited freedoms, including small-scale private enterprise. In 1928–1929, however, Joseph Stalin, who gradually strengthened his powers after Lenin's death in 1924, ended NEP by beginning his own "revolution from above." This Stalin revolution ended private enterprise, accelerated industrialization, and introduced a command economy in which the government decided which products and how many of them were going to be produced throughout the Soviet Union. Stalin also began the forced collectivization of agriculture, which was strongly, sometimes violently, opposed by many peasants. In many ways, Stalin's revolution changed the lives of Soviet citizens (four-fifths of them were still peasants in 1928) as much or more than had the revolutions of 1917.

The following two readings reflect first the utopian hopes of the communists and their supporters in 1917 and then the grim and brutal reality faced by peasants and others during Stalin's revolution. While some scholars have argued that the sufferings experienced by peasants during the collectivization of agriculture followed naturally from the communism introduced by Lenin, others have countered by insisting that Stalin's policies represented just one of many possible approaches that could have been taken by communist leaders following Lenin's death.

READING 7.1

John Reed Describes the Establishment of Communist Power in Russia in 1917

John Reed was a radical U.S. journalist sympathetic to the communist revolution. (See Reading 5.2 for more on him.) In 1917 he was in Petrograd (St. Petersburg) to witness the events described in the reading. After his death in Russia in 1920, the communist government buried him with great ceremony near the Kremlin Wall in Moscow. The events he describes, with his reporter's eye and revolutionary enthusiasm, occurred on November 7 and 8, while Russia was still at war against Germany. They took place at the Smolny Institute while troops under the control of the Bolshevik-dominated Petrograd Soviet (Council) of Workers' and Soldiers' Deputies were overthrowing the Provisional Government and taking control of Petrograd.

What Reed describes deals primarily with the actions of the Second All-Russian Congress of Soviets, which began with 670 delegates from about 400 soviets (councils) from different parts of Russia. The soviets had sprung up during 1917, gradually becoming more radical, and by November the Bolsheviks could count on a majority of the delegates to support their positions and the takeover they engineered. As Reed indicates, many delegates from other socialist parties, including the moderate Marxist Mensheviks, objected to the takeover. At the congress, Lenin speaks of the "self-determination of peoples," but, as indicated earlier (see Chapter 6), he did not intend for it to be universally applicable, and his new communist government prevented many of the nationalities of the former Russian empire from breaking with Soviet Russia. Lenin also speaks of the need for peace, and a German-Soviet armistice was soon forthcoming, followed by a separate German-Soviet peace treaty in March 1918. On the other hand, he indicates "we are not afraid of a revolutionary war." In fact, both he and Trotsky believed that only by bringing about revolution in more technologically advanced areas, especially Germany, could their new communist government survive with help from abroad. On November 9, after the events described in the reading, the delegates who remained approved the new government, with Lenin as its head, Trotsky as foreign commissar (a less bourgeois-sounding term than minister), and Joseph Stalin as commissar of nationalities. The following selection is from Reed's influential *Ten Days That Shook the World.*

The massive façade of Smolny blazed with lights as we drove up, and from every street converged upon it streams of hurrying shapes dim in the gloom. Automobiles and motorcycles came and went; an enormous elephant-coloured armoured automobile, with two red flags flying from the turret, lumbered out with screaming siren. It was cold, and at the outer gate the Red Guards had built themselves a bon-fire. At the inner gate, too, there was a blaze, by the light of which the sentries slowly spelled out our passes and looked us up and down. . . .

The Petrograd Soviet of Workers' and Soldiers' Deputies, saluting the victorious Revolution of the Petrograd proletariat and garrison, particularly emphasises the

Reed, John. *Ten Days That Shook the World.* New York: International Publishers, 1919, pp. 84–97, 91, 93–94, 109–10, 125–27, 131.

Smolny Institute, with statue of Lenin in front. In 1917 this building, once housing a school for noblewomen, became the headquarters of the Petrograd Soviet and the site of the Second All-Russian Congress of Soviets. Walter Moss

unity, organisation, discipline, and complete cooperation shown by the masses in this rising; rarely has less blood been spilled, and rarely has an insurrection succeeded so well.

The Soviet expresses its firm conviction that the Workers' and Peasants' Government which, as the government of the Soviets, will be created by the Revolution, and which will assure the industrial proletariat of the support of the entire mass of poor peasants, will march firmly toward Socialism, the only means by which the country can be spared the miseries and unheard-of horrors of war.

The new Workers' and Peasants' Government will propose immediately a just and democratic peace to all the belligerent countries.

It will suppress immediately the great landed property, and transfer the land to the peasants. It will establish workmen's control over production and distribution of manufactured products, and will set up a general control over the banks, which it will transform into a state monopoly.

The Petrograd Soviet of Workers' and Soldiers' Deputies calls upon the workers and the peasants of Russia to support with all their energy and all their devotion the Proletarian Revolution. The Soviet expresses its conviction that the city workers, allies of the poor peasants, will assure complete revolutionary order, indispensable to the victory of Socialism. The Soviet is convinced that the proletariat of the countries of Western Europe will aid us in conducting the cause of Socialism to a real and lasting victory.

"You consider it won then?"

He lifted his shoulders. "There is much to do. Horribly much. It is just beginning. . . ."

On the landing I met Riazanov, vice-president of the Trade Unions, looking black and biting his grey beard. "It's insane! Insane!" he shouted. "The European working-class won't move! All Russia—" He waved his hand distractedly and ran off. . . .

So we came into the great meeting-hall, pushing through the clamorous mob at the door. In the rows of seats, under the white chandeliers, packed immovably in the aisles and on the sides, perched on every window-sill, and even the edge of the platform, the representatives of the workers and soldiers of all Russia waited in anxious silence or wild exultation the ringing of the chairman's bell. There was no heat in the hall but the stifling heat of unwashed human bodies. A foul blue cloud of cigarette smoke rose from the mass and hung in the thick air. Occasionally some one in authority mounted the tribune and asked the comrades not to smoke; then everybody, smokers and all, took up the cry "Don't smoke, comrades!" and went on smoking. . . .

On behalf of the Mensheviki, Khintchuk then announced that the only possibility of a peaceful solution was to begin negotiations with the Provisional Government for the formation of a new Cabinet, which would find support in all strata of society. He could not proceed for several minutes. Raising his voice to a shout he read the Menshevik declaration:

"Because the Bolsheviki have made a military conspiracy with the aid of the Petrograd Soviet, without consulting the other factions and parties, we find it impossible to remain in the Congress, and therefore withdraw, inviting the other groups to follow us and to meet for discussion of the situation!". . .

Kameniev [a Bolshevik leader] jangled the bell, shouting, "Keep your seats and we'll go on with our business!" And Trotzky, standing up with a pale, cruel face, letting out his rich voice in cool contempt, "All these so-called Socialist compromisers, these frightened Mensheviki, Socialist Revolutionaries, *Bund*—let them go! They are just so much refuse which will be swept into the garbage-heap of history!". . .

The assembly decided to ignore the withdrawal of the factions, and proceed to the appeal to the workers, soldiers and peasants of all Russia:

TO WORKERS, SOLDIERS AND PEASANTS

The Second All-Russian Congress of Soviets of Workers' and Soldiers' Deputies has opened. It represents the great majority of the Soviets. There are also a number of Peasant deputies. Based upon the will of the great majority of the workers', soldiers and peasants, based upon the triumphant uprising of the Petrograd workmen and soldiers, the Congress assumes the Power.

The Provisional Government is deposed. Most of the members of the Provisional Government are already arrested.

The Soviet authority will at once propose an immediate democratic peace to all nations, and an immediate truce on all fronts. It will assure the free transfer of landlord, crown and monastery lands to the Land Committees, defend the soldiers' rights, enforcing a complete democratisation of the Army, establish workers' control over production, ensure the convocation of the Constituent Assembly at the proper date, take means to supply bread to the cities and articles of first necessity to the villages, and secure to all nationalities living in Russia a real right to independent existence.

The Congress resolves: that all local power shall be transferred to the Soviets of Workers', Soldiers' and Peasants' Deputies, which must enforce revolutionary order. . . .

It was just 8.40 when a thundering wave of cheers announced the entrance of the presidium, with Lenin—great Lenin—among them. A short, stocky figure, with a big head set down in his shoulders, bald and bulging. Little eyes, a snubbish nose, wide, generous mouth, and heavy chin; clean-shaven now, but already beginning to bristle with the well-known beard of his past and future. Dressed in shabby clothes, his trousers much too long for him. Unimpressive, to be the idol of a mob, loved and revered as perhaps few leaders in history have been. A strange popular leader—a leader purely by virtue of intellect; colourless, humourless, uncompromising and detached, without picturesque idiosyncrasies—but with the power of explaining profound ideas in simple terms, of analysing a concrete situation. And combined with shrewdness, the greatest intellectual audacity. . . .

. . . Now Lenin, gripping the edge of the reading stand, letting his little winking eyes travel over the crowd as he stood there waiting, apparently oblivious to the long-rolling ovation, which lasted several minutes. When it finished, he said simply, "We shall now proceed to construct the Socialist order!" Again that overwhelming human roar.

"The first thing is the adoption of practical measures to realise peace. . . . We shall offer peace to the peoples of all the belligerent countries upon the basis of the Soviet terms—no annexations, no indemnities, and the right of self-determination of peoples. At the same time, according to our promise, we shall publish and repudiate the secret treaties. . . . The question of War and Peace is so clear that I think that I may, without preamble, read the project of a Proclamation to the Peoples of All the Belligerent Countries. . . ."

His great mouth, seeming to smile, opened wide as he spoke; his voice was hoarse—not unpleasantly so, but as if it had hardened that way after years and years of speaking—and went on monotonously, with the effect of being able to go on forever. . . . For emphasis he bent forward slightly. No gestures. And before him, a thousand simple faces looking up in intent adoration. . . .

. . . Something was kindled in these men. One spoke of the "coming World-Revolution, of which we are the advance guard"; another of "the new age of brotherhood, when all the peoples will become one great family. . . ." An individual member claimed the floor. "There is contradiction here," he said. "First you offer peace without annexations and indemnities, and then you say you will consider all peace offers. To consider means to accept. . . ."

Lenin was on his feet. "We want a just peace, but we are not afraid of a revolutionary war. . . . Probably the imperialist Governments will not answer our appeal—but we shall not issue an ultimatum to which it will be easy to say no. . . . If the German proletariat realises that we are ready to consider all offers of peace, that will perhaps be the last drop which overflows the bowl—revolution will break out in Germany.

READING 7.2

A Soviet Writer Describes Stalin's Revolution in the Countryside

Vasily Grossman (1905–1964) was a Soviet writer born into a Ukrainian Jewish family. As a war correspondent during World War II, his pieces were widely read. After the war, he wrote several controversial novels. One of them, *Life and Fate,* which dealt with the World War II battle of Stalingrad, was seized in manuscript form by Soviet authorities in 1961. Although it paid tribute to the heroism and goodness of ordinary people, it also indicated many similarities between nazism and communism. It was not published until a Western publisher came out with it in 1980. Grossman worked on another novel, *Forever Flowing,* which was not published until 1970 and then not in the USSR but in West Germany. It is excerpts from this novel that appear in this reading. Although a novel, the picture Grossman paints in it of collectivization and peasant starvation is true-to-life and an accurate portrayal of the type of events that occurred.

The first part of the selection deals with Stalin's policy that insisted that the kulaks must be "liquidated as a class." Kulaks were theoretically rich peasants, but under Stalin the Communist party applied the term to all types of peasants who opposed Stalin's collectivization policies or were suspected of opposing them. As Grossman points out, a peasant might be labeled a kulak because someone denounced him or her as such. Many of those labeled kulaks were killed or exiled, sometimes to forced labor camps. While in 1928 less than 3 percent of Russia's farming was under the control of collective or state farms, by July 1936, 90 percent of all peasant households were working on such farms. Both types of farms were tightly controlled by party-state functionaries, and the peasants on them lost most of the rights they previously had over household strips of land, their produce, and farm animals. Rather than turn their farm animals over to the new farms, many peasants killed and ate them. In 1933, there were less than half the number of cattle, horses, hogs, goats, and sheep that had existed in 1929.

The second part of the selection deals primarily with the effects of Stalin's policies in 1932 and 1933 that led to the starvation of millions of people, primarily in Ukraine. The government's exorbitant crop demands often left peasants nothing to eat. While millions starved, the government continued to export grain during the 1932–1933 famine, partly to help pay for imported goods for Stalin's rapid industrialization efforts. (Decades later in China, during Mao Zedong's Great Leap Forward, Mao pursued a similar policy, which again resulted in millions of needless deaths.)

The campaign to liquidate the kulaks began at the end of 1929, and the height of the drive came in February and March of 1930. . . .

Perhaps in other provinces things went differently. But in our province here is exactly how it happened. They began to arrest the heads of families only. Most of those arrested first had served in the cavalry under Denikin [a civil war general]. The arrests were carried out solely by the GPU [secret police]. Party activists had no part in this at all. All those rounded up in this first stage were shot—to a man.

Grossman, Vasily. *Forever Flowing.* Trans. Thomas P. Whitney. New York: Harper & Row Publishers, Inc., 1972, pp. 140–51, 153, 155, 157, 160.

Those arrested at the end of December were held in prison for two or three months and then sent off to special resettlement colonies. . . .

. . . Then, at the beginning of 1930, they began to round up the families too. This was more than the GPU could accomplish by itself. All Party activists were mobilized for the job. They were all people who knew one another well and knew their victims, but in carrying out this task they became dazed, stupefied. They would threaten people with guns, as if they were under a spell, calling small children "kulak bastards," screaming "Bloodsuckers!" And those "bloodsuckers" were so terrified they had hardly any blood of their own left in their veins. They were as white as clean paper. The eyes of the Party activists were glassy, like the eyes of cats. They were in the majority after all, and they were dealing with people who were acquaintances and friends. True, they were under a spell—they had sold themselves on the idea that the so-called "kulaks" were pariahs, untouchables, vermin. They would not sit down at a "parasite's" table; the "kulak" child was loathsome; the young "kulak" girl was lower than a louse. They looked on the so-called "kulaks" as cattle, swine, loathsome, repulsive: they had no souls; they stank; they all had venereal diseases; they were enemies of the people and exploited the labor of others. . . .

And there was no pity for them. They were not to be regarded as people. . . . The [Party] activist committee included all kinds—those who believed the propaganda and who hated the parasites and were on the side of the poorest peasantry, and others who used the situation for their own advantage. But most of them were merely anxious to carry out orders from above. They would have killed their own fathers and mothers simply in order to carry out instructions. And the worst were not those who really believed the destruction of the kulaks would bring about a happy life. For that matter, the wild beasts were not the most poisonous among them either. The most poisonous and vicious were those who managed to square their own accounts. They shouted about political awareness—and settled their grudges and stole. And they stole out of crass selfishness: some clothes, a pair of boots. It was so easy to do a man in: you wrote a denunciation; you did not even have to sign it. All you had to say was that he had paid people to work for him as hired hands, or that he had owned three cows. . . .

. . . What torture was meted out to them! In order to massacre them, it was necessary to proclaim that kulaks are not human beings. . . .

And so, at the beginning of 1930, they began to liquidate the kulak families. The height of the fever was in February and March. They expelled them from their home districts so that when it was time for sowing there would be no kulaks left, so that a new life could begin. That is what we all said it would be: "the first collective farm spring."

It is clear that the committees of Party activists were in charge of the expulsions. There were no instructions as to how the expulsions should be carried out. One collective farm chairman might assemble so many carts. . . .

From our village, on the other hand, the "kulaks" were driven out on foot. They took what they could carry on their backs: bedding, clothing. The mud was so deep it pulled the boots off their feet. It was terrible to watch them. They marched along in a column and looked back at their huts, and their bodies still held the warmth from their own stoves. What pain they must have suffered! . . .

In the district center there was no space left in the prisons. Yes, and when you get down to that, what kind of prison was there in the district center anyway? A hole in the

"Kulaks" being deported as part of Stalin's campaign against them. The banner in the upper left corner mouths Stalin's slogan of liquidating the kulaks as a class. The Illustrated London News/The British Library.

wall. And there were many more coming than just this one column—a column from each village. The movie theater, the club, the schools were all inundated with prisoners. But they did not keep them there long. They drove them to the station, where trains of empty freight cars were waiting on the sidings. They were driven there under guard—by the militia and the GPU—like murderers: grandfathers and grandmothers, women and children, but no fathers, for the fathers had already been taken away in the winter. And people whispered: "They are driving off the kulaks." Just as if they were wolves. And people even shouted: "Curses on you!" But the prisoners had already stopped weeping. They had become like stone. . . .

They were transported in sealed freight cars, and their belongings were transported separately. They took with them only the food they had in their hands. . . . The railways were full of trainloads of similar peasants. Peasants were being transported from all over Russia. They were all tightly packed. There were no berths in the cattle cars. Those ill died en route. But they did get fed. At the main stations along the way they were given a pail of gruel and about seven ounces of bread per person. . . .

The guard consisted of military units. The guards were not vicious. They merely treated them like cattle, and that was that. . . .

. . . The provincial authorities scattered them in the Siberian taiga. Wherever a small village was nearby, the ailing and handicapped were put into huts as crowded as the prisoner- transport trains. And where there was no village nearby, they were simply set down right there on the snow. The weakest died. And those able to work began to cut down timber and didn't bother to take out the stumps. They hauled out the tree trunks and built shacks, lean-tos, makeshift sheds and dwellings. They worked almost without sleeping so that their families would not freeze to death. . . .

Meanwhile back at home our new life began without the so-called "kulaks." They started to force people to join the collective farms. Meetings were under way from morning on. There were shouts and curses. Some of them shouted: "We will not join!" Others shouted: "All right, we will join, but we are not going to give up our cows." . . .

And we thought, fools that we were, that there could be no fate worse than that of the kulaks. How wrong we were! The ax fell upon the peasants right where they stood, on large and small alike. The execution by famine had arrived. . . . As a Party activist, I was sent to the Ukraine in order to strengthen a collective farm. In the Ukraine, we were told, they had an instinct for private property that was stronger than in the Russian Republic. And truly, truly, the whole business was much worse in the Ukraine than it was with us. . . .

How was it? After the liquidation of the kulaks the amount of land under cultivation dropped very sharply and so did the crop yield. But meanwhile people continued to report that without the kulaks our whole life was flourishing. The village soviet lied to the district, and the district lied to the province, and the province lied to Moscow. Everything was apparently in order, so Moscow assigned grain production and delivery quotas to the provinces, and the provinces then assigned them to the districts. And our village was given a quota that it couldn't have fulfilled in ten years! In the village soviet even those who weren't drinkers took to drink out of terror. It was clear that Moscow was basing its hopes on the Ukraine. And the upshot of it was that most of the subsequent anger was directed against the Ukraine. What they said was simple: you have failed to fulfill the plan, and that means that you yourself are an unliquidated kulak.

Of course, the grain deliveries could not be fulfilled. Smaller areas had been sown, and the crop yield on those smaller areas had shrunk. So where could it come from, that promised ocean of grain from the collective farms? The conclusion reached up top was that the grain had all been concealed, hidden away. By kulaks who had not yet been liquidated, by loafers! The "kulaks" had been removed, but the "kulak" spirit remained. Private property was master over the mind of the Ukrainian peasant.

Who was it who then signed the act which imposed mass murder? . . . For the decree required that the peasants of the Ukraine, the Don, and the Kuban be put to death by starvation, put to death along with their tiny children. The instructions were to take away the entire seed fund. Grain was searched for as if it were not grain but bombs and machine guns. The whole earth was stabbed with bayonets and ramrods. Cellars were dug up, floors were broken through, and vegetable gardens were turned over. From some they confiscated even the grain in their houses—in pots or troughs. They even took baked bread away from one woman, loaded it onto the cart, and hauled it off to the district. Day and night the carts creaked along, laden with the confiscated grain, and dust hung over the earth. And there were no grain elevators to accommodate it, and they simply dumped it out on the earth and set guards around it. By winter the grain had been soaked by the rains and began to ferment—the Soviet government didn't even have enough canvas to cover it up! . . .

So then I understood: the most important thing for the Soviet government was the plan! Fulfill the plan! Pay up your assessment, make your assigned deliveries! The state comes first, and people are a big zero.

Fathers and mothers wanted to save their children and hid a tiny bit of grain, and they were told: "You hate the country of socialism. You are trying to make the plan fail, you parasites, you pro-kulaks, you rats." They tried to answer, but it was to no avail: "We aren't trying to sabotage the plan. All we want is to feed our children and to save ourselves. After all, everyone has to eat." . . .

With the autumn people began to use up their potatoes, and, since there was no bread, they disappeared very quickly. By Christmas they began to slaughter their cattle. The cattle were by then mostly skin and bones anyway, and the meat was stringy and tough. Then, of course, they killed the chickens. All the meat went swiftly. Not a drop of milk was to be had. Not an egg was left in the village either. But the worst thing was that there was no grain, no bread. They had taken every last kernel of grain from the village. . . .

The starving people were left to themselves. The state had abandoned them. In the villages people went from house to house, begging from each other. The poor begged from the poor, the starving begged from the starving. . . . And the state gave not one tiny kernel to the starving. Though it was on the grain of the peasants that the state was founded, that it stood. . . .

And now they ate anything at all. They caught mice, rats, snakes, sparrows, ants, earthworms. They ground up bones into flour, and did the same with leather and shoe soles; they cut up old skins and furs to make noodles of a kind, and they cooked glue. And when the grass came up, they began to dig up the roots and eat the leaves and the buds. . . .

Deaths from starvation mowed down the village. First the children, then the old people, then those of middle age. At first they dug graves and buried them, and then as things got worse they stopped. Dead people lay there in the yards, and in the end they remained right in their huts. Things fell silent. The whole village died.

DISCUSSION QUESTION

Compare and contrast the picture Reed presents of the Bolsheviks (communists) in 1917 with Grossman's depiction of the activity of the Communist party in its relations with the peasants between 1929 and 1933.

CHAPTER EIGHT

Social Conflicts in the United States

The United States emerged from World War I as a major global power. Americans immediately demanded a "return to normalcy," seeking to forget the horrors of war and to enjoy their newfound wealth and glory. In rich urban areas in the United States and around the world, the 1920s often "roared" as those who could afford to do so embarked on a frenzy of conspicuous consumption, partying, drinking, and self-indulgence. However, the seeming prosperity masked major economic and social problems.

Throughout the history of the United States, no problem has been more persistent and difficult to solve than the issue of racial equality. The reading by W.E.B. DuBois, one of the founders of the National Association for the Advancement of Colored People (NAACP), directly addresses this issue. It is an open letter to newly elected President Warren G. Harding, in which DuBois made an impassioned plea for equal rights and an end to discrimination and oppression. Almost forty years later, President Lyndon Johnson would reiterate many of the same demands before a joint session of Congress (see Reading 17.1 in Part 3).

During his long and extremely productive career, W.E.B. DuBois (1868–1963) remained a committed spokesperson, not only for racial equality in the United States, but for human rights throughout the world. DuBois graduated sum laude with a degree in philosophy from Harvard University and was a guiding figure in many African American movements. In this selection, DuBois writes about the wrongs of racial segregation (uses the then preferred terminology "Negro race").

In the post–World War I era, the conflict between those espousing new scientific theories and those firmly wedded to traditional religious beliefs also continued. The struggle between people who accepted Darwinian theories of evolution and selective adaptation and traditionalists who believed in the divine creation of all life, humans in particular, was especially persistent and virulent. These two contradictory positions were brought into vivid focus during the 1925 Scopes Trial, in which a biology teacher in Tennessee was tried for having broken the law when he taught Darwin's theory of evolution in a public school. Reading 8.2 offers a critique of the controversy by a zoologist who testified at the trial.

READING 8.1

W.E.B. DuBois on Race Relations

The following reading is from an open letter to President Harding published in *The Crisis,* a monthly journal and official publication of the NAACP, aimed at an educated African American audience. The journal was an immediate success from its first issue in 1910. Under W.E.B. DuBois' editorship, it addressed such crucial issues as lynching, economic problems, and segregation. As early as 1911, *The Crisis* featured an article on black sources of the ancient Egyptian civilization, an issue that has been debated until the present day. The journal also introduced many African American writers, including Langston Hughes, to a wider audience. In his popular editorials and essays, DuBois not only addressed the issue of racial relations but also supported women's rights, including the right to vote.

During the interwar years, most African Americans lived under a repressive system of racial segregation. Eighty-five percent of the 10 million African Americans lived in Southern states, where they were disfranchised; attended segregated schools, churches, and other institutions; and were sometimes subjected to physical attacks and even lynchings. While DuBois advocated increased education as a means for African Americans to improve their living standards, he also addressed the major issues of racism and economic inequality, not only in the United States but in the Caribbean and elsewhere. He called for an end to the discriminatory "Jim Crow" laws of the South and fought for the enactment of more stringent antilynching legislation.

In the struggle for racial equality, African Americans differed over whether they should follow policies of accommodation and slow change or adopt more dynamic and confrontational strategies. As he grew older, DuBois supported more activist approaches to the question of race relations.

DuBois also supported the Pan African movement and was one of the organizers of the 1919 Pan African Congress, which met in Paris at the same time as the Paris Peace Conference. In spite of considerable opposition from the British and United States governments, the Pan African Congress submitted its resolutions recommending that the League of Nations oversee the former German colonies in Africa.

In the interwar years, DuBois traveled widely and expressed his sympathy for the Soviet Union. DuBois' increasingly leftist positions alienated the more conservative elements in the NAACP. In 1932, *The Crisis* was reorganized under new editorship; DuBois formally resigned from the organization in 1934. In 1961, he moved permanently to the newly independent West African nation of Ghana. When DuBois died in 1963, Kwame Nkrumeh, the Ghanaian nationalist leader, gave a moving oratory lauding his contributions as the foremost African American intellectual and lifelong champion of human rights.

AN OPEN LETTER TO WARREN GAMALIEL HARDING [HARDING HAD BEEN ELECTED AS PRESIDENT OF THE UNITED STATES]

March 1921

Sir:

By an unprecedented vote you have been called to the most powerful position in the gift of mankind. Of the more than hundred million human beings whose destiny rests so largely with you in the next four years, one in every ten is of Negro descent.

Your enemies in the campaign sought to count you among this number and if it were true it would give us deep satisfaction to welcome you to the old and mystic chrism of Negroland, whence many mighty souls have stepped since time began.

But blood and physical descent are little and idle things as compared with spiritual heritage. And here we would see you son of the highest: a child of Abraham Lincoln and Lloyd Garrison and Frederick Douglass; a grandson of Thomas Jefferson and John Quincy Adams; and a lineal descendant of the martyred Fathers of the Free of all times and lands.

We appeal to you: we the outcast and lynched, the mobbed and murdered, the de-spoiled and insulted; and yet withal, the indomitable, unconquered, unbending and unafraid black children of kings and slaves and of the best blood of the workers of the earth—

WE WANT THE RIGHT TO VOTE.
WE WANT TO TRAVEL WITHOUT INSULT.
WE WANT LYNCHING AND MOB-LAW QUELLED FOREVER.
WE WANT FREEDOM FOR OUR BROTHERS IN HAITI.

We know that the power to do these things is not entirely in your hands, but its begin-nings lie there. After the fourth of March, on you more than on any other human being rests the redemption of the blood of Africa and through it the peace of the world. All the cruelty, rape and atrocities of slavery; all the groans and humiliations of half-freedom; all the theft and degradation of that spirit of the Ku Klux mob that seeks to build a free Amer-ica on racial, religious and class hatred—the weight of all this woe is yours.

You, Sir, whether you will or no, stand responsible. You are responsible for the truth back of the pictures of the burning of Americans circulated in European drawing-rooms; for the spectacle of 82% of the voters of the South disfranchised under a government called a democracy; for the hypocrisy of a nation seeking to lend idealism to the world for peace when within its own borders there is more murder, theft, riot and crucifixion than was ever even charged against Bolshevik Russia.

In the name of our fathers, President Harding, our fathers black and white who toiled and bled and died to make this a free and decent nation, will you not tear aside the cob-webs of politics, and lies of society, and the grip of industrial thieves, and give us an ad-ministration which will say and mean: *the first and fundamental and inescapable prob-lem of American democracy is Justice to the American Negro.* If races cannot live

DuBois, W.E.B. "Open Letter to President Warren Gamaliel Harding," *The Crisis,* March 1921, pp. 197–98.

During his long and extremely productive career, W.E.B. DuBois was an outspoken champion for the civil rights movement in the United States; he also wrote extensively on causes as diverse as independence for African and Caribbean nations, votes for women, and educational and economic reforms. Archive Photos

together in peace and happiness in America, they cannot live together in the world. Race isolation died a century ago. Human unity within and without Nations, must and will succeed—and you, Sir, must start bringing this to pass.

READING 8.2

Darwinian Theory and the Scopes Trial

In the famous 1925 Scopes Trial, a high school biology teacher, who had volunteered to be a "test case" for the American Civil Liberties Union (ACLU), was indicted on criminal charges for teaching Darwinian theory rather than the traditional Christian religious interpretation of creation. The trial—the first trial nationally broadcast over the radio in the United States—became another "trial of the century," along with the Lindbergh kidnapping and, much later, the O.J. Simpson murder trials.

At the trial, William Jennings Bryan, a former secretary of state, a noted orator, and the nation's best-known populist leader, argued for the prosecution. As a populist, Bryan had supported numerous progressive social causes, including votes for women, but he was concerned that Darwinian theory could be misused to justify the continued exploitation of the disadvantaged. So-called Social Darwinists, including English writer Herbert Spencer and many others, misapplied Darwinian theories of "survival of the fittest" to argue that the poor were poor because they were "less fit" and that the rich deserved their wealth and position because they were "more fit."

Clarence Darrow, an equally famous lawyer and defender of the underdog, argued for the accused. In now famous exchanges, Bryan and Darrow clashed over the meaning of Scripture. Although they disagreed with many of Bryan's progressive social stances, many Christian fundamentalists rallied to his defense of biblical Scripture. The Scopes trial also raised basic questions regarding issues of individual rights over the will of the majority. Although Darrow lost the case, many of the issues raised at the trial continue to resonate today.

In the following reading, a zoologist, Edward L. Rice, focuses on the arguments between the supporters and opponents of Darwin's evolutionary theories. Writing soon after the trial, Rice emphasizes that those with new or revolutionary ideas were attacked or even persecuted throughout much of history. He concludes that evolutionary theory has come to stay and that, based on historical experience, there is no reason to fear that religious belief would be destroyed because of it.

Subsequent events supported Rice's contention. During the 1930s, scientists, including C.D. Darlington and J.B.S. Haldane, synthesized knowledge about genetics and cell structure, thereby laying the foundations for future discoveries of DNA and the basic composition of cells. During the 1950s, further discoveries were made about the molecular structure of genes, with scientists demonstrating that genes were, in fact, long strands of digital information, carrying a genetic code far more complex and vast than modern computers.

This "new" biology went far toward proving Darwinian theories on evolution, but those who held to the belief in divine creation of all life continued to attack those who fully accepted the new scientific findings. Although Darwinian theory has been generally accepted, its teaching in schools, not only in the United States, is still challenged periodically.

With the adjournment of the Eighteenth Tennessee Circuit Court in the Rhea County Court House, Dayton, on July 21, 1925, following the conviction and sentence of John T. Scopes, the curtain fell on the first act of a most astonishing drama, perhaps, rather, on the first of a series of one-act plays. While the managers are determining the location and setting of the next performance, we may well consider some of the lessons of the completed act.

Of the dramatic character of the trial there is no question; but was it tragedy, or comedy, or vaudeville? The views are as varied as the critics. Whatever it was as a drama, as a lawsuit it was, as the headlines defined it, a "comedy of errors." Was the defendant really Mr. Scopes, and was the charge the infringement of a specific law of Tennessee, forbidding the teaching of evolution? Or was the State of Tennessee under charges of infringement of her own Constitution or that of the United States? Or was the theory of evolution at the bar, charged with violating the Fundamentalist interpretation of Genesis [the first book of the Bible]? Or was it a personal duel between Clarence Darrow and William Jennings Bryan? Judge Raulston's decision to exclude scientific and theological experts indicated that he considered the case merely one of infringement of the Tennessee law as it stands; but, whether through undue leniency or from confusion under the attacks and counter-attacks of the lead-

Rice, Edward L. "From the Standpoint of Science," *Current History Magazine,* September 1925, pp. 889–91.

ing attorneys, he failed to hold the trial to this interpretation. The constant effort of the defense was to draw in the broader questions of constitutionality, while the prosecution, after its sensational preliminary challenge to a duel of science and fundamentalism, became the strictest of strict constructionists.

PROGRESS VS. CONSERVATISM

Whatever the legal right and wrong in this trial, and whatever the further legal developments, it is not the legal question which has caught the popular interest of this country and of the civilized world. It is not as the trial of an individual, but as one episode in the world's struggle for freedom of thought that the Scopes case becomes significant. Throughout the ages, two diametrically opposed spirits have been in constant contrast. On the one hand, progress going forth in the adventurous spirit of the knight errant, has been ever striving to force back the powers of moral and intellectual darkness encircling humanity; on the other hand, conservatism has been consolidating the positions already won. Both may be right; indeed, both are necessary to the highest human development; but each may easily go wrong. In the drive for new truth, progress may become reckless, and may mistake the merely new for the true; in zeal for old truth, conservatism is in danger of refusing new truth, and in even greater danger of clinging to old error no less tenaciously than to old truth. It is the truth of an idea, not its age, which is important. In a letter to the Thessalonian Church, Paul expressed with telegraphic brevity the right relation of these contrasting spirits: "Prove all things; hold fast that which is good."

Unfortunately, the dominant theology of the Middle Ages forgot Paul's first injunction, and stood for conservatism in its most extreme form. On the birth of progressive modern science, a conflict became inevitable. With militant modern fundamentalism as the lineal descendant of medieval theology, the continuation of the conflict was no less inevitable. The trial of Galileo [who insisted that the earth revolved around the sun] in 1615 and the trial of Scopes in 1925 are but two picturesque incidents in this age-long warfare. . . .

IDEA, NOT MAN, ON TRIAL

The parallel is amazing. In 1925, as in 1615, an idea rather than a man was on trial. The spirit of intolerance and persecution was identical; fortunately, however, there has been a marked evolution in penal practice, a money fine and banishment from the public educational system of Tennessee taking the place of excommunication and torture popular in the seventeenth century. . . .

The history of the relation of science and theology in the past might well give pause to those who think to stop the progress of the evolution theory today by legislative act and civil trial. The theory of evolution has come to stay. No inductive argument permits a demonstrative proof like that of a problem in geometry; but the mass of cumulative evidence for evolution is such that its probability, like that of the theories of gravitation and the conservation of energy, has become a practical certainty.

Evolution, i.e., the derivative origin of plants and animals, including man, has the all but unanimous assent of those who have given it serious study; and it is inconceivable to modern biologists that this theory will ever be discarded. On the other hand, there still is and long will be the widest divergence of opinion on the details of its application and on the theories as to its method. The exact determination of lines of descent is often very obscure, as, for instance, in the origin of vertebrates from invertebrates; "Darwinism," in its proper significance as an explanation of the method of evolution through natural selection and sexual selection, is still far from its final evaluation, as is the contrasted theory of Lamarck, with its dependence upon the inheritance of acquired characters. But this confusion regarding details and methods must not be mistaken for doubt concerning the main fact of evolution. Gradually many of the present problems will be solved; more and more of truth will be discovered. But this sifting of the true from the false can be accomplished only by the patient experimentation and careful induction of trained biologists; the truth of a scientific theory is not to be determined by legislative enactment, by jury trial, or by popular majority.

To those who honestly feel that the evolution theory is dangerous to religion, the history of past conflicts between science and theology should bring comfort and encouragement. One scientific advance after another has been first viewed with horror as heretical, but, on better acquaintance, has proved harmless or even helpful to true religion; so may new scientific advances prove equally harmless or helpful in the future. In England the evolution theory reached this stage a generation ago; the "heresy" of Darwin's time is the orthodoxy of today. And it was in 1884 that a great American, John Fiske, wrote: "As with the Copernican astronomy, so with the Darwinian biology, we rise to a higher view of the workings of God and of the nature of Man than was ever attainable before."

DISCUSSION QUESTION

Discuss the conflicting points of view over two of the major social issues confronting society in the United States during the twentieth century, namely racial equality and the conflict between science and tradition.

CHAPTER NINE

The Global Depression

In 1929 the world plunged into a serious and prolonged economic crisis; this Great Depression persisted through the 1930s. The general perception is that the collapse of the New York stock market in October 1929 signalled the beginning of the Great Depression. The deeper causes of this shattering world event, however, are rooted in weakness in the world economy that had persisted through the 1920s. The economic recovery after World War I had been limited in scope, and industrial unemployment had remained high in western European countries. In fact, several economies, including the Japanese, had been in a depressed state for several years prior to 1929.

The agricultural sector was another vulnerable area before 1929. Dropping prices in world food staples had dramatically undercut the farmers' ability to purchase manufactured goods. The weakness of agricultural prices and an excess in the production of industrial goods that could not be sold had dramatic consequences when a financial crisis erupted.

Between 1919 and 1929, the United States, which had emerged from World War I with no civilian damages and increased industrial capacity, led the world in prosperity. American banks profited by making huge short-term loans to German and other European governments and businesses at high interest rates. Profits were plowed into the stock market, and, as stock prices soared, more people purchased stocks on borrowed money. German government loans from U.S. banks had partially financed its reparation payments and had allowed German businesses to expand.

When the speculative boom on the Wall Street stock exchange ended in a crash, the ensuing panic led to the collapse of the American economy, with dramatic repercussions in Europe, especially in Germany. Many German banks closed when new supplies of American money ended and U.S. banks demanded the repayment of loans as soon as they became due. The collapse of German banks resulted in great losses to banks in other countries, especially those in Great Britain and the United States. As a result, Britain was forced to abandon the gold standard in 1931, marking the end of an epoch when the British currency was literally as good as gold. The weakening of the British economy would damage Great Britain's international clout in countering Nazi Germany's aggressions during the late 1930s (see Reading 13.1).

Another result of the depression was the abandonment of free trade in favor of protectionism and the quest for autarchy (economic self-sufficiency). In Japan, where a domestic depression had begun in 1926, the world depression exacerbated an already failing economy. Exports halved between 1929 and 1931 and farm income dropped by two thirds, leaving 3 million Japanese unemployed. Although Japan was the first industrial power to recover, the depression fatally weakened the newly established elected party governments and encouraged the rising militarists to seek long-term economic solution in imperialism (see Reading 13.2).

The prevailing view on combating the depression was for governments to follow a deflationary policy of restricting credit, lessening spending, and balancing budgets. These policies, however, did not create new jobs, and people without jobs and incomes could not afford to buy goods. Thus, the number of the unemployed rose rapidly in all industrialized countries, to 3 million in Great Britain in 1931 and 6 million in Germany in 1933, where industrial production was half in that year of what it had been in 1929.

In the United States, the Republican administration under President Herbert Hoover followed the same deflationary policy as most European countries, with the result that the U.S. economy continued to stagnate. It was only with the election of Democratic president Franklin Roosevelt in 1933 that the U.S. government began a "New Deal," inaugurating massive public works programs that gradually lifted the country from the depth of the depression. Whereas the United States under President Roosevelt was able to pursue a New Deal to foster economic recovery, the German government was unwilling to prime the German economic pump for fear of inflation because of its earlier experience with hyperinflation in 1923.

The global economic crisis was a turning point in the interwar years. It weakened the democratic and internationalist forces that had prevailed in the 1920s, especially in Japan and Germany, and replaced them with militarists and ultranationalists. It also weakened the will of the established democratic nations, such as Great Britain, France, and the United States, to lead the world in maintaining international order and resisting aggression. They opted to appease the aggressors instead. The 1930s became increasingly turbulent, even as economic recovery progressed. Before the end of the decade, the world had plunged into another world war.

READING 9.1

The Great Depression in the United States

The prosperity and sense of security enjoyed by many Americans in the 1920s came to a crashing halt on October 24, 1929, when the stock market began to collapse. The economy plunged into a downward spiral for the next three years, characterized by rising unemployment and bankruptcies.

Unable to turn the economy around, Republican President Herbert Hoover lost his bid for a second term in 1932. When Democrat Franklin Roosevelt was inaugurated as president in March 1933, unemployment stood at 25 percent. To avert further economic disaster and suffering, Roosevelt immediately proposed legislation to extend the federal government's regulatory powers to provide relief and stimulate recovery. With bipartisan support in Congress, he enacted a program called the New Deal, which gradually caused a turnaround.

To boost public confidence, Roosevelt resorted to a novel practice by talking to the American people regularly on radio. He called these informal talks fireside chats. Reading 9.1A is taken from his second fireside chat, in which he tells the nation about his plans for economic recovery and the legislation he has proposed to Congress. This chat took place on May 7, 1933, less than two months after he assumed office.

Reading 9.1B records the experiences of people during the depression. It begins with an account by a young female social worker who describes what she encounters in her work among the unemployed. It is part of a collection of oral history of the Great Depression titled *Hard Times,* compiled by Studs Terkel. It is followed by two letters appealing for help, addressed to President and Mrs. Roosevelt, respectively. They were among thousands of letters sent to the White House, compiled in a collection edited by Robert S. McElvaine, titled *Down and Out in the Great Depression, Letters from the "Forgotten Man."*

READING 9.1A: PRESIDENT ROOSEVELT'S FIRESIDE CHAT

Tonight . . . I come for the second time to give you my report; in the same spirit and by the same means to tell you about what we have been doing and what we are planning to do. . . . A prompt program applied as quickly as possible seemed to me not only justified but imperative to our national security. The Congress, and when I say Congress I mean the members of both political parties, fully understood this and gave me generous and intelligent support. The members of Congress realized that the methods of normal times had to be replaced in the emergency by measures which were suited to the serious and pressing requirements of the moment. . . .

The legislation which has been passed or is in the process of enactment can properly be considered as part of a well-grounded plan.

First, we are giving opportunity of employment to one-quarter of a million of the unemployed, especially the young men who have dependents, to go into the forestry and flood-prevention work. This is a big task because it means feeding, clothing and caring

Roosevelt, Franklin D. *The Public Papers and Addresses of Franklin D. Roosevelt, with a Special Introduction and Explanatory Notes by President Roosevelt: Vol. Two, The Years of Crisis, 1933.* New York: Random House, 1938, pp. 160–63, 165.

for nearly twice as many men as we have in the regular army itself. In creating this civilian conservation corps we are killing two birds with one stone. We are clearly enhancing the value of our natural resources, and we are relieving an appreciable amount of actual distress. This great group of men has entered upon its work on a purely voluntary basis; no military training is involved and we are conserving not only our natural resources, but our human resources. One of the great values to this work is the fact that it is direct and requires the intervention of very little machinery.

Second, I have requested the Congress and have secured action upon a proposal to put the great properties owned by our Government at Muscle Shoals to work after long years of wasteful inaction, and with this a broad plan for the improvement of a vast area in the Tennessee Valley. It will add to the comfort and happiness of hundreds of thousands of people and the incident benefits will reach the entire Nation.

Next, the Congress is about to pass legislation that will greatly ease the mortgage distress among the farmers and the home owners of the Nation, by providing for the easing of the burden of debt now bearing so heavily upon millions of our people.

Our next step in seeking immediate relief is a grant of half a billion dollars to help the States, counties and municipalities in their duty to care for those who need direct and immediate relief. . . .

We are planning to ask the Congress for legislation to enable the Government to undertake public works, thus stimulating directly and indirectly the employment of many others in well-considered projects. . . .

Depression breadline, Los Angeles, early 1930s. Archive Photos/American Stock

Further legislation has been taken up which goes much more fundamentally into our economic problems. The Farm Relief Bill seeks by the use of several methods, alone or together, to bring about an increased return to farmers for their major farm products, seeking at the same time to prevent in the days to come disastrous overproduction which so often in the past has kept farm commodity prices far below a reasonable return. This measure provides wide powers for emergencies. The extent of its use will depend entirely upon what the future has in store. . . .

We are working toward a definite goal, which is to prevent the return of conditions which came very close to destroying what we call modern civilization. The actual accomplishment of our purpose cannot be attained in a day. Our policies are wholly within purposes for which our American Constitutional Government was established 150 years ago.

READING 9.1B: PERSONAL ACCOUNTS OF THE DEPRESSION

I was twenty-one when I started and very inexperienced. My studies at school didn't prepare me for this. How could I cope with this problem? We were still studying about immigrant families. Not about mass unemployment. The school just hadn't kept up with the times. We made terrible blunders. I'm sure I did.

There was a terrible dependence on the case worker. What did they feel about a young girl as their boss? Whom they had to depend on for food, a pitiful bare minimum? There was always the fear of possibly saying the wrong thing to her. The case worker represented the Agency. We seemed powerful because we were their only source of income. Actually, there was little we could do.

I had a terrible guilt feeling. I was living rather well sharing a nice apartment with two other girls. My top pay was $135 a month, which made me well off. Yet there were constant layoffs. I always felt that if I lost my job, I might go on relief, too. So I never really had a sense of security myself.

I think most case workers felt as I did. Though there were quite a few who were self-righteous. They felt some of the people weren't looking hard enough for work. Or they were loafers. They believed some of the stuff that came out in the newspapers. Even then. They sometimes made it very difficult for the clients. There was a lot of hypocrisy and sham.

I worked with both whites and blacks. One could say the blacks were more accustomed to poverty. But they still said, "I wouldn't come here if I had work." There was a lot of waiting around the relief offices. Where they came to pick up their food orders. These places were mostly old warehouses, very dismal. That was another thing, dispiriting. Sitting around and waiting, waiting, waiting. . . .

The case worker was often the object of their anger. Where else could they give vent to their feelings? So they took it out on us. They didn't know the cause of their problems. Of course, there were tensions. At one time, my job was to cover the entire city. I

Terkel, Studs. *Hard Times: An Oral History of the Great Depression.* New York: Random House, 1970, pp. 419–20; McElvaine, Robert S., ed. *Down and Out in the Great Depression: Letters from the "Forgotten Man."* Chapel Hill: The University of North Carolina Press, 1983, pp. 83, 102–3.

often worked at night. I found myself in very strange neighborhoods at all hours. I took it as a matter of course. Yet I knew when these people felt put upon. . . .

In 1934, a case worker was killed by her client, while sitting in the chair at his home. A youngish white man living with his mother. The story is: she had promised him a job. CWA was coming in. He was so overwhelmed by his joblessness he became maddened to the point where he shot her. He dragged his mother to the district office. He killed the supervisor, a clerical worker and then killed his mother and himself.

We were all frightened. Bulletins were issued to all the offices: case workers could take a moratorium on visits. We weren't told we *must not* visit. So I decided I'd go anyway. I was young and felt the clients needed me. (Laughs softly.) If this were to happen now, would I go? I don't know.

I remember, for a time after that, peering into the window, before I rang the bell. I guess I was pretty scared. One family said to me it was terrible, but some case workers deserve to be killed. He looked at me and smiled, "But not you, Miss Barth."

Reidsville. Ga Oct 19th 1935

Hon. Franklin D. Roosevelt.
President of U.S.
Washington D.C.
Dear Mr. President
Would you please direct the people in charge of the releaf work in Georgia to issue the provisions + other supplies to our suffering colored people. I am sorry to worrie you with this Mr. President but hard as it is to believe the releaf officials here are using up most every thing that you send for them self + their friends. they give out the releaf supplies here on Wednesday of this week and give us black folks, each one, nothing but a few cans of pickle meet and to white folks they give blankets, bolts of cloth and things like that. I dont want to take to mutch of your time Mr president but will give you just one example of how the releaf is work down here   the witto Nancy Hendrics own lands, stock holder in the Bank in this town and she is being supplied with Blankets cloth and gets a supply of cans goods regular   this is only one case but I could tell you many. Please help us mr President because we cant help our self and we know you is the president and a good Christian man   we is praying for you. Yours truly   cant sign my name Mr President   they will beat me up and run me away from here and this is my home

[Anonymous]

Sept 7—1934.
Webbville Ky

Mrs Roosevelt:
I am riting you in regard to my Condition and the Reason that I am riting you is that I think that Women is more Sympathetic than men for the old and distressed people. if there is any Way or any thing that you Could do or say that would help me a little in my last days I would be Verry thankful. I have allmost lived out my three score and ten and have bin in ill health for 2 years not able to Work any—I have no income at all I have a wife and tow Children looking to me for suport—
I was on the federal relief a part of last Winter and by fraud or some reason I was Cut off in March not noing the Cause and I think if there is any one that acutal needs help I

am one of them We are destitute of food and raiment With no income no relation able to help me. Just on the mercies of the people and I have two statements from two doctors in the Committees office at the County Seat Shoeing my disability

Mrs Roosevelt you have a talk with the president and see if there is any Way for me I red your speech in the paper in regard to old age pension I sure would be glad if it does become a law to give all old aged people that are in distress a living in their last days as for my Self I would be glad to get it for a short time that I Will not need it long my time is a bout up if you could give me any advise that would help me in any Way I sure Would appreciate it and Stand by any Candidate that Stands for the old age pension.

Respect yours

J. C. G. [male]

READING 9.2

The Depression Devastates Germany

The German economy, increasingly powerful before 1914, was severely damaged by defeat in World War I. Postwar German economic recovery was hampered by the huge reparation payments Germany was required to make to some of the victor nations; the payments also hampered Germany's economic recovery. To jump start its economy so that it could meet the payments, the Weimar Republic took massive foreign loans, principally from the United States. As economist John Maynard Keynes said, "Reparations and interallied debts are being mostly settled on paper and not in goods. The United States lends money to Germany, Germany transfers its equivalent to the allies, the allies pass it back to the United States government. Nothing really passes—no one is a penny worse." However, the loans had to be repaid with interest, and the Germans had to earn the interest with exports. Before 1923, and again between 1924 and 1929, foreign loans, mostly from the United States, enabled Germany to recover economically and to continue making its reparation payments. Germany could make the payments as long as the world economy was expanding and there was demand for German goods.

When the collapse of the U.S. stock market that began on October 24, 1929, triggered a worldwide depression, U.S. banks withdrew credit, which had a ripple effect on the European banking system that was most disastrous in Germany. In 1932, 6 million Germans were out of work. The inability of Germany's democratically elected governments to reverse the economic catastrophe turned many Germans against the Weimar Republic. Desperate people turned to a leader with radical solutions. As Chancellor Franz von Pappen correctly predicted in 1932,

> What is particularly fatal is that an ever-growing number of young people have no possibility and no hope of finding employment and of earning their livelihood. Despair and the political radicalization of the youthful section of the population are the consequence of this state of things.

The desperation felt by millions of Germans helps explain the appeal of National Socialism and the rise of Adolf Hitler only one year later.

The following selections come from contemporary German newspapers' accounts of the Great Depression as it affected Germany. The first article is titled "Bank Failure," published in late 1929. The second, titled "The Unemployed," published in 1933, is an account of the effects of unemployment.

BANK FAILURE

Rushes on the banks are beginning. Savers have been seized by panic. They fear, no, they are certain that their money, for which they have saved and slaved, is lost. They stand as early as midnight in endless lines to be the first when the cash drawers open. The earlier one arrives the better the chances of still saving something. The ordered life of the banks is being torn apart. All personnel must be mobilized to disburse payments. No one makes deposits. All credit is being called in. Banks in other countries are receiving imploring cables to help out with fluid money and with checks. All the reserves of the national banking association are being called up. But the lines in front of the banks grow longer.

And then the banks begin to crash, because they cannot make the payments. The money has been leant out; for when the bank is not able to make loans then it cannot pay interest to its small savers. The little banks crash first. The larger ones still get by, limiting banking hours first to two hours, then to one. Then the larger banks begin to crash.

And behind all of this chaos is no sudden disappearance of a continent, no gigantic natural catastrophe that destroys values irretrievably. Behind this whole collapse of economic order and economic security, which is under constant threat by agitators, is nothing other than the disrupted notions of those who have something, the suddenly insecure hope of those who possess much, and of those who possess little. Everything that is now taking place on Wall Street is based on nothing but the fact that thoughts have suddenly, too suddenly, taken on unexpected turn. Mass hypnosis. Mass suggestion. The suggestion, the notion: "I can lose!" tears this beautiful economic system, willed by God, blessed by God, protected by God, to shreds. And nonetheless all values remain the same. Values have not changed. There is just as much cash in the world as before. All the money is still there, and not a single cent has fallen off the globe into space, where it cannot be fished back onto land. All the buildings are still standing. All the forests. All the waterfalls. All the oceans. The railroads and the ships all remain intact. And hundreds of thousands of strong and healthy people are willing to work and to produce and to increase the available wealth of the world. Not a single engineer has lost the ability to design new machines. No vein of coal has been hidden by the forces of nature. The sun rises bright and warm in the sky as always. It rains as always. The grain waves in the fields and ripens as always. The fields of cotton extend in splendor. Nothing has changed in the available value of earthly riches. People, seen as a whole, are just as wealthy as yesterday. And for the simple reason, and only the simple reason, that the property of individuals is in danger of changing and shifting does a catastrophe overtake humanity as a whole. [. . .]

An economic system, an economic order, created by people who claim to possess intelligence. People, however, who, despite all the highly developed technology they cre-

Kaes, Anton, Martin Jay, and Edward Dimendberg, eds. *The Weimar Republic Sourcebook.* Berkeley: University of California Press, 1994, pp. 74–75, 84–85.

ated, have still not overcome primitiveness as far as a studied and well-regulated economic system is concerned.

THE UNEMPLOYED

An almost unbroken chain of homeless men extends the whole length of the great Hamburg-Berlin highway.

There are so many of them moving in both directions, impelled by the wind or making their way against it, that they could shout a message from Hamburg to Berlin by word of mouth.

It is the same scene for the entire two hundred miles, and the same scene repeats itself between Hamburg and Bremen, between Bremen and Kassel, between Kassel and Würzburg, between Würzburg and Munich. All the highways in Germany over which I traveled this year presented the same aspect.

The only people who shouted and waved at me and ran along beside my automobile hoping for a ride during their journey were the newcomers, the youngsters. They were recognizable at once. They still had shoes on their feet and carried knapsacks, like the *Wandervögel*. [. . .]

But most of the hikers paid no attention to me. They walked separately or in small groups with their eyes on the ground. And they had the queer, stumbling gait of barefoot people, for their shoes were slung over their shoulders. Some of them were guild members—carpenters with embroidered wallets, knee breeches, and broad felt hats; milkmen with striped red shirts, and bricklayers with tall black hats—but they were in a minority. Far more numerous were those to whom one could assign no special profession or craft—unskilled young people for the most part who had been unable to find a place for themselves in any city or town in Germany, and who had never had a job and never expected to have one. There was something else that had never been seen before—whole families that had piled all their goods into baby carriages and wheelbarrows that they were pushing along as they plodded forward in dumb despair. It was a whole nation on the march.

I saw them—and this was the strongest impression that the year 1932 left with me—I saw them, gathered into groups of fifty or a hundred men, attacking fields of potatoes. I saw them digging up the potatoes and throwing them into sacks while the farmer who owned the field watched them in despair and the local policeman looked on gloomily from the distance. I saw them staggering toward the lights of the city as night fell, with their sacks on their backs. What did it remind me of? Of the war, of the worst period of starvation in 1917 and 1918, but even then people paid for the potatoes. [. . .]

I entered the huge Berlin municipal lodging house in a northern quarter of the city. [. . .] Dreary barracks extended to the edge of the sidewalk and under their dripping roofs long lines of men were leaning against the wooden walls, waiting in silence and staring at a brick structure across the street.

This wall was the side of the lodging house and it seemed to blot out the entire sky. [. . .] There was an entrance arched by a brick vaulting, and a watchman sat in a little wooden sentry box. His white coat made him look like a doctor. We stood waiting in the corridor. Heavy steam rose from the men's clothes. Some of them sat down on the floor, pulled off their shoes, and unwound the rags that bound their feet. More people were constantly pouring in the door, and we stood closely packed together. Then another door opened. The crowd pushed forward, and people began forcing their way almost eagerly through this door, for it was warm in there. Without knowing it I had already caught the rhythm of the municipal lodging house. It means waiting, waiting, standing around, and then suddenly jumping up.

We now stand in a long hall. [. . .] There under yellow lamps that hang from the ceiling on long wires sit men in white smocks. We arrange ourselves in long lines, each leading up to one of these men, and the mill begins to grind. [. . .]

What does the man in the white smock want to know? All these fellows in white smocks belong to a very special type of official. The way they let the line flow by while they work so smoothly together is facile, lazy, almost elegant. The way they say "Mr." to the down-and-outers from the street is full of ironic politeness. [. . .] The whole impersonal manner of the officials makes them as incomprehensible as a cash register. [. . .]

Then come the questions. When and where were you born, and where have you come from? Name of your parents? Ever been in a municipal lodging house before? Where have you spent the last three nights? Where did you work last? Have you begged? The first impression that these questions and answers make on me is that it is just like the army. [. . .]

My second impression is the helplessness of the men on my side of the bar and the shocking ruthlessness with which the men on the other side of the bar insult this helplessness. Eight out of every ten men on my side of the bar are young fellows and about a third of these are mere boys. [. . .]

The official presses a white card into my hand and tells me to go to the desk of another clerk with the sign, "adjuster," over it. While waiting in line I look at my white card. It is divided into squares and has my name at the top and all kinds of mysterious symbols underneath. [. . .] I do not remember what the "adjuster" said to me—there was some inconsistency in my papers, I believe. [. . .] [Hauser was sent on to a police examiner, but eventually was cleared.]

When I come out I am holding a check that has been given me for a night's sleep and food in the lodging house. [. . .] The bare walls of the room that we have entered are lined with iron bedsteads. There are no windows but a sloping roof with skylights that reminds me of a factory. We sit down on the bedsteads along the middle of the room, closely packed together. A voice near me whispers, "What was the matter with you, buddy?"

"My papers."

"Say, you had luck to get out again. They kept the fellow that went in with you. He spent his dole of eighteen marks [about $4.30] in two days. Oh, boy, think of it! Eighteen marks! . . ."

I look at the clock again. Our reception ceremony lasted an hour and a half, and we now sit here another half hour, which makes two hours. They do not make it easy for you to get supper and a bed in a municipal lodging house.

DISCUSSION QUESTION

What common characteristics were shared by the unemployed in Germany and in the United States during the Great Depression?

CHAPTER TEN

Asia Between the World Wars

World War I accelerated the forces of nationalism and anticolonialism in Asia and worldwide. The three readings in this chapter focus on the changes at work in Asia during the interwar years. Nationalism, already a force in many parts of the continent before 1914, became dominant continentwide after 1918. Whereas the European empires had been too strong to challenge before 1914, the bloodletting between the major European nations, the dramatic defeat of Germany, and the overthrow of the Russian monarchy so reduced European power that Asian nationalists were emboldened to seek independence after 1918. The Russian Revolution and the establishment of the Soviet Union, with its dramatically different ideas on the economy, political order, and the relationship between social classes, inspired many Asians to seek a Marxist solution to their society's problems.

Thus, anticolonialism is the major theme in all of the three readings that follow. In India, the Western-oriented and democratically inspired Indian National Congress led the way among colonized peoples toward independence. Mohandas K. Gandhi emerged during this period as the leading light of India's nonviolent struggle to win freedom from Great Britain. Gandhi's personality and philosophy gave the Indian nationalist movement a unique moral force that is still admired and emulated today. Reading 10.1 has Gandhi's own words on his ideal of nonviolence; it also contains statements about Gandhi by two of his leading followers, Mrs. Sarojini Naidu and Jawaharlal Nehru.

Multifaceted nationalist movements emerged in "semicolonial" China. China's nationalist struggle began with Western-educated Sun Yat-sen's Nationalist party (Kuomintang), which overthrew the Manchu dynasty in 1911 and replaced it with a republic. Sun sought to create a modern China by harnessing the forces of nationalism, democracy, and economic reform. Reading 10.2 begins with Sun's lectures on nationalism; it was the first of his Three People's Principles, because to Sun nationalism was the essential force in China's struggle against imperialism. The impotence of the warlord-dominated early Chinese republic resulted in the student-led May 4th Movement and Intellectual Revolution of 1919, which demanded improvements in China's status internationally, modernization, and women's emancipation. Reading 10.2 continues with the manifesto of the May 4th Movement, a university student's recollections of his role in the events, and a woman's recollections of her quest for emancipation.

Reading 10.3 deals with the rise of Marxism as an ideology and political movement in Asia and consists of the writings of Mao Tse-tung (Mao Zedong) and Ho Chi Minh, leaders of the Communist parties of China and Vietnam, respectively. The disillusionment that many Chinese felt about China's treatment at the Paris Peace Conference by the Western powers resulted in the formation of the Chinese Communist party in 1921. Mao was a founding member of the Chinese Communist party, and he contributed to world communism by changing its focus from the urban proletariat to the poor peasant in nonindustrial China. In French Indochina, Marxism inspired Ho and the Vietnamese Communist party to work toward social change, as well as independence from France. Ho's Marxist vision would color Vietnam's struggle and its postindependence course.

Demand for social change was strong throughout Asia during the interwar years. In India the progress of this force is seen in the emergence of women political leaders such as Mrs. Sarojini Naidu, first female president of the Indian National Congress and first female governor of an Indian province (Reading 10.1). In China, a broadening movement for women's emancipation is demonstrated in the writing of Mao Yen-wen, who as a young girl participated in the antifoot binding movement and a young people's revolt to end marriages arranged by parents (Reading 10.2).

Other trends in Asia between the world wars include advances in the sciences, technology, and modern education. New industries also spread across many Asian lands, creating unionized industrial workforces that demanded change. Thus, in India, Gandhi could marshall large numbers of workers in nonviolent strikes and marches (Reading 10.1). In China, the student demonstrators of the May 4th Movement were supported by striking workers and by merchant associations that organized trade boycotts (Reading 10.2).

READING 10.1

Gandhi's Impact on India

Mohandas K. Gandhi (1869–1948) was commonly called Mahatma by Indians, a title of respect meaning Great Soul or Holy One. Raised in a devout upper-class Hindu family, he went to Great Britain to study, receiving a law degree. His British education also exposed him to the writings of other religions and philosophies. While practicing law in South Africa, he developed a nonviolent movement to help his fellow Indians overcome racially discriminatory laws. This nonviolent movement was called *satyagraha,* meaning truth force. After returning to India and becoming leader of the Indian National Congress, Gandhi used nonviolent techniques in India's independent movement against British rule and in his crusade for social reforms.

The first excerpt (10.1A) is from Gandhi's autobiography, *The Story of My Experiments with Truth.* It illustrates his ideals and the principle that the end never justifies the means. In strict adherence to this precept, Gandhi would unhesitatingly call off a successful civil disobedience camping when it turned violent. This frustrated some of his followers, who lamented that he thereby delayed the attainment of Indian independence.

The next two excerpts are about Gandhi, the man and his contributions, by two of his famous disciples. The first, titled "The Father of Modern India: An Appreciation" (10.1B) is by Mrs. Sarojini Naidu, poet, orator, politician, and women's leader. Born in 1879 and educated at London and Cambridge Universities, she was elected the first woman president of the Indian National Congress in 1925 and participated in all important negotiations in India's independence movement. She became governor of the United Provinces in 1947 and later served in the cabinet of Prime Minister Jawaharlal Nehru. Reading 10.1C is titled "The Spirit of India." It was written by J. Nehru, Gandhi's best-known disciple and India's longest serving postindependence prime minister (1947–1964).

READING 10.1A: GANDHI ON THE MEANING OF SATYAGRAHA

Thus, while on the one hand the agitation against the Rowlatt Committee's report [1918, to crack down on protests] gathered volume and intensity, on the other the Government grew more and more determined to give effect to its recommendations. . . . I earnestly pleaded with the Viceroy. I addressed him private letters as also public letters, in the course of which I clearly told him that the Government's action left me no other course except to resort to Satyagraha. But it was all in vain. . . .

We daily discussed together plans of the fight, but beyond the holding of public meetings I could not then think of any other programme. I felt myself at a loss to discover how to offer civil disobedience against the Rowlatt Bill. . . . One could disobey it only if the Government gave one the opportunity for it. Failing that, could we civilly disobey other laws? And if so, where was the line to be drawn? . . .

Gandhi, Mohandas K. *Autobiography: The Story of My Experiments with Truth.* Trans. Mahadev Desai. New York: Dover Publications, 1983, pp. 413–18, 422–25.

The idea came to me . . . to call upon the country to observe a *hartal*. Satyagraha is a process of self-purification, and ours is a sacred fight, and it seems to me too in the fitness of things that it should be commenced with an act of self-purification. Let all the people of India, therefore, suspend their business that day and observe the day as one of fasting and prayer. . . . The date of the *hartal* was . . . fixed on 6th April. . . . On that day the whole of India from one end to the other, towns as well as villages, observed a complete *hartal*. It was a most wonderful spectacle. . . .

On the morning of the 6th the citizens of Bombay flocked in their thousands to the Chowpati for a bath in the sea, after which they moved on in a procession to Thakurdvar. The procession included a fair sprinkling of women and children, while the Musalmans joined it in large numbers. From Thakurdvar some of us who were in the procession were taken by the Musalman friends to a mosque near by, where Mrs. Naidu and myself were persuaded to deliver speeches. . . .

Needless to say the *hartal* in Bombay was a complete success. Full preparation had been made for starting civil disobedience. Two or three things had been discussed in this connection. It was decided that civil disobedience might be offered in respect of such laws only as easily lent themselves to being disobeyed by the masses. The salt tax was extremely unpopular and a powerful movement had been for some time past going on to secure its repeal. I therefore suggested that the people might prepare salt from sea-water in their own houses in disregard of the salt laws. My other suggestion was about the sale of proscribed literature, two of my books, viz., *Hind Swaraj* and *Saravodaya* (Gujrati adaptation of Ruskin's *Unto This Law*), which had already been proscribed, came in handy for this purpose. To print and sell them openly seemed to be the easiest way of offering civil disobedience. A sufficient number of copies of the books was therefore printed, and it was arranged to sell them at the end of the monster meeting that was to be held that evening after the breaking of the fast.

On the evening of the 6th an army of volunteers issued forth accordingly with this prohibited literature to sell it among the people. . . . All the copies were soon sold out. The proceeds of the sale were to be utilized for furthering the civil disobedience campaign. . . . It was duly explained to the people that they were liable to be arrested and imprisoned for purchasing the proscribed literature. But for the moment they had shed all fear of jail-going.

It was subsequently learnt that the Government had conveniently taken the view that the books that had been proscribed by it had not in fact been sold, and that what we had sold was not held as coming under the definition of proscribed literature. The reprint was held by the Government to be a new edition of the books that had been proscribed, and to sell them did not constitute an offence under the law. This news caused general disappointment. . . .

[Elsewhere the protests had turned violent.] I learnt that an attempt had been made to pull up the rails near the Nadiad railway station, that a Government officer had been murdered in Viramgam, and that it was under martial law. The people were terror-stricken. They had indulged in acts of violence and were being made to pay for them with interest. . . .

[Gandhi persuaded the police commissioner to rescind martial law and to let him address a public rally.] Addressing the meeting, I tried to bring home to the people the sense of their wrong, declared a penitential fast of three days for myself, appealed to the people to go on a similar fast for a day, and suggested to those who had been guilty of acts of violence to confess their guilt.

I saw my duty as clear as daylight. It was unbearable for me to find that the labourers, amongst whom I had spent a good deal of my time, whom I had served, and from whom I had expected better things, had taken part in the riots, and I felt I was a sharer in their guilt.

Just as I suggested to the people to confess their guilt, I suggested to the Government to condone the crimes. Neither accepted my suggestion. . . . I made up my mind to suspend Satyagraha so long as people had not learnt the lesson of peace. . . .

There were, however, others who were unhappy over the decision. They felt that, if I expected peace everywhere and regarded it as a condition precedent to launching Satyagraha, mass Satyagraha would be an impossibility. I was sorry to disagree with them. If those amongst whom I worked, and whom I expected to be prepared for nonviolence and self-suffering, could not be nonviolent, Satyagraha was certainly impossible. I was firmly of opinion that those who wanted to lead the people to Satyagraha ought to be able to keep the people within the limited nonviolence expected of them. I hold the same opinion even today.

Almost immediately after the meeting I went to Nadiad. It was here that I first used the expression "Himalayan miscalculation" which obtained such a wide currency afterwards . . . that I had committed a grave error in calling upon the people in the Kheda district and elsewhere to launch upon civil disobedience prematurely. . . . My confession brought down upon me no small amount of ridicule. But I have never regretted having made that confession. . . .

Let us now see what that Himalayan miscalculation was. Before one can be fit for the practice of civil disobedience one must have rendered a willing and respectful obedience to the state laws. For the most part we obey such laws out of fear of the penalty for their breach, and this holds good particularly in respect of such laws as do not involve a moral principle. . . . Such compliance is not, however the willing and spontaneous obedience that is required of a Satyagrahi. A Satyagrahi obeys the laws of society intelligently and of his own free will, because he considers it to be his sacred duty to do so. It is only when a person has thus obeyed the laws of society scrupulously that he is in a position to judge as to which particular rules are good and just and which unjust and iniquitous. Only then does the right accrue to him of the civil disobedience of certain laws in well-defined circumstances. My error lay in my failure to observe this necessary limitation. I had called on the people to launch upon civil disobedience before they had thus qualified themselves for it, and this mistake seemed to me of Himalayan magnitude. . . . I realized that before a people could be fit for offering civil disobedience, they should thoroughly understand its deeper implications. That being so, before re-starting civil disobedience on a mass scale, it would be necessary to create a band of well-tried, pure-hearted volunteers who thoroughly understand its deeper implications. . . . I realized that the progress of the training in civil disobedience was not going to be as rapid as I had at first expected.

READING 10.1B: THE FATHER OF MODERN INDIA: AN APPRECIATION

My first meeting with Mahatma Gandhi took place in London on the eve of the great European War of 1914, when he arrived fresh from his triumphs in South Africa, where he had initiated his principle of passive resistance and won a victory for his countrymen, who were at that time chiefly indentured labourers, over the redoubtable General Smuts. I had not been able to meet his ship on his arrival, but the next afternoon I went wandering round in search of his lodging in an obscure part of Kensington and climbed the steep stairs of an old, unfashionable house, to find an open door framing a living picture of a little man with a shaven head, seated on the floor on a black prison blanket and eating a messy meal of squashed tomatoes and olive oil out of a wooden bowl. . . . I burst instinctively into happy laughter at this amusing and unexpected vision of a famous leader, whose name had already become a household word in our country. He lifted his eyes and laughed back at me, saying: "Ah, you must be Mrs. Naidu!" Who else dare be so irreverent? "Come in," said he, "and share my meal." "No thanks," I replied, sniffing: "what an abominable mess it is!" In this way and at that instant commenced our friendship, which flowered into real comradeship, and bore fruit in a long, loving, loyal discipleship, which never wavered for a single hour through more than thirty years of common service in the cause of India's freedom.

How shall I find words of adequate beauty and power that might serve, even approximately, to portray the rare and exquisite courtesy and compassion, courage, wisdom, humour and humanity of this unique man? . . . This man of God [who] inspired in us awe and veneration because of his supreme greatness [and] endeared himself to us and evoked our warmest love by the very faults and follies which he shared with our frail humanity?

I love to remember him as a playmate of little children, as the giver of solace to the sorrowful, the oppressed and the fallen. I love to recall the picture of him at his evening prayers, facing a multitude of worshippers, with the full moon slowly rising above a silver sea, the very spirit of immortal India; and, with a brief interval, to find him seated with bent brows, giving counsel to statesmen responsible for the policies and programmes of political India, the very spirit of nascent India demanding her equal place among the world's nations. But perhaps the most poignant and memorable of all is the last picture of him walking to his prayers at the sunset hour on 30 January, 1948, translated in a tragic instant of martyrdom from mortality to immortality.

READING 10.1C: THE SPIRIT OF INDIA

He came to represent India to an amazing degree and to express the very spirit of that ancient and tortured land. Almost he was India, and his very failings were Indian failings. . . . He represents the peasant masses of India; he is the quintessence of the con-

Polak, H.S.L., H.N. Brailsford, and Lord Pethick-Lawrence. *Mahatma Gandhi, with a Forward and Appreciation by Her Excellency Sarojini Naidu.* London: Odhams Press Limited, 1948, pp. 6–8.

Tendulkar, D.G., et al., eds. *Gandhiji: His Life and Work.* Bombay: Karnatak Publishing House, 1948, pp. 2–4.

scious and subconscious will of those millions. . . . Of course, he is not the average peasant. A man of the keenest intellect, of fine feeling and good taste, wide vision; very human, and yet essentially the ascetic who has suppressed his passions and emotions, sublimated them and directed them in spiritual channels; a tremendous personality, drawing people to himself like a magnet, and calling our fierce loyalties and attachments—all this so utterly unlike and beyond a peasant. And yet withal he is the great peasant, with a peasant's outlook on affairs and with a peasant's blindness to some aspects of life. But India is peasant India, and so he knows his India well and reacts to her lightest tremors, and gauges a situation accurately and almost instinctively, and has a knack of acting at the psychological moment.

What a problem and a puzzle he has been not only to the British Government but to his own people and his closest associates! . . . Many of us had cut adrift from this peasant outlook, and the old ways of thought and customs and religion had become alien to us. We called ourselves moderns, and thought in terms of "progress" and industrialisation and a higher standard of living and collectivisation. We considered the peasant's view-point reactionary. . . . How came we to associate ourselves with Gandhiji politically, and to become, in many instances, his devoted followers? . . . He attracted people, but it was ultimately intellectual conviction that brought them to him and kept them there. They did not agree with his philosophy of life, or even with many of his ideals. Often they did not understand him. But the action that he proposed was something tangible which could be understood and appreciated intellectually . . . and effective action with an ethical halo about it had an irresistible appeal, both to the intellect and the emotions. Step by step he convinced us of the rightness of the action, and we went with him, although we did not accept his philosophy.

READING 10.2

Sun Yat-sen's Impact on China

Sun Yat-sen (1866–1925) is the Father of the Chinese Republic. A Western-educated medical doctor, he dedicated his life to changing China. Sun formed a revolutionary organization called the Kuomintang, or Nationalist party, with an ideology called the Three People's Principles (nationalism, democracy, and livelihood). Nationalism, the strongest unifying force in China during the twentieth century, was initially directed against the minority ethnic group called Manchus who ruled China as the Ch'ing or Manchu dynasty until 1911, then against Western and Japanese imperialism. Reading 10.2A is from Sun's writings on nationalism.

Reading 10.2B is the Manifesto of the May 4th Movement, a student-led event of seminal importance in twentieth-century China. On May 4th, 1919, university students in Peking staged a protest against the awarding of China's Shantung province, seized by Germany in 1898, to Japan at the Paris Peace Conference. It was a move contrary to self-determination and a victory for Japanese imperialism. This student protest became a nationalist, antiimperialist, and reform movement. It influenced Sun to reorganize and redirect his then out of power Nationalist party; it also led to the formation of the Chinese Communist party by intellectuals disillusioned with the United States and other Western powers. The movement expanded to become the Intellectual Revolution, which helped launch the women's movement for equality and other social reforms. The Manifesto became the rallying call for the reformers.

Reading 10.2C is from the *Memoirs of Shen I,* a university student in Shanghai in 1919. He recounts how students in universities and schools in Shanghai rallied to the call of fellow students in Peking and how other groups in China rose to support the students. Shen went on to a distinguished career as a hydraulic engineer, heading important projects in China and for the United Nations.

Reading 10.2D shows Sun's impact on Chinese women's quest for emancipation, which first manifested itself during the 1911 revolution. It is by a pioneering professional woman who successfully resisted foot binding and an arranged marriage. She went on to obtain a modern education, including graduate studies in the United States, and then to a long and distinguished career in education and public service.

READING 10.2A: SUN YAT-SEN ON NATIONALISM

The next ten years will be crucial for the survival of our Chinese race. We will only be able to survive if we can free ourselves from the political and economic oppression of the great powers. . . . We have been the victims of European and American oppression for almost a hundred years. . . . During this period we have lost enormous amounts of territory, the most recent being Weihaiwei, Lushun, Dalien, Tsingtao, Kowloon, and Kwangchow-wan. . . . Although these were only small pieces of land [ports along the coast], the imperialist powers considered them worth seizing, to serve as bases for the future partition of China. Since our revolution the Great Powers have changed their minds about the feasibility of partitioning China. . . . They have redirected their might to economic oppression. . . .

Yet my fellow countrymen still comfort and delude themselves by saying that China is only a semi-colony. In fact as a semi-colony China suffers greater economic oppression than the true colonies of the powers. We say that Korea is a Japanese colony and the Koreans are slaves of Japan, that Annam is a French colony and the Annamese are slaves of France. We do not realize that in fact our plight is worse than those of the Koreans and Annamese. . . . That is because any nation that has signed an [unequal] treaty with China is in fact China's master. This way China is not the colony of one nation, but of all nations; making the Chinese not slaves of one nation, but of all nations. Is it better to be slaves of one nation or of many nations? Masters feel an obligation to give assistance and lessen the suffering of their slaves in times of natural disasters. . . . However when natural disasters struck northern China recently, no foreign nation felt obligated to help. . . . That is why China is worse off than Annam and Korea, that is why it is far better to be the slaves of one nation than of many. That is why it is incorrect to call China a semi-colony. I have therefore coined a new word from chemistry, "Hyper-colony," to describe China's humiliating position. . . .

Sun, Wen. *San-min Chu-i.* Trans. Jiu-Hwa Lo Upshur. Taipei: Central Committee of the Kuomintang, 1985, pp. 19, 21–23, 68, 71–72.

At this moment of supreme crisis, can we strive to save ourselves? We certainly can. But first of all we must awaken to the dire straights we are in. That is why we advocate nationalism to our 400 million compatriots. Even a doomed animal will put up a last ditch fight, how can we as a people not do the same when we are faced with national extinction? . . .

Foreigners often compare the Chinese with loose sand because we lack the sense of national cohesiveness. . . . However, as I have said before, we Chinese have a very deep sense of belonging to family and clan . . . and to the localities we come from. . . . Thus we can build up our sense of nationhood by starting from our small bases, by building upon our foundations of loyalty to family, clan, and locality. This way we can expand our loyalty to the whole nation and revive our sense of nationhood. . . .

The reason that we have so far been unsuccessful in resisting foreign oppression is because we have not awakened to our dire plight, and have therefore not organized our whole race. However when we do link up our small loyalties into one that binds all our 400 million people, then we will not find it difficult to resist foreign oppression. Take India for example. Under British rule, Indians have no effective political weapon to resist Great Britain. But Gandhi has devised a way to resist Britain's economic exploitation. How? By economic non-cooperation. In other words, not supplying labor to produce what Britain wants, not buying what Britain produces, and relying on Indians' own handicraft industries. Britain did not take Gandhi seriously at first, but in time non-cooperation by Indians has had a very serious effect on Britain's economy. That is why the British have put Gandhi in jail. Even though they are under British control, yet Indians have been able to organize themselves effectively to resist British rule through non-cooperation. We Chinese are still an independent nation. We can certainly carry out an economic boycott against the foreign imperialists by not working for their companies, not buying their goods, and not using their banks and currencies; instead buying and using Chinese products. . . . We can resist foreign oppression in two ways. One method is through direct action—rousing our people's nationalistic awareness, demanding democracy, and working toward improvements in the people's livelihood. The other is passive resistance, by non-cooperation, thereby hurting the profits the imperialist nations have made at our expense. By these means we can maintain the position of our race and avoid national extinction.

READING 10.2B: THE MANIFESTO OF THE MAY 4TH MOVEMENT

The Japanese have scored a major diplomatic victory at the International Peace Conference. They have won their demand to takeover Tsingtao and all rights [that had been seized by Germany from China] in Shantung. Our country has suffered a major diplomatic defeat. The loss of Shantung will be a blow to China's territorial integrity and will eventually lead to China's loss of independence. This is why we students are marching to

Lo, Chia-lun. *Lo Chia-lun hsien-sheng wen chen, vol. 1*. Trans. Jiu-Hwa Lo Upshur. Taipei: Academia Historica, 1976, p. 1.

the diplomatic quarters to demand that the nations of the world step forward to maintain justice. We hope that all farmers, laborers, and merchants of our nation will rise up, and convene a National Assembly that will fight for China's sovereignty among the nations and rid China of its traitorous government leaders. China's survival will depend on our action. Today we swear this covenant before our compatriots:

1. China's territories can be conquered from us but cannot be given away.
2. The Chinese people can be killed, but will never bow their heads.

Rise up compatriots, save our country from extinction!

READING 10.2C: REMEMBERING THE MAY 4TH MOVEMENT

We students in Shanghai immediately responded to the news [of student demonstrations on May 4th] from Peking. Led by students from Futan University, a Student Union was soon organized. . . . After one month of planning, Shanghai erupted into a wave of students led unrest on June 3. It began with a student strike that closed schools, and spread like wildfire into a merchant strike, and a nationwide anti-Japanese boycott. . . .

Day after day public rallies were held at the sports arena at the West Gate of the city. Students from various schools marched to the rallies holding flags and banners. . . . As I recall the early days of the movement, I am still touched by the warm support we received from all sectors of society. They treated us like soldiers marching to war, lining the streets and offering us tea and snacks. On June 3 the merchants in the Chinese city as well as those in the concessions, led by the major department stores, supported us with shutting down their shops. During the merchant strike the normally busy main commercial streets were filled with milling people. The usually formidable foreign policemen, including Indian officers, could do nothing to control the crowds. The Student Union organized large numbers of its members to patrol the streets during the merchant strike—ostensibly to help maintain order, but with an additional mission to exert pressure on individual merchants so no one would break the strike. Whenever a crowd appeared to become unruly and unamenable to police control, we student representatives would come forth, say a few words and the crowd would do as we asked. The foreign authorities were initially pleased with our intervention, until they learned that our true purpose was to enforce the solidarity of the strike. Then they told us we could no longer patrol the main intersections. But by then the strike had achieved its purpose. I still smile when I recall how we had duped the foreign authorities on this occasion.

I remember taking part in patrolling the streets. Two people formed a team; my team mate was Juan Shan-chen, also from Tungchih University and our sector was Nanking Road to the Ball Park. We all wore white uniforms and armbands on which we had written in English the words "maintain strict discipline." As we patrolled, the salespeople from the closed shops would invite us in and offer us tea and give us patent medicine.

Shen, I. *Shen I Chih-shu.* Trans. and ed. Jiu-Hwa Lo Upshur. Taipei: Chuan-chi wenh-sueh, 1985, pp. 35–38.

Students at Peking universities demonstrated on May 4, 1919, to protest China's treatment at the Paris Peace Conference. The ensuing May 4th Movement set off an intellectual revolution that would have profound effects on China. Jiu-Hwa Lo Upshur

Many citizens, some riding to town in rickshaws, would stuff fresh fruit into our pockets, not allowing us to refuse. The offices in our schools were similarly filled with fruits, sweets, and other edibles the good hearted people kept on giving us. It is impossible to describe their warm support which touched us deeply. . . .

I remember one day being elected to lead the Tungchih contingent in a rally. As we marched down the streets, students from other schools began to break ranks. They entered shops to smash Japanese made crockery and to confiscate such items as Japanese made textiles. We from Tungchih were firmly opposed to such undisciplined and lawless behavior and maintained our contingent in strict marching order. Our discipline earned us cheers and applause from onlookers as we marched past. Those who had confiscated Japanese made textiles from shops took them to the sports stadium which was our destination. There they piled the stuff into a huge mound, adding to items already there, and set them on fire. Newspaper articles next day criticized the students for what they had done, likening it to mob action. Regretably such behavior decreased public support for the students in the coming days.

With the foreign authorities now forbidding student patrols in the shopping areas we students changed our tactics. We decided to send students to Chapei and South Shanghai to make speeches to rouse public support. Our goal was to get ourselves arrested, so that news of our arrest would lead to a widening of the student protest movement throughout the nation. We had even prepared a statement to the nation to denounce the massive arrest of student speakers. Unfortunately our strategy was discovered by the authorities, who ordered the police not to interfere. I remember going to the City Temple with three other students where we made inflammatory speeches and got no response from the patrolling policemen. My frustrated teammate finally went up to a policeman and asked him why he wasn't arresting us. The policeman just laughed at him. After a full day of speechmaking, there was not a single arrest throughout the city! I remember later being sent to make speeches at Wusung, a little town near to the Tungchih University campus. Several tens of our school mates came to listen to us, far outnumbering the townspeople. We talked for a long time, really only converting the already converted. When I recall what happened then, I still cannot refrain from laughing. . . .

Tungchih University's students also began to publish a journal, called *The Self-Awareness Weekly*. . . . It was considered the best student publication in Shanghai. I became interested in writing at that time and began to contribute to various journals. One day I sent an article to the Women's Magazine of the *Shanghai Times* in which I called on women to stop binding their chests [to promote a lithe, delicate appearance], and it got published. That provoked a lot of teasing on the part of my class mates. They asked me: "What has that to do with you? Why do you interest yourself in things that are none of your business?" Ten years later [in 1929] I remember reading about an order issued by Mr. Chu Chia-hua, then Director of the Department of Civil Affairs of Chekiang province, which forbade the practice of chest binding. I finally felt vindicated.

READING 10.2D: THE REVOLUTION AND WOMEN'S EMANCIPATION

All schools throughout the country closed down in October 1911 with the outbreak of the revolution. As a result all the boys from Chiangshan who were studying in Hang-chow, Peking, and other cities returned home. Having been exposed to new ideas in the big cities, they were unhappy that Chiangshan had no schools for girls, and hoped to remedy the situation. But they had no money, nor any buildings for setting up a girls' school. Luckily the Mao clan came to the rescue. We were a wealthy clan in Chiangshan and had buildings to spare. Since several of the young men who proposed to organize a girls' school belonged to the Mao clan, they approached the clan officers to borrow a vacant building to house a girls' school. The clan officers consented and the girls' school came into being. It was called Hsiho Girls' School; I became one of the twenty odd pupils. All the boys on enforced vacation became teachers, one of them, Mao Hsien, was elected principal. All the boys however returned to their own studies early the next year when their schools reopened. Our school remained open nevertheless; one of my aunts, Mrs. Chu, then took over as principal. . . .

One new idea the young teachers brought to the school was that marriages arranged by parents were wrong. . . . One day at lunch break "principal" Mao Hsien said to another student Mao Fu-ming and me: "You two remain behind please. Chun-i [a boy teacher] and I want to talk to you."

Mao, Yen-wen. *Wang Shih*. Trans. and ed. Jiu-Hwa Lo Upshur. Taipei: Yung-yu Publishing Co., 1989, pp. 4–6, 8.

When the four of us were alone Mao Hsien continued: "Chun-i and I didn't sleep last night because we were discussing matters concerning you two. Do you two know that your parents have already arranged your betrothal?"

We nodded.

He added: "Do you know what to be betrothed means?"

When we replied no, he told us: "It means that one day you will be married to men you don't even know."

We started to cry. Mao Hsien then said:

"Don't cry. You are not old enough to be married yet. Oppose your parents when the time comes, and then ask them to annul your engagement. This is called a family revolution." . . .

During the early years of the republic many people were concerned with how to improve public education. In response many county governments rushed to open new schools, but these schools often lacked qualified teachers. To remedy the defect our Chekiang provincial government ordered the Hangchow Women's Normal School to add two two-year classes to train elementary teachers and guaranteed one full scholarship to each county, stipulating that the recipient must be between 20 and 25 years old and must agree to return to her county and teach in a local elementary school after graduation. I applied and faked my age as twenty though I was then not yet sixteen, and luckily won a scholarship.

This is how I came to be chosen. In 1913, a Natural Foot Movement [antifoot binding for girls] was launched throughout Chiangshan county and a meeting at the Temple of the City God was planned to kick-off the event. . . . I was chosen as a student representative to give a speech against foot-binding and I spent several days practising a speech a Mr. Hsu had written for me. . . . On that day the Temple was crammed full of people. County magistrate Mr. Yao Ying-tai sat at the center of the platform, flanked by rows of local leaders. The sight of the huge crowd and the array of dignitaries gave me such stage-fright when I mounted the podium that after bowing to the audience and saying my opening sentence, I forgot everything else in my speech. Then I remembered that I had one silver dollar that I planned to present as my contribution to the movement. So I quickly dug out the dollar from my pocket, put it on the podium and said: "I shall kick off the drive with my one dollar contribution." Then I bowed and walked off the stage. Magistrate Yao asked his neighbor seated on the dais: "Who is this little girl? Even though stage-fright made her forget her speech she didn't burst into tears and knew how to make a graceful exit! She is a bright child!" This good impression Magistrate Yao formed of me stood me in good stead when he came to judge the applicants for the scholarship and saw my name.

My winning a full scholarship to attend the Women's Normal School in Hangchow was a big event in those days, and many people in Chiangshan felt proud because of me. On the other hand those counties that could find no suitable candidates felt they had lost face. Henceforth all counties tried hard to find qualified girls to attend the normal school; some parents sent their daughters without scholarships.

READING 10.3

The Birth of Communist Parties in China and Vietnam

The Bolshevik Revolution in Russia and the results of World War I were crucial to the formation of Communist parties in China and Vietnam, which would play major roles in shaping the course of contemporary history throughout Asia. Prior to the Russian Revolution, very few Asians had known about Karl Marx and Friedrich Engels as the founders of "scientific socialism." In 1919 some Chinese intellectuals who were disillusioned with the Paris Peace Treaties turned to Marxism because it gave them a rationale for simultaneously rejecting both the West and their own indigenous traditions. They believed that the dramatic success of the Russian communist revolution demonstrated the effectiveness of Marxist ideology. Lenin's analysis that imperialism was a capitalist device to postpone the inevitable proletarian revolution in the industrialized countries, Soviet offers of friendship and help to fellow revolutionaries and its forming of the Third International to coordinate communist movements throughout the world, and the psychological and intellectual appeals of Marxism provided impetus to the formation of Communist parties in China in 1921 and Vietnam in 1930.

Reading 10.2A features the writings of Mao Tse-tung (Mao Zedong, 1893–1976) and Ho Chi Minh (c. 1892–1967), founders of the Chinese and Vietnamese Communist parties, respectively. Both men were nationalists in that they worked for their country's political independence; they also shared the Marxist political and economic vision. In 1921, disappointed with China's treatment at the Paris Peace Conference, Mao, who was then a library assistant at Peking University, became a founding member of the Chinese Communist party. Ho Chi Minh began as a young revolutionary (he also went by the name Nguyen Ai Quoc, "Nguyen the patriot"), helped form the French Communist party in 1920, went to Moscow to study in the University for the Toilers of the East in 1923, and organized the Vietnamese (soon broadened into Indochinese) Communist party in 1930.

Reading 10.3A is from a report Mao wrote in 1927 after investigating the peasant movement in Hunan, his home province. His contribution to Marxism-Leninism lies in recognizing the importance of poor peasants as the key revolutionary force in nonindustrial China and, by implication, in other nonindustrialized parts of the world.

Ho Chi Minh recounts in Reading 10.3B his frustration with the unwillingness of the United States and France to help the Vietnamese people realize their quest for equality and freedom at the Paris Peace Conference. Later he found in Lenin's writings the inspiration that would guide him for the rest of his life. His successful combination of Vietnamese nationalism and the right of self-determination that U.S. President Woodrow Wilson promised for oppressed peoples in his Fourteen Points, but which the Paris Peace Treaties denied for Vietnam, with Marxism would culminate in France's ouster from Vietnam and the establishment of a communist regime in that country.

Although both Mao and Ho talked about the great peasant-led, antigentry, and antiimperialist revolutions that would lead to communist victories, it was the cataclysm of World War II that finally toppled the Nationalist government in China and French colonial rule in Indochina and led to the triumph of communism in both lands.

Mao Tse-tung (Zedong) became interested in Marxism while working as a library assistant at Peking University in 1919. He was a founding member of the Chinese Communist party and played a key role in Chinese history until his death in 1976. Archive Photos

READING 10.3A: MAO ON ORGANIZING PEASANTS FOR REVOLUTION

During my recent visit to Hunan I made a first-hand investigation of conditions. . . . I called together fact-finding conferences in villages and county towns, which were attended by experienced peasants and by comrades working in the peasant movement, and I listened attentively to their reports and collected a great deal of material. . . .

The present upsurge of the peasant movement is a colossal event. In a very short time, in China's central, southern and northern provinces, several hundred million peasants will rise like a mighty storm, like a hurricane, a force so swift and violent that no power, however great, will be able to hold it back. They will smash all the trammels that bind them and rush forward along the road to liberation. They will sweep all the imperialists, warlords, corrupt officials, local tyrants and evil gentry into their graves. . . .

Almost half the peasants in Hunan are now organized. . . . It was on the strength of their extensive organization that the peasants went into action and within four months brought about a great revolution in the countryside, a revolution without parallel in history. The main targets of attack by the peasants are the local tyrants, the evil gentry . . . the patriarchal ideas and institutions . . . bad practices and customs in the rural areas. . . . As a result, the privileges which the feudal landlords enjoyed for thousands of years are being shattered to pieces. . . . With the collapse of the power of the landlords, the peasant associations have now become the sole organs of authority and the popular slogan "All power to the peasant associations" has become a reality. Even trifles such as a quarrel between husband and wife are brought to the peasant association. Nothing can be

Mao Tse-tung. *Report on an Investigation of the Peasant Movement in Hunan.* Peking: Foreign Language Press, 1965, pp. 1, 3–4, 12–14, 37.

settled unless someone from the peasant association is present. The association actually dictates all rural affairs, and, quite literally "whatever it says, goes." . . .

We said previously that the peasants have accomplished a revolutionary task . . . but has this important revolutionary work been performed by all the peasants? No. There are three kinds of peasants, the rich, the middle and the poor peasants. The three live in different circumstances and so have different views about the revolution. . . . Only under the impact of all this [threats] are the rich peasants tardily joining the associations. . . . But there are quite a number of die-hards who have not joined to this day. . . . After joining, the rich peasants are not keen on doing any work for the associations. They remain inactive throughout.

How about the middle peasants? Theirs is a vacillating attitude. They think that the revolution will not bring them much good. They have rice cooking in their pots and no creditors knocking on their doors at midnight. . . . They show up better in the associations than the rich peasants but are not as yet very enthusiastic. . . .

The poor peasants have always been the main force in the bitter fight in the countryside. . . . They are the most responsive to Communist Party leadership. They are deadly enemies of the camp of the local tyrants and evil gentry and attack it without the slightest hesitation. . . . According to the survey of Changsha County, the poor peasants comprise 70 percent, the middle peasants 20 percent, and the landlords and the rich peasants 10 percent of the population in the rural areas. . . . This great mass of poor peasants, or altogether 70 percent of the rural population, are the backbone of the peasant associations, the vanguard in the overthrow of the feudal forces. . . .

The spread of political propaganda throughout the rural areas is entirely an achievement of the Communist Party and the peasant associations. Simple slogans, cartoons and speeches have produced such a widespread and speedy effect among the peasants that every one of them seems to have been through a political school. According to the reports of comrades engaged in rural work, political propaganda was very extensive at the time of the three great mass rallies, the anti-British demonstration, the celebration of the October Revolution and the victory celebration for the Northern Expedition [led by the Kuomintang under Chiang Kai-shek to oust the warlords and unify China]. On these occasions, political propaganda was conducted extensively wherever there were peasant associations, arousing the whole countryside with tremendous effect. From now on care should be taken to use every opportunity gradually to enrich the content and clarify the meaning of those simple slogans.

READING 10.3B: HO CHI MINH ON WHY HE BECAME A COMMUNIST

When the Great War ended the Vietnamese people like other peoples were deceived by Wilson's "generous" declaration on the right of peoples to self-determination. A group of Vietnamese, which included myself, sent the following demands to the French Parliament and to all delegations to the Versailles Conference . . . :

1. Amnesty for all Vietnamese political detainees;

Ho, Chi Minh. *Selected Writings, 1920–1969.* Hanoi: Foreign Language Press, 1973, pp. 22–23.

2. Reform of the Indochinese judicial system by giving the Vietnamese the same judicial safeguards as to the Europeans and completely and definitely abolishing the special tribunals which are instruments of terror and oppression against the most honest part of the Vietnamese people;

3. Freedom of the press and freedom of opinion;

4. Freedom of association and freedom of assembly;

5. Freedom to emigrate and travel abroad;

6. Freedom of teaching and creation in all provinces of technical and vocational schools for natives;

7. Replacement of the regime of decrees by that of laws;

8. Presence in the French Parliament of a permanent delegation elected by the natives to keep it informed of their aspirations! . . .

However, after a time of waiting and study, we realized that the "Wilson doctrine" was but a big fraud. The liberation of the proletariat is the necessary condition for national liberation. Both these liberations can only come from Communism and world revolution.

After World War One, I made my living in Paris, at one time as an employee at a photographer's, at another as painter of "Chinese antiques" (turned out by French shops). I often distributed leaflets denouncing the crimes committed by the French colonialists in Vietnam.

At the time, I supported the October Revolution only spontaneously. I did not yet grasp all its historic importance. I loved and respected Lenin because he was a great patriot who had liberated his fellow-countrymen; until then I had read none of his books.

The reason for my joining the French Socialist Party was because . . . my comrades [there] . . . had shown their sympathy with me, with the struggle of the oppressed peoples. But I had no understanding as yet of what a party, a trade-union, and communism, were. . . .

One [comrade] gave to me to read Lenin's "Theses on the national and colonial questions" printed in *l'Humanite.*

In those Theses, there were political terms that were difficult to understand. But by reading them again and again finally I was able to grasp the essential part. What emotion, enthusiasm, enlightenment and confidence they communicated to me! I wept for joy. Sitting by myself in my room, I would shout as if I were addressing large crowds: "Dear martyr compatriots! This is what we need, this is our path to liberation!"

Since then, I had entire confidence in Lenin, in the Third International.

Formerly, during the cell meetings, I had only listened to the discussion. . . . But from then on, I also plunged into the debates and participated with fervour in the discussions. Though my French was still too weak to express all my thoughts, I hit hard at the allegations attacking Lenin and the Third International. My only argument was: "If you do not condemn colonialism, if you do not side with the colonial peoples, what kind of revolution are you then waging?" . . .

There is a legend, in our country as well as in China, about the magic "Brocade Bag". When facing great difficulties, one opens it and finds a way out. For us Vietnamese revolutionaries and people, Leninism is not only a miraculous "Brocade Bag", a compass, but also a radiant sun illuminating our path to final victory, to socialism, and communism.

DISCUSSION QUESTION

Compare and contrast the ideals and approaches of M.K. Gandhi, Sun Yat-sen, Mao Tse-tung, and Ho Chi Minh to their countries' problems.

CHAPTER ELEVEN

Anticolonialism in the Middle East and Africa

During World War I, nationalist groups across Africa and the Middle East struggled, sometimes violently, against the imperial powers. With their superior military and economic power, the imperial nations were able to suppress all the movements for self-determination in their overseas empires in opposition to U.S. President Woodrow Wilson's calls for self-determination during World War I.

At the Paris Peace Conference after the war, Wilson largely ignored the pleas of nationalists, including the Arabs and others, who were struggling for independence. Instead, Wilson compromised on his demands for the self-determination of peoples around the world in order to obtain support for the creation of the League of Nations. Wilson then pinned his hope—in vain, as it turned out—on the League to oversee and guide the nations under imperial control toward independence. Partly because the United States did not join the League, the imperial powers, notably Great Britain and France, continued to rule and, in Africa and the Middle East, to expand their empires without interference from other major powers until after World War II.

As the victors in World War I, Great Britain and France enlarged their empires in Africa and the Middle East by taking over territories of the losing Central Powers: Germany and the Ottoman Empire. Although in the Middle East Britain granted nominal independence to Iraq and Egypt in the 1920s, it retained military control over them through treaties of alliance that allowed continued military presence in these countries. In contrast, France kept direct control over all of its overseas territories.

The first three readings in this chapter (11.1A, 11.1B, 11.1C) deal with the conflicting agreements regarding the disposition of Arab territories made by the British during World War I. These agreements sowed the seeds for conflicts that remain unresolved.

129

Reading 11.2 describes the diplomatic and political struggles of Kenyan nationalists against British domination. The methods adopted by the Kenyan nationalists, including Jomo Kenyatta, the author of Reading 11.2, were typical of those used by other African leaders across the continent.

During the interwar years, most nationalist leaders in Africa hoped to achieve their goals through diplomatic and political means. Consequently, African nationalists entered into protracted negotiations with the imperial powers, but, although these negotiations sometimes led to limited reforms, none resulted in the realization of independence. In some cases, as in Morocco in the 1920s and Egypt in 1919, nationalists launched armed rebellions against the Western imperial powers, but combined French and Spanish forces crushed the Rif rebellion in Morocco, while the British defeated the popular revolution in Egypt. In western, eastern, and southern Africa, nationalist leaders continued to press for increased political participation and economic reforms. The oldest of these movements, the South African Native National Congress (subsequently the African National Congress, ANC), established in 1912, tried nonviolent means to achieve full political participation, but, when decades of nonviolent struggle failed to achieve the hoped for reforms, even the ANC reluctantly turned to armed struggle. Similarly, Kenyan nationalists turned to violent means in order to achieve full independence (see Chapter 19 in Part 3).

READING 11.1

Conflicting Agreements Regarding the Middle East

During World War I, Great Britain made three conflicting agreements regarding the future of territories in the Middle East held by the Ottoman Empire, commonly known as the "Sick Man of Europe." When the Ottoman Empire joined Germany and the Central Powers in World War I, many foresaw that the Sick Man would not survive the war and that its empire would finally collapse. Great Britain and France saw the war as an opportunity to enlarge their empires in the Middle East, a region with vast petroleum resources and geo-strategic importance. Numerous peoples within the Ottoman Empire—including Armenians, Kurds, and Arabs, who were the largest single population group within the empire—also hoped to gain national independence after the war.

With this goal in mind, Sherif Husayn, an Arab national and religious leader in the Muslim holy city of Mecca, entered into a correspondence with the British in 1915 and 1916 to secure their support for the creation of one unified, independent Arab nation after the war. In return, Sherif Husayn proposed to lead his fellow Arabs in revolt against the Ottomans and to fight on the side of the Allies. Had the Ottomans discovered Sherif Husayn's proposals, he would have been hanged for treason. The British wanted Arab support in the war effort but, for imperial reasons, did not want to include the Arab territories of present-day Lebanon, where the French had interests, or Iraq, where the British knew there was petroleum, in Husayn's proposed Arab state.

Henry McMahon, the British high commissioner in Egypt, represented Great Britain in the negotiations with Sherif Husayn, and the resulting correspondence bears their names. Sherif Husayn's letter in which he discusses the borders of the proposed Arab state is included as the first reading in this chapter. After protracted negotiations, the British and Sherif Husayn secretly agreed to delay a final decision on the future of the territories of Iraq and Lebanon. In 1916 many Arabs in Arabia and the Ottoman provinces of greater Syria (present-day Lebanon, Syria, Jordan, and Israel—none of which existed as independent states in 1916) rose up against the Ottomans. They fought on the side of the Allies for the duration of the war, believing that they would receive an independent Arab state when the war ended. The letter included here indicates that the Arabs and the British were not in full agreement and that problems over the disposition of Arab lands might arise in the future.

A second secret agreement, the Sykes-Picot Agreement of 1916, created further complications. The British, represented by Sir Mark Sykes, and the French, represented by Georges Picot, agreed to divide the Arab territories of the Ottoman Empire. Great Britain was allocated direct control over Iraq, Palestine, and Jordan and a "sphere of influence" over Arabia. In 1916 no one knew there was petroleum in Arabia; therefore, indirect control appeared to be adequate for what was generally considered to be an unimportant region. The French were to receive direct control over present-day Lebanon and Syria. The portion of the Sykes-Picot Agreement that pertains to the Arabs is included as the second reading in this chapter.

As the documents indicate, portions of the first two secret agreements contradict one another. However, as the third reading shows, the British complicated matters still further by making a third agreement regarding the Middle East. Just as the Arabs and others sought to create independent states after the war, so, too, did the Zionists, or Jewish nationalists, seek to establish an independent Jewish state, Israel, in the Ottoman territory of Palestine. The Zionists, led by Chaim Weizmann, had approached the British government and Foreign Secretary Lord Balfour to secure their support. In

1917 the British government issued a public statement, the Balfour Declaration, that seemed to support the creation of a Jewish state in Palestine.

The declaration took the form of a purposely vaguely worded letter from Balfour to Lord Rothschild, a leading British Zionist. The Palestinian Arabs, almost 90 percent of the population of Palestine, were not consulted about the declaration in which they were not even mentioned by name. Not surprisingly, the Palestinians opposed the statement that threatened to dispossess them. Other Arabs also opposed the Balfour Declaration, arguing that the British were not even in control of Palestine when they seemingly promised it to the Zionists and that, furthermore, the territory had already been included in the Arab state proposed by Sherif Husayn.

For their part, the British downplayed or denied the contradictions in the three agreements. The British viewed the agreements as (1) a means to strengthen their war effort against the Central Powers and (2) a way to enlarge their imperial holdings in the Middle East after the war. In the end, the imperial powers prevailed, and the Arab territories were divided between Great Britain and France as indicated in the Sykes-Picot Agreement (see Reading 11.1B and map). Although the Arabs fought against foreign domination, their small, ill-equipped armies were quickly defeated by the better-armed and far wealthier French and British forces. As a consequence, the Arabs not only were denied national independence but were divided into separate nations controlled by the British and French. These divisions became solidified into separate nation states that remain the source of many still unresolved conflicts. Although the British gave some support to the Zionist efforts in Palestine, a Jewish state, Israel, was not created until after World War II (see Chapter 20).

READING 11.1A: SHERIF HUSAYN TO MCMAHON

Translation of a Letter from the Sherif of Mecca to Sir H. McMahon, His Majesty's High Commissioner, Cairo, dated 27 el Hijj, 1333 [November 5, 1915].

[LITERAL TRANSLATION.]

(In the name of God the Merciful the Compassionate.)

To his Excellency the most exalted and eminent Minister who is endowed with the highest authority and soundness of opinion. May God guide him to do His Will!

I RECEIVED with great pleasure your honoured letter, dated 15th Zul Hijj (24th October, 1915), to which I beg to answer as follows:—

1. In order to facilitate an agreement and to render a service to Islam, and at the same time to avoid all that may cause Islam troubles and hardships—seeing moreover that we have great consideration for the distinguished qualities and dispositions of the Government of Great Britain—we renounce our insistence on the inclusion of vilayets of Messina and Adana in the Arab Kingdom. But the provinces of Aleppo and Beyrut and

Key portion of Sherif Husayn's *Third Letter to Sir Henry McMahon,* November 5, 1915, Great Britain, Public Record Office, CAB 21/154.

their sea-coasts are purely Arab provinces, and there is no difference between a Moslem and a Christian Arab; they are both descendants of one forefather.

We Moslems will follow the footsteps of the Commander of the Faithful, Omar Ibn Khattab, and other Khalifs succeeding him, who ordained in the laws of the Moslem faith that Moslems should treat the Christians as they treat themselves. He, Omar, declared with reference to Christians "they will have the same privileges and submit to the same duties as ourselves." They will thus enjoy their civic rights in as much as it accords with the general interest of the whole nation.

2. As the provinces of Irak are parts of the pure Arab Kingdom and were in fact the seat of its Governments in the time of Ali Ibn Abu Talib, and in the time of all Khalifs who succeeded him; and as in them began the civilisation of the Arabs, and as their towns in those provinces were the first towns built in Islam where the Arab power became so great; therefore these provinces are greatly valued by all Arabs far and near, and their traditions cannot be forgotten by them. Consequently we cannot satisfy the Arab nations or make them submit to give up such a title to nobility. But in order to render an accord easy, and taking into consideration the assurances mentioned in the fifth article of your letter, to keep and guard our mutual interests in that country as they are one and the same, for all these reasons we might agree to leave under the British administration for a short time those districts now occupied *by the British troops* without the rights of either party being prejudiced thereby (especially those of the Arab nation, which interests are to it economic and vital) and against a suitable sum paid as compensation to the Arab Kingdom for the period of occupation, in order to meet the expenses which every new kingdom is bound to support, at the same time respecting your agreements with the Sheikhs of those districts, and especially those which are essential.

3. In your desire to hasten the movement we see not only advantages, but grounds of apprehension. The first of these grounds is the fear of the blame of the Moslems of the opposite party, as has already happened in the past, who would declare that we have revolted against Islam and ruined its forces. The second is that, standing in the face of Turkey, which is supported by all the forces of Germany, we do not know what Great Britain and her Allies would do if one of the *Entente* Powers were weakened and obliged to make peace. We fear that the Arab nation will then be left alone in the face of Turkey together with her Allies, but we would not at all mind if we were to face the Turks alone. Therefore it is necessary to take these points into consideration in order to avoid a peace being concluded in which the parties concerned may decide the fate of our people as if we had taken part in the war without making good our claims to official consideration. . . .

READING 11.1B: SYKES-PICOT AGREEMENT
Arab Proposals.

Amended Version.

1. THAT France and Great Britain are prepared to recognise and protect an independent Arab State or a Confederation of Arab States in the areas (*a*) and (*b*) marked on the annexed map, under the suzerainty of an Arab chief. That in area (*a*) France, and in area

Great Britain. Public Record Office, CAB17/176, 232–1.

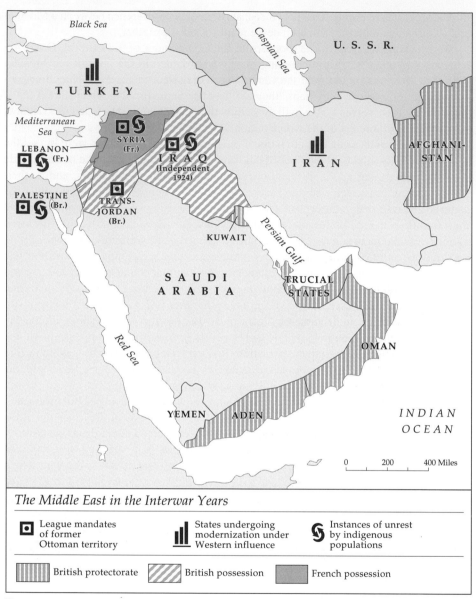

The Middle East in the Interwar Years

League mandates of former Ottoman territory

States undergoing modernization under Western influence

Instances of unrest by indigenous populations

British protectorate

British possession

French possession

The failure to grant independence to the Arab provinces of the old Ottoman Empire and the division of the region into separate states sowed the seeds for long-term conflicts, some of which persist until the present day.

In Reading 11.1B: Sykes-Picot Agreement, Zone A (the French Area) essentially included Syria and Lebanon, and Zone B (the British area) included Iraq, Palestine, and Transjordan.

(*b*) Great Britain, shall have priority of right of enterprise and local loans. That in area (*a*) France, and in area (*b*) Great Britain, shall alone supply advisers or foreign functionaries at the request of the Arab State or Confederation of Arab States.

2. That in the Blue area France, and in the Red area Great Britain, shall be allowed to establish such direct or indirect administration or control as they desire and as they may think fit to arrange with the Arab State or Confederation of Arab States.

3. That in the Brown area there shall be established an international administration, the form of which is to be decided upon after consultation with Russia, and subsequently in consultation with the other Allies, and the representatives of the Shereef of Mecca.

4. That Great Britain be accorded (1) the ports of Haifa and Acre, (2) guarantee of a given supply of water from the Tigris and Euphrates in area (*a*) for area (*b*). His Majesty's Government on their part undertake that they will at no time enter into negotiations for the cession of Cyprus to any third Power without the previous consent of the French Government.

5. That Alexandretta shall be a free port as regards the trade of the British Empire, and that there shall be no discrimination in port charges or facilities as regards British shipping and British goods; that there shall be freedom of transit for British goods through Alexandretta and by railway through the Blue area, whether those goods are intended for or originate in the Red area, or (*B*) area, or area (*A*); and there shall be no discrimination, direct or indirect, against British goods on any railway or against British goods or ships at any port serving the areas mentioned.

That Haifa shall be a free port as regards the trade of France, her dominions and protectorates, and there shall be no discrimination in port charges or facilities as regards French shipping and French goods. There shall be freedom of transit for French goods through Haifa and by the British railway through the Brown area, whether those goods are intended for or originate in the Blue area, area (*a*), or area (*b*), and there shall be no discrimination, direct or indirect, against French goods on any railway, or against French goods or ships at any port serving the areas mentioned.

6. That in area (*A*) the Bagdad Railway shall not be extended southwards beyond Mosul, and in area (*B*) northwards beyond Samarra, until a railway connecting Bagdad with Aleppo via the Euphrates Valley has been completed, and then only with the concurrence of the two Governments.

7. That Great Britain has the right to build, administer, and be sole owner of a railway connecting Haifa with area (*B*), and shall have a perpetual right to transport troops along such a line at all times.

It is to be understood by both Governments that this railway is to facilitate the connection of Bagdad with Haifa by rail, and it is further understood that, if the engineering difficulties and expense entailed by keeping this connecting line in the Brown area only make the project unfeasible, that the French Government shall be prepared to consider that the line in question may also traverse the polygon Banias–Keis Marib–Salkhad Tell Otsda–Mesmie before reaching area (*B*).

8. For a period of twenty years the existing Turkish customs tariff shall remain in force throughout the whole of the Blue and Red areas, as well as in areas (*A*) and (*B*), and no increase in the rates of duty or conversion from *ad valorem* to specific rates shall be made except by agreement between the two Powers.

There shall be no interior customs barriers between any of the above-mentioned areas. The customs duties leviable on goods destined for the interior shall be collected at the port of entry, and handed over to the administration of the area of destination.

9. It shall be agreed that the French Government will at no time enter into any negotiations for the cession of their rights, and will not cede such rights in the Blue area to any third Power, except the Arab State or Confederation of Arab States, without the previous agreement of His Majesty's Government, who on their part will give a similar undertaking to the French Government regarding the Red area.

10. The British and French Governments, as the protectors of the Arab State, shall agree that they will not themselves acquire, and will not consent to a third Power acquiring territorial possessions in the Arabian peninsula, nor consent to a third Power constructing a naval base on the islands or the east coast of the Red Sea. This, however, shall not prevent such adjustment of the Aden frontier as may be necessary in consequence of recent Turkish aggression.

11. The negotiations with the Arabs as to the boundaries of the Arab State or Confederation of Arab States shall be continued through the same channel as heretofore on behalf of the two Powers.

12. It is agreed that measures to control the importation of arms into the Arab territories will be considered by the two Governments.

READING 11.1C: THE BALFOUR DECLARATION

I have much pleasure in conveying to you, on behalf of his Majesty's Government, the following declaration of sympathy with Jewish Zionist aspirations which has been submitted to and approved by the Cabinet—

His Majesty's Government view with favour the establishment in Palestine of a national home for the Jewish people, and will use their best endeavours to facilitate the achievement of this object, it being clearly understood that nothing shall be done which may prejudice the civil and religious rights of existing non-Jewish communities in Palestine, or the rights and political status enjoyed by Jews in any other country.

I should be grateful if you would bring this declaration to the knowledge of the Zionist Federation.

READING 11.2

Kenyatta Describes the Nationalist Struggle in Kenya

The following reading, from *Suffering Without Bitterness: The Founding of the Kenya Nation,* is a firsthand account of the struggle for Kenyan independence by Jomo Kenyatta, one of the foremost Kenyan nationalist leaders. Kenyatta's experiences typify those of other leaders who fought against imperialism in the twentieth century. Jomo

Public statement by the British government, November 2, 1917.

Kenyatta (c. 1897–1978) was a Kikuyu, one of the major ethnic groups in Kenya. An agricultural people, the Kikuyu had lost vast tracts of land in the valuable Kenyan highlands to British-supported European settlers. A recently dispossessed group, they were in the vanguard of the Kenyan nationalist movement against British control. Educated in a mission school, Kenyatta became a clerk in the Nairobi Municipal Council and was active in the Kikuyu Central Association (KCA), a nationalist organization. He represented the Kikuyu in negotiations with the British in London in the 1920s.

During the interwar years, Kenyatta studied anthropology, published a book, *Facing Mount Kenya,* that remains a classic study of Kenyan society; visited the Soviet Union several times; and was an active spokesperson for Kikuyu interests. After World War II, he returned to Kenya as one of the leading figures in the Kenyan nationalist movement. During the 1950s, sectors within the Kenyan nationalist movement, particularly the Mau Mau, became increasingly violent (see Chapter 19 in Part 3). Although Kenyatta had publicly opposed the Mau Mau, he was arrested and sentenced to seven years hard labor by the British authorities, who feared his growing popularity. This reading (11.2) is an excerpt from Kenyatta's testimony during his 1953 trial, in which he recalled his long involvement in the nationalist struggle and the goals of the KCA.

Like many other nationalist leaders in Africa and Asia, Kenyatta spent long years in prison or under close surveillance by the imperial powers. His political acumen and long-term commitment to the nationalist cause made him the recognized leader of the nation. When the British withdrew and granted Kenya independence in 1964, Kenyatta became the president of the newly created nation; he held that position until his death in 1978.

The principal examination of Jomo Kenyatta, as a witness in the Kapenguria trial, began on January 26, 1953. A Court transcript must necessarily note all interjections, repetitions and verbal stumbles. While these are here ignored, what follows—from this transcript— is an accurate reproduction, in condensed form, of Mzee's opening testimony on that day:

'The East African Association in 1921, with which I sympathised, opposed such things as forced labour of both African men and women, and the Registration Certificate introduced soon after the war. It was also concerned about land, and that people should have better wages, education, hospitals and roads. The Association worked by constitutional means, making representations to the Government in the most peaceful way we possibly could.

'The Kikuyu Central Association, from about 1925 onwards, pursued the same aims and objects, but by 1928 more grievances were added. Most of us had become aware of the Crown Lands Ordinance of 1915, which said something like: "all land previously occupied by native people becomes the property of the Crown, and the Africans or natives living thereon become tenants at the will of the Crown". When we realised this, we started a demand for its abolition, on the grounds that it was unfair for our people, because we were not informed of its enactment and had no say in its provisions.

'We were also protesting against the country's status being changed to that of a Colony, instead of a Protectorate. We knew the Africans would have less legal claim to their territory in a Colony than in a Protectorate, since the latter would be guided by the British Government until we could be left to our own affairs. We were told that everybody would have rights in a Colony, but Africans would have the least rights.

Kenyatta, Jomo. *Suffering Without Bitterness: The Founding of the Kenya Nation.* Nairobi: East African Publishing House, 1968, pp. 24–28.

'If you woke up one morning and found that somebody had come to your house, and had declared that house belonged to him, you would naturally be surprised, and you would like to know by what arrangement. Many Africans at that time found that, on land which had been in the possession of their ancestors from time immemorial, they were now working as squatters or as labourers.

'I became a member of the Kikuyu Central Association in 1928, after the visit of the Hilton Young Commission which came to investigate land problems in Kenya. My people approached me saying they would like me to represent them, so I left Government service and joined the KCA. I immediately started a paper—the first newspaper in this part of the world published by Africans—called "Muigwithania".

'The KCA sought the redress of grievances through constitutional means: by making representations to the Government of Kenya, to various Commissions, and to the home Government in England.

'In 1929, I was asked if I could go to England to represent my people. By then our demands had increased, to include direct representation of the African people in Legislative Council. We were told when we approached the Government: "well, you know, we have no objection to you coming to Legislative Council or any other place of Government, providing you have education". We badly wanted to educate our children, so another reason why I went to Europe was to seek ways and means of establishing our schools.

'When I arrived in London, I prepared my case, sent a memorandum to the Secretary of State—then Lord Passfield—and made contact with Members of Parliament. There were many negotiations. A White Paper was then published saying, in essence, that the Government has decided no more African land would be taken away from them, and what was left to them would remain their land for ever. I think this reaffirmed as well another declaration—by the Duke of Devonshire in 1923—to the effect that: "Kenya is an African territory and the African interest must be paramount, and whenever the interests of the African people and those of the immigrant races conflict, the African interests will always prevail".

'I think this 1930 White Paper was known as: "Native Policy in East Africa". But I have been placed at a great disadvantage because I cannot get my papers to present my case, so I have to rely on what I can remember. All my documents and files were taken away . . . *(Note: Mzee Kenyatta's personal files and documents were never returned to him by the Administration or the Police. An exhaustive search since Independence has proved fruitless, and the assumption can only be that they were destroyed.)*

'While in Europe, I had published the correspondence as between the KCA and the Secretary of State. I also had the opportunity of going to meet the Archbishop of Canterbury, and went to Edinburgh for an interview with the Moderator of the Church of Scotland.

'Speaking to a Committee of the House of Commons, I said we could take some of the good European and Indian customs, and those of our customs which were good, and see how we could build a new kind of society in Kenya.

'Whereas formerly it had been illegal for us to establish a school, we were now given permission by the Government to do so, if we could find land to build on, find the money to build, and find money to pay teachers. From about 1930, the Kikuyu Independent

Schools Association and the Karinga ISA came into being. When I came back, I found they had over 300 schools educating more than 60,000 children, with no financial help at all from the Government.

'I went to Europe again in 1931 and stayed till 1946, when I found the KCA had been proscribed. I saw the Governor . . . *(Note: the late Sir Philip Mitchell)* . . . twice on this question, and had interviews with the Chief Native Commissioner several times to investigate the position. The Governor told me the matter would be reconsidered. He said he himself could see no reason why the Association should not start functioning, but he left the matter to his officials and to the Member of Legislative Council representing African interests. The Chief Native Commissioner said some people had behaved rashly and got themselves into trouble, so the matter was dropped.

'Our files show that the KCA was a constitutional organization, but the Police are keeping them.

'Early in 1947, when I was very busy in the activities of schools, I came to know about and joined the Kenya African Union. At the annual meeting in June, I was elected as President. The aims of KAU were to unite the African people of Kenya; to prepare the way for introduction of democracy in Kenya; to defend and promote the interests of the African people by organizing and educating them in the struggle for better working and social conditions; to fight for equal rights for all Africans and break down racial barriers; to strive for extension to all African adults of the right to vote and to be elected to parliamentary and other representative bodies; to publish a political newspaper; to fight for freedom of assembly, press and movement.

'To fight for equal rights does not mean fighting with fists or with a weapon, but to fight through negotiations and by constitutional means. We do not believe in violence at all, but in discussion and representation.

'We feel that the racial barrier is one of the most diabolical things that we have in the Colony, and we see no reason at all why all races in this country cannot work harmoniously together without any discrimination. If people of goodwill can come together, they can eliminate this evil. God put everybody into this world to live happily, and to enjoy the gifts of Nature that God bestowed upon mankind. During my stay in Europe— and especially in England—I lived very happily, and made thousands of good friends. I do not see why people in this country cannot do the same thing. To my mind, colour is irrelevant.

'Some time ago, I invited about 40 Europeans to meet me, and spent a whole day with them at our school at Githunguri. One of them said they expected to be chased away; then he apologised for the hatred that he had felt for us, and for believing that we hated the Europeans. That was a common attitude of many settlers who had never met me. I told him I was just an ordinary man, striving to fight for the rights of my people, and to better their conditions, without hating anybody.'

DISCUSSION QUESTION

Discuss the contradictions and potential conflicts created by the three separate agreements made regarding the Middle East during World War I. How did these agreements differ from or correspond with imperial policies in Africa?

TWELVE

Stalin and Hitler and the "Enemies of the People" in the 1930s

To many people in the 1930s, communism and nazism were ideological opposites, the former on the far left, the latter on the far right and usually thought of as the most extreme form of fascism. Such a view was especially prevalent during the Spanish Civil War (1936–1939), a classic confrontation between national and international forces of the left and right. Indeed, there were profound historical and ideological differences between nazism and communism. For example, the former emphasized racial and nationalistic ideas, while the latter stressed international class conflict. However, under Adolf Hitler in Germany and Joseph Stalin in the Soviet Union during the 1930s, the two systems also displayed numerous similarities.[1]

After coming to power in 1933, Hitler soon became a dictator; Stalin also became increasingly dictatorial during the 1930s. Some historians have referred to their systems of control as totalitarian; though the term is not entirely accurate, it remains useful. Neither man *totally* controlled what occurred in his country, but both men did rely on terror and control of a single party and the government, the military, the police, educational and cultural institutions, the media, and much of the economy to come closer to total control than did dictators elsewhere. In both the Soviet Union and Germany, the law became a tool of the government and offered little or no protection to individuals arrested by security forces. In Reading 12.1, Eugenia Ginzburg recounts her personal experiences with such terror and control in the Soviet Union.

---

[1]The fact that these similarities were later sometimes emphasized for political reasons by American anticommunists should not prevent us from acknowledging that they existed. See, for example, Alan Bullock, *Hitler and Stalin: Parallel Lives* (New York: Vintage Books, 1993) and Ian Kershaw and Moshe Lewin, eds., *Stalinism and Nazism: Dictatorships in Comparison* (New York: Cambridge University Press, 1997).

The Ginzburg selection also indicates that Stalin labeled many Soviet citizens as "enemies of the people." Partly because of his highly suspicious nature, Stalin believed that many conspiracies against him actually existed. He was especially fearful of Trotskyite plots, supposedly masterminded from abroad by his former rival for power, the exiled Leon Trotsky. However, even in Lenin's day the communist system had focused on enemies, foreign and domestic, real and imagined, and such a focus helped to solidify and energize the new Soviet system. Soviet communism, at least under Lenin and Stalin, was a powerful mixture of utopian dreams and class hatred directed against capitalists and other opponents. After Stalin came to power in the late 1920s, he increased the list of enemies. We have already seen how he applied the term "kulaks" to many peasants who resisted his collectivization policies (review Reading 7.2). By the late 1930s, the "enemies of the people" included an ever-widening circle, including many members of the Communist party, such as Eugenia Ginzburg. And, the more enemies uncovered, even though in reality many of them were loyal to the system and Stalin himself, the greater the terroristic methods used by the state.

In Germany, Hitler also targeted "enemies of the people" (*volk* in German); like communism, nazism was a potent combination of utopian dreams mixed with hatred. Like Stalin, Hitler accused many people, at home and abroad, of being enemies of the people. The foreign powers that had imposed the Treaty of Versailles on Germany after

This poster depicts various "Enemies of the 5-Year Plan," a plan first introduced in late 1928 as part of Stalin's "revolution from above" (see Chapter 7). Thus, even by the end of the 1920s, Stalin's list of "enemies" was already broad, though it would widen even more later. Poster by Deni 1929. British Museum, London. Photo Thames and Hudson Ltd., London.

World War I were certainly among those Hitler pointed to as enemies of the German *volk.* From the beginning, however, as can be seen from Hitler's *Mein Kampf* (written in the 1920s), he pointed to Jews and communists as the chief enemies, and to Hitler's mind Jews were the founders and chief proponents of communism (see Reading 12.2B). After the Great Depression had put one out of every three Germans out of work, many Germans were looking for scapegoats upon whom to blame their problems and vent their frustrations, but they were also seeking bold new visions. Hitler provided both.

The readings in 12.2 indicate how extensive Nazi racism and antisemitism were, even prior to World War II. Although those targeted by Stalin as enemies in the 1930s were sometimes members of minority Soviet nationalities, race was not a Soviet criterion for selection as an "enemy of the people." Nevertheless, those murdered under Stalin prior to World War II outnumbered those who suffered a similar fate under Hitler in those years. During World War II, however, Hitler's death camps and squads killed millions of innocent Jews in the Holocaust, as well as Gypsies, Slavs, and others that Hitler considered racially inferior. Thus, "enemies of the people" and terror were important ingredients of both Hitler's nazism and Stalin's communism.

One final comparison is that despite all the scholarship and recent revelations, the debate continues as to the extent of the responsibility of others besides the two dictators for the many deaths that occurred under them. Daniel Goldhagen's *Hitler's Willing Executioners: Ordinary Germans and the Holocaust* (1996) and J. Arch Getty's works beginning with his *Origins of the Great Purges: The Soviet Communist Party Reconsidered, 1933–1938* (1985) have especially stimulated controversy.

READING 12.1

The Great Terror in the Soviet Union: One Woman's Experience

Following the assassination of Sergei Kirov, Leningrad Communist party chief, in December 1934 (an assassination Stalin probably approved of), Stalin used the killing to escalate his use of terror. From 1936 to 1939, millions of arrests, executions, imprisonments, and deportations to forced-labor camps terrorized the Soviet people. An especially high percentage of Communist party leaders and military leaders lost their lives, at least partly because the highly suspicious Stalin distrusted any potential competition to his leadership and sometimes perceived plots against him where none existed.

However, not just top political and military leaders suffered; so did intellectuals, national minorities, and ordinary citizens who sometimes were subject to "arrest quotas." In the midst of the Great Terror, writer Isaac Babel, who was arrested in 1939, remarked, "Today a man talks frankly only with his wife—at night with the blanket pulled over his head." Because Stalin and those loyal to him controlled the media of the time, however, many Soviet citizens failed to realize that he was primarily responsible for the terror.

Eugenia Ginzburg (1896–1980) was caught up in it when she was arrested in February 1937. In her first volume of memoirs, *Journey into the Whirlwind,* from which excerpts appear in this reading, this scholar and Communist party member shares her feelings during the months prior to her arrest. In 1935, she was reprimanded by higher party officials for not having earlier criticized a recently arrested fellow faculty member who had been labeled a Trotskyite.

Soon after being imprisoned, Ginzburg's husband was also arrested, leaving their children without a free parent. After months of imprisonment in Kazan, she was transferred to a Moscow prison, where she first saw the charges against her and feared she would be put to death. On August 1, 1937, however, she was relieved when a military tribunal sentenced her instead to ten years imprisonment in solitary confinement, plus loss of civil rights for five more years. Shortly after receiving her sentence, she was once again transferred, this time to a prison in Yaroslavl. The last part of the reading recounts the slogans she saw from a train while heading there. After two years imprisonment in Yaroslavl, she was sent with seventy-five others in a boxcar on a month-long train trip to the Vladivostok area, where she was further transported (again under atrocious conditions) by ship to Siberia's infamous Kolyma area. There, where winter temperatures sometimes reached −50°F, she was placed in the women's forced-labor camp, where at first she almost died because she was unable to chop down enough trees to earn sufficient rations for survival.

Ginzburg was subsequently fortunate enough to be assigned other work, described in her second volume of memoirs, *Within the Whirlwind.* In 1947 she was released from forced labor but remained in exile. She was joined in Siberia by her youngest son, Vasya, who later became world famous as writer Vassily Aksyonov. Ginzburg did not return to European Russia until 1955, two years after the death of Stalin. She was rehabilitated the following year, as were millions of others returning from the camps and exile, where they had been unjustly sent under Stalin.

The last year of my former existence, which came to an end in February 1937, was very confused, but it was perfectly clear that I was heading straight for disaster, particularly after the Zinovyev-Kamenev trial, the Kemerovo affair, the trial of Pyatakov and Radek.*

The news burned, stung, clawed at one's heart. After each trial, the screw was turned tighter. The hideous term "enemy of the people" came into use. Every region and every national republic was obliged by some lunatic logic to have its own crop of enemies so as not to lag behind the others, for all the world as though it were a campaign for deliveries of grain or milk.

I myself was marked, I felt, and I wasn't allowed to forget it for a single moment. . . .

The bolt clicked open. A young officer stood in the doorway and thrust a piece of paper at me.

"Read this." Before I could ask him anything, he had locked me in again.

"This" was my charge sheet. . . .

I ran my eyes over the "preamble" to the act of accusation. There was nothing special here—the usual newspaper claptrap: "A Trotskyist terrorist counter-revolutionary group . . . dedicated to the restoration of capitalism and the physical annihilation of Party and government leaders." These formulae, repeated millions of times over, had lost their power to shock and now inspired only a vague nausea: they affected the mind almost like a refrain, or like some oft-repeated fairy tale. People skipped them and would wait with bated breath for the real story to begin, for the ogre to appear. . . .

In my case, after the ritual introduction came a list of "members of the counter-revolutionary Trotskyist terrorist organization among the editorial staff of the newspaper *Red Tartary.*" Again not the slightest attempt at plausibility. Some of the people on the list had never worked on the newspaper; others had long since moved to other towns and were nowhere near at the time of the crime. As I later found out, those who had moved away far enough were never arrested. . . .

I read on. Ah, here was the real story, here came the ogre at last. "On the basis of these facts, the case is referred to the military tribunal . . . in accordance with sections 8 and 11 of Article 58, of the Criminal Code and the law of December 1, 1934."

By now the flutter in my temples had changed to a slow, reverberating throb. What law was this? Its date boded no good. . . .

The young officer opened the door of my kennel again. This time I was able to take in his appearance: he had a sharp little nose and a toothbrush mustache, like the comic policeman in Gorky's play *Enemies.* . . . As if from very far off, I heard him asking for the second time: "Have you acquainted yourself with the indictment? Is it quite clear?"

"No, it isn't. I don't know what the law of December 1, 1934, says."

He looked astonished, as if I had asked him what the sun or the moon were. Then he replied with a shrug:

"It says that the sentence must be carried out within twenty-four hours of its being pronounced."

*Grigory Zinovyev, 1883–1936, Lev Kamenev, 1883–1936, Grigory Pyatakov, 1890–1937, and Karl Radek, 1885–1939, were all prominent Bolshevik leaders. The Kemerovo affair was one of the many cases of alleged industrial sabotage.

Ginzburg, Eugenia Semyonovna. *Journey into the Whirlwind.* Trans. Paul Stevenson and Max Hayward. San Diego: Harcourt, Brace, Jovanovich, 1967, pp. 26, 172–75, 178–81, 199.

Twenty-four hours—plus another twenty-four between now and my trial. (They had told me in the cell that people were usually tried on the day after they were shown the indictment.) That made forty-eight hours in all—forty-eight hours to live.

There was once a little girl called Genia [the author]. Her mother used to braid her hair, and she grew up and fell in love and tried to discover what life was about. And she lived as a grown-up woman for two whole years, till she was twenty-eight. And she had two sons, Alyosha and Vasya. . . .

I checked the time at the beginning and end of the trial. Seven minutes. That, neither more nor less, was the time it took to enact this tragicomedy.

The voice of the president of the court—Dmitriev, People's Commissar for Justice of the Russian Republic—resembled the expression of his eyes. If a frozen codfish could talk, that is undoubtedly what it would sound like. There was not a trace here of the animation, the zest which my interrogators had put into their performances: the judges were merely functionaries earning their pay. No doubt they had a quota, and were anxious to overfulfill it if they could.

"You have read the indictment?" said the president in tones of unutterable boredom. "You plead guilty? No? But the evidence shows . . ."

He leafed through the bulky file and muttered through his teeth: "For instance the witness Kozlov . . ."

"Kozlova. It's a woman—and, I may add, a despicable one."

"Kozlova, yes. Or again, the witness Dyachenko . . ."

"Dyakonov."

"Yes. Well, they both state . . ."

But what they stated the judge was too pressed for time to read. Breaking off, he asked me:

"Any questions you wish to ask the court?"

"Yes, I do. I am accused under section 8 of Article 58, which means that I am charged with terrorism. Will you please tell me the name of the political leader against whose life I am supposed to have plotted?"

The judges were silent for a while, taken aback by this preposterous question. They looked reproachfully at the inquisitive woman who was holding up their work. Then the one with grizzled hair muttered:

"You know, don't you, that Comrade Kirov was murdered in Leningrad?"

"Yes, but I didn't kill him, it was someone called Nikolayev. Anyway, I've never been in Leningrad. Isn't that what you call an alibi?"

"Are you a lawyer by any chance?" said the gray-haired man crossly.

"No, I'm a teacher."

"You won't get anywhere by quibbling. You may never have been in Leningrad, but it was your accomplices who killed him, and that makes you morally and criminally responsible."

"The court will withdraw for consultation," grunted the president. Whereupon they all stood up, lazily stretching their limbs. . . .

I looked at the clock again. They couldn't even have had time for a smoke! In less than two minutes the worshipful assembly was back in session. The president had in his hand a large sheet of paper of excellent quality, covered with typescript in close spacing. The text, which must have taken at least twenty minutes to copy, was my sentence:

the official document setting forth my crimes and the penalty for them. It began with the solemn words: "In the name of the Union of Soviet Socialist Republics," followed by something long and unintelligible. Oh, yes, it was the same preamble as in the indictment, with its "restoration of capitalism," "underground terrorist organization," and all the rest. Only wherever that document had said "accused," this one said "convicted." . . .

The president went on in a whining nasal voice. How slowly he read! He turned over the page. Here it comes . . . any moment now he would utter the words "supreme penalty . . ."

Again I heard the trees rustling. For a moment I felt as if all this were part of a film. How could they possibly be going to kill me for no reason at all—me, Mother's Genia, Alyosha's and Vasya's mother. By what right . . .

I thought I must have screamed, but no—I stood and listened in silence, and all these other strange things were taking place inside me.

A sort of darkness came over my mind; the judge's voice sounded like a muddy torrent by which I might be swamped at any moment. In my delirium I noticed a thoughtful move by the two warders who were joining hands behind my back—evidently so that I should not hit the floor when I fainted. Why were they so sure I would faint? Oh, well, they must know from experience, doubtless many women fainted when they heard their death sentence read out.

The darkness closed in again—for the last time, surely. And then, all of a sudden—

What was it? What had he said? Like a blinding zigzag of lightning cutting across my mind. He had said . . . Had I heard right? . . .

"Ten years' imprisonment in solitary confinement with loss of civil rights for five years . . ."

The world around me was suddenly warm and bright. Ten years! That meant I was to live!

". . . and confiscation of all personal property."

To live! Without property, but what was that to me? Let them confiscate it—they were brigands anyway, confiscating was their business. They wouldn't get much good out of mine, a few books and clothes—why, we didn't even have a radio. . . .

At last our train started. Greedily I drank in the sight of the Moscow suburbs as they drifted by. Every station had its red banner printed with a slogan. All the slogans spoke of sabotage: "Liquidating the effects of sabotage in the transport system, we pledge ourselves to . . ." Here was a store with the slogan: "We shall stamp out sabotage in the retail-trade network," and on a power station: "Liquidating the effects of sabotage in industry, we resolve to exceed the norm. . . ."

READING 12.2

German Prewar Policy Directed Against the Jews and "Unsound"

This collection of readings indicates Nazi racism, specifically toward the Jews, and the Nazi desire to foster so-called Aryan supremacy. Antisemitism in Europe certainly did not begin with Hitler; it had existed for centuries, partly as a result of the minority status of Jews in overwhelmingly Christian countries. Economic factors and nineteenth-century pseudoscientific racist ideas also contributed to antisemitism. The persecution of Jews in the Russian Empire before World War I was especially notable. They were discriminated against in various ways and occasionally victimized by pogroms characterized by mob violence. By 1914, almost one-third of about 5 million Jews (in the 1897 census) had emigrated, primarily to the United States. In this same period, antisemitism was also clearly visible in Austria, where Hitler was born and spent his youth, and in France, where the Dreyfus Case split public opinion regarding the guilt or innocence of a Jewish army officer charged with treason.

However, Nazi policies culminating in the wartime Holocaust went far beyond previous persecutions. In *Mein Kampf,* Hitler had written that the main reason for the German collapse in 1918 was "the failure to recognize the racial problem and especially the Jewish menace." In 1925, there were a little over 550,000 Jews in Germany, about 1 percent of Germany's population. After coming to power in January 1933, Hitler wasted little time in enacting policies directed against them. A series of laws enacted in 1933 resulted in the dismissal of Jews from government, educational, entertainment, and media positions, as well as from some other selected professions. In addition, the percentage of Jews allowed to enter higher educational establishments was limited to 1.5 percent of admissions, and Jews were prohibited from owning farms.

In September-November 1935, a new series of anti-Jewish laws were enacted, usually referred to as the Nuremberg Laws. The most significant portions of a September 15, 1935, law to protect "German blood and honor" are presented as Reading 12.2A. In November 1935, a new citizenship law stated specifically that "a Jew cannot be a citizen" or vote.

From 1935 to 1938, the Nazis imposed new restrictions on the Jews and encouraged hatred of them. Along with Jews, communists had been a long-time target of Nazi propaganda—and, in Germany, of persecution. In a 1938 Year Book of the Hitler Youth, the link between Soviet communists and Jews is so greatly exaggerated (Reading 12.2B) that it presents a false portrayal of the Soviet government and society. The Nazis also gradually escalated and allowed others to increase violent actions against the Jews. In a few days beginning with November 9, 1938, Nazi thugs and others destroyed or ransacked more than 10,000 Jewish shops, homes, and synagogues; killed scores of Jews; and arrested and sent tens of thousands of Jews to concentration camps. Because of all the windows broken on the night of November 9, the Nazis labeled it Crystal Night.

Just a few days after November 9, Hitler's economic overseer, Field Marshall Herman Goering, convened a meeting of several high-ranking Nazis at his Air Force headquarters. He told those gathered that Hitler wanted the "Jewish question" solved "one way or another." Among those present at the meeting were Hitler's propaganda minister Joseph Goebbels and SS General Reinhard Heydrich, whose Security Service had played a leading role in Crystal Night. A partial transcript of their meeting (Reading 12.2C) highlights the Nazi hostility toward the Jews. At this meeting, Goering declared that the problem was primarily an economic one, and he instituted a stepped-up effort to confiscate remaining Jewish businesses and assets. One means for the government to enrich itself at Jewish expense was by collecting and confiscating various amounts from Jews wishing to emigrate—by the beginning of World War II, in September 1939, about half the number of Jews living in Germany in 1933 had emigrated, including such notables as Albert Einstein.

Although the Jews were the main target of Nazi laws designed to protect and foster Aryan supremacy, the Nazis also took such measures as the forced sterilization of people they considered defective. Reading 12.2D is an excerpt from a 1937 textbook on racial science, genetics, and racial policy that illustrates the Nazi government's thinking about such "unsound" people. Among other victims of sterilization were some of Germany's homosexuals.

READING 12.2A: NUREMBERG LAWS

Section 1

1. Marriages between Jews and nationals of German or kindred blood are forbidden. Marriages concluded in defiance of this law are void, even if, for the purpose of evading this law, they are concluded abroad.

2. Proceedings for annulment may be initiated only by the Public Prosecutor.

Section 2

Relation outside marriage between Jews and nationals of German or kindred blood are forbidden.

Section 3

Jews will not be permitted to employ female nationals of German or kindred blood in their household.

Section 4

1. Jews are forbidden to hoist the Reichs and national flag and to present the colors of the Reich.

2. On the other hand they are permitted to present the Jewish colors. The exercise of this authority is protected by the State.

Section 5

1. A person who acts contrary to the prohibition of section 1 will be punished with hard labor.

2. A person who acts contrary to the prohibition of section 2 will be punished with imprisonment or with hard labor.

3. A person who acts contrary to the provisions of sections 3 or 4 will be punished with imprisonment up to a year and with a fine or with one of these penalties.

Excerpted from U.S. Chief of Counsel for the Prosecution of Axis Criminality. *Nazi Conspiracy and Aggression.* Washington, D.C.: U.S. Government Printing Office, 1946, vol. 4, doc. no. 2000-PS, p. 637.

READING 12.2B: NAZI VIEW OF JEWS IN THE SOVIET UNION*

The Jewish Dictatorship.

A situation has developed which was recognizable since the foundation of this country [USSR], that is, the development toward dictatorial power of one individual man and his circle. At the same time the real power was taken over by that race which played a decisive role in the downfall of the old Reich and in the formation of the new republic: the Jewish race! Whoever considers Soviet Russian affairs must, in order to understand these happenings, concern himself with the Jewish race. Because everywhere in the decisive key positions of the Soviet system and of the communist party are Jews.

The liquidation of 15 million Russians and the extermination of the intelligensia and Russian leadership are also a product of the Jewish race, like the bombastic propaganda with which the actual needs, the existings gaps, the insufficiency in the organization of the state administration are being covered up. Bolshevism and Judaism are one thing, because the Jewish element is the authoritative and decisive element in the leadership of Bolshevism. Now as before Jews are represented five to fifteen times as much in the leading offices of the party and state administration as among the party mass, and ten to thirty times stronger than according to their population ratio. They are the representatives of the new bourgeois in Soviet Russia, the only ones who actually benefit from this system; and the politics and tactics they pursue are intended to remove systematically the Russian spirit from the schools and institutions of education and replace it with the Jewish one. Russia, today, is under a Jewish alien sovereignty; it is true that Stalin is no Jew, but all important key positions, be they in foreign politics or in the secret police (GPU, Tsheka) or in the internal administration, or in the political set-up of the Red Army, are occupied by Jews. . . . It is a question of the crimes of the Jewish race in Soviet Russia which is connected inseparably with the spilled blood of millions of dead in history. From it emanate the powers of destruction which guide Russia into the world. They act according to the program of their racial comrade Marx. It is they who oppress the worker and peasant and carry out a system which today rests like one heavy chain on the Russian people and makes impossible all efforts of a self-deliverance.

READING 12.2C: A NAZI MEETING ON THE "JEWISH QUESTION," NOVEMBER 1938**

Goebbels: Number 2. In almost all German cities synagogues are burned. New, various possibilities exist to utilize the space where the synagogues stood. Some cities want to build parks in their place, others want to put up new buildings.

Goering: How many synagogues were actually burned?

Heydrich: Altogether there are 101 synagogues destroyed by fire; 76 synagogues demolished; and 7,500 stores ruined in the Reich.

*First appeared in 1938 Year Book of the Hitler Youth, translated in U.S. Chief of Counsel for the Prosecution of Axis Criminality. *Nazi Conspiracy and Aggression.* Washington, D.C.: U.S. Government Printing Office, 1946, vol. 5, doc. no. 2440-PS, pp. 140–41.

**From a Stenographic Report of the Meeting in U.S. Chief of Counsel for the Prosecution of Axis Criminality. *Nazi Conspiracy and Aggression.* Washington, D.C.: U.S. Government Printing Office, 1946, vol. 4, doc. no. 1816-PS, pp. 431–34.

Goering: What do you mean "destroyed by fire?"

Heydrich: Partly, they are razed, and partly gutted.

Goebbels: I am of the opinion that this is our chance to dissolve the synagogues. All these not completely intact, shall be razed by the Jews. The Jews shall pay for it. There in Berlin, the Jews are ready to do that. The synagogues which burned in Berlin are being leveled by the Jews themselves. We shall build parking lots in their places or new buildings. That ought to be the criterion for the whole country, the Jews shall have to remove the damaged or burned synagogues, and shall have to provide us with ready free space.

Number 3: I deem it necessary to issue a decree forbidding the Jews to enter German theaters, moving houses, and circuses. I have already issued such a decree under the authority of the law of the chamber for culture. Considering the present situation of the theaters, I believe we can afford that. Our theaters are overcrowded, we have hardly any room. I am of the opinion that it is not possible to have Jews sitting next to Germans in movies and theaters. One might consider, later on, to let the Jews have one or two movie houses here in Berlin, where they may see Jewish movies. But in German theaters they have no business anymore.

Furthermore, I advocate that the Jews be eliminated from all positions in public life in which they may prove to be provocative. It is still possible today that a Jew shares a compartment in a sleeping car with a German. Therefore, we need a decree by the Reich Ministry for Communications stating that separate compartments for Jews shall be available; in case where compartments are filled up, Jews cannot claim a seat. They shall be given a separate compartment only after all Germans have secured seats. They shall not mix with Germans, and if there is no more room, they shall have to stand in the corridor.

Goering: In that case, I think it would make more sense to give them separate compartments.

Goebbels: Not if the train is overcrowded!

Goering: Just a moment. There'll be only one Jewish coach. If that is filled up, the other Jews will have to stay at home.

Goebbels: Suppose, though, there won't be many Jews going on the express train to Munich, suppose there would be two Jews in the train and the other compartments would be overcrowded. These two Jews would then have a compartment all themselves. Therefore, Jews may claim a seat only after all Germans have secured a seat.

Goering: I'd give the Jews one coach or one compartment. And should a case like you mention arise and the train be overcrowded, believe me, we won't need a law. We'll kick him out and he'll have to sit all alone in the toilet all the way!

Goebbels: I don't agree. I don't believe in this. There ought to be a law. Furthermore, there ought to be a decree barring Jews from German beaches and resorts. Last summer . . .

Goering: Particularly here in the Admiralspalast very disgusting things have happened lately.

Goebbels: Also at the Wannsee beach. A law which definitely forbids the Jews to visit German resorts!

Goering: We could give them their own.

Goebbels: It would have to be considered whether we'd give them their own or whether we should turn a few German resorts over to them, but not the finest and best, so we cannot say the Jews go there for recreation.

Part of the former Auschwitz-Birkenau Concentration Camp complex, near Krakow, Poland. During World War II, many Jews and other prisoners were brought here from other areas and gassed to death. Altogether, about 6 million Jews were killed in World War II. Walter Moss

It'll also have to be considered if it might not become necessary to forbid the Jews to enter the German forests. In the Grunewald, whole herds of them are running around. It is a constant provocation and we are having incidents all the time. The behavior of the Jews is so inciting and provocative that brawls are a daily routine.

Goering: We shall give the Jews a certain part of the forest, and the Alpers shall take care of it that various animals that look damned much like Jews—the Elk has such a crooked nose, —get there also and become acclimated.

Goebbels: I think this behavior is provocative. Furthermore, Jews should not be allowed to sit around in German parks. I am thinking of the whispering campaign on the part of Jewish women in the public gardens at Fehrbelliner Platz. They go and sit with German mothers and their children and begin to gossip and incite.

Goebbels: I see in this a particularly grave danger. I think it is imperative to give the Jews certain public parks, not the best ones—and tell them: "You may sit on these benches" these benches shall be marked "For Jews only." Besides that they have no business in German parks. Furthermore, Jewish children are still allowed in German schools. That's impossible. It is out of the question that any boy should sit beside a Jewish boy in a German gymnasium and receive lessons in German history. Jews ought to be eliminated completely from German schools; they may take care of their own education in their own communities.

READING 12.2D: THE PREVENTION OF "HEREDITARILY UNSOUND PROGENY"

The Fight Against Degeneration:

It is a great fortune, that the leadership of our people has not only recognized the danger of the situation, but also has made a strict decision to combat it. He who wants to live as a member of our community, is not only obliged to put all his efforts at the service of this community, but also must make sacrifices. He must tolerate encroachments on his personal rights, if the need of the community demands it. It is one of the first duties of the community, to see to it, that the increase of those, inferior by heredity, is stopped. At our stage of culture, we cannot think of it of course, to expect them from our community, but we can easily see to it, that they are not propagated and give their inferior heritage to new generations. To prevent this, the law exists for the prevention of hereditarily unsound progeny. This gives the right to the national community, to exclude those men and women from propagation with whom it can be expected with certainty through knowledge of the heredity laws, that their offspring will to a great extent be physically, mentally and spiritually inferior.

Fig. 27, Costs of welfare in comparison to average earnings [Page 39].

The daily cost of a			Criminals	=	3.50 M
Deaf mute	=	6.00 M	The daily earnings of a		
Cripple	=	6.00 M	Laborer	=	2.50 M
Reform School			Employee	=	2.50 M
inmate	=	4.85 M	Civil Servant	=	4.00 M
Mentally Sick	=	4.50 M			

Only comparatively simple medical intervention is necessary for that, which will not effect the well being and ability to live of the person at all. The law enumerates a whole series of hereditary diseases, in case of which the prevention of procreation can be carried out. Into this class belong in the first place serious physical disabilities such as hereditary blindness and deaf-muteness, but also a series of serious mental diseases, especially hereditary feeblemindness and idiocy. Of course, in every case, before such intervention is ordered by the state, all circumstances must be thoroughly examined by a court, appointed especially for the purpose.

These measures, of course, cannot show their results immediately, but in the course of many years, the health of the heritage of our people will improve, and the tremendous burden, which is placed today on the community by taking care of the inferior ones, will decrease more and more. Actually, today it is so, that the state spends more for the existence of these actually worthless compatriots, than the salary for the work of a healthy man, with which he must bring up a healthy family. . . .

Streche, O. *Lehrbuch der Rassenkunde, Verebungslehre, und Rassenplege,* Leipzing, 1937, translated in U.S. Chief of Counsel for the Prosecution of Axis Criminality. *Nazi Conspiracy and Aggression.* Washington, D.C.: U.S. Government Printing Office, 1946, vol. 5, doc. no. 2442-PS, pp. 176–77.

Racial Hygiene:

When choosing a mate, for marriage, we also take the obligation, to keep in mind the racial composition of our national substance. The six basic races, which we have learned to know previously, are so mixed in our national community and their participation in the construction of our culture cannot easily be separated, that we cannot easily put them against each other in strong contrast. We have previously seen that the Nordic race distinguishes itself by a special leadership talent and that it has certainly played an outstanding part in the development of our national substance. The result is that today, we have relatively many Nordic people among the leading strata of our people. If, therefore, an increase of these strata is helped along, the share of Nordic blood within, it will become a greater one. But it is very essential, that we avoid, as best as we can, the penetration of elements of alien races into our national body.

DISCUSSION QUESTION

Compare and contrast the government attitudes toward and treatment of "enemies of the people" in Germany and in the Soviet Union in the 1930s.

THIRTEEN

Axis Aggressions and World War II

Aggressions by Japan in Asia and Germany and Italy in Europe and Africa during the 1930s culminated in World War II. In Japan, ultranationalist officers assassinated domestic opponents, including more moderate senior officers, and destroyed the fragile parliamentary government led by the political parties. Blatant Japanese aggressions against China netted large territorial gains and won widespread public support. Italy under the vainglorious Fascist leader Benito Mussolini conquered Ethiopia and Albania and incorporated them into the Italian empire. The League of Nations condemned both Japan and Italy; it demanded that Japan restore Manchuria (conquered in 1931) to China and instituted an embargo of strategic materials to Italy. Neither move was enforced, and both Japan and Italy showed their contempt for international law by resigning from the League.

In Germany, Nazi leader Adolf Hitler brought an end to the democratic Weimar Republic and made himself the supreme dictator. He systematically violated the Treaty of Versailles by rearming and militarizing Germany, annexing Austria, and then dismembering Czechoslovakia. Japan, Germany, and Italy became allies in the Anti-Comintern Pact, also called the Rome-Berlin-Tokyo Axis. Their acts plunged the world into another world war.

China, Ethiopia, Czechoslovakia, and other victim nations were too weak to offer effective resistance. The major Western powers did not act to stop the aggressors for several reasons. One was genuine hatred and horror of war after the bloodletting of World War I, as expressed by British Prime Minister Neville Chamberlain. Another was reluctance to be dragged into wars by problems and conflicts in remote places such as China and Czechoslovakia, especially when Britain was not militarily prepared and had no strong allies (see Reading 13.1). The depression and its lasting debilitating effects also restrained leaders of the Western democracies from taking effective measures to halt aggression (review Reading 8.1). Because of these and other reasons, Britain responded to German aggression with appeasement, and the United States retreated to isolationism.

Reading 13.1A pertains to the Munich Agreement of September 1938, whereby Great Britain, France, and Italy agreed to Germany's dismemberment of Czechoslovakia by annexing the Sudetenland, a part of Czechoslovakia bordering on Germany. Although it had a majority of ethnic German inhabitants, the Sudetenland had never been part of Germany. The Munich Agreement has come to epitomize appeasement, with British Prime Minister Neville Chamberlain as its foremost apologist. In Reading 13.1B, Czech President Edvard Benes provides an anguished explanation of why his country acquiesced in its own destruction without resort to arms.

World War II began in Asia when Japan launched an all-out attack on China in 1937. Between 1931 and 1937, Japan had gradually conquered parts of northeastern China. Frantically attempting to unify and modernize so that China could resist Japanese aggression, China's leader, Chiang Kai-shek, had promised to fight to the end when national survival was at stake. When Japan began its attack in 1937, the Chinese government and people determined that the moment had come. Reading 13.2 is an autobiographical account by a Chinese boy who joined the army at age twelve in the wake of Japan's attack. This account represents the will of millions of Chinese to sacrifice and resist, which persisted for eight years and took millions of lives.

World War II began in Europe when Nazi Germany attacked Poland in 1939, provoking Great Britain and France to declare war on Germany. The United States entered World War II when Japan attacked Pearl Harbor in 1941. All belligerent countries totally mobilized all human and material resources during World War II. Most able-bodied men were drafted to fight; others worked in vital and defense-related industries. Women were not drafted. Some joined the military; millions contributed to the war effort in the home front, in all aspects of production, including the vital war-related industries.

Reading 13.3 is by an American homemaker, one of millions of women in the United States and throughout the world who took part in wartime production. The participation by large numbers of women in jobs hitherto held exclusively by men not only contributed significantly to the war effort, but it also changed social patterns and relations between men and women that would continue in the postwar world.

READING 13.1

Hitler Seizes the Sudetenland

Nazi German leader Adolf Hitler began to tear up the Treaty of Versailles soon after assuming power in 1933. In 1935 he instituted conscription to build up Germany's armed forces, in 1936 he remilitarized the Rhineland, and in 1938 he annexed Austria. During the summer of 1938, Hitler demanded that Czechoslovakia cede the Sudetenland to Germany, threatening to take it by force if his demands were not met. The territory consisted mainly of ethnic Germans; it bordered on but had never belonged to Germany. Desperate to avoid war for which his country was not prepared, British Prime Minister Neville Chamberlain flew to Germany three times during September 1938 to meet with Hitler. The third meeting took place on September 29 at Munich, where Hitler and Chamberlain were joined by French Premier Eduard Deladier (who was also anxious to appease Hitler) and Italy's Benito Mussolini (who was firmly in Hitler's camp). Czechoslovakia, whose fate was being decided, was not invited to participate, nor was the Soviet Union, which had an agreement with Czechoslovakia (together with France) to come to its defense in case of aggression. The Munich Agreement granted Hitler the Sudetenland. Hitler in return promised not to make additional territorial demands, and all signatories guaranteed the independence of what remained of Czechoslovakia. In retrospect, appeasement was doomed because it was based on the assumption that Hitler had a few territorial demands in Europe, whereas, in fact, his ambitions were limitless.

In Reading 13.1A, Prime Minister Chamberlain explains to the British parliament and people why Great Britain was willing to agree to some of Hitler's demands. In Reading 13.1B, Czech President Edvard Benes reflects on the tragic events that first dismembered and then destroyed his nation.

READING 13.1A: CHAMBERLAIN'S APPEASEMENT POLICY

"My first duty now that I have come back [from his second meeting with Hitler] is to report to the British and French Governments the result of my mission, and until I have done that, it would be difficult for me to say anything about it.

"I will only say this. I trust all concerned will continue their efforts to solve the Czechoslovakian problem peacefully, because on that turns the peace of Europe in our time. . . .

". . . How horrible, fantastic, incredible it is that we should be digging trenches and trying on gas masks here because of a quarrel in a far-away country between people of whom we know nothing. It seems still more impossible that a quarrel which has already been settled in principle should be the subject of war.

"I can well understand the reasons why the Czech Government have felt unable to accept the terms which have been put before them in the German memorandum. Yet I believe after my talks with Herr Hitler that, if only time were allowed, it ought to be possible for the arrangements for transferring the territory that the Czech Government has agreed to give to Germany to be settled by agreement under conditions which would assure fair treatment to the population concerned.

"You know already that I have done all that one man can do to compose this quarrel. After my visits to Germany I have realised vividly how Herr Hitler feels that he

Chamberlain, Neville. *In Search of Peace.* London: Putnam and Sons, 1939, pp. 172, 174–76.

On his return from the Munich Conference, Prime Minister Neville Chamberlain displays a British-German declaration and makes a brief airport speech, declaring "Peace in our time." Imperial War Museum/Archive Photos

must champion other Germans, and his indignation that grievances have not been met before this. He told me privately, and last night he repeated publicly, that after this Sudeten German question is settled, that is the end of Germany's territorial claims in Europe. . . .

"However much we may sympathise with a small nation confronted by a big and powerful neighbour, we cannot in all circumstances undertake to involve the whole British Empire in war simply on her account. If we have to fight it must be on larger issues than that. I am myself a man of peace to the depths of my soul. Armed conflict between nations is a nightmare to me; but if I were convinced that any nation had made up its mind to dominate the world by fear of its force, I should feel that it must be resisted. Under such a domination life for people who believe in liberty would not be worth living; but war is a fearful thing, and we must be very clear, before we embark on it, that it is really the great issues that are at stake, and that the call to risk everything in their defence, when all the consequences are weighed, is irresistible. . . .

"I think I should add that before saying farewell to Herr Hitler I had a few words with him in private, which I do not think are without importance. In the first place he repeated to me with great earnestness what he had said already at Berchtesgaden, namely, that this was the last of his territorial ambitions in Europe and that he had no wish to include in the Reich people of other races than Germans. . . .

"There are only two things I want to say. First of all I received an immense number of letters during all these anxious days—and so has my wife—letters of support and approval and gratitude; and I cannot tell you what an encouragement that has been to me. I want to thank the British people for what they have done. Next I want to say that the settlement of the Czechoslovak problem which has now been achieved is, in my view, only a prelude to a larger settlement in which all Europe may find peace."

READING 13.1B: CZECH PRESIDENT BENES' STATEMENT ON THE MUNICH AGREEMENT

"I have no intention of analyzing the whole political situation which has led me to this decision. I shall only say, in short, that the system of balance of power in Europe, established after the war, has been steadily weakening for several years. In the last three years it has changed basically to the disadvantage of ourselves and our friends. . . .

"It became clear that a world catastrophe might ensue. You know that under these circumstances four great powers met together and agreed among themselves on the sacrifice they would demand from us in the interest of peace. We had to accept.

"I do not wish to criticize. Nor must you expect from me a single word of recrimination in any direction. History will be our judge.

"I shall only say this, which we all feel very painfully: the sacrifices demanded of us with such emphasis were excessive and unjust. The nation will never forget this, although it has borne everything with a calmness and self-control that have aroused universal admiration and proved the strength and moral greatness of the whole people. . . .

"I turn to you, finally, with an appeal which comes from my heart. The homeland of the Czechs and Slovaks is indeed in danger today. It would be in much greater danger if at this moment we failed to hold together. It is above all necessary for Czechs to reach full unity with Slovaks. Slovaks, too, are in danger. . . .

"The decree of Munich was imposed upon us. Our soldiers, airmen and the members of a responsive and intelligent citizen army were ready for action. With the aid of her Allies and friends, Czechoslovakia could have helped to bring the German war machine crumbling to destruction. But in the hour of crisis she stood alone. . . .

"There is nothing that I want to change. If we were to alter any part of our basic principles and their purpose, we definitely should lose thereby.

"Here (i.e., in Western Europe) they may still believe that peace was saved at Munich. But soon they will discover that war has already begun.

"Munich made war inevitable. I do not know when it will break out; personally I doubt that it will take more than a year.

"The first to suffer the blow will be Poland. Beck has helped and still helps Hitler against us, but actually he is helping Hitler against Poland and the rest. France will pay horribly for her betrayal of us. And Chamberlain—he will live to see the results of his appeasement of Hitler and Mussolini. Hitler will attack all—in the West and even Russia—and in the end the United States, too, will be in it."

Benes, Edvard. *My Country.* New York: Czech American National Alliance, 1944, pp. 35–37.

READING 13.2

Father-Son Soldiers

When Japan attacked China in 1937, it expected to win within six months. Instead, the Sino-Japanese War lasted for eight years. It became part of World War II after Japan attacked the U.S. naval base at Pearl Harbor and U.S., British, and Dutch colonial holdings in Southeast Asia, and it ended with the defeat of Japan. Between 1937 and 1941 China fought alone, trading space for time, resorting to scorched earth tactics, and retreating to the interior, bogging down the mechanized Japanese war machine.

China mobilized 14 million men for the regular army; many more joined guerrilla units. It suffered a total military casualty of over 3 million; civilian casualties were much greater, and the amount of property damage and losses were incalculable.

Reading 13.2 is the reminiscence of a soldier who fought in that war. The son of an army officer, he joined the army at age twelve and became the youngest soldier in his unit.

For four of the eight years of our War of Resistance against Japanese Aggression, or for over a thousand days, I served in the army side by side with my father. I grew up to be a man and became strong from serving in the army. I also lost the father I loved and re-spected in the war. . . .

I was only twelve when I joined the army, the youngest among all the soldiers. It hap-pened this way. . . . My home town Hsiaohsien was captured by the Japanese army. . . . At the time Father had been on leave from his army unit to be with Grandma who had been ill. We had fled our home and taken refuge at Auntie's home in the country. In a hurry to return to his unit which had just received orders to regroup, Father said to Grandma and Mother:

"Life under Japanese occupation will be most difficult. There will be no school for our boy to go to. . . . I think it would be better if I take him with me now."

Mother replied that nothing would make her part from me. But Grandmother was less emotional. She said to Mother:

"I'm sure the Japanese devils will be here before the year's out. When they come they will as usual kill many Chinese. Do you think they will spare him? Rather than staying home and waiting to be killed, it's better to let him go fight with his father. I know he's your only son, as his father is mine. Maybe he will survive and even do his bit in de-feating the Japanese so we can all live in peace again."

Mother shook her head and continued to cry. Father could say nothing that comforted her. After two days' impasse, whether because she had been persuaded by Grandma's ar-guments or she had changed her mind on her own, Mother called me. Standing me in front of her and swallowing her tears, she said:

"Go with your father. Obey him and take care of yourself!"

Shi-tu, Fu, et al. *K'ang-chan Sui-yueh.* Taipei: Central Daily News, 1985, pp. 32–41, "Fu-tz'u-ping" (Father-Son Soldiers) by Ch'eng Chun-ling (translated and edited by Jiu-Hwa Lo Upshur).

I nodded my head. Though I was terribly excited about going to war, the thought of leaving Grandma and Mother also filled my heart with sadness and I began to cry. . . .

Father and I headed for Chiangpu but could find no news of where his unit was. We were almost out of money. Father then called on Mr. Wang Kung-yu, the Special Commissioner and Chief of Security of the Third District, who had in an earlier posting been magistrate of our county. Mr. Wang's office was just then organizing a company of security forces, and since Father was an artillery officer, Mr. Wang asked him to take the position of company commander. He had a hundred men in his unit and was issued three light artillery pieces, three heavy machine guns, plus over a hundred other weapons, including light machine guns, rifles, and pistols. . . .

I became a private second class in Father's company and was given a rifle and a pouch of bullets, a suit of uniform, puttees, a sack, a blanket, a water bottle, and other personal items. My army identification card had my name, rank and unit on one side, the reverse side had our motto: "We love our country and people, we do not fear death and we do not covet wealth." Even the smallest size uniform was far too big for me and I had to roll up the sleeves and pant legs. The rifle stood half a head taller than me. Father laughed wryly at the sight I made. . . .

Although he was allowed private quarters and separate mess facilities because of his rank, Father ate with his men and slept on the floor alongside them. Although he shared their hardships he was nevertheless a strict disciplinarian, and he personally supervised the rigorous training of the men he commanded. I could not keep up with the men in our daily early morning exercises which included running with our full packs. When I fell, Father would gently urge me to get up, saying:

"You can take it slowly, but see that you don't damage your rifle."

After the exercise ended he would call in the medic and help wipe clean my cuts and scrapes and apply medicine over them. I became very discouraged and said:

"I don't want to train any more!"

He was clearly annoyed as he replied: "If you can't even persevere through physical training, how can you ever learn to be a soldier and fight?"

In this way he helped me to understand what it was to be a soldier. I learned not to complain and to persevere. Before long I had mastered the basic drills, skills, and the use of various weapons. I felt proud of what I could do. . . .

Father found a sergeant in his unit to tutor me in my spare time. He was an accomplished scholar in the classics, poetry, and calligraphy, and knew some English and mathematics. He was also a strict teacher. He would grade my homework everyday and then show them to Father. Father would smile with pleasure when I did well and would reprimand me when I did not. Once Father went away for a month on assignment; I took the opportunity to spend all my spare time playing with the village children, neglecting my homework. We climbed trees, caught birds, and played in the ponds. Father found out about my behavior on his return and lectured me angrily:

"So you don't want to study. Do you want to be a private second class for the rest of your life?"

Father then explained that he wanted me to study so that I could later qualify for high school, and eventually go to a military academy. I realized that I did not want to be a private second class for the remainder of my life. So I studied every evening by the light of an oil lamp and did not go to bed until three changes of the watch had taken place. . . .

After several months of training [our unit received orders to] . . . support the guerrillas under Double-Gun Huang Pa-mei [Eighth Sister Huang] against a Japanese sweep aimed at the people in her region. Her job was to ambush them in the woods near the Lin Bridge. Father received his orders at dusk and we set out immediately on a fifty *li* [about 16 miles] forced march, arriving at our destination at around midnight. The guerrillas were waiting for us with more than ten barrels filled with cooked rice, noodles, and condiments which smelled and tasted wonderful. We were famished and had no trouble wolfing everything down. As we ate Huang Pa-mei briefed us as follows:

"There are over three hundred Japanese troops who are still several li away. We have over five hundred. With your support, we expect to win this engagement. Please eat quickly so we can get moving."

We had barely finished eating when gun fire sounded in the distance. Father quickly found a commanding hill site that covered the Lin Bridge below and from which we could beat an easy retreat if necessary. He deployed our artillery pieces and machine guns on the hill, and assigned a lieutenant to lead the remaining men to assist the guerrillas in combat.

The battle centered on control of the bridge. In bloody hand to hand combat, we charged and the enemy counter-charged; troops of both sides roared their battle cries, the cannons and guns boomed, and amidst all the noise, there was Father shouting his orders: "Target—distance—fire!" Finally the defeated enemy retreated, abandoning more than two hundred of their dead. Over a hundred of our people were dead or wounded. We captured two Japanese officers; they were bound and brought to the village clearing. The local people crowded around them, some cursed, others went up and slapped their faces. They loudly demanded revenge, some advocating ripping out their hearts and cutting them to pieces. . . . Then Huang Pa-mei stepped forward and said:

"Don't harm them. We will deliver them to headquarters!"

Because they respected her, the villagers obeyed her orders and stopped. But a crowd lingered at the square until the prisoners had been taken away.

Although everyone was happy at our victory, we were nevertheless saddened by the death of a guerrilla commander named Chu Lung, a fighter famous throughout northern Kiangsu province. Having lost his right hand in an earlier battle, he had learned to shoot so well with his left hand that reputedly he could hit a thrown coin. The government ordered Lin Bridge to be renamed Chu Lung Bridge to honor his memory. I learned that the Japanese never attempted to sweep that area again.

Both guerrillas and local militias operated against enemy lines in the Southern Kiangsu Guerrilla Zone. The Third Military Region command supplied all our weapons and ammunitions. With its hilly terrain and many small rivers, this area was well suited to guerrilla operations. . . . The guerrillas had good information, moved frequently to shelter in safe areas, avoided combat except when conditions suited them, and concentrated on wearing down the enemy. . . . Japanese units in the region came to resemble caged animals because they seldom dared venture out of their strongholds. . . .

During my third year in the army, many schools in guerrilla controlled areas . . . were resuming operation. My teacher, who had become a village chief [in free China] wrote to Father, promising to look after me if he would let me go study in the good Wartime Secondary School at Chenchiashih, near to where he worked. He assured Father that the school was located well away from the nearest Japanese army post, and near to the Chinese army base at Tapiehshan, where the students could be evacuated if necessary. . . . After thinking it over, Father wrote to accept the offer and said that he would take me to the school before the beginning of the next academic year. I was very happy that at last I would have a chance to resume my education. But it was not to be. . . .

Father, who had until now been so strong and healthy, fell ill, and had to hand over command to his deputy while he and I remained at our base. Soon we got news that several thousand enemy troops were headed westward and would pass our base village en route. We were ordered to evacuate immediately, and to head toward Chiuhua Mountain to join our forward unit there. Father and I set off, each carrying a rifle. . . . But he was too ill and weak to walk fast. No sooner had we crossed one hill than we were spotted by Japanese soldiers on the next hill top. A barrage of machine gun fire followed. Father yelled:

"Down!"

But it was too late for him. He was hit in the chest, blood spurted from his wound and he fell down. I pulled him to a gully and asked:

"Daddy, is it bad?"

In his accustomed tone of command, he said: "Fire back, hurry!"

I fired and fired until the barrel of my rifle became too hot and jammed. Then I turned to my wounded father and called out: "Daddy, Daddy," while gently stroking him. He replied in a weak voice:

"I . . . I am through! Tell them to cremate my remains. After we've won the war, take my ashes home. I want to rest near your Grandmother and Mother!" . . .

Next day we were discovered by our search party. They carried Father back on a stretcher, the field doctor tried to save him but it was too late. He had lost too much blood. That was how I lost my father. . . . I told Father's last wish to the deputy company commander and the men. They cremated him as he had wanted.

Holding the urn that contained Father's ashes and wearing heavy mourning, I walked to Pukow, got on the Tientsin-Pukow train and headed for home. Japanese military policemen at checkpoints let me through because of my mourning clothes and the urn of ashes I carried: perhaps they were afraid of the spirits of the dead, having killed so many Chinese. Mother clung to the urn that held Father's ashes and cried until she was faint. As usual my brave Grandmother was the first to wipe away her tears and say:

"The Japanese have killed so many of my people. But my son died in battle after he had killed many Japanese. He died in a worthwhile cause. It was a very worthwhile sacrifice!"

I buried Father in our ancestral burial ground amidst a grove of ancient trees. Then just as I was wondering how to tell Mother that I wanted to leave, she said to me:

"It's time for you to go. Remember to kill many Japanese. You have to avenge your Father's death!"

Mother and I clung to each other for a long time and we both cried. Then I said good bye to Grandmother and Mother and made my way back to my unit. I had just turned sixteen. Later my unit sponsored me for officer training at the military academy. By the time we celebrated victory at the end of the war I was wearing the badge of a first lieutenant of the army.

READING 13.3

Women and Wartime Production

World War II changed social patterns the world over. When most young male office and factory workers were drafted to fight, women were recruited to replace them. Recruiting women, especially married women, for the workplace challenged traditional cultural ideals. In the United States, opposition to women working outside the home was enhanced by postdepression prejudices that they were taking scarce jobs away from men.

The campaign encouraging women to join the workplace, however, was successful for two main reasons. One was the strong patriotic appeal of helping in the war effort. Another was the emphasis on the temporary nature of women's wartime work, and the belief that they would return to be full-time homemakers once the war was over. In time one-third of the workers in U.S. defense industries were women. Women were then dubbed "Rosie the Riveter" (a person who drove rivets that joined pieces of metal).

The ability to earn a good wage changed women's attitudes and enhanced their confidence. The shortage of workers also brought southern rural African Americans and Mexican Americans into high-paying industrial jobs, inevitably breaking down racial and regional barriers. A 1944 survey of former homemakers among female workers showed that half wanted to continue working after the war. However, large numbers of both men and women were laid off after the war because of changing peacetime needs, or because returning servicemen had been promised their former jobs. Nevertheless, many women continued in the full-time workforce, showing the permanent effect World War II had on social change and changing gender roles.

Reading 13.3 is from an oral history project that interviewed former female defense industry workers. Charlcia Neuman was a young, traditional housewife who returned to be a full-time homemaker after the war. She recounted the reasons she went to work, her family's concerns about her working, and her experiences working in an aircraft factory.

I started defense work in '42. I think a lot of it was because one of my neighbors found out about it, and she wanted me to go with her. I thought, "Well, now, this would take care of the situation." I still was getting along on next to nothing; it was still difficult. . . .

My husband didn't like it. He was one of these men that never wanted his wife to work. He was German and was brought up with the idea that the man made the living; the woman didn't do that. . . .

And my brother, especially my youngest brother, he thought it was terrible. My father, oh, he was very upset. He said, "You can't work amongst people like that." They were people just like me, but they thought it was people that were rough and not the same type I'm used to being with. They just couldn't see me going over and working in a factory and doing that type of work. . . .

Gluck, Shema Berger. *Rosie the Riveter: Women, the War, and Social Change.* Boston: Twayne Publishers, 1987, pp. 163–66, 168–70.

I went over and took tests to see about getting a job at Vultee. When I took the test, as far as using the hands and the eye and hand movements, I passed just about the highest. See, anything using my hands—I could take a little hand drill and go up and down these holes as fast as you could move, just go like that, where most people would break a drill. It was a very simple thing. The riveting is the same way. It's just a matter of rhythm. So it was easy to do.

They had a school set up in Downey to show us how to do assembly work and riveting and the reasons for things—what was a good rivet and what wasn't. We went there about two weeks before we started to work. It was mostly women on these jobs. See, so many young men were in the service that it didn't leave very many of them to do these types of jobs; the ones that were kept out of the service could do the more specialized work. They had to have men to make these jigs and to make the forms for the ribs. That was beyond us.

I was started on this jig. The P-38 that Lockheed put out was a twin engine, and we worked on the center part between the two hulls. It was a much heavier rivet that went into this. It was what they call cold riveting; you took them out of the icebox real cold and riveted it. That was harder work. . . .

Vultee was the first plant of this type in the area to hire a black girl. She was a very nice person. Wilhelmina was her first name, but I can't remember her last name. Her mother was a schoolteacher and she was from Los Angeles. . . .

. . . In that three years that I was there, then they began coming from the South. You could really tell the difference. The ones coming from the South were shy. It was very hard for them to mix with people. It was a very hard situation for them, but they were treated nice. . . .

When these black people were beginning to come in pretty steadily, I went over to show them how to do smaller types of assembly work, get them used to working with people and like that. . . .

Then there were the Mexican girls. They were treated just like we were. There was no such thing as brown; they were white as far as we were concerned. There again, they were very nice. . . .

I was laid off in September of '45. I just got a slip of paper saying that I wouldn't be needed again. Most of us went at the same time; it was just a matter that there was no more work. There were a few jobs that they kept open but most of the women were off then—and men, too. It wasn't discriminatory; it was what they happened to have left.

The idea was for the women to go back home. The women understood that. And the men had been promised their jobs when they came back. I was ready to go home. I was tired. . . .

The women got out and worked because they wanted to work. And they worked knowing full well that this was for a short time. We hoped the war would be over in a very short time and that we could go back home and do what we wanted to do. So that was what I felt.

DISCUSSION QUESTION

Based on the readings in this chapter, what differences do you discover in the responses of the Czech president, the Chinese soldier, and the American worker to their countries' plight as victims of aggression?

THREE

The Era of the Cold War and the Collapse of Empires

Two major political trends dominated the world after World War II. First, the Cold War embroiled the two superpowers, the United States and the Soviet Union, in a global diplomatic, political, and economic rivalry and an arms race that would last for over forty years. Second, the major European empires collapsed as nation after nation in Asia and Africa achieved independence. Meanwhile, technological, scientific, and social changes occurred at a dizzying pace.

At the beginning of the century, Western societies generally believed that scientific and technological advances would lead to higher standards of living for people around the globe. The work of pioneers such as the Wright brothers in aviation and Henry Ford in the automotive industry (review Readings 1.1 and 1.2) changed lifestyles for millions around the world. In Reading 17.2, David Brinkley, a noted journalist and political commentator, details the enormous cultural changes caused by television, another major innovation of the twentieth century. Television and other forms of electronic media continue to have an astounding impact on societies throughout the world.

In contrast, only a few intellectuals, such as Tolstoy (review Reading 1.3), questioned the unmitigated benefits provided by faster means of transportation and the production of a myriad of new consumer goods, but, by the end of the century, the steady growth of consumerism and its accompanying environmental pollution had become a major concern. In Reading 14.2, Alan Durning addresses the complex interrelationships between consumerism and environmental degradation.

The struggle for gender equality has been another major trend of the twentieth century. In the beginning of the century, Emmeline Pankhurst and the suffragists fought for the right to vote (review Reading 2.2). In the 1990s, women are still organizing to demand equal pay for equal work, improved education and health care for themselves and their families, and better legal protections. Reports from the United Nations on the world's women (Reading 14.1) and from the International Conference on Women in Beijing (Reading 21.1A) both focus on these vital issues. Readings 18.3A and 18.3B describe specific problems of Indian women working in agricultural and professional jobs. The problems faced by Indian women are typical of most women in poor, predominantly agricultural nations in the Southern Hemisphere. Reading 21.1B offers a similar first-hand account by a Native American woman on the struggles of indigenous peoples.

In the United States, standards of living and consumerism rose for many, but numerous social and racial problems remained. The struggle for racial equality and equal rights for all citizens had been an ongoing one. In the beginning of the century, W. E. B. DuBois and others organized and fought for greater rights for African Americans, other people of color, and women (review Reading 8.1). During the 1950s and 1960s, a vibrant civil rights movement emerged to demand many of the same reforms. Martin Luther King, Jr.'s program of nonviolence mirrored programs advocated by M. K. Gandhi (review Reading 10.1), the Indian nationalist leader. King was one of the most effective voices in the civil rights movement. For his work in the nonviolent civil rights movement, King was awarded the Nobel Peace Prize in 1964. The civil rights movement led to government legislation to provide at least partial legal guarantees for equal rights. In what many consider his most moving address, President Lyndon Johnson urged Congress, in an unprecedented joint session, to adopt the Civil Rights Bill of 1965 (Reading 17.1). Johnson's support for civil rights legislation and his behind-the-scenes "politicking" undoubtedly helped to secure the passage of the then highly controversial bill.

The readings in Chapter 15 focus on the Cold War, offering two conflicting responses to the conflict from American and Soviet perspectives (Readings 15.1A and 15.1B). The impact of the Berlin Wall, long the visual symbol of the Cold War, is described in Reading 15.2A, while the collapse of the Berlin Wall in 1989, which in many ways marked the end of the Cold War, is explained in Reading 15.3. The Cuban Missile Crisis, the most dangerous confrontation of the Cold War, is described in President Kennedy's response to the placement of Soviet missiles in Cuba (Reading 15.2B).

Western and other nations were also confronted by divisions between conservative and socialist forces throughout the century (review Readings 2.1 and 4.3). In many European nations and the United States, voters tend to shift from liberal or leftist to conservative parties and then back again. The socialist West German chancellor (1969–1974), Willy Brandt (Reading 16.2), and the conservative British prime minister (1979–1990), Margaret Thatcher, who moved to dismantle the British welfare state (Reading 16.3), represented these two opposing forces. In France, Charles de Gaulle, the president from 1958 to 1969, preceded Brandt in attempting to overcome the rigidity of Cold War divisions that had divided Europe in half. The readings by de Gaulle and Brandt (16.1 and 16.2) both address crucial aspects of Europe's role in the Cold War.

Governments in much of Latin and South America also swung from right to left. Readings 17.3A and 17.3B highlight this trend, describing the populist regime of Juan and Eva Peron in Argentina and Che Guevara's support for Marxist revolutions in Cuba and Bolivia. Peron's personalist dictatorship was typical of many military, one-man dictatorships in other Latin and African nations. At the same time, some Asian and African nations adopted socialist and revolutionary programs (review Reading 10.2; see 19.1). After Japan's defeat in World War II, the United States dismantled Japan's rightist regime and instituted a new democratic constitution, which proved remarkably durable and became the underpinnings for Japan's remarkable economic recovery (Reading 18.1).

By the 1970s, most of the nations of Asia, the Middle East, and Africa had gained their independence and had begun the long and often arduous task of political and economic development. Frantz Fanon, one of the foremost spokespersons for revolutionary struggles, articulated the negative legacies of imperialism and the goals of Third World peoples in *The Wretched of the Earth* (Reading 19.1A) and a host of other essays. Fanon's works had an enormous impact on young people and political leaders in the 1960s and 1970s. In Kenya, the Mau Mau movement and Jomo Kenyatta led armed and political struggles against British domination and white settlers, much as the Irish had fought against British control in earlier decades (review Reading 6.2). Reading 19.1B describes the reaction of one young Kenyan student to the independence movement during this era of upheaval and change. In Reading 19.2A, Julius Nyerere, leader of the newly independent nation of Tanzania, highlights the importance of education and self-reliance for African nations.

Readings 20.1A and 20.1B detail similar struggles against imperial control in Egypt and describe the popular support for Egyptian leader Gamal Abdul Nasser's calls for secular nationalism and Arab unity. Like other African and Arab leaders, Nasser also sought to destroy the remnants of feudalism, to institute land reform, and to modernize his nation.

The struggle for self-determination in southern Africa and the conflict between the Israelis and Palestinians proved to be two of the most intractable problems of the century. In his autobiography, *Long Walk to Freedom,* Nelson Mandela, leader of the African National Congress (ANC) and president of South Africa from 1995, traces his long fight against the apartheid system and his support of full political suffrage for all South Africans, regardless of their color (Reading 19.2B). In Readings 20.2A and 20.2B, Golda Meir and Hanan Ashrawi describe their respective commitments to Israeli and Palestinian nationalism. Both movingly comment on their emotional responses to the declaration of independence of their respective nations. Both are also keenly aware that major problems remain unresolved in the complex Israeli-Palestinian relationship.

The last two readings (21.2A and 21.2B) focus on present and future problems from historical perspectives. Wole Soyinka, the Novel Prize–winning Nigerian novelist, presents an overview of nationalism—one of the most enduring trends of the twentieth century. Soyinka compares and contrasts the political development of many nations in Africa and Europe. He concludes with a basic question: "What is a nation?" In *Summer Meditations,* Vaclav Havel, a noted author and president of the Czech republic, addresses many of the same issues. Like the long imprisoned and now exiled Chinese dissident, Wei Jingsheng (Reading 18.2), Havel, once an impassioned dissident himself, makes a plea for human rights. Havel concludes that nations should be founded on morality, democracy, and civility in political discourse. Thus, as the century draws to a close, the struggles for human dignity and equal rights continue around the world.

CHAPTER FOURTEEN

Women, Households, Consumption, and the Environment: Interrelated Issues in the Postwar Era

In the decades after World War II, impressive and far-reaching changes occurred in scientific-technological spheres, such as space travel, electronics, and genetics. Some of these developments were stimulated by wartime occurrences and the Cold War that followed. Space exploration was one example. In 1969, U.S. astronauts reached and explored the moon. This event was watched by millions around the world on their television sets. The development of television, computers, and other electronic devices helped usher in an Information Age, which transformed the ways people obtained information and spent their working and leisure time.

These and other scientific-technological developments had a significant impact on many other economic, social, political, and cultural aspects of life. The development and spread of the contraceptive pill, for example, had important repercussions for women and family planning. Numerous technological innovations greatly increased the production of consumer products. Already, at the beginning of the century, Leo Tolstoy had stated that "industry is more and more diverted to the production of the most unnecessary, stupid, depraving products . . . and no end can be foreseen to these inventions." (Review Reading 1.3.) Mass production, however, was just beginning, and, as it picked up speed throughout the century, so, too, did mass consumption, despite some temporary downturns, such as the Great Depression (review the introduction to Part 2 and Chapter 9). After World War II, the development of television and television advertising greatly stimulated increased consumption around the world. Unfortunately, however, increased consumption also caused many environmental problems.

The first reading deals with the most important changes affecting women and households; the second reading concentrates on increased consumption and its effect on the environment. Neither selection deals much with the subject of the other, yet obvious links exist. Already, in 1915, almost 90 percent of U.S. consumer spending was done by women. In 1969, one feminist wrote, "Women are essential to the economy not only as free labor, but also as consumers. The American system of capitalism depends for its survival on the consumption of vast amounts of socially wasteful goods, and a prime target for the unloading of this waste is the housewife. She is the purchasing agent for the family."[1] The second reading notes, "Some 93% of American teenage girls surveyed in 1987 deemed shopping their favorite pastime." Just as in Chapter 4, where the question of gender differences regarding war and peace arose, so, too, here the question arises of gender differences regarding consumers and consumption. Do women shop more than men? If so, is this true globally or only in certain societies? How is the type of purchases made related to one's gender and self-identification?

[1] Dixon, Marlene. "The Rise of Women's Liberation" in *Masculine/Feminine: Readings in Sexual Mythology and the Liberation of Women,* eds. Betty Roszak and Theodore Roszak (New York: Harper Colophon Books, 1969), p. 194. The 1915 figure is from Thomas J. Schlereth, *Victorian America: Transformations in Everyday Life, 1876–1915* (New York: HarperCollins Publishers, 1991), p. 141.

READING 14.1

A United Nations Report on the World's Women, 1970–1990

In the 1960s, U.S. women sharply escalated their demands for equality. One indication of this was the formation (in 1966) and subsequent activities of the National Organization for Women (NOW). In their quest for equality, women's movement leaders in the United States and other countries also soon began looking beyond national borders and lobbied international bodies such as the United Nations. By 1975, the United Nations had become increasingly active in promoting the equality of women. It declared 1975 as International Women's Year and convened an International Women's Year Conference in Mexico City. In December of that year, the UN declared that the decade 1976 to 1985 was to be the "UN Decade for Women." The first UN women's conference in 1975 was followed by others in 1980 (Copenhagen), 1985 (Nairobi), and 1995 (Beijing). (See Reading 21.1A for more on the Beijing Conference.) Although the results of these international conferences often failed fully to satisfy women's movement advocates, the conferences did help to globalize women's networks and issues.

The following selection not only presents UN data on women from 1970 to 1990 but also clearly advocates the need for more progress in obtaining gender equality. The reading, however, is primarily concerned with the position of women in Africa, Asia, and Latin America. To supplement these data and illustrate tendencies in countries such as the United States and those of western Europe, it is helpful to cite some statistics relating to U.S. women, family life, and households. In 1960, about 35 percent of all college graduates were women; by 1991, the percentage had shot up to 54 percent. In this same period, the average age of U.S. women when first married rose from 20.3 to 24.1; the birth rate declined by about one-third; the divorce rate more than doubled; births to unwed mothers increased as a fraction of total births from about 1 in 20 to about 6 in 20; and, among married women residing with their husbands, the proportion of those who were employed outside the home went from about one-fourth to about two-thirds. In the early 1990s, more than half of all U.S. children were spending at least some of their childhood in single-parent households. Outside of the United States, similar trends were evident in other major, technologically advanced countries.

Consider this: the number of illiterate women rose from 543 million in 1970 to 597 million in 1985, while the number of illiterate men rose from 348 million to 352 million.

And this: women work as much as or more than men everywhere—as much as 13 hours, on average, more each week according to studies in Asia and Africa.

And this: of 8,000 abortions in Bombay after parents learned the sex of the fetus through amniocentesis, only one would have been a boy.

Numbers can thus give words considerable power—the power to change.

The World's Women, 1970–1990: Trends and Statistics. New York: United Nations, 1991, pp. 1–7. Footnotes appearing in the text are not included.

REGIONAL TRENDS: 1970–1990

Over the past 20 years there have been important changes in what women do—out of choice or necessity, depending on the hardships and opportunities they face.

In *Latin America and the Caribbean,* women in urban areas made some significant gains according to indicators of health, child-bearing, education and economic, social and political participation. But there was little change in rural areas, and the serious macroeconomic deterioration of many Latin American countries in the 1980s undercut even the urban gains as the decade progressed.

In *sub-Saharan Africa,* there was some improvement for women in health and education, but indicators in these fields are still far from even minimally acceptable levels in most countries. Fertility remains very high, and there are signs that serious economic decline—coupled with rapid population growth—is undermining even the modest gains in health and education. Women's economic and social participation and contribution is high in sub-Saharan Africa. But given the large differences between men and women in most economic, social and political indicators at the start of the 1970s, the limited progress in narrowing those differences since then and the general economic decline, the situation for women in Africa remains grave.

In *northern Africa and western Asia,* women made gains in health and education. Fertility declined slightly but remains very high—5.5 children in northern Africa and 5.3 in western Asia. Women in these regions continue to lag far behind in their economic participation and in social participation and decision-making.

In *southern Asia,* women's health and education improved somewhat. But as in Africa, indicators are still far from minimally acceptable levels—and are still very far from men's. Nor has economic growth, when it has occurred, helped women—apparently because of their low social, political and economic participation in both urban and rural areas.

In much of *eastern and south-eastern Asia,* women's levels of living improved steadily in the 1970s and 1980s. Many of the inequalities between men and women—in health, education and employment—were reduced in both urban and rural areas and fertility also declined considerably. Even so, considerable political and economic inequalities persist in much of the region—because women are confined to the lowest paid and lowest status jobs and sectors and because they are excluded from decision-making.

Throughout the *developed regions,* the health of women is generally good and their fertility is low. But in other fields, indicators of the status of women show mixed results. Women's economic participation is high in eastern Europe and the USSR, northern Europe and northern America—lower in Australia, Japan, New Zealand and southern and western Europe. Everywhere occupational segregation and discrimination in wages and training work very much in favour of men. In political participation and decision-making, women are relatively well represented only in northern Europe and (at least until recently) eastern Europe and the USSR.

GAPS IN POLICY, INVESTMENT AND PAY

. . . Major gaps in policy, investment and earnings prevent women from performing to their full potential in social, economic and political life.

Policy Gaps

Integration of Women in Mainstream Development Policies.   The main policy gap is that governments seldom integrate the concerns and interests of women into mainstream policies. Development policies typically emphasize export-oriented growth centered on cash crops, primary commodities and manufactures—largely controlled by men. Those policies typically neglect the informal sector and subsistence agriculture—the usual preserve of women. Even when women are included in mainstream development strategies, it is often in marginal women-in-development activities.

Much of this gap is embodied in laws that deny women equality with men in their rights to own land, borrow money and enter contracts. Even where women now have *de jure* equality, the failures to carry out the law deny equality de facto. Consider Uganda, which has a new constitution guaranteeing full equality for women. One women's leader there had this assessment: "We continue to be second-rate citizens—no, third-rate, since our sons come before us. Even donkeys and tractors sometimes get better treatment."

Counting Women's Work.   A second policy gap is that governments do not consider much of women's work to be economically productive and thus do not count it. If women's unpaid work in subsistence agriculture and housework and family care were fully counted in labour force statistics, their share of the labour force would be equal to or greater than men's. And if their unpaid housework and family care were counted as productive outputs in national accounts, measures of global output would increase 25 to 30 per cent.

Even when governments do consider women's work to be economically productive, they overlook or undervalue it. . . .

Investment Gaps

Education.   There also are big gaps between what women could produce and the investments they command. Households—and governments—almost always invest less in women and girls than in men and boys. One measure of this is enrollment in school: roughly 60 per cent of rural Indian boys and girls enter primary school, but after five years, only 16 per cent of the girls are still enrolled, compared with 35 per cent of the boys.

The losses from investing less in girls' education are considerable. . . .

One consequence of women's low educational achievement is that it puts them at a disadvantage to their husbands when making major life decisions about the work they do, the number of children they have and the way they invest family income.

Health Services.   Another investment gap is in health services. Women need, and too seldom receive, maternal health care and family planning services. And families often give lower priority to the health care of girls than boys. Where health services are being cut back, as they so often are under economic austerity programmes, the health needs of women are typically neglected.

Productivity.   These gaps in investing in women's development persist in the investments that governments might make to increase their economic productivity. Governments give little or no support to activities in which women predominate—notably, the informal sector and subsistence agriculture. Indeed, government policies typically steer women into less productive endeavours. The infrastructure that might underpin their work is extremely inadequate. And the credit available to them from formal lending institutions is negligible. Often illiterate, usually lacking collateral and almost always discriminated against, women must rely on their husbands or on high-priced money-lenders if they want to invest in more productive ventures.

Pay Gaps

Lower Pay.   There also are big gaps between what women produce and what they are paid. Occupational segregation and discrimination relegate women to low-paying, low-status jobs. And even when women do the same work as men, they typically receive less pay—30 to 40 per cent less on average world-wide. Nor are their prospects for advancement the same as men's, with deeply rooted prejudices blocking them from the top.

No Pay.   Another pay gap is that much of women's work is not paid and not recognized as economically productive. The work is considered to be of no economic importance and is not counted, which brings the discussion back to policy gaps.

TRENDS IN CHILD-BEARING AND FAMILY LIFE

Giving women the means to regulate their child-bearing enhances their ability to shape their own lives. Modern family planning methods make it far easier for women today to limit their fertility—and as important, to pick the timing and spacing of their births. Almost everywhere, the access to and the use of family planning are increasing, but not as rapidly as they might.

Fertility rates are declining in many developing countries but remain at quite high levels in most countries in Africa, in the southern Asia region and in countries of western Asia. Influencing the falling rates are broader use of effective family planning methods, changing attitudes about desired family size and reductions in infant mortality. With the spread of modern contraception, women are better able to limit their fertility. But safe contraception must be available and accepted by both women and men, and in some societies men often do not allow women to practice family planning.

The child-bearing gap between developed and developing regions remains wide. In Asia and Africa, a woman typically has her first child at about age 19 or even earlier, her last at 37, for a child-bearing span of 18 years. In some countries—such as Bangladesh, Mauritania, Nigeria, the Sudan and Yemen—girls often start having children at age 15. Compare this with developed regions, where a woman typically has her first child at 23 and her last at 30, for a span of only seven years. Women in developed regions have fewer children over a shorter span of years and thus need to devote a smaller part of their lives to child-bearing and parenting.

Family planning and health services have helped women in many ways—improving their overall health status and that of their children and increasing their opportunities to take an expanded role in society.

Child-bearing exposes women to a particular array of health risks. But the broader availability of family planning and maternal health services has reduced some of the risks of pregnancy and childbirth. . . . Complications from child-bearing nevertheless remain a major (avoidable) cause of death for women in many developing countries—especially where family planning services are poor or hard to reach, where malnutrition is endemic among pregnant women and where births are not attended by trained personnel.

Healthier mothers are more likely to have full-term pregnancies and strong children. With more resources, they are better able to nurture their children. Better educated mothers are more likely to educate their children. The positive outcome: healthier, better educated families.

Poor women generally miss out on this positive cycle. Because they have little or no education, they have little knowledge of health practices and limited economic opportunities. They have no collateral for borrowing to invest in more productive activities. Simply trying to ensure that the family survives takes all their time. The unhappy outcome: sick, poorly educated families—and continuing poverty.

Poor teenage girls, the most vulnerable of mothers, face even greater obstacles. Cultural pressures, scant schooling and inadequate information about and access to family planning make them most likely to have unhealthy or unwanted pregnancies. In developed and developing countries alike, mothers aged 15–19 are twice as likely to die in childbirth as mothers in their early twenties, and those under 15 are five times as likely. They are less likely to obtain enough education or training to ensure a good future for themselves and their children.

Trends in Marriages and Households

In developed and developing regions alike, women now spend less time married and fewer years bearing and rearing children. Couples are marrying later and separating or divorcing more, in part because of their increased mobility and migration.

Throughout much of the world—the exceptions are in Asia and the Pacific—households are getting smaller and have fewer children. There are fewer multigenerational households, more single-parent families and more people living alone. Smaller households suggest the gradual decline of the extended family household, most evident in western developed countries, but also beginning to be apparent in developing countries. Also evident is a decline in the strength of kinship and in the importance of family responsibility combined with greater reliance on alternative support systems and greater variations in living arrangements.

Because more women are living (or forced to live) alone or as heads of households with dependents, their responsibility for their family's survival and their own has been increasing since 1970. Motherhood is more often unsupported by marriage and the elderly are more often unsupported by their children—trends that increase the burden on women. And even for women living with men, the man's income is often so inadequate that the woman must take on the double burden of household management and outside work to make ends meet.

Women face another burden that is invisible to the outside world: domestic violence. It is unmeasured but almost certainly very extensive. Domestic violence is masked by secretiveness and poor evidence, and there are social and legal barriers to its active prevention. Men's attacks on women in their homes are thought to be the least reported of crimes—in part because such violence is seen as a social ill, not a crime. Women's economic independence—and the corresponding ability to leave an abusive man—are essential for preventing violence and for fostering self-esteem. And as the awareness of women's rights becomes more universal and enforceable, more women will be opposing domestic violence.

ECONOMIC LIFE

Economic growth in many of the developed regions has provided new opportunities for women in economic participation, production and income—despite persistent occupational and wage discrimination and the continuing exclusion of women's unpaid housework from economic measurement.

Some countries in Asia and a few in other developing regions were also able to sustain strong economic growth rates, again providing new opportunities for women despite even more pervasive social and economic obstacles. . . . And whether in circumstances of economic growth or decline, women have been called on to bear the greater burdens, and receive the fewest benefits.

Women are the first to be dismissed from the salaried labour force by economic downturns and the contractions under stabilization and adjustment programmes. With essentials less affordable because of rising inflation and falling subsidies, women have little choice but to work harder and longer. And when the demand for workers rises, as in Brazil in the late 1980s, the men find jobs at their old wages while the women must take jobs at even lower pay than before.

Women's Working World

Women's working world continues to differ from men's in the type of work, the pay, the status and the pattern of entering and leaving the work force. The biggest difference is that women continue to bear the burden of managing the household and caring for the family—and that men continue to control the resources for production and the income from it. In agriculture, for example, women continue to be left labour-intensive tasks that consume the most time.

Women everywhere contribute to economic production. As officially measured, 41 per cent of the world's women aged 15 and over—828 million—are economically active. At least another 10–20 per cent of the world's women are economically productive but not counted as part of the labour force because of inadequate measurement.

Women are left to provide child care, to provide food and health care, to prepare and process crops, to market goods, to tend gardens and livestock and to weave cloth, carpets and baskets. Much of this work does not benefit from investment, making it very inefficient and forcing women to work very hard for meagre results. In the worst cases, technological investments end up exploiting women—improving their productivity but barring them from any access or control over the profits.

In Africa and many other parts of the world, women perform most of the agricultural labor, especially in cases in which the men in their family take jobs off the land. Courtesy CARE

The pattern, then, is that women work as much or more than men. Although women spend less time in activities officially counted as economically productive and make much less money, they spend far more in home production. If a woman spends more time in the labour force, she still bears the main responsibility for home and family care, and sleep and leisure are sacrificed.

Economic Participation

Men's participation in the labour force has fallen everywhere. Women's, by contrast, has fallen significantly only in sub-Saharan Africa, where economic crises have been most widespread. Women's share in the total labour force is increasing in most regions.

In many parts of the developed regions, there have been increases in women's economic activity rates over the past two decades. Women's highest shares in wage and salaried employment are in eastern Europe and the Soviet Union, something that could change as new economic policies create widespread unemployment there.

In Africa, most public and wage employees are men, leaving women either in subsistence agriculture or to create whatever opportunities they can in the informal sector.

In Asia and the Pacific, the picture is mixed. Women's economic activity rates (in official statistics) are very low (under 20 per cent) in southern and western Asia, but fairly high (35–40 per cent) in eastern and south-eastern Asia. Women's wage and salary employment rose considerably (from 44 to 57 per cent of the total, excluding southern Asia), reflecting significant expansion of economic opportunities for women.

In Latin America, women's economic participation grew fastest but remained at low levels (31 per cent in urban areas, 14 per cent in rural). The increase reflects greater opportunities in towns and cities as well as greater economic necessities arising from the ongoing economic crisis of the 1980s.

Occupational Segregation and Wage Discrimination

Everywhere in the world the workplace is segregated by sex. Women tend to be in clerical, sales and domestic services and men in manufacturing and transport. Women work in teaching, care-giving and subsistence agriculture and men in management, administration and politics. Looking at job categories in more detail reveals even sharper segregation. For example, in teaching, women predominate in elementary or first level education while men predominate in higher education.

Women hold a mere 10–20 per cent of managerial and administrative jobs worldwide and less than 20 per cent of the manufacturing jobs. In Singapore barely 1 per cent of working women are in managerial work, compared with nearly 10 per cent for a much larger number of working men. Even when women work in male-dominated occupations, they are relegated to the lower echelons. Among all the organizations of the United Nations system, for example, women hold only 3 per cent of the top management jobs and 8 per cent of senior management positions, but 42 per cent of the entry-level civil service slots, suggesting that women are not usually promoted or hired directly into higher levels. Of the top 1,000 corporations in the United States, only two are headed by a woman, a mere 2/10 of 1 per cent.

In every country having data, women's non-agricultural wage rates are substantially lower than men's. In some countries, the gap is around 50 per cent and only in very few is it less than 30 per cent. The average gap is between 30 per cent and 40 per cent and there is no sign that it is substantially narrowing.

Even where women have moved into occupations dominated by men, their income remains lower. Take Canada, where women have made solid inroads into administration, management, engineering, physical sciences, university teaching and law and medicine. Between 1971 and 1981 they accounted for nearly a third of the growth in these professions. Women in these professions earned about 15 per cent more than women in other professional categories but they still lagged 15–20 per cent behind their male counterparts. . . .

PUBLIC LIFE AND LEADERSHIP

Women are poorly represented in the ranks of power, policy and decision-making. Women make up less than 5 per cent of the world's heads of State, heads of major corporations and top positions in international organizations. Women are not just behind in political and managerial equity, they are a long way behind. This is in spite of the fact that women are found in large numbers in low-level positions of public administrations, political parties, trade unions and businesses.

The picture barely improves at other decision-making levels. Fifty United Nations member States have no woman in any of their top echelons of government. Although women have made some incursions in the past 20 years in parliaments and at middle management levels, their representation in these areas still averages less than 10 per cent and less than 20 per cent respectively. . . .

Women continue to be denied equal access to high-status and high-paying positions but there has been some progress since the United Nations Decade for Women began in 1976. Many countries have set up special offices to review complaints of discriminatory practice in political parties, parliaments, unions and professional organizations. Israel, Venezuela and several European countries have quotas to guarantee women more equal participation in the leadership of political parties. Trade unions in Canada, Norway and the United Kingdom have reserved a designated percentage of political seats for women. Women are also defining their own paths in politics. Increasing numbers are entering political life through non-governmental organizations, women's movements and associations of professional women. And women are increasingly active in the politics of their communities and locales.

Community and grass-roots participation have long been an extension of women's traditional place in the community and responsibility for the health and well-being of their families. The past 20 years have seen a burgeoning of groups headed by or heavily made up of women. Discriminatory practices, increasing poverty, violence against women, environmental threats, military build-ups, family and economic imperatives and the negative consequences of economic adjustment and stabilization programmes have all increased women's needs to band together to change conditions or policies. Women in both the developed and the developing regions have discovered that they can translate their efforts to protect themselves into effective political action.

DEMANDS FOR EQUAL STATUS

International efforts to establish the rights of women culminated in 1979 with the General Assembly's adoption of the Convention on the Elimination of All Forms of Discrimination against Women. . . .

Even with progress in legislation, women—especially poor women—are still a long way from receiving social recognition for what they do. De facto discrimination on the grounds of sex is insidious but widespread. For example, the Bangladesh Constitution guarantees the equal rights of men and women and sanctions affirmative action programmes in favour of women but as the data in the following chapters reveal, the status of women in Bangladesh is among the lowest in the world. It is encouraging, then, that policy makers there have stepped up efforts to implement programmes for women, particularly in health and education.

Many societies deny women independence from family and male control, particularly where girls are married at a very young age to much older men. According to estimates from the World Fertility Survey, almost half the women in Africa, 40 per cent in Asia and 30 per cent in Latin America are married by the age of 18. Men are on average four to eight years older. And a woman's social status is often linked entirely to her reproductive role. Failure to bear children—or even to bear sons—is cause for ostracism, divorce and even brutality in areas of Africa and southern Asia.

BOX 1.1

MILESTONES OF ADVOCACY FOR WOMEN'S EQUALITY

Women, more than ever, are on the global agenda, as a result of 30 years of constant advocacy and pressure.

1946 The United Nations Commission on the Status of Women is formed to monitor the situation of women and promote women's rights around the world.

1952 The Commission initiates the Convention on the Political Rights of Women, the first global mandate to grant women equal political rights under the law—the right to vote, hold office and exercise public functions.

1957 and **1962** Conventions initiated on the equality of married women, guaranteeing them equal rights in marriage and in dissolving marriage.

1967 Declaration on the Elimination of Discrimination against Women.

1975 International Women's Year. The World Conference on Women in Mexico City proclaims 1976–1985 as the United Nations Decade for Women: Equality, Development, Peace. Agencies are asked to collect thorough statistical information on women for the first time.

1979 The United Nations General Assembly adopts the Convention on the Elimination of all Forms of Discrimination against Women.

1980 The World Conference on Women in Copenhagen adopts the Programme of Action for the Second Half of the United Nations Decade for Women: Equality, Development and Peace. Agencies are asked to prepare the most recent data and time-trend analyses on the situation of women.

1985 The Nairobi World Conference reviews progress during the decade for women and adopts the Forward-looking Strategies for the Advancement of Women.

READING 14.2

Increasing Consumption and the Environment

Since the end of World War II, certainly one of the most important changes affecting everyday life, especially in the more affluent regions of the world, has been the production of a vast array of new products, such as televisions and computers. It is mainly because of the widespread use of such products that many people believe they are more fortunate than earlier generations. In the following selection, however, Alan Durning raises questions similar to those which Tolstoy (quoted by Durning) raised in Reading 1.3 in Part 1: Are the better-off people of the world consuming too much? How does increased consumption affect different parts of the world? Has the availability of so many new products led to greater happiness? Durning is a senior researcher at the Worldwide Institute, a group that focuses on environmental concerns, and his article reflects such concerns more than does Tolstoy's earlier piece, even though Tolstoy was more environmentally aware than most writers of his time—not until the 1960s did environmental awareness begin spreading beyond a small number of people. Both the Durning and Tolstoy selections, however, are responses to the ever-increasing ability of modern technology to provide more and more goods; both pieces criticize certain practices of capitalism that contribute to "overconsumption," and both challenge, primarily from a moralistic position, overwhelmingly popular consumption tendencies.

Durning's selection stimulates thought and questions on numerous related issues. Although he writes of "the tidal wave of consumer demand" that has arisen after the collapse of communist regimes in eastern Europe and of the negative environmental impact of overconsumption, which capitalism encourages, he does not mention the terrible environmental record of communist governments. Is it not true that both capitalist and communist systems have failed to provide adequate incentives to safeguard the environment? Can capitalism produce more widespread prosperity without also bringing about an ever-increasing global consumption that causes serious environmental degradation?

Increasing consumption not only has produced severe environmental consequences but has also had a major impact on culture and the way we think and relate to others. Historian Eric Hobsbawm has cited the "universal triumph of the society of mass consumption" as a major factor undermining "classical high culture." He adds, "From the 1960s on the images which accompanied human beings in the Western world—and increasingly in the urbanized Third World—from birth to death were those advertising or embodying consumption or dedicated to commercial mass entertainment."[1] By the mid-1990s, the average U.S. citizen by age twenty had been bombarded by 1 million commercials.

By the 1990s, mass consumption and mass entertainment (including sports) had become inextricably interwoven, especially in the United States. Popular entertainers often benefitted from some of the same type of marketing that sold popular products. Advertisers had a strong impact on television programming, and movie, television, and sports personalities increasingly advertised a wide range of products (sometimes, as with golfers, simply by displaying a brand name or logo on their clothing). As Durning indicates, sports stadiums and arenas displayed a growing number of advertisements. Even many schools beamed ads at their students in exchange for the educational programs that accompanied these advertisements. Celebrities excelling in one area increasingly took advantage of their fame to cross over into other media spheres: for example, a sports hero popularized in part by television and the press might act in films or write (or have ghostwritten) an autobiography. It is hardly surprising that in the 1990s many of the highest incomes in the United States were earned by those engaged in sports or other forms of entertainment and that "celebrityitis" had reached unprecedented levels.

Early in the age of affluence that followed World War II, an American retailing analyst named Victor Lebow proclaimed, "Our enormously productive economy . . . demands that we make consumption our way of life, that we convert the buying and use of goods into rituals, that we seek our spiritual satisfaction, our ego satisfaction, in consumption. . . . We need things consumed, burned up, worn out, replaced, and discarded at an ever increasing rate." Americans have responded to Mr. Lebow's call, and much of the world has followed. . . .

---

[1]*The Age of Extremes: A History of the World, 1914–1991* (New York, Vintage Books, 1996), p. 513.

Durning, Alan. "Asking How Much Is Enough," *State of the World 1991*. Eds. Lester R. Brown et al. New York: W. W. Norton & Company, 1991, pp. 153–165. References and charts appearing in the text are not included.

Overconsumption by the world's fortunate is an environmental problem unmatched in severity by anything but perhaps population growth. Their surging exploitation of resources threatens to exhaust or unalterably disfigure forests, soils, water, air, and climate. Ironically, high consumption may be a mixed blessing in human terms too. The time-honored values of integrity of character, good work, friendship, family, and community have often been sacrificed in the rush to riches. Thus, many in the industrial lands have a sense that their world of plenty is somehow hollow—that, hoodwinked by a consumerist culture, they have been fruitlessly attempting to satisfy what are essentially social, psychological, and spiritual needs with material things. . . .

THE CONSUMING SOCIETY

Skyrocketing consumption is the hallmark of our era. The headlong advance of technology, rising earnings, and consequently cheaper material goods have lifted overall consumption to levels never dreamed of a century ago. The trend is visible in statistics for almost any per capita indicator. Worldwide, since mid-century the intake of copper, energy, meat, steel, and wood has approximately doubled; car ownership and cement consumption have quadrupled; plastic use has quintupled; aluminum consumption has grown sevenfold; and air travel has multiplied 32 times.

Moneyed regions account for the largest waves of consumption since 1950. In the United States, the world's premier consuming society, on average people today own twice as many cars, drive two-and-a-half times as far, use 21 times as much plastic, and travel 25 times as far by air as did their parents in 1950. Air conditioning spread from 15 percent of households in 1960 to 64 percent in 1987, and color televisions from 1 to 93 percent. Microwave ovens and video cassette recorders found their way into almost two thirds of American homes during the eighties alone. . . .

Japan and Western Europe have displayed parallel trends. . . . The collapse of socialist governments in Eastern Europe, meanwhile, unleashed a tidal wave of consumer demand that had gone unsatisfied in the region's ossified state-controlled economies. A young man in a Budapest bar captured his country's mood when he told a western reporter: "People in the West think that we in Hungary don't know how they live. Well, we do know how they live, and we want to live like that, too." Says German banker Ulrich Ramm, "The East Germans want cars, videos and Marlboros." . . .

The late eighties saw some poor societies begin the transition to consuming ways. In China, the sudden surge in spending on consumer durables shows up clearly in data from the State Statistical Bureau: between 1982 and 1987, color televisions spread from 1 percent to 35 percent of urban Chinese homes, the share with washing machines quadrupled from 16 to 67 percent, and refrigerators grew in prevalence from 1 percent to 20 percent of homes.

Meanwhile, in India, the emergence of a middle class with perhaps 100 million members, along with liberalization of the consumer market and the introduction of buying on credit, has led to explosive growth in sales of everything from automobiles and motorbikes to televisions and frozen dinners. The *Wall Street Journal* gloats, "The traditional conservative Indian who believes in modesty and savings is gradually giving way to a new generation that thinks as freely as it spends."

Few would begrudge anyone the simple advantages of cold food storage or mechanized clothes washing. The point, rather, is that even the non-western nations with the longest histories are increasingly emulating the high-consumption style of life. The lure of "modern" things is hard to resist: Coca-Cola soft drink is sold in more than 160 countries, and "Dallas," the television series that portrays the richest class of Americans, is avidly followed in many of the world's poorest nations.

Long before all the world's people could achieve the American dream, however, the planet would be laid waste. The world's 1 billion meat eaters, car drivers, and throw-away consumers are responsible for the lion's share of the damage humans have caused to common global resources. . . . Industrial nations account for close to two thirds of global use of steel, more than two thirds of aluminum, copper, lead, nickel, tin, and zinc, and three fourths of energy.

Those in the wealthiest fifth of humanity have built more than 99 percent of the world's nuclear warheads. Their appetite for wood is a driving force behind destruction of the tropical rain forests, and the resulting extinction of countless species. Over the past century, their economies have pumped out two thirds of the greenhouse gases that threaten the earth's climate, and each year their energy use releases perhaps three fourths of the sulfur and nitrogen oxides that cause acid rain. Their industries generate most of the world's hazardous chemical wastes, and their air conditioners, aerosol sprays, and factories release almost 90 percent of the chlorofluorocarbons that destroy the earth's protective ozone layer. Clearly, even 1 billion profligate consumers is too much for the earth.

Beyond the environmental costs of acquisitiveness, some perplexing findings of social scientists throw doubt on the wisdom of high consumption as a personal and national goal: rich societies have had little success in turning consumption into fulfillment. Regular surveys by the National Opinion Research Center of the University of Chicago reveal, for example, that no more Americans report they are "very happy" now than in 1957. The share has fluctuated around one third since then, despite a doubling of personal consumption expenditures per capita. Whatever Americans are buying, it does not seem to be enough. . . .

Measured in constant dollars, the world's people have consumed as many goods and services since 1950 as all previous generations put together. . . . Since 1940 Americans alone have used up as large a share of the earth's mineral resources as did everyone before them combined. . . .

IN SEARCH OF SUFFICIENCY

Some guidance on what the earth can sustain emerges from an examination of current consumption patterns around the world. For three of the most ecologically important types of consumption—transportation, diet, and use of raw materials—the world's people are distributed unevenly over a vast range. Those at the bottom clearly fall below the "too little" line, while those at the top, in what could be called the cars-meat-and-disposables class, clearly consume too much. . . .

. . . The world's automobile class is relatively small: only 8 percent of humans, about 400 million people, own cars. Their vehicles are directly responsible for an estimated

Junked cars in the United States, where more cars are driven than anywhere else in the world, symbolize many aspects of the consuming and disposing society. EPA Documeria

13 percent of carbon dioxide emissions from fossil fuels worldwide, along with air pollution, acid rain, and a quarter-million traffic fatalities a year.

Car owners bear indirect responsibility for the far-reaching impacts of their chosen vehicle. The automobile makes itself indispensable: cities sprawl, public transit atrophies, shopping centers multiply, workplaces scatter. . . . Today, working Americans spend nine hours a week behind the wheel. To make these homes-away-from-home more comfortable, 90 percent of new cars have air-conditioning, doubling their contribution to climate change and adding emissions of ozone-depleting chlorofluorocarbons. . . .

The global food consumption ladder has three rungs. At the bottom, the world's 630 million poorest people are unable to provide themselves with a healthy diet according to the latest World Bank estimates. On the next rung, the 3.4 billion grain eaters of the world's middle class get enough calories and plenty of plant-based protein, giving them the healthiest basic diet of the world's people. They typically receive less than 20 percent of their calories from fat, a level low enough to protect them from the consequences of excessive dietary fat.

The top of the ladder is populated by the meat eaters, those who obtain close to 40 percent of their calories from fat. These 1.25 billion people eat three times as much fat per person as the remaining 4 billion, mostly because they eat so much red meat. . . . The meat class pays the price of its diet in high death rates from the so-called diseases of affluence—heart disease, stroke, and certain types of cancer. . . .

The earth also pays for the high-fat diet. Indirectly, the meat-eating quarter of humanity consumes nearly 40 percent of the world's grain—grain that fattens the livestock they eat. Meat production is behind a substantial share of the environmental strains induced by the present global agricultural system, from soil erosion to overpumping of underground water. In the extreme case of American beef, producing 1 kilogram of steak requires 5 kilograms of grain and the energy equivalent of 9 liters of gasoline, not to mention the associated soil erosion, water consumption, pesticide and fertilizer runoff, groundwater depletion, and emissions of the greenhouse gas methane. . . .

Processing and packaging add further resource costs to the way the affluent eat. Extensively packaged foods are energy gluttons. . . .

Global beverage consumption reveals a similar pattern. The 1.75 billion people at the bottom are clearly deprived: they have no option but to drink water that is often contaminated with human, animal, and chemical wastes. Those in the next group up, in this case nearly 2 billion people, take more than 80 percent of their liquid refreshment in the form of clean drinking water, with the remainder coming from commercial beverages such as tea, coffee, and, for children, milk. At the quantities consumed, these beverages pose few environmental problems; they are packaged minimally, and transport energy needs are low because they are moved only short distances or in a dry form.

In the top class once again are the billion people in industrial countries. At a growing rate, they imbibe soft drinks, bottled water, and other prepared commercial beverages packaged in single-use containers and transported over great distances—sometimes even across oceans. Ironically, where tap water is purest and most accessible, its use as a beverage is declining. It now typically accounts for only a quarter of drinks in industrial countries. In the extreme case of the United States, per capita consumption of soft drinks rose to 176 liters in 1989 (nearly seven times the global mean), compared with water intake of 141 liters. Americans now drink more soda pop than water from the kitchen sink.

In raw material consumption, the same pattern emerges. . . .

. . . At the top of the heap is the throwaway class, which uses raw materials extravagantly. A typical resident of the industrialized fourth of the world uses 15 times as much paper, 10 times as much steel, and 12 times as much fuel as a Third World resident. The extreme case is again the United States, where the average person consumes most of his or her own weight in basic materials each day—18 kilograms of petroleum and coal, 13 kilograms of other minerals, 12 kilograms of agricultural products, and 9 kilograms of forest products.

In the throwaway economy, packaging becomes an end in itself, disposables proliferate, and durability suffers. Four percent of consumer expenditures on goods in the United States goes for packaging—$225 a year. Likewise, the Japanese use 30 million "disposable" single-roll cameras each year, and the British dump 2.5 billion diapers. Americans toss away 180 million razors annually, enough paper and plastic plates and cups to feed the world a picnic six times a year, and enough aluminum cans to make 6,000 DC-10 airplanes.

Where disposability and planned obsolescence fail to accelerate the trip from cash register to junk heap, fashion sometimes succeeds. Most clothing goes out of style long before it is worn out; lately, the realm of fashion has even colonized sports footwear. Kevin Ventrudo, chief financial officer of California-based L.A. Gear, which saw sales multiply 50 times over in four years, told the *Washington Post,* "If you talk about shoe performance, you only need one or two pairs. If you're talking fashion, you're talking endless pairs of shoes."

In transportation, diet, and use of raw materials, as consumption rises on the economic scale so does waste—both of resources and of health. Bicycles and public transit are cheaper, more efficient, and healthier transport options than cars. A diet founded on the basics of grains and water is gentle to the earth and the body. And a lifestyle that makes full use of raw materials for durable goods without succumbing to the throwaway mentality is ecologically sound while still affording many of the comforts of modernity. Yet despite these arguments in favor of modest consumption, few people who can afford high consumption levels opt to live simply. What prompts us, then, to consume so much?

THE CULTIVATION OF NEEDS

"The avarice of mankind is insatiable," wrote Aristotle 23 centuries ago, describing the way that as each of our desires is satisfied a new one seems to appear in its place. That observation, on which all of economic theory is based, provides the most obvious answer to the question of why people never seem satisfied with what they have. If our wants are insatiable, there is simply no such thing as enough. . . .

. . . Russian novelist Leo Tolstoy [wrote] "Seek among men, from beggar to millionaire, one who is contented with his lot, and you will not find one such in a thousand. . . . Today we must buy an overcoat and galoshes, tomorrow, a watch and a chain; the next day we must install ourselves in an apartment with a sofa and a bronze lamp; then we must have carpets and velvet gowns; then a house, horses and carriages, paintings and decorations."

What distinguishes modern consuming habits from those of interest to . . . Tolstoy, some would say, is simply that we are much richer than our ancestors, and consequently have more ruinous effects on nature. There is no doubt a great deal of truth in that view, but there is also reason to believe that certain forces in the modern world encourage people to act on their consumptive desires as rarely before. Five distinctly modern factors seem to play a role in cultivating particularly voracious appetites: the influence of social pressures in mass societies, advertising, the shopping culture, various government policies, and the expansion of the mass market into the traditional realm of household and local self-reliance.

In the anonymous mass societies of advanced industrial nations, daily interactions with the economy lack the face-to-face character that prevails in surviving local communities. Traditional virtues such as integrity, honesty, and skill are too hard to measure to serve as yardsticks of social worth. By default, they are gradually supplanted by a simple, single indicator—money. As one Wall Street Banker put it bluntly to the *New York Times,* "Net worth equals self-worth." Under this definition, consumption becomes a treadmill, with everyone judging their status by who is ahead and who is behind.

Psychological data from several nations confirm that the satisfaction derived from money does not come from simply having it. It comes from having more of it than others do, and from having more this year than last. Thus, the bulk of survey data reveals that the upper classes in any society are more satisfied with their lives than the lower classes are, but they are no more satisfied than the upper classes of much poorer countries—nor than the upper classes were in the less-affluent past.

More striking, perhaps, most psychological data show that the main determinants of happiness in life are not related to consumption at all: prominent among them are satisfaction with family life, especially marriage, followed by satisfaction with work, leisure, and friendships.

Beyond social pressures, the affluent live completely enveloped in proconsumption advertising messages. The sales pitch is everywhere. One analyst estimates that the typical American is exposed to 50–100 advertisements each morning before nine o'clock. Along with their weekly 22-hour diet of television, American teenagers are typically exposed to 3–4 hours of TV advertisements a week, adding up to at least 100,000 ads between birth and high school graduation.

Marketers have found ever more ways to push their products. Advertisements are broadcast by over 10,000 television and radio stations in the United States, towed behind airplanes, plastered on billboards and in sports stadiums, bounced around the planet from satellites. They are posted on chair-lift poles on ski slopes, and played through closed circuit televisions at bus stops, in subway stations, and on wall-sized video screens at shopping malls.

Ads are piped into classrooms and doctors' offices, woven into the plots of feature films, placed on board games, mounted in bathroom stalls, and played back between rings on public phones in the Kansas City airport. . . .

Advertising has been one of the fastest growing industries during the past half-century. In the United States, ad expenditures rose from $198 per capita in 1950 to $498 in 1989. Total global advertising expenditures, meanwhile, rose from an estimated $39 billion in 1950 to $237 billion in 1988, growing far faster than economic output. Over the same period, per person advertising expenditures grew from $15 to $46. . . . In developing countries, the increases have been astonishing. Advertising billings in India jumped fivefold in the eighties, and South Korea's advertising industry has recently grown 35–40 percent annually. . . .

Particularly in the United States, shopping seems to have become a primary cultural activity. Americans spend 6 hours a week doing various types of shopping, and they go to shopping centers on average once a week—more often than they go to church or synagogue. Some 93 percent of American teenage girls surveyed in 1987 deemed shopping their favorite pastime. . . .

Shopping centers are sprouting across the landscape in many industrial lands. . . .

. . . National economic goals are built squarely on the assumption that more is better. National statistics, for example, refer to people more frequently as consumers than as citizens. Economic policy, because it is based on modern economics' system of partial accounting, views as healthy growth what is often feverish and debilitating overconsumption.

Finally, the sweeping advance of the commercial mass market into realms once dominated by family members and local enterprise has made consumption far more wasteful than in the past, as American history illustrates. . . .

. . . More and more, flush with cash but pressed for time, households opt for the questionable "conveniences" of prepared, packaged foods, miracle cleaning products, and disposable everything—from napkins to shower curtains. All these things, while saving the householders time, cost the earth dearly, and change households from the primary unit of the economy to passive, consuming entities. Shifting one economic activity after another out of the home does boost the gross national product (GNP)—but that is largely a fiction of bookkeeping, an economic sleight of hand.

Like the household, the community economy has atrophied—or been dismembered—under the blind force of the money economy. Shopping malls, superhighways, and "strips" have replaced corner stores, local restaurants, and neighborhood theaters—the very things that help to create a sense of common identity and community in an area. Traditional vegetable stands and fish shops in Japan are giving way to supermarkets and convenience stores; along the way styrofoam and plastic film have replaced yesterday's newspaper as fish wrap. Even in France, where the passion for fresh foods is legend, the microwave and the *grande surface* (shopping mall) are edging out bakeries, dairies, and farmers' markets.

The recycling ethos of the past was built upon a materials economy that valued things, and it embodied that value in institutions. Not long ago in western lands—and to this day in nonindustrial regions—rag pickers, junkyard dealers, scrap collectors, and dairy deliverers kept used materials and containers flowing back into the economy. In the United States, where the demise of local economies is furthest advanced, many neighborhoods are little more than a place to sleep. Americans move, on average, every five years, and develop little attachment to those who live near them.

The search for social status in massive and anonymous societies, omnipresent advertising messages, a shopping culture that edges out nonconsuming alternatives, government biases favoring consumption, and the spread of the commercial market into most aspects of private life—all these things nurture the acquisitive desires that everyone has.

DISCUSSION QUESTION

Changes in the status and conditions of women and households changed greatly in the decades following World War II, as did changes in world consumption patterns and the environmental effects of such changes. Which of these changes do you think will have the greatest long-term effects?

FIFTEEN

The Cold War and Its Impact from the 1940s to the 1980s

Toward the end of World War II, tensions and suspicions between the Soviet Union and its Western allies began to increase; once their mutual wartime enemies were defeated, their chief reason for coming together no longer existed. Differing ideologies, economic and geopolitical interests, and the personalities of U.S. President Harry Truman and Soviet leader Joseph Stalin all played a part in the widening rift that developed. In 1947, U.S. financier and statesman Bernard Baruch declared that "we are in the midst of a cold war." The term came into increasing use after that and referred to the postwar tensions between the USSR-led bloc of communist countries and the Western nations that formed the North Atlantic Treaty Organization (NATO) in 1949.

The Cold War—or "cruel peace," as one historian has labeled it—lasted until the late 1980s. At that point, the actions of Soviet leader Mikhail Gorbachev and numerous others, including opponents of communism in eastern Europe and elsewhere, helped bring it to an end. Although there were many causes of the Gorbachev initiatives that helped end the Cold War, economic considerations were perhaps utmost in his mind. The Soviet economy was stagnating, and Cold War spending was a far greater burden for Soviet citizens than for U.S. citizens. Being a poorer country than the United States, the USSR spent a higher percentage of its national wealth for Cold War purposes. For similar reasons, eastern Europeans suffered more than western Europeans.

During the four decades it existed, the Cold War affected so many spheres of life that it is difficult to imagine how different the world might have become if it had not existed. International affairs, scientific and technological developments, ideological beliefs, governments' relations with their societies, and social and cultural life in numerous countries were all altered by the Cold War.

The following readings indicate some of these Cold War effects. Reading 15.1 points to the Cold War's early influence on cultural life and the intolerance and ideological rigidity it helped to foster on both sides of the "iron curtain"—a term made popular in 1946 by former British Prime Minister Winston Churchill when he spoke of the ideological divide that had come to separate eastern from western Europe.

During the Cold War, both sides realized, as Truman stated in 1950, that it was a "struggle . . . for the minds of men." One of the visible signs of this struggle was the efforts of the U.S. government's Voice of America (VOA), which began Russian language radio broadcasting beamed at the USSR in 1947. In subsequent years, the Soviet government spent millions of dollars attempting to prevent reception by jamming, and the United States reciprocated by also spending large amounts to frustrate and overcome Soviet jamming efforts. When communist governments finally collapsed from 1989 to 1991 in eastern Europe and the Soviet Union, there was little doubt that the appeal of Western culture had played a part. VOA, Radio Free Europe, the British Broadcasting Corporation (BBC), and other Western media and cultural influences had the effect of increasing dissatisfaction with communist life and enticing more imitation of the West, especially among young and better-educated communist citizens.

In 1961, a more concrete symbol of the iron curtain came into existence—the Berlin Wall (see Reading 15.2A). Its erection by communist authorities in August 1961 created the Berlin Crisis of that year. This crisis along with the Cuban Missile Crisis a year later made 1961–1962 the most dangerous period of the Cold War. U.S. President John Kennedy later said that at the time of the Cuban Missile Crisis he thought the chances of the Soviet Union going to war (rather than backing down from the forceful Kennedy response indicated in Reading 15.2B) were between "one out of three and even."

The Berlin Wall stood for almost three decades. Isolating West Berlin from East Berlin and other parts of East Germany, it symbolized the division not only of Berlin but also of Germany, Europe, and a good part of the world beyond. In early November 1989, East German forces and individuals began knocking down portions of the wall (see Reading 15.3). Its collapse and the reunification of Germany in 1990 clearly signalled the end of the Cold War.

Although the readings relating to Berlin depict some of the suffering experienced by its people, Cold War casualties extended far beyond Berlin. Numerous "hot wars," including the Korean War and Vietnam War, were intertwined with the Cold War, killing millions of Asians, roughly 100,000 U.S. soldiers, and unknown numbers of others in areas such as Latin America and Africa. Besides the deaths of these individuals, mostly young men, and the legacy of pain it caused their families, people throughout the world suffered from the diversion of tremendous economic and human resources and energies for Cold War purposes.

It is impossible, however, to know what would have happened if the Cold War had not existed, and some of the phenomena that occurred in this period might have come about regardless. As we have seen in earlier selections, Soviet citizens suffered even more before the Cold War began, not only in World War II but even in the 1930s. Now that the Cold War is over, many nations still allocate great sums of money for military purposes. By far the largest expenditures in recent years have been by the only superpower remaining, the United States. Even without the Cold War, technology and nationalistic rivalries might have led to expensive arms races. Furthermore, scholars still debate the allocation of blame for the Cold War, though there is general agreement that the Soviet Union lost the "war." A more complex question is whether the United States and its allies "won" it or if, as one recent book title suggests, "We All Lost the Cold War."

READING 15.1

Cultural Repercussions of the Cold War in the United States and USSR

As the Cold War developed, its effects were increasingly felt at home (on both sides of the iron curtain), as well as abroad. In the United States, concern with communist subversive activities stimulated President Truman in 1947 to establish a loyalty program. This program led to the resignation or dismissal of more than 3,000 federal employees. Congress also became increasingly active in the fight against subversion. Although recently discovered Russian archival material has demonstrated substantial Soviet subversive activity in the United States, the U.S. government's response sometimes violated U.S. citizens' civil liberties and confused real dangers with imagined ones.

One of the most active congressional bodies in this struggle was the House Committee on Un-American Activities (HUAC). In a series of public hearings, HUAC attacked the Hollywood film industry. In 1947, the committee, which included future president Richard Nixon, cited ten Hollywood personalities, mainly film writers, for contempt because they refused to answer whether or not they were or had been members of the U.S. Communist party. As unpopular as such membership was to most U.S. citizens, the "Hollywood Ten" did have a constitutional right to belong to the party, which they had exercised. A court, however, subsequently convicted the Ten of contempt of Congress, and they were sentenced, most of them to one year's imprisonment. After their release, they discovered that Hollywood studios no longer wished to employ them. In 1951–1952, HUAC conducted more Hollywood hearings. In both sets of hearings, many famous screen personalities appeared, some of them bowing to committee pressure and naming individuals they suspected of being involved in Communist party activities.

In the early 1950s, however, a Wisconsin senator named Joseph McCarthy became even more famous for his anticommunist activities, which became known as McCarthyism. From 1950 to 1954, he charged various individuals with being communists or communist sympathizers. As Republican President Dwight Eisenhower later wrote, "No one was safe from charges recklessly made. . . . Teachers, government employees, and even ministers became vulnerable." Eventually, in December 1954, the U.S. Senate condemned McCarthy for his recklessness. As Reading 15.1A makes clear, however, HUAC continued its activities.

In Nixon's family:
"What's the matter with you, Dick?"
"I dreamt that you were a Communist!"

This cartoon from the Soviet humor magazine *Krokodil* pokes fun at Vice-President (1953–1961) Richard Nixon, suggesting that his anticommunism was obsessive. *Krokodil* cartoons of the 1950s and early 1960s (and beyond) often depicted the United States in an unfavorable light, exaggerating, for example, the extent of the racism, crime, and unemployment that did, indeed, exist within its borders. Courtesy Rodger Swearingen

As a result of HUAC and McCarthyism, Hollywood studios shied away from making any films that might be construed as too leftist, while at the same time producing
more anticommunist films such as *The Red Menace* (1949) and *I Married a Communist* (1950). Various Hollywood organizations, including the Screen Actors Guild
(then headed by future U.S. president Ronald Reagan) and the Motion Picture Alliance for the Preservation of American Ideals (whose members included director John
Ford and actors John Wayne and Clark Gable) displayed a willingness to cooperate
with HUAC in its battle against suspected communist influences in Hollywood. In the
first selection (15.1A), the executive director of the Motion Picture Alliance, screen-
writer Maurice Ries, testifies to his organization's views in a paper prepared for
HUAC and released in 1956.

The second selection (15.1B) points out that the Cold War also influenced culture
in the Soviet Union. Although censorship and persecution of anyone refusing to follow Stalinist guidelines predated the Cold War, the tensions heightened by it led to
new crackdowns against Western influences—this was indicated in a minor way by re-
naming French bread "city bread." Stalin especially feared the West's impact because
the Soviet Union temporarily had relaxed its usual vigilance against the West after the
United States and Great Britain became Soviet allies during World War II. In August
1946, the Soviet government unleashed a major attack against Soviet writers, artists,
and composers for kowtowing to Western cultural influences. The author of 15.1B is
Michel Gordey, a knowledgeable French correspondent of Russian parentage who
spent two months in the Soviet Union in 1950.

READING 15.1A: SEEING RED IN HOLLYWOOD

Yes, there still is communism in Hollywood. Not much. Not nearly so much as there
was once.

But *any* communism is too much communism.

So virulent is the Red disease that even a trace of its infection holds peril. And this is
doubly true when you are dealing with media of propaganda as important as motion pictures. Most psychological warfare specialists think films are the world's most powerful
potential propaganda tool. . . .

Friends and defenders of communism say Communists never succeeded in getting Red
messages into United States films. Although this claim may be debated, it isn't the main
point. Communists never succeeded in gaining undisputed control in Hollywood; but if the
Kremlin ever does attain its goal of dominating the United States motion-picture industry,
does any sane person believe there would be no Communist-line films *then?*

The second aspect of Red infiltration of the motion-picture industry arises out of
man's perfectly natural desire to make a profit on his labor. With its great risks and sometimes fantastic returns, the motion-picture industry in the United States is one of the most
keenly competitive on earth. When producers (meaning the big studios and independent
film makers alike) put money into a picture, they want all the insurance they can get. To
get it, unfortunately, a few will hire any talented individual likely to bring the producer

Ries, Maurice. "Seeing Red in Hollywood," in *Soviet Total War: "Historic Mission" of Violence and De-
ceit.* Washington, DC: Committee on Un-American Activities, United States House of Representatives, 1956,
Vol. 1, pp. 160, 162–68. Footnotes appearing in the text are not included.

sufficient financial reward, regardless of whether he, or she, has a record of affinity for organizations and activities the United States Government has labeled as subversive.

True, making money always has been a premise of the capitalist system and in the United States of America capitalism is the economic way of life. But capital has its responsibilities and should have its standards of morality. In addition to being treasonable, it is quite literally unmoral to give aid and comfort to your country's enemies. And all Communists are enemies.

Enemies, too, are those persons who are not members of the Communist Party but who submit to Communist discipline, and those who, identified under oath as party members, nonetheless manage to squirm through a loophole in the Constitution when they are asked to cooperate with the Government of the United States.

During World War II, any United States citizen who hired a known Japanese spy or one of Adolf Hitler's saboteurs would have been regarded at the very least as insane. Moreover, he would have been held to be dangerous to national security—which he certainly would have been. Today, we are on the defensive in a far more deadly war with international communism. Is it, then, less wrong to give help to these more dangerous foes?

The two aspects of persisting Red influences in Hollywood operate simultaneously— the organized Communist efforts to infiltrate filmdom, and the employment of Communists and pro-Communists on an opportunistically selfish or boxoffice basis. They operate in relation to each other because the first makes the second easier. For if Communists were not seeking systematically to infest the motion-picture industry, there would be few Reds or their stooges on hand for cynical producers to hire. Here is the way that dollar softness on subversion works:

A major studio gives a 7-year writer-producer-director contract to a man who has a public record of being connected with *47* Communist "fronts." Admittedly, this is a man of considerable talent—but what price genius itself when the result helps to destroy freedom? That 7-year contract now links Hollywood with nearly half a hundred organizations working night and day to tear down the Government of the United States and substitute in its place the Red fascism of the Kremlin. Has the studio a conscience? . . .

Hollywood Communist fighters regard the New York stage, together with television there, as prime sources of Red reinfection. To that city have gravitated many former film folk now *persona non grata* on the west coast motion-picture lots by reason of hiding (after being identified under oath as Communists) behind the first and/or fifth amendments to the Constitution. These displaced personages find work in New York, since the live theater there apparently lacks some of the scruples of the screen city. At the same time, television—particularly on the east coast, though TV in Los Angeles has plenty of guilt of its own—appears to be considerably softer on communism than is Hollywood. And, with TV and motion pictures drawing closer and closer to each other, what is more natural than that some television folk should bring renewed Red influences into the film capital? In fact, Chairman Francis Walter, of the House Committee on Un-American Activities, has stated as recently as August 1955 that "During the course of numerous hearings conducted in Los Angeles between 1951 and 1955, it was learned that many individuals alleged to have knowledge of Communist Party activities within this field came to Hollywood from the city of New York.

The Committee on Un-American Activities is so very right in keeping an inquiring eye on the United States entertainment industry. From end to end of the world the industry is enormously influential. . . .

. . . Starting about the middle of 1936, Communist progress was such that by the late thirties and early forties Moscow secretly had clamped a firm grip on the entire American [film] industry. There was a well-organized Hollywood branch of the party, important enough to bypass Communist headquarters in Los Angeles and operate under direct orders from CPUSA headquarters in New York. . . . Iceberg-like, the Hollywood command operated for the most part submerged. Whatever portion was visible appeared in the guise of a legitimate organization of some sort. These "fronts" always were strong and effective—until continuing anti-Communist activities, such as the 1947 and 1951 hearings conducted in the film capital by the House Committee on Un-American Activities, caused them (if the iceberg simile may be belabored a bit) to melt away.

Since 1936 there have been dozens of "fronts" in Hollywood—motion-picture committees for this, citizens against that, and Hollywood's councils on the other. It is significant that today there are none concentrating on the motion-picture industry.

This does not mean Hollywood is "clean." How wonderful if it were. Nonetheless, the situation has improved. If leftwing efforts to wreck the Nation's security program can be blocked . . . it may be possible to check similar, subsidiary destruction in the motion-picture field—and hold onto the victories that have been won in the past 10 years.

Subversive influences in the United States motion-picture industry are far fewer than in some other areas of the Nation's business and professional life: Fewer than in education, for example, or the press. But they exist. Getting rid of them presents a problem. . . .

. . . There are liberals today who are hard on communism abroad while being soft on communism in the United States. They simply refuse to believe that *their* friends can be Communists.

Many who were caught, even lightly, in the Red web in Hollywood appear genuinely unable to comprehend that what they did was bad. It does not matter to them that history has proved it was bad. Some did not know, at the time, that they were being used, and they act as if they do not know it now. Others are well aware that they were had, but, as working members of the Hollywood intelligensia, panic at the thought of admitting any error in judgment. Still others have become anti-anti-Communists as a result of their earlier aberrations in world politics. They fear their onetime association with groups and individuals later unveiled as puppets of Moscow may arise some day to point ghostly fingers at them across the years. Accordingly, they fear and oppose anyone, or any organization, likely to open a closet and let a skeleton out.

Naturally, such professional bleeding hearts as the Fund for the Republic wail that these poor, deluded Hollywoodites, having got themselves into the mess, have been put on "the blacklist." This is supposed to be a shameful, secret catalog operated in the entertainment field by witch-hunting anti-Communists. In the dialectic of dogmatic liberals all anti-Communists are witch hunters and, since witches don't exist, all anti-Communists must be wrong. This disposes of the need for security measures.

Aside from a monumental naivete on the part of the Fund for the Republic and its associated bleeders, just one thing is amiss with this theory that unrepentant wrongdoers in the motion-picture industry are listed somewhere, and blackly, as never, never to be hired again: *There isn't any blacklist.* Motion-picture people who are unemployable made themselves unemployable. . . .

As to why the motion-picture industry should indulge in these horrid "blacklisting practices" (the term belongs to the fund's probers), the foreword to the two-volume "Report on Blacklisting" states the case remarkably well. Anti-Communists, the foreword says, believe that—

> Communist and pro-Communist infiltration into the entertainment industries represented a serious peril to the American system of law and governance, and therefore to the freedoms which it enshrines. The peril might be direct, through giving Communists access to mass media into which they could introduce subversive propaganda, or which they might even sabotage given the proper circumstances. It might be only indirect, permitting Communist sympathizers to enjoy popular esteem, earning incomes which would help support Communist causes, operating their own blacklists against anti-Communists—

and here we interrupt to lift three rousing cheers for the verity of this last statement—

> and promoting the interests of an international conspiracy directed toward the destruction of all liberties. In any case * * * the extirpation from the entertainment industries of proven members of the Communist conspiracy and of all who were considered to have lent their support or had been indifferent to its dangers (and remained impenitent) was essential as a protection to American institutions.

Hollywood's really convinced Communist-fighters make no bones about believing Reds and those who toady to Reds have no place in the motion-picture industry. For that matter, they do not believe any subversives, or the proponents of any totalitarianism, should be a part of an industry which deals with the communication of ideas.

And Hollywood does deal with ideas. Back in 1944 Harry M. Warner, president of Warner Bros. Studios, said: "Whether a producer makes a picture for pleasure or for profit, for pure entertainment or for pure education—or just for art's sake—he is up against the incontrovertible fact that his picture will produce some effect, for good or bad, on its audiences."

The anti-Communist thesis in Hollywood is that communism is a cancer. And with the soundest logic in the world, the men and women who fight communism point out that no one can coexist with a cancer.

Efforts to combat Communist influences and Communist reinfection in the film world continue vigorously. Rather discouragingly, however, the greatest single obstacle to success is not communism, as you would expect it to be, but doctrinaire liberalism: not Communists but the civil libertines exalted by the Fund for the Republic.

. . . Piously they [Hollywood liberals] announce that they are going to protect the individual against "group pressures," even if they have to form bigger and better pressure groups to do it. And they strike their carefully noble pose between Communists and anti-Communist, always willing to hamper those who would fight to preserve freedom, but, oddly enough, rarely interfering with the conspirators openly dedicated to enslaving the world. The illiberal Liberal thinks it is wrong to be anti-Communist. He thinks it is right to be *anti*-anti-Communist.

Staunchest outside help to Hollywood's embattled Communist-fighters comes from two sources: Governmental agencies and (largely by way of the national patriotic organizations) the public. Most vigorous internal resistance to communism within the motion-picture industry is provided by individuals and organizations firm in the belief that communism is evil; that a world Communist conspiracy is the greatest peril of our time; and that every freeman and every free industry must fight this danger unceasingly.

What are these organizations? And how effective are they? All of Hollywood's guilds and unions now have anti-Communist clauses in their constitutions, though these range from pallidly lukewarm to the bright glow of genuine conviction. . . .

While the United States motion-picture industry has its phony liberals and its great hearts that bleed promptly on the hour, every hour, it also has something few other industries possess (if, indeed, *any* other industry can match it): a full-time organization devoted to fighting communism.

This is the voluntary, unofficial, 13-year-old Motion Picture Alliance for the Preservation of American Ideals.

READING 15.1B: ANTI-AMERICAN PLAYS IN THE USSR

Four years of "cold war" have given rise in the Soviet Union to a whole anti-American literature, the most striking expression of which is probably to be found in the theater. Anti-imperialist or anti-capitalist plays are no novelty in the USSR: the Soviet playwrights had produced a certain number of them before the Second World War. These older plays, however, used to refer for the most part to the history of the Revolution, and more particularly to the foreign intervention during the Civil War. At the present time the anti-American theater chooses strictly contemporaneous subjects. With the encouragement of the party, twenty-eight anti-American plays were written and presented from the end of the war up into 1950. The subjects of these plays have to do with American life or with the Soviet-American struggle in Europe. This new theatrical genre is an instrument of domestic propaganda to combat the sympathetic feeling for the United States engendered by the Russian-American war alliance, and to put the Soviet public on guard against the "perfidy" and the hostility of that country, which is represented (not only in the theater, but also in the press, in films, on the radio, and in books) as the worst enemy of the Soviet Union and of peace in general.

I saw six of these plays. It would have been possible to see a score of them. The content of the piece interested me, every time, in an equal measure with the public reaction. These evenings in the theater revealed to me many things concerning the essential problem of the world today: relations between Russia and America. It would be a mistake to think that the authors of the twenty-eight anti-American plays represent Soviet public opinion; but in carrying out the wishes of the regime, these authors disclose a certain attitude, fix certain directives, and seek to create in the public certain reactions desired by the party. The quality of their productions depends, obviously, on their respective talents. For a spectator who knows America, some of these works would be seen to be filled with monstrosities, monumental psychological and political errors. The majority of the supposedly American characters represented in these tragedies or comedies have no relation

Gordey, Michel. *Visa to Moscow.* Trans. Katherine Woods. New York: Alfred A. Knopf, 1952, pp. 147–48, 151, 413.

whatever to reality in America. But what proportion of the Soviet playgoers has even the slightest acquaintance with the United States? Surely not more than one in ten thousand. The Soviet dramatists are thus quite free to create totally artificial American types and invent situations and predicaments that could never have occurred in America. The fact is that the Americans exhibited in the Soviet theater greatly resemble most Soviet cartoons, from which ferocity has erased—at least for a Western eye—every trace of humor. Will the tricks and lying of the anti-American propaganda that abounded in the Soviet theater in 1950 be able to bring about important results? Certain small signs I observed do not allow me to think it is doing so yet. But a continuous barrage of fire directed always toward the same target must in the long run produce effects. . . .

From this stylized picture of America what idea can the Soviet spectator form of a country that is unknown to him? The United States must appear to his vision as a nation implacably hostile to the Soviet Union, ruled by fascists and gangsters who are making ready for anti-Soviet war and who do not recoil from the most sordid crimes that may help them carry out their plans. The American people are thus divided into criminals, imbeciles, and dollar-chasers, who make up the majority, and a small minority of Communist-oriented citizens (pursued, persecuted, and oppressed) who are struggling "to save the peace." Even in its exaggeration of the importance of this latter group the picture of the whole is disquieting if not portentous. An average spectator, who in one year will have seen a dozen plays and films of this type, is not likely to be reassured about the future. There is nothing for him to do but behave like a good Soviet patriot and approve the policy of his government, which is resisting the "implacable enemy" by every means in its power. He will demonstrate his patriotism by being—more than ever—suspicious of the several Westerners whom he may run into in the streets of Moscow. After all, how can he know—he, the ordinary citizen—whether these Westerners are good or bad? If he judges by his last visit to the theater, there is a big chance that the Westerner he sees before him may be an enemy of his country: a spy, a potential saboteur, a man who wants to make war against him. . . .

Considerable campaigns have been launched since 1946 against kowtowing to the West, against what is called, in an all-encompassing epithet, "bourgeois cosmopolitanism." Purges and Communist calls to order have taken place successively in the domains of literature, music, painting, architecture, and pure and applied science. From biology to philology, including history and medicine on the way, there has been a loud glorification of Soviet scholars faithful to the party line. Diatribes against the scholars or artists of the Western countries went hand in hand with this.

There is no need to review and refute each of these themes of Bolshevist propaganda. Much more important is the general impression created in the Soviet mind: the West is feeble, its culture is moribund, it no longer produces anything valuable or great. The Soviet *kultura* [culture], on the contrary, is dynamic, creative, and productive in all fields. It is in the vanguard of human thought and creation.

READING 15.2

The Berlin Wall and Cuban Missile Crisis

The erection of the Berlin Wall in 1961 was not the first Cold War crisis to affect the divided city. In June 1948, the Soviet Union closed rail and highway access from West German zones of occupation through East Germany to West Berlin, thus threatening Western supply lines to civilian and military forces in the western zones of the city. Western governments responded to this Berlin blockade with the Berlin Airlift, in which planes sometimes flew into West Berlin every few minutes to deliver a mind-boggling amount of supplies. The blockade and airlift continued until May 1949. From then until 1961, especially after Nikita Khrushchev became head of the Communist party in the Soviet Union in 1953, there were additional threats of crises over Berlin.

In 1958, Khrushchev was determined to reduce what he considered a serious nuclear threat in West Germany. U.S.-led NATO forces there possessed nuclear weapons, and there was talk within NATO of allowing West Germany to have its own such weapons. From 1958 to 1961, Khrushchev used various tactics and threats to arrive at a settlement regarding Germany. He hinted at another blockade and proposed that a free and demilitarized Berlin could replace the four-power occupation of the city. He also suggested that both East and West Germany should withdraw from their respective military alliances, retaining only minimal self-defense forces.

A different type of threat perceived by Khrushchev and East German authorities was the increase in numbers of East Berliners and other East Germans pouring into West Berlin. In early August 1961 alone more than 20,000 refugees, many of them professional and skilled people, fled to West Berlin, threatening a brain drain and an economic crisis in East Germany. It was this mass exodus that was primarily responsible for the Soviet and East German decision to construct the wall, which was announced on August 13.

To the dismay of Berlin's mayor, Willy Brandt (see Reading 16.1 for more on Brandt), the response of the West Berlin occupying powers (the United States, Great Britain, and France) was not as forceful as he desired, and the construction of the wall and other barriers went forward. Despite his disappointment, Brandt along with more than 1 million other West Berliners welcomed U.S. President John Kennedy to their city in 1963. In the memorable speech he made there, Kennedy referred to the wall as "the most obvious and vivid demonstration of the failures of the communist system, for all the world to see . . . an offense against humanity, separating families, dividing husbands and wives and brothers and sisters and dividing a people who wish to be joined together."

In a second major showdown, the Cuban Missile Crisis, Kennedy was more forceful, as Reading 15.2B indicates. The crisis developed because of Khrushchev's decision to place in Cuba medium- and intermediate-range nuclear missiles targeted on the United States. In his memoirs, Khrushchev stated that he took the step to safeguard Cuba against the United States and to equalize the "balance of power." Fidel Castro's Marxist forces had turned back a U.S.-supported invasion of Cuban exiles in 1961, and, fearful of another attempt, Khrushchev was determined to maintain this bastion of Marxism in the Western hemisphere. He was also far behind the United States in nuclear weapons and perceived his country as encircled by hostile nuclear placements, including U.S. nuclear missiles in Turkey, just across the Black Sea from the Soviet Union.

After U.S. spy planes discovered Soviet missile installations being constructed in Cuba, Kennedy had several choices. Some advisers advocated a military attack, others a blockade, and still others a private communication to Khrushchev, which would allow him an opportunity to remove the missiles and thereby relieve Kennedy of the need to present a public ultimatum. After detailed discussions, Kennedy decided on a blockade, or naval "quarantine," as he called it in his radio address to the American people on October 22, 1962 (see Reading 15.2B). Kennedy believed that such a quarantine stood the best chance of obtaining his objectives—preventing the Soviet missile deployment and displaying U.S. resolve—without causing war. However, Kennedy and his advisers realized that such a step, if less risky than attacking Cuba, nevertheless could provoke war. They also feared the crisis might lead to increased pressures on West Berlin, and Kennedy warned in his radio address against any hostile move against the city.

For almost a week after Kennedy's address, the threat of nuclear war hung in the air, until Khrushchev finally backed down. In exchange for a U.S. promise not to attack Cuba, and an unofficial (and nonpublicized) assurance that the United States would remove its missiles from Turkey in four or five months, Khrushchev agreed to dismantle Soviet missile sites in Cuba and return them to the USSR.

In subsequent years, the Cuban Missile Crisis was often assessed and reassessed. Today there is little doubt that both Khrushchev and Kennedy made some miscalculations and that Kennedy and the world were indeed fortunate that Khrushchev backed down. It was the response Kennedy hoped for, but given Khrushchev's unpredictable nature it is little wonder that Kennedy thought the odds of his not backing down and that war would occur were almost as high.

In Reading 15.2A, Norman Gelb, who was a correspondent in Berlin during the time the Berlin Wall was constructed, describes the wall and its significance. Reading 15.2B is excerpted from John Kennedy's television and radio address of October 22, 1962.

READING 15.2A: THE WALL

Grim and forbidding, the Wall snakes through the city of Berlin like the backdrop to a nightmare. In certain respects, that's exactly what it is. Tears have been shed here, curses uttered, threats snarled, blood spilled, lives snuffed out. The Wall has been standing a long time now—more than two decades. It has become part of the political architecture of modern times, a concrete barrier planted across the middle of the biggest city between Paris and Moscow, a dramatic statement as well as a grotesque edifice. It is an awkward thing, outlandish and unloved, a numbing fact of life, a fortification thrown up in panic to keep people in rather than out. . . .

. . . Berlin was, after all, the place described by Soviet Premier Nikita Khrushchev as 'the testicles of the West. When I want the West to scream, I squeeze on Berlin.' It was the place about which President John F. Kennedy growled, 'If Khrushchev wants to rub my nose in the dirt, it's all over.' Berlin was where the Cold War had begun with a So-

Gelb, Norman. *The Berlin Wall: Kennedy, Khrushchev, and a Showdown in the Heart of Europe.* New York: Times Books, 1986, pp. 3–7.

viet blockade [1948–1949], where Soviet and American tanks faced each other virtually snout-to-snout for the first—and hopefully only—time [October 1961], and where the grisly game of nuclear brinkmanship was introduced.

For a brief moment, the Berlin Wall was the focus of the whole world's attention. Spawned in an atmosphere of bluster and defiance, it generated a mood of deepest anxiety and profoundest despair. Everywhere, hawks and doves debated its significance and consequences. In Moscow, the Russians, who had authorized its erection in violation of international agreement, kept nervous watch as this most remarkable, most presumptuous urban redevelopment scheme—chopping a city in two—was implemented. They needn't have worried. In Washington, despite rumours of secret American connivance, the White House, State Department, Pentagon and Central Intelligence Agency, having expected something else, struggled but failed to fix on a suitable response. Deplored and reviled, but unchallenged, the Wall stood and grew and grew.

Swarms of journalists and news photographers descended on Berlin to see and record the erection of what was quickly designated either the 'Wall of Shame' or the 'Wall of Peace'—depending on where you stood ideologically. Pundits and politicians, generals and spymasters converged on it like impious pilgrims come to marvel at a blasphemous miracle. People marvel at it still and wonder—did its erection halt a downhill tumble toward a catastrophic war which might have engulfed the globe, or would the world be a better place today had it been immediately, unceremoniously, defiantly demolished?

The great Wall of Berlin is more than just an emotionally-charged geopolitical spectacle. Made of reinforced concrete, ten to thirteen feet high, it is a very remarkable structure. Meandering through the heart of the metropolis, turning corners, winding and bending, it hacks the old capital of Germany into two distinct entities, and then curls to enfold all of the western half of Berlin in its concrete embrace. If straightened, the Wall would measure 103 miles long, which is greater than the distance from New York to Philadelphia or London to Calais. But that doesn't give a truly accurate picture of the situation.

There is more to the Wall than this one edifice. Behind it, one hundred yards deeper into Communist territory, is another concrete barrier, almost as formidable. The levelled area between the two is a desolate, dangerous no-man's-land, patrolled by kalashnikov-toting guards, dotted with free-fire machine-gun emplacements, and sown in places with landmines. It is punctuated by 285 elevated watchtowers, more suited to prison camps than city centres, and by a series of dog runs where ferocious, long-leashed alsatians effectively run free. It is not a safe place to be.

Before reaching the Wall from the East, a person would have to get over the interior concrete barrier, evade the guards, dogs, minefields and/or automatically-triggered guns, and sidestep strategically positioned devices designed to set off both sound alarms and light signals when activated. When that person finally reached the Wall on the border undetected, he would have to get a firm grip on it to lever himself over, despite the thick, smooth-surfaced, ungrippable cement tubing affixed to its top to prevent him from doing just that. Some would-be escapers, having remarkably got that far, have been foiled by this last refinement.

Floodlights and searchlights are positioned along the Wall to illuminate it at night—an eerie sight. Specially reinforced obstructions have been erected at the handful of

A portion of the Berlin Wall fortifications first constructed in 1961. Walter Moss

official border crossing points to discourage people emboldened by pipe-dreams of crashing through in vehicles, which a daring few did during the Wall's early days.

All this vigilance is not directed against criminals. The object of these extraordinary precautions are the people of East Germany. When the Iron Curtain was lowered by the Communists along the border between East Germany and West Germany after the Second World War, Berlin—though deep within Communist East Germany—was spared this division. It remained under joint control of the victorious Russians, Americans, British and French, each with their own sector of the city, each with their own military garrison stationed in that sector, but with right of unrestricted movement throughout the German capital guaranteed by East–West agreement.

That meant that East Germans, seeking more from life than they believed was being offered to them in their Communist homeland but unable to cross the Iron Curtain directly into West Germany, could still find a way out. They could make their way to East Berlin—the Soviet Sector of the city—and then cross without fuss or ceremony into West Berlin, where the dividing line between the American, British and French sectors had become largely irrelevant, where freedom of speech, belief and mobility was protected by law, and which was recovering from the war's devastation at a dazzling pace. American correspondents in Berlin at the time called their cross-over the 'five cent subway ride to freedom'. Having come across, the refugees could stay in West Berlin or, if they wished, they could be flown out to West Germany—to waiting jobs and new lives well beyond reach of the Communists from whom they had fled.

They came in the thousands over the years, tens of thousands, hundreds of thousands, millions. So great was the flight that the continued existence of the Communist East German state was threatened. The Wall was erected around West Berlin to stop the exodus and thereby save the Soviet Union and its East European empire from the consequences of an East German collapse.

Many things have happened since that summer's night in 1961 when, in a blitz operation, thousands of armed guards took up positions along the border, and the first barbed wire was strung across the middle of the city to mark the spot where the Wall would stand. But East Berlin is still walled off from West Berlin. The people behind the Wall are still being shielded from the temptations and distractions so glitteringly displayed just a few minutes away. They are still locked in.

Not all people in East Berlin and East Germany have accepted this situation. Despite all the obstacles, many have managed to get across the Wall, over it or under it, since it was built. But more than three thousand East Germans are known to have failed in their effort to escape and to have been arrested by the Vopos (*Volkspolizisten*—People's Police) for trying to get across town to West Berlin. At least sixty persons are known to have been shot dead in the attempt. How many more have lost their lives or have been wounded trying to escape is just a guess. The East German authorities do not publicize such things. People wounded and caught are led or carried away by the border guards. Rarely is news of their subsequent fate made public. However, it is known—through observation from afar and reports brought across by successful escapers and western visitors—that dozens of persons have been wounded in abortive, often foolhardy bids to break through to West Berlin.

The Wall has regularly been strengthened, with points deemed penetrable reinforced and other sections merely tidied up. There is continuous maintenance along its entire length. So efficient has this maintenance been that escape attempts have now practically ceased, though a reckless or desperate person still occasionally tries to find or make a way through, and occasionally still succeeds. Not long ago, an East Berlin border guard was jailed in West Berlin for shooting dead another guard before fleeing over the Wall. He said he had not wanted to kill the man, only disable him so that he could make his get-away without fear of being shot himself. Two East Germans soared over the Wall on a pulley attached to a steel cable strung from the roof of a building in East Berlin and fixed by a friend to a car hidden behind a West Berlin house. The East German authorities are continually alert for new schemes, new devices, new subterfuges for trying to get over the Wall. Not for nothing have they outlawed hang-gliding.

READING 15.2B: KENNEDY'S RESPONSE TO SOVIET MISSILES IN CUBA[1]

Good evening, my fellow citizens. This Government, as promised, has maintained the closest surveillance of the Soviet military buildup on the island of Cuba. Within the past week unmistakable evidence has established the fact that a series of offensive missile sites is now in preparation on that imprisoned island. The purpose of these bases can be none other than to provide a nuclear strike capability against the Western Hemisphere. . . .

Kennedy, John F. "The Soviet Threat to the Americas," *Department of State Bulletin,* November 12, 1962, pp. 715–16, 718.
[1]Delivered from the White House by television and radio on Oct. 22 (White House press release; as-delivered text).

The characteristics of these new missile sites indicate two distinct types of installations. Several of them include medium-range ballistic missiles capable of carrying a nuclear warhead for a distance of more than 1,000 nautical miles. Each of these missiles, in short, is capable of striking Washington, D.C., the Panama Canal, Cape Canaveral, Mexico City, or any other city in the southeastern part of the United States, in Central America, or in the Caribbean area.

Additional sites not yet completed appear to be designed for intermediate-range ballistic missiles capable of traveling more than twice as far—and thus capable of striking most of the major cities in the Western Hemisphere. . . .

Initial Steps Proposed

Acting, therefore, in the defense of our own security and of the entire Western Hemisphere, and under the authority entrusted to me by the Constitution as endorsed by the resolution of the Congress, I have directed that the following *initial* steps be taken immediately:

First: To halt this offensive buildup, a strict quarantine on all offensive military equipment under shipment to Cuba is being initiated. All ships of any kind bound for Cuba from whatever nation or port will, if found to contain cargoes of offensive weapons, be turned back. This quarantine will be extended, if needed, to other types of cargo and carriers. We are not at this time, however, denying the necessities of life as the Soviets attempted to do in their Berlin blockade of 1948.

Second: I have directed the continued and increased close surveillance of Cuba and its military buildup. The Foreign Ministers of the OAS [Organization of American States] in their communique of October 3 rejected secrecy on such matters in this hemisphere. Should these offensive military preparations continue, thus increasing the threat to the hemisphere, further action will be justified. I have directed the Armed Forces to prepare for any eventualities; and I trust that, in the interest of both the Cuban people and the Soviet technicians at the sites, the hazards to all concerned of continuing this threat will be recognized.

Third: It shall be the policy of this nation to regard any nuclear missile launched from Cuba against any nation in the Western Hemisphere as an attack by the Soviet Union on the United States, requiring a full retaliatory response upon the Soviet Union.

Fourth: As a necessary military precaution I have reinforced our base at Guantanamo, evacuated today the dependents of our personnel there, and ordered additional military units to be on a standby alert basis.

Fifth: We are calling tonight for an immediate meeting of the Organ of Consultation, under the Organization of American States, to consider this threat to hemispheric security and to invoke articles 6 and 8 of the Rio Treaty in support of all necessary action. The United Nations Charter allows for regional security arrangements—and the nations of this hemisphere decided long ago against the military presence of outside powers. Our other allies around the world have also been alerted.

Sixth: Under the Charter of the United Nations, we are asking tonight that an emergency meeting of the Security Council be convoked without delay to take action against this latest Soviet threat to world peace. Our resolution will call for the prompt dismantling and withdrawal of all offensive weapons in Cuba, under the supervision of U.N. observers, before the quarantine can be lifted.

Seventh and finally: I call upon Chairman Khrushchev to halt and eliminate this clandestine, reckless, and provocative threat to world peace and to stable relations between our two nations. I call upon him further to abandon this course of world domination and to join in an historic effort to end the perilous arms race and transform the history of man. He has an opportunity now to move the world back from the abyss of destruction—by returning to his Government's own words that it had no need to station missiles outside its own territory, and withdrawing these weapons from Cuba—by refraining from any action which will widen or deepen the present crisis—and then by participating in a search for peaceful and permanent solutions.

This nation is prepared to present its case against the Soviet threat to peace, and our own proposals for a peaceful world, at any time and in any forum—in the OAS, in the United Nations, or in any other meeting that could be useful—without limiting our freedom of action.

READING 15.3

The Collapse of the Berlin Wall, 1989

In the following reading, Timothy Garton Ash, one of England's leading experts on eastern and central Europe, describes the collapse of the Berlin Wall, which he witnessed, and the events leading up to it and flowing from it (up to early 1990). His book was finished before German reunification formally occurred in October 1990, but he foresaw that events were moving in that direction. Among the causes that he mentions for the collapse of the wall are the East Germans' hatred of it and their demonstrations in 1989, the belief that Soviet leader Mikhail Gorbachev would not send in Soviet troops to put down demonstrations, and, less significantly, the example of Poles and Hungarians who had overthrown communist controls in 1989. Ash also mentions East Germans' dissatisfaction with their economic conditions, which were worse than many Western analysts then realized.

Since 1989, there has been considerable additional analysis regarding the causes of the revolutionary events of that year and the end of the Cold War, which was intertwined with them. Although many differences of interpretation remain, there is little doubt that both the actions of the opponents of communist rule in eastern and central Europe and those of Gorbachev were among the most important of the many causes of these momentous occurrences.

On the morning of Sunday, 12 November [1989] I walked through the Wall . . . with a crowd of East Berliners, a watchtower to our left, Hitler's bunker to our right. Bewildered border-guards waved us through. (As recently as February their colleagues had shot dead a man trying to escape.) Vertical segments of the wall stood at ease where the crane had just dumped them, their multicoloured graffiti facing east for the first time. A crowd of West Berliners applauded as we came through, and a man handed out free city plans. Then I turned round and walked back again, past more bewildered borderguards and customs officers. . . .

By nightfall, West Berlin workers had dismantled the famous platform, like an un-needed prop. Europe's *Mousetrap* had ended its twenty-eight-year run. Clear the stage for another show.

Everyone has seen the pictures of joyful celebration in West Berlin, the vast crowds stopping the traffic on the Kürfurstendamm, *Sekt* corks popping, strangers tearfully embracing—the greatest street-party in the history of the world. Yes, it was like that. But it was not only like that. Most of the estimated two million East Germans who flooded into West Berlin over the weekend simply walked the streets in quiet family groups, often with toddlers in pushchairs. They queued up at a bank to collect the 100 Deutschmarks 'greeting money' (about thirty-five pounds) offered to visiting East Germans by the West German government, and then they went, very cautiously, shopping. Generally they bought one or two small items, perhaps some fresh fruit, a Western newspaper and toys for the children. Then, clasping their carrier-bags, they walked quietly back through the Wall, through the grey, deserted streets of East Berlin, home.

It is very difficult to describe the quality of this experience because what they actually did was so stunningly ordinary. . . . Berliners walked the streets of Berlin. What could be more normal? And yet, what could be more fantastic! 'Twenty-eight years and ninety-one days,' says one man in his late thirties strolling back up Friedrichstrasse. Twenty-eight years and ninety-one days since the building of the Wall. On that day, in August 1961, his parents had wanted to go to a late-night Western in a West Berlin cinema, but their eleven-year-old son had been too tired. In the early hours they woke to the sound of tanks. He had never been to West Berlin from that day to this. A taxi-driver asks me, with a sly smile: 'How much is the ferry to England?' The day before yesterday his question would have been unthinkable.

Everyone, but everyone, on the streets of East Berlin has just been, or is just going to West Berlin. A breathless, denim-jacketed couple stop me to ask, 'Is this the way out?' They have come hot-foot from Leipzig. 'Our hearts are going pitter-pat,' they say, in broad Saxon dialect. Everyone looks the same as they make their way home—except for the tell-tale Western carrier-bag. But everyone is inwardly changed, changed utterly. 'Now people are standing up straight,' says a hotel porter. 'They are speaking their minds. Even work is more fun. I think the sick will get up from their hospital beds.' And it was in East rather than West Berlin that this weekend had the magic, pentecostal quality which I last experienced in Poland in autumn 1980. Ordinary men and women find

Ash, Timothy Garton. *The Magic Lantern: The Revolution of '89 Witnessed in Warsaw, Budapest, Berlin, and Prague.* New York: Vintage Books, 1993, pp. 61–66, 68–69, 75–76.

their voice and their courage—*Lebensmut,* as the porter puts it. These are moments when you feel that somewhere an angel has opened his wings.

They may have been ordinary people doing very ordinary things, but the Berliners immediately grasped the historical dimensions of the event. 'Of course the real villain was Hitler,' said one. A note stuck to a remnant of the Wall read: 'Stalin is dead, Europe lives.' The man who counted twenty-eight years and ninety-one days told me he had been most moved by an improvised poster saying: 'Only today is the war really over.'

Bild newspaper—West Germany's *Sun*—carried a black-red-gold banner headline declaring 'Good Morning, Germany,' and underneath it an effusive thank-you letter from the editors to Mikhail Gorbachev. The East Germans also felt grateful to Gorbachev. But more important, they felt they had won this opening for themselves. For it was only the pressure of their massive, peaceful demonstrations that compelled the Party leadership to take this step. 'You see, it shows Lenin was wrong,' observed one worker. 'Lenin said a revolution could succeed only with violence. But this was a peaceful revolution.' And even the Party's Central Committee acknowledged at the beginning of its hastily drafted Action Programme that 'a revolutionary people's movement has set in motion a process of profound upheavals.'

Why did it happen? And why so quickly? No one in East Germany predicted it. . . .

. . . At the very least, one can list in order some factors that brought the cup of popular discontent to overflowing. In the beginning was the Wall itself: the Wall and the system it both represented and preserved. The Wall was not round the periphery of East Germany, it was at its very centre. And it ran through every heart. It was difficult even for people from other East European countries to appreciate the full psychological burden it imposed. An East Berlin doctor wrote a book describing the real sicknesses—and of course the suicides—that resulted. He called it *The Wall Sickness.* In a sense, the mystery was always why the people of East Germany did not revolt.

The second causal factor, both in time and importance, was Gorbachev. The 'Gorbachev effect' was strongest in East Germany because it was more strongly oriented towards—and ultimately dependent on—the Soviet Union than any other East European state. It was not for nothing that a 1974 amendment to the constitution proclaimed: 'The German Democratic Republic is for ever and irrevocably allied with the Union of Soviet Socialist Republics.' East Germany's young people had for years been told, *Von der Sowjetunion lernen heisst siegen lernen*—'To learn from the Soviet Union is to learn how to win.' So they did! For several years East Germans had been turning the name of Gorbachev, and the Soviet example, against their rulers. And Gorbachev personally gave the last push—on his visit to join the fortieth-anniversary celebrations of the GDR [German Democratic Republic, East Germany's formal name] on 7 October—with his carefully calculated utterance that 'Life itself punishes those who delay', the leaked news that he had told Honecker [GDR communist leader] Soviet troops would not be used for internal repression and (according to well-informed West German sources) his direct encouragement to the likes of Egon Krenz and the Berlin Party chief Günter Schabowski, to move to depose Honecker.

The Polish and Hungarian examples were not so important. To be sure, everyone learned about them, in great detail, from the West German television they watched nightly. To be sure, developments in those two countries demonstrated that fundamental changes were possible. But for most people the economic misery in Poland more than cancelled out the political example. Hungary—a favoured holiday destination for East Germans, with a better economic situation and a history (and, dare one say, national character) less fatefully at odds with Germany's—Hungary perhaps had a greater impact. Yet the crucial Hungarian input was not the example of its internal reforms, but the opening of its frontier with Austria.

As soon as the Hungarians started cutting the barbed wire of the 'iron curtain', in May, East Germans began to escape across it. As the numbers grew, and East Germans gathered in refugee camps in Budapest, the Hungarian authorities decided, in early September, to let them leave officially (suspending a bilateral consular agreement with the GDR). The trickle turned into a flood: some 15,000 crossed the border in the first three days, 50,000 by the end of October. Others sought an exit route via the West German embassies in Prague and Warsaw. This was the final catalyst for internal change in East Germany. . . .

To say the growth of popular protest was exponential would be an understatement. It was a non-violent explosion. Those extraordinary, peaceful, determined Monday evening demonstrations in Leipzig—always starting with 'peace prayers' in the churches—grew week-by-week, from 70,000 to double that, to 300,000, to perhaps half a million. The whole of East Germany suddenly went into labour, an old world—to recall Marx's image—pregnant with the new. From that time forward the people acted and the Party reacted. . . .

Yet the opening of the Berlin Wall on 9 November, and subsequently of the whole inter-German frontier, changed the terms of the revolution completely. Before 9 November, the issue had been how this state—the German Democratic Republic— should be governed. The people were reclaiming their so-called people's state. They were putting the D for Democratic into the GDR. After 9 November, the issue was whether this state should continue to exist at all. . . .

For the overwhelming fact of East German political life at the beginning of 1990 was the flood-tide towards a re- or rather new-unification with West Germany. . . . And then there were innumerable examples of practical co-operation and joint enterprise across the inter-German frontier and through the Wall: new air links, bus routes, joint ventures.

This was most dramatically visible in Berlin. Where previously a West Berlin underground line ran through ghostly, sealed underground stations in East Berlin, the doors of the train now opened and East Berliners leapt aboard. The whole mental geography of Berlin changed overnight. What had been the edge became the centre. It was one city again. But it was also true all around the German-German borders. Unification was happening from below.

DISCUSSION QUESTION

Indicate some of the most important effects of the Cold War and how the city of Berlin and the Berlin Wall served as a fitting symbol for the Cold War.

CHAPTER SIXTEEN

Three Western European Leaders: de Gaulle, Brandt, and Thatcher

In western Europe, the postwar years produced several influential leaders. French President Charles de Gaulle (1890–1970) was the dominant head of state in the 1960s. Willy Brandt (1913–1992) became West Germany's foreign minister in 1966 and chancellor in 1969 and was perhaps the most influential European statesman of the early 1970s. And British Prime Minister Margaret Thatcher (b. 1925) was the paramount western European political figure of the 1980s. The issues that concerned these three varied. Each of them, however, dealt forcefully with foreign policy matters that included Cold War problems and the relationship of his or her country with other western European nations and the United States, especially relations that pertained to the North Atlantic Treaty Organization (NATO) and the Common Market.

In dealing with the Cold War, both de Gaulle and Brandt pursued a policy of détente (relaxation of tensions) before the term became linked with the efforts of U.S. President Richard Nixon and Soviet leader Leonid Brezhnev during the early 1970s. Although Thatcher was one of the first Western leaders to recognize that Mikhail Gorbachev was "a man you can do business with," her conservative tendencies led her to proceed slowly in responding to Gorbachev's initiatives to end the Cold War during the late 1980s.

Like de Gaulle, Brandt favored close German-French relations and attempted to pursue a foreign policy less dependent on the United States, but, like Thatcher later, he supported NATO. In contrast, de Gaulle withdrew French forces from NATO. The Common Market—more formally, the European Economic Community (EEC) and later the European Community (EC)—was founded in 1957. Initially, it included France, West Germany, Italy, Belgium, the Netherlands, and Luxembourg. De Gaulle, unlike Brandt, was against British entry into it, and it was not until 1973 that Great Britain, Ireland, and Denmark became members of the organization. In 1981, Greece joined and, in 1986,

Spain and Portugal (as the European Union, or EU, it has continued to expand during the 1990s). The Common Market's main accomplishment was to create a free trade zone for its members. As the organization grew, bodies within it, such as its Council of Ministers and European Parliament, increased in significance. Being strong nationalists, both de Gaulle and Thatcher were opposed to allowing such institutions any powers that would seriously threaten national sovereignty. They both supported a *Europe des patries* (Europe of states), as opposed to a more integrated European federation.

Brandt was less fearful than the other two leaders of any supranational threat to national sovereignty. He was also among the most important socialist leaders in Europe. Like the British Labour party, Brandt's Social Democratic party expanded government responsibility for the welfare of its citizens, a European trend that Thatcher believed had gone much too far by the time she became prime minister in 1979. By the time she left office in 1990, criticism of expensive government social welfare programs and extensive government controls had become common throughout Europe.

READING 16.1

The Foreign Policy of Charles de Gaulle

After France had been ruled by twenty-seven governments from 1945 to 1958, Charles de Gaulle, the general who had led Free-French forces during World War II, came to power in 1958. He did so under a new constitution intended to provide more stability to French political life. It accomplished its aim, and de Gaulle remained president for eleven years.

One of his first major accomplishments was to extricate France from a costly Algerian war of independence against France. De Gaulle's main goal was to strengthen France's position as a major power. To accomplish this task, he refused to echo U.S. policies and initiatives and set out to establish France as the leader of a more independent western Europe. Under de Gaulle, France not only withdrew French forces from the U.S.-dominated NATO but also developed its own nuclear weapons. Great Britain's close ties to the United States contributed to de Gaulle's continuing opposition to British entry into the Common Market. Toward West Germany, however, he was more cordial. Along with West German leaders, especially Chancellor (1949–1963) Konrad Adenauer, he significantly contributed to overcoming the longtime Franco-German distrust that had helped bring about two wars in the twentieth century. In 1964, de Gaulle preceded the United States by fifteen years when he extended diplomatic recognition to Communist China. And years before the U.S. and Soviet governments established détente, de Gaulle had made it a high priority in his relations with the Soviet Union; in 1966, he told Willy Brandt that he thought that West Germany and other parts of western Europe should also work toward achieving it. After Brandt began pursuing détente, the cumulative efforts of de Gaulle and Brandt placed increasing pressure on the United States to also pursue such a policy or risk weakening its influence in western Europe. Except for the last portion of the following reading, which is from de Gaulle's December 31, 1963, radio and television address to the French people, the other three sections of the reading are from de Gaulle's press conference of January 14, 1963.

THE BRITISH AND THE COMMON MARKET

... [A]fter having put some pressure on the Six [member states of the Common Market] in order to prevent the application of the Common Market from really getting started ... Britain ... in its turn [in 1961] requested membership, but on its own conditions.

This undoubtedly raises for each of the six States and for England problems of a very great dimension.

England is, in effect, insular, maritime, linked through its trade, markets and food supply to very diverse and often very distant countries. Its activities are essentially industrial and commercial, and only slightly agricultural. It has, throughout its work, very marked and original customs and traditions. In short, the nature, structure and economic context of England differ profoundly from those of the other States of the Continent.

Major Addresses, Statements, and Press Conferences of General Charles de Gaulle, May 19, 1958–January 31, 1964. New York: French Embassy, Press and Information Division, 1964, pp. 213–14, 217–18, 220–21, 244.

What is to be done so that Britain, such as it lives, such as it produces and such as it trades, be incorporated into the Common Market such as it has been conceived and such as it functions?

For example, the means by which the people of Great Britain nourish themselves is in fact by importing foodstuffs purchased at low prices in the two Americas or in the former dominions, while still granting large subsidies to British farmers. This means is obviously incompatible with the system the Six have quite naturally set up for themselves. . . .

One was sometimes led to believe that our British friends, in applying for membership in the Common Market, agreed to change their own ways even to the point of applying all the conditions accepted and practiced by the Six, but, the question is to know if Great Britain can at present place itself, with the Continent and like it, within a tariff that is truly common, give up all preference with regard to the Commonwealth, cease to claim that its agriculture be privileged and, even more, consider as null and void the commitments it has made with the countries that are part of its free trade area. That question is the one at issue.

One cannot say that it has now been resolved. Will it be so one day? Obviously Britain alone can answer that.

The question is raised all the more since, following Britain, other States which are, I repeat, linked to it in the Free Trade Area, for the same reasons as Great Britain, would or will want to enter the Common Market.

It must be agreed that the entry first of Great Britain and then that of those other States will completely change the series of adjustments, agreements, compensations and regulations already established between the Six, because all these States, like Britain, have very important traits of their own. We would then have to envisage the construction of another Common Market. But the 11-member, then 13-member and then perhaps 18-member Common Market that would be built would, without any doubt, hardly resemble the one the Six have built.

Moreover, this Community, growing in that way, would be confronted with all the problems of its economic relations with a crowd of other States, and first of all with the United States.

It is foreseeable that the cohesion of all its members, who would be very numerous and very diverse, would not hold for long and that in the end there would appear a colossal Atlantic Community under American dependence and leadership which would soon completely swallow up the European Community. . . .

AN INDEPENDENT NUCLEAR FORCE FOR FRANCE

. . . [T]he [nuclear] deterrent is now a fact for the Russians as for the Americans, which means that in the case of a general atomic war, there would inevitably be frightful and perhaps fatal destruction in both countries. In these conditions, no one in the world— particularly no one in America—can say if, where, when, how and to what extent the American nuclear weapons would be employed to defend Europe. . . .

Thus principles and realities combine to lead France to equip herself with an atomic force of her own. This does not all exclude, of course, the combination of the action of this force with the action of the similar forces of its allies. But, for us, in this specific case, integration is something that is unimaginable. Indeed, as you know, we have begun with our own and only means to invent, test and construct atomic bombs and the vehicles for launching them.

It is completely understandable that this French undertaking does not appear to be highly satisfactory to certain American circles. In politics and in strategy, as in the economy, monopoly quite naturally appears to the person who holds it to be the best possible system. Then we hear a multiple choir of Americans—unofficial persons, experts and journalists—violently and strongly attacking our autonomous armament. "The atomic force with which France intends to equip herself is and will remain," they say, "insignificant in relation to those of the United States and Russia. To build it up is thus to waste a lot of effort and money for nothing. And then, within the Alliance, the United States has an overwhelming superiority, therefore no one should run counter to its strategy through any divergent action."

It is quite true that the number of nuclear weapons with which we can equip ourselves will not equal, far from it, the mass of those of the two giants of today. But since when has it been proved that a people should remain deprived of the most effective weapon for the reason that its chief possible adversary and its chief friend have means far superior to its own?

France, when formerly it was its turn to be world colossus, often experienced the worth of either the resistance of a less powerful but well-equipped adversary, or the support of an ally lining up inferior but well-tempered and well-employed weapons. . . .

FRANCO-GERMAN RELATIONS

Among the new elements that are in the process of shaping the world at present, I believe that there is none more striking and more fruitful than the French-German pact. [This treaty of cooperation was formally signed on January 22, 1963.] Two great peoples, which have for so long and so terribly opposed and fought each other, are now turning toward each other with the same impulse of sympathy and understanding. It is not only a question of a reconciliation demanded by circumstances. What is happening in reality is a kind of mutual discovery of two neighbors, each noticing the extent to which the other is valid, worthy and attractive.

It is from this then that springs the desire for a rapprochement manifest everywhere in the two countries which conforms with reality and which commands politics, because for the first time in many generations, the Germans and Gauls realize their solidarity. This solidarity exists obviously from the standpoint of their security, since the same threat of foreign domination confronts them and because their territories constitute a single strategic area. It exists from the economic standpoint because, for each of them, mutual trade is an essential and preponderant element. It exists from the standpoint of their cultural influence and development, for in thought, philosophy, science, the arts and technology they are complementary. . . .

The French-German meeting that will shortly be held here [to sign the treaty of cooperation] will permit, us, we most sincerely hope, to organize our cooperation better than it is organized already.

On the right, German Foreign Minister Willy Brandt and (next to him) French President Charles de Gaulle, along with Kurt-Georg Kiesinger (West German chancellor, 1966–1969) and French Prime Minister Georges Pompidou, at a Paris conference in January 1967. Archive Photos/Archive France

FRANCE'S WORLD ROLE

. . . France, because she can do so, because everything invites her to do so, because she is France, should conduct amidst the world a world policy. Throughout the year which is beginning, we will thus work toward the three major tasks incumbent upon us. The union of Europe, including as soon as possible the regular and organized cooperation of Germany, Italy, the Netherlands, Belgium, Luxembourg and France in the domains of politics, defense and culture, as will be the case in that of economics. The progress of the developing countries, above all those which, in Africa, are already linked to us through special agreements and those on the same or other continents which will be so. Lastly, a contribution to the maintenance of peace.

As for this last objective, there are conditions imposed upon us. Firstly, we must pursue the effort which should equip us with a thermonuclear arsenal, the only one with a power adequate to the threat of aggression and consequently the only one which allows us independence. Next, we must assist our Western Europe, from the time that it is united, in practicing with America a truly concerted political, economic and strategic entente. Lastly, we must, without giving in to the illusions in which the weak lull themselves, but without losing the hope that human liberty and dignity will in the end prevail everywhere, we must envisage the day when, perhaps in Warsaw, in Prague, . . . in Budapest, in Bucharest, in Sofia, in Belgrade, in Tirana, in Moscow, the Communist totalitarian regime, which still succeeds in constraining confined peoples, will gradually come to an evolution compatible with our own transformation. Then there would be open to Europe as a whole prospects in keeping with its resources and its capacities.

Women and men of France, it is in all serenity that I wish each and every one of you a good and happy 1964. And since, by reason of our history, as well as of my office, I have the honor and the duty of speaking in our name to all, I extend to France, once again, the most eager and most confident wishes of her children.

Vive la République! Vive la France!

READING 16.2

Willy Brandt: Seeker of a New Europe

Willy Brandt was a generation younger than Charles de Gaulle, and he spent the Hitler years in Scandinavia, an influence which moderated his socialist ideas. After the war, he returned to Germany, served in the West German legislature, and for a while edited a Berlin newspaper. From 1957 to 1966, he was the mayor of West Berlin, and the Berlin Crisis of 1961 (see Reading 15.2) greatly influenced his views. He was deeply disappointed at the lack of a more forceful U.S. response to the erection of the Berlin Wall. This failure helped give birth to the *Ostpolitik* (Eastern policy) he would later champion as German foreign minister (1966–1969) and finally as chancellor (1969–1974).

Between 1970 and 1972, he fully implemented this détente policy of improving relations with the Soviet Union and its eastern European satellites, including East Germany. In this three-year period, West Germany signed nonaggression treaties with the Soviet Union and Poland, agreeing to existing boundaries; improved West Germany's access to West Berlin; increased human and other contacts between East and West Berlin; and established virtually complete diplomatic relations with East Germany. For his efforts, in 1971 Brandt was awarded the Nobel Peace Prize.

Brandt viewed his efforts as steps toward the eventual reunification of Germany, a dream he lived long enough to see fulfilled in 1990, two years before his death. In 1970, his government issued "a letter on German unity" to accompany the treaty it signed with the Soviet Union. This letter emphasized the long-standing West German commitment to continue working for the "free self-determination" of the German people. Two decades later, West German Chancellor Helmut Kohl reiterated this commitment to German self-determination, and Mikhail Gorbachev agreed to Germany's right to it. The term Woodrow Wilson had first popularized after World War I (review Reading 5.1) still proved relevant more than seventy years later.

Gorbachev spoke at Brandt's funeral in 1992, and in his memoirs the former Soviet leader referred to Brandt as "an example of wisdom, decisiveness, and responsibility in a political leader . . . the highest example of morality in politics." The following selection is from Brandt's Report on the State of the Nation to the Bundestag (the lower house of the West German parliament), January 28, 1971.

As you know, I was in Paris at the beginning of this week, together with the Foreign Minister and other Cabinet colleagues. We were reminded once again of the friendly understanding which accompanies our efforts. "France supports you unreservedly," President Pompidou [who replaced de Gaulle in 1969] said in his speech, which—a noble gesture which we should not forget—was made in German. These latest talks in France have made abundantly clear the interdependence of our Western and Eastern policies and how much they belong together. In other words: West European cooperation and union—which, as everyone knows, we are actively encouraging—do not prevent us from developing better relations with the East; they are indeed the basis for such—we are convinced—necessary efforts.

Our policies directed towards reduction of tensions and the organization of peace are being followed with great interest and understanding by many governments, influential personalities and the Press in neutral countries and in wide areas of the Third World. Many people know that Europe will be able to achieve more in the field of international cooperation if these efforts lead to success.

Even in the eastern world, it is today hardly doubted that German policy is directed towards peace. And it is known that we are making no exceptions, not even in the case of the G.D.R. [East Germany], in our efforts to reach understanding.

Seen from this point of view, it was only logical, when signing the Moscow Treaty on the 12th August last year, to declare our agreement with the Soviet Union that all treaties we may want to conclude with the partners of the Warsaw Pact [alliance of USSR and Soviet European satellites] will form a political whole.

No one will be able to speak of effective relaxation of tension in Central Europe until all these elements are present.

Over and above this, I want to establish here that these treaties—to be exact, the treaty with the Soviet Union and that with the People's Republic of Poland—in no way contradict our position as a member of the European Community or as an ally of N.A.T.O. In neither West nor East, North nor South are there particular German interests or special German reservations, which could diminish or influence our decision in favour of a policy of settlement. However, we made it clear in Moscow that no treaty either can or may prevent us from striving for a state of peace in which our nation can recover its unity in freedom and self-determination. This reflects the task laid down in our constitution as well as our own convictions. But no one believes that aspirations come any nearer to fulfilment by being committed to paper.

We also have German interests in the widest sense at heart in our relationship to Poland, in doing what we can to ensure that the name of Germany shall no longer be used as a symbol of injustice and horror, but as a sign of hope for reconciliation and peaceful coexistence. That this hope is not in vain may be seen in the number of Germans who will cross to the Federal Republic in the coming months. [In 1970, Poland agreed to allow "several tens of thousands" of Polish ethnic Germans to emigrate.]

With regard to relations with the G.D.R.: as laid down in the principles of the United Nations regarding relations between states, peaceful settlement of relations on the basis

Brandt, Willy. *Peace: Writings and Speeches of the Nobel Peace Prize Winner, 1971*. Bonn: Verlag Neue Gesellschaft, 1971, pp. 14–16, 18–19.

of human rights, equality, peaceful coexistence and non-discrimination must occupy the foreground of all efforts in this case as well.

The meetings at Erfurt and Kassel were important for the neighbourly coexistence of the two systems of government on German soil, even though they were only the beginning of a discussion. We consequently reached an arrangement with the Government of the G.D.R., at the end of October, to conduct an official exchange of opinions on questions whose settlement would serve the cause of relaxation of tension in Central Europe and which are of interest to both states.

We stand by all this. Here is a basis, which is not bound by any pre-condition and on which we can work in 1971. . . .

This survey of developments since my last report a year ago makes clear the extent to which the settlement of relations between the Federal Republic of Germany and the G.D.R. must be seen in relation to the whole. An isolated solution to the problems affecting our people is just as impossible as, say, an attempt to secure peace on our own. History has taught us that crises can be created by one, but the maintenance of peace requires the cooperation of all.

What is possible between the states of Europe must also be possible between the two states in Germany; the artificial severance which has now lasted more than two decades has brought neither stability nor tranquility. On the contrary, it has aroused tensions and crises which must now be overcome in the interests of Europe and Germany. . . .

. . . I would like to remind you here of what I said in my government policy statement on 28th October, 1969:

> "This government believes that the problems resulting for the German people from the Second World War and the national betrayal by the Hitler Regime can only be finally resolved in a European peace settlement. No one, however, can dissuade us that the Germans have the same right to self-determination as all other peoples. The task of practical policy in the years which lie ahead of us is to uphold the unity of the nation by freeing relations between the two parts of Germany from their present state of regidity."

And in my last speech on the state of the nation a year ago, on 14th January, 1970, I added:

> "25 years after the unconditional capitulation of Hitler's Reich, the concept of nationhood binds divided Germany. . . . A nation is based on the continuous feeling of belonging together of people. No one can deny that, in this sense, there is a German nation and will continue to be one as far as we can see into the future."

These conclusions formed the basis of my statements in Erfurt and Kassel and also the basis of the talks which the Foreign Minister and I and our colleagues conducted in Moscow and Warsaw. There could not and cannot be any question of ignoring the elements of our historical development for tactical, let alone opportunist reasons.

Nor is there any question for us of adjusting the concept of nationhood to apparently contemporary or short-term necessities.

READING 16.3

Margaret Thatcher: Critic of the Welfare State and European Federalism

Margaret Thatcher was Great Britain's first female prime minister and served in that office (1979–1990) longer than anyone else in the twentieth century. At Oxford, she studied chemistry but, after graduation, studied law and became a tax lawyer. In 1959, she was elected to the House of Commons as a member of the Conservative party. In the early 1970s, she served as minister of education and science under Prime Minister Edward Heath, and after the Conservatives were defeated in 1974 she soon replaced him as the head of the Conservative party.

Sometimes referred to as the "iron lady," her admirers emphasized that she acted forcefully on her principles, even if they were unpopular at the moment. Her detractors claimed she was an unfeeling ideologue, more concerned with the "haves" than the "have-nots." Ideologically, her views were similar to those of U.S. President Ronald Reagan. While she was prime minister, Britain's economic growth rate was among the best in Europe, and inflation declined. She broke the power of unions and privatized many previously government-run operations, such as those controlling electricity and water. Although some of Thatcher's critics claimed that rising North Sea oil production deserved more credit than she for Britain's growing economy, there is little doubt that some of her policies improved Britain's competitive position in an increasingly global economy. Nevertheless, during her last few years in power, inflation, interest rates, and the trade deficit all rose, as compared with earlier figures. Her tax policies, criticized for favoring the rich, and her resistance to faster Common Market integration also caused increasing public dissatisfaction. Under pressure from her party, she resigned as prime minister in November 1990.

In the following selection, Thatcher describes her background and views shortly before coming to power in 1979 and later discusses her attitude toward the Common Market.

. . . [T]he Britain that woke up on the morning after 1945 was not only a nation drained by two great military efforts in defence of common civilization, but also one suffering from a prolonged bout of economic and financial anaemia.

With the election of Attlee's Labour Government [in 1945], however, there began a sustained attempt, which lasted over thirty years, to halt this relative decline and kick-start a resurgence along lines which . . . represented a centralizing, managerial, bureaucratic, interventionist style of government. Already large and unwieldy after its expansion in two world wars, the British Government very soon jammed a finger in every pie. It levied high rates of tax on work, enterprise, consumption, and wealth transfer. It planned development at every level—urban, rural, industrial and scientific. It managed the economy, macro-economically by Keynesian methods of fiscal manipulation, microeconomically by granting regional and industrial subsidies on a variety of criteria. It nationalized industries, either directly by taking ownership, or indirectly by using its powers of regulation to constrain the decisions of private management in the direction the Government wanted. . . . It made available various forms of welfare for a wide range of

Thatcher, Margaret. *The Downing Street Years.* New York: HarperCollins, 1993, pp. 5–12, 536.

Margaret Thatcher with Mikhail Gorbachev after a discussion at Brize Norton RAF Airport, England, December 1987. Reuters/Nick Didlick/Archive Photos

contingencies—poverty, unemployment, large families, old age, misfortune, ill-health, family quarrels—generally on a universal basis. And when some people preferred to rely on their own resources or on the assistance of family and friends, the Government would run advertising campaigns to persuade people of the virtues of dependence.

The rationale for such a comprehensive set of interventions was, to quote the former Labour Cabinet minister, Douglas Jay, that 'the gentleman in Whitehall really does know better what is good for the people than the people know themselves.' A disinterested civil service, with access to the best and latest information, was better able to foresee economic eventualities and to propose responses to them than were the blind forces of the so-called 'free market'.

Such a philosophy was explicitly advocated by the Labour Party. It gloried in planning, regulation, controls and subsidies. It had a vision of the future: Britain as a democratic socialist society, third way between east European collectivism and American capitalism. And there was a rough consistency between its principles and its policies—both tending towards the expansion of government—even if the pace of that change was not fast enough for its own Left.

The Tory [Conservative] Party was more ambivalent. At the level of principle, rhetorically and in Opposition, it opposed these doctrines and preached the gospel of free enterprise with very little qualification. Almost every post-war Tory victory had been won on slogans such as 'Britain Strong and Free' or 'Set the People Free'. But in the fine print of policy, and especially in government, the Tory Party merely pitched camp in the long march to the left. It never tried seriously to reverse it. Privatization? The Carlisle State Pubs were sold off. Taxation? Regulation? Subsidies? If these were cut down at the start of a Tory government, they gradually crept up again as its life ebbed away. The welfare state? We boasted of spending more money than Labour, not of restoring people to independence and self-reliance. The result of this style of accommodationist politics, as my colleague Keith Joseph complained, was that post-war politics became a 'socialist ratchet'—Labour moved Britain towards more statism; the Tories stood pat; and the next Labour Government moved the country a little further left. The Tories loosened the corset of socialism; they never removed it. . . .

No theory of government was ever given a fairer test or a more prolonged experiment in a democratic country than democratic socialism received in Britain. Yet it was a miserable failure in every respect. Far from reversing the slow relative decline of Britain *vis-à-vis* its main industrial competitors, it accelerated it. We fell further behind them, until by 1979 we were widely dismissed as 'the sick man of Europe'. The relative worsening of our economic position was disguised by the rising affluence of the West as a whole. We, among others, could hardly fail to benefit from the long economic expansion of the post-war western world led by the United States. But if we never had it so good, others—like Germany, France, Italy, Denmark—increasingly had it better. And, as the 1970s wore grimly on, we began to fail in absolute as well as relative terms.

Injections of monetary demand, which in the 1950s had produced a rise in real production and a fall in unemployment before causing a modest rise in prices, now went directly into high rates of inflation without so much as a blip on the charts for production and unemployment. State subsidies and direction of investment achieved progressively more inefficient industries and ever lower returns on capital. Laws giving protective immunity to the trade unions at the turn of the century were now abused to protect restrictive practices and over-manning, to underpin strikes, and to coerce workers into joining unions and participating in industrial action against their better judgement. Welfare benefits, distributed with little or no consideration of their effects on behaviour, encouraged illegitimacy, facilitated the breakdown of families, and replaced incentives favouring work and self-reliance with perverse encouragement for idleness and cheating. The final illusion—that state intervention would promote social harmony and solidarity or, in Tory language, 'One Nation'—collapsed in the 'winter of discontent' [1978–1979] when the dead went unburied, critically ill patients were turned away from hospitals by pickets, and the prevailing social mood was one of snarling envy and motiveless hostility. To cure the British disease with socialism was like trying to cure leukaemia with leeches.

Another approach was needed—and for international reasons as well as domestic ones. Britain's weakened economic position meant that its international role was bound to be cramped and strained as well. . . .

What made this more dangerous in the late 1970s was that the United States was undergoing a similar crisis of morale following its failure in Vietnam. In fact, the 'Vietnam Syndrome' . . . embodied the conviction that the United States was *fortunately* incapable of intervention abroad since such intervention would almost certainly be inimical to morality, the world's poor, or the revolutionary tides of history. Hobbled by this psychological constraint and by a Congress also deeply influenced by it, two presidents saw the Soviet Union and its surrogates expand their power and influence in Afghanistan, southern Africa and Central America by subversion and outright military invasion. In Europe, an increasingly self-confident Soviet Union was planting offensive missiles in its eastern satellites, building its conventional forces to levels far in excess of NATO equivalents. It was also constructing a navy that would give it global reach. . . .

Taken together, these three challenges—long-term economic decline, the debilitating effects of socialism, and the growing Soviet threat—were an intimidating inheritance for a new Prime Minister [as of May 1979]. I ought perhaps to have been more cowed by them in my imagination than in fact I was. . . .

My background and experience were not those of a traditional Conservative prime minister. I was less able to depend on automatic deference, but I was also perhaps less intimidated by the risks of change. My senior colleagues, growing to political maturity in the slump of the 1930s, had a more resigned and pessimistic view of political possibilities. They were perhaps too ready to accept the Labour Party and union leaders as authentic interpreters of the wishes of the people. I did not feel I needed an interpreter to address people who spoke the same language. And I felt it was a real advantage that we had lived the same sort of life. I felt that the experiences I had lived through had fitted me curiously well for the coming struggle.

I had grown up in a household that was neither poor nor rich. We had to economize each day in order to enjoy the occasional luxury. My father's background as a grocer is sometimes cited as the basis for my economic philosophy. So it was—and is—but his original philosophy encompassed more than simply ensuring that incomings showed a small surplus over outgoings at the end of the week. My father was both a practical man and a man of theory. He liked to connect the progress of our corner shop with the great complex romance of international trade which recruited people all over the world to ensure that a family in Grantham could have on its table rice from India, coffee from Kenya, sugar from the West Indies and spices from five continents. Before I read a line from the great liberal economists, I knew from my father's accounts that the free market was like a vast sensitive nervous system, responding to events and signals all over the world to meet the ever-changing needs of peoples in different countries, from different classes, of different religions, with a kind of benign indifference to their status. Governments acted on a much smaller store of conscious information and, by contrast, were themselves 'blind forces' blundering about in the dark, and obstructing the operations of markets rather than improving them. The economic history of Britain for the next forty years confirmed and amplified almost every item of my father's practical economics. In effect, I had been equipped at an early age with the ideal mental outlook and tools of analysis for reconstructing an economy ravaged by state socialism.

My life, like those of most people on the planet, was transformed by the Second World War. In my case, because I was at school and university for its duration, the transformation was an intellectual rather than a physical one. I drew from the failure of appeasement the lesson that aggression must always be firmly resisted. But how? The ultimate victory of the Allies persuaded me that nations must co-operate in defence of agreed international rules if they are either to resist great evils or to achieve great benefits. That is merely a platitude, however, if political leaders lack the courage and farsightedness, or—what is equally important—if nations lack strong bonds of common loyalty. Weak nations could not have resisted Hitler effectively—indeed, those nations that were weak did not stand up to him. So I drew from the Second World War a lesson very different from the hostility towards the nation-state evinced by some post-war European statesmen. My view was—and is—that an effective internationalism can only be built by strong nations which are able to call upon the loyalty of their citizens to defend and enforce civilized rules of international conduct. An internationalism which seeks to supersede the nation-state, however, will founder quickly upon the reality that very few people are prepared to make genuine sacrifices for it. It is likely to degenerate, therefore, into a formula for endless discussion and hand-wringing. . . .

TWO VISIONS OF EUROPE

The wisdom of hindsight, so useful to historians and indeed to authors of memoirs, is sadly denied to practising politicians. Looking back, it is now possible to see the period of my second term as Prime Minister [1983–1987] as that in which the European Community subtly but surely shifted its direction away from being a Community of open trade, light regulation and freely co-operating sovereign nation-states towards statism and centralism. I can only say that it did not seem like that at the time. For it was during this period that I not only managed to secure a durable financial settlement of Britain's Community budget imbalance and began to get Europe to take financial discipline more seriously, but also launched the drive for a real Common Market free of hidden protectionism. It was clear to me from the start that there were two competing visions of Europe: but I felt that our vision of a free enterprise *Europe des patries* was predominant.

Now I see the period somewhat differently. For the underlying forces of federalism and bureaucracy were gaining in strength as a coalition of Socialist and Christian Democrat governments in France, Spain, Italy and Germany forced the pace of integration and a commission, equipped with extra powers, began to manipulate them to advance its own agenda. It was only in my last days in office and under my successor that the true scale of the challenge has become clear.

DISCUSSION QUESTION

In what ways were Brandt's views similar to or different from those of de Gaulle or Thatcher?

SEVENTEEN

Post–World War II Trends
in the Americas

Profound political, social, technological, and economic changes have occurred in the half century after World War II. Many of these changes followed patterns already set earlier in the century, but at a faster pace. The United States led the way and set the pace in many of the changes.

One area of fast change is the realization of equality by hitherto oppressed peoples, both national groups who obtained independence after World War II and minority or other disadvantaged groups within nations who had been denied full rights. In the United States, African Americans had been denied full citizens' rights, by law in the South and by custom, usage, and other factors in the North. Like many other movements for liberation, the civil rights movements for equality for African Americans gained momentum in the 1950s and 1960s.

While every president after the end of World War II contributed to reforms that gave African Americans more rights, President Lyndon B. Johnson sponsored the most far reaching legislation toward equality for African Americans. Prodded and backed by such civil rights leaders as Martin Luther King, Jr., of the southern Baptist Movement, President Johnson introduced and Congress enacted the landmark Civil Rights Act in 1964 that banned legal inequality on the basis of race. In 1965, President Johnson made a powerful speech before Congress, urging it to enact a Voting Rights Act, which banned harassment and subterfuge by the white-dominated authorities in many southern states that denied African Americans the right to vote. As a result of this act, massive voter registration drives were launched in the South; with African Americans voting in large numbers, many of the injustices that had been perpetrated against them and other minority groups began to crumble. Thus, the civil rights movement and Voting Rights Act were as important for African Americans in the United States as the Suffragette Movement and the gaining of the right to vote were for women in Great Britain. Reading 17.1 quotes from President Lyndon Johnson's speech before Congress, advocating passage of the Voting Rights Act.

Technological advances also accelerated after World War II. They would change the pace of life and improve the overall standard of living for most people globally. Because many of the scientific and technological innovations first came about in the United States, and because the majority of the prosperous American population could increasingly afford the new inventions, the innovations came to be associated with the comforts that accompany material wealth and materialism.

Communications have made amazing advances. Just as radio changed lives and culture in an earlier era, television changed life after 1945. Televisions brought visual images in ever clearer living color and finer definition from anywhere in the world and from space and other planets to almost every family's living room. Other vital changes in means of communicating, especially via the computer, would follow.

The second reading in this chapter is taken from a recent work by veteran television anchor and commentator David Brinkley, who pioneered and participated in TV reporting from its inception. Two generations of Americans grew accustomed to Brinkley's face as he presented the evening news and, later, gave his personal interpretations of them. Reading Brinkley's account of the early TV coverage of political conventions (Reading 17.2), one becomes deeply aware of how this medium has influenced and changed the political culture of the United States. His account of the coverage of the private lives of leaders shows great changes in social mores during the past several decades.

Latin America experienced dramatic and profound political changes in the second half of the twentieth century. The region as a whole suffered from a heritage of economic underdevelopment and great economic disparity between the few rich and a majority of disenfranchised poor. Such economic inequities contributed to political instability. Even when there were elections in Latin American nations, they were often dishonest and rigged. Coup d'etats and strong-men rule were prevalent throughout the region.

Not all strong men were reactionaries; some espoused economic and social reforms. In Argentina, charismatic dictator Juan Peron rigged elections but was also admired by many of his poor, urban compatriots, partly because of his social welfare programs. Many of these programs, however, could not be fully implemented or sustained because Argentina's resources were inadequately developed and Peron's policies created economic difficulties, such as inflation. Reading 17.3A is a statement of some Peronist ideas.

In Cuba, dramatic changes under Fidel Castro were inspired by Marxism and were carried out with violence and massive aid from the Soviet Union. Committed Latin American revolutionaries, such as Fidel Castro of Cuba and Che Guevara (an Argentinian who worked alongside Castro), not only sought to change Cuban society according to the Marxist model but also aimed at expanding the movement throughout South America. Bolivia, with its sharply divided social classes and an indigenous Marxist movement, seemed a likely place for a Marxist social revolution. In 1966 and 1967, Che Guevara and a small band of dedicated supporters struggled to create a communist guerrilla insurgency in Bolivia. They failed because the local people saw them as foreigners; the peasants did not rise up to support them; and, in the Cold War struggle against the

Soviet Union, the United States helped the Bolivian government to destroy the insurgency. Reading 17.3B is a firsthand account of the last days of the Guevara-led insurgency in Bolivia.

In the closing decades of the twentieth century, most Latin American countries rejected both military juntas, strong-men rule, and Marxist insurgencies and moved toward democratically elected governments. Although Peronists survived in Argentina, as has Castroism in Cuba, both seemed increasingly anachronistic and divorced from their respective original ideologies.

READING 17.1

The Voting Rights Bill

Racial tensions heightened in the United States during the 1950s because African Americans who still faced discrimination legally in the South and practically throughout the land were beginning to press hard for redress. Building on the foundations laid by earlier leaders such as W.E.B. DuBois (review Reading 8.1), the civil rights movement by African Americans and their white allies gained momentum as the 1960s progressed. Its greatest leader during this period was Baptist minister Martin Luther King, Jr., who patterned his nonviolent protests after the earlier ones in India led by Mohandas K. Gandhi (review Reading 10.1A). The goal of the civil rights movement was to end segregation against African Americans in public housing, schools, and transportation, as well as at the polling place. The movement persevered despite violent persecution by southern white authorities and prosegregation mobs.

Taking office after the assassination of President John F. Kennedy in November 1963, President Lyndon B. Johnson introduced landmark legislation that significantly advanced the civil rights movement. The most important civil rights message President Johnson presented to Congress accompanied the Right to Vote Bill, which he personally delivered to a joint session of the legislature on March 15, 1965. He called on Democrats and Republicans for bipartisan support to correct a glaring omission in the Civil Rights Bill of the previous year, which had failed to protect the right of African Americans to vote. The passage of this bill, procivil rights legal interpretations by the Supreme Court, and the registration of large numbers of African Americans to vote ultimately ensured the gradual realization of equal protection of all citizens under the law. Victories in the civil rights movement for African Americans also advanced the causes of other hitherto discriminated against groups, such as the Native Americans, Mexican Americans, and poor people. Thus, the 1960s witnessed the expansion of individual civil liberties throughout the United States. This reading excerpts key passages from President Johnson's address, which accompanied his presentation of the Voting Rights Bill to Congress.

Mr. Speaker, Mr. President, Members of the Congress:

I speak tonight for the dignity of man and the destiny of democracy.

I urge every member of both parties, Americans of all religions and of all colors, from every section of this country, to join me in that cause. . . .

Our mission is at once the oldest and the most basic of this country: to right wrong, to do justice, to serve man.

In our time we have come to live with moments of great crisis. Our lives have been marked with debate about great issues; issues of war and peace, issues of prosperity and depression. But rarely in any time does an issue lay bare the secret heart of America itself. Rarely are we met with a challenge, not to our growth or abundance, our welfare or our security, but rather to the values and the purposes and the meaning of our beloved Nation.

Johnson, Lyndon B. *Public Papers of the Presidents of the United States, Containing the Public Messages, Speeches, and Statements of the President, 1965* (in two books), *Book I*—January 1 to May 31, 1965. Washington, DC: U.S. Government Printing Office, 1966, pp. 281–84, 286.

The issue of equal rights for American Negroes is such an issue. And should we defeat every enemy, should we double our wealth and conquer the stars, and still be unequal to this issue, then we will have failed as a people and as a nation. . . .

For with a country as with a person, "What is a man profited, if he shall gain the whole world, and lose his own soul?"

There is no Negro problem. There is no Southern problem. There is no Northern problem. There is only an American problem. And we are met here tonight as Americans—not as Democrats or Republicans—we are met here as Americans to solve that problem.

This was the first nation in the history of the world to be founded with a purpose. The great phrases of that purpose still sound in every American heart, North and South: "All men are created equal"—"government by consent of the governed"—"give me liberty or give me death." Well, those are not just clever words, or those are not just empty theories. In their name Americans have fought and died for two centuries, and tonight around the world they stand there as guardians of our liberty, risking their lives.

Those words are a promise to every citizen that he shall share in the dignity of man. This dignity cannot be found in a man's possessions; it cannot be found in his power, or in his position. It really rests on his right to be treated as a man equal in opportunity to all others. It says that he shall share in freedom, he shall choose his leaders, educate his children, and provide for his family according to his ability and his merits as a human being.

To apply any other test—to deny a man his hopes because of his color or race, his religion or the place of his birth—is not only to do injustice, it is to deny America and to dishonor the dead who gave their lives for American freedom. . . .

Our fathers believed that if this noble view of the rights of man was to flourish, it must be rooted in democracy. The most basic right of all was the right to choose your own leaders. The history of this country, in large measure, is the history of the expansion of that right to all of our people.

Many of the issues of civil rights are very complex and most difficult. But about this there can and should be no argument. Every American citizen must have an equal right to vote. There is no reason which can excuse the denial of that right. There is no duty which weighs more heavily on us than the duty we have to ensure that right.

Yet the harsh fact is that in many places in this country men and women are kept from voting simply because they are Negroes.

Every device of which human ingenuity is capable has been used to deny this right. . . .

Experience has clearly shown that the existing process of law cannot overcome systematic and ingenious discrimination. No law that we now have on the books—and I have helped to put three of them there—can ensure the right to vote when local officials are determined to deny it.

In such a case our duty must be clear to all of us. The Constitution says that no person shall be kept from voting because of his race or his color. We have all sworn an oath before God to support and to defend that Constitution. We must now act in obedience to that oath. . . .

Wednesday I will send to Congress a law designed to eliminate illegal barriers to the right to vote. . . .

This bill will strike down restrictions to voting in all elections—Federal, State, and local—which have been used to deny Negroes the right to vote.

This bill will establish a simple, uniform standard which cannot be used, however ingenious the effort, to flout our Constitution.

It will provide for citizens to be registered by officials of the United States Government if the State officials refuse to register them.

It will eliminate tedious, unnecessary lawsuits which delay the right to vote.

Finally, this legislation will ensure that properly registered individuals are not prohibited from voting. . . .

This time, on this issue, there must be no delay, no hesitation and no compromise with our purpose.

We cannot, we must not, refuse to protect the right of every American to vote in every election that he may desire to participate in. And we ought not and we cannot and we must not wait another 8 months before we get a bill. We have already waited a hundred years and more, and the time for waiting is gone.

So I ask you to join me in working long hours—nights and weekends, if necessary—to pass this bill. And I don't make that request lightly. For from the window where I sit with the problems of our country I recognize that outside this chamber is the outraged conscience of a nation, the grave concern of many nations, and the harsh judgment of history on our acts.

But even if we pass this bill, the battle will not be over. What happened in Selma is part of a far larger movement which reaches into every section and State of America. It is the effort of American Negroes to secure for themselves the full blessings of American life.

Their cause must be our cause too. Because it is not just Negroes, but really it is all of us, who must overcome the crippling legacy of bigotry and injustice.

And we shall overcome. . . .

The bill that I am presenting to you will be known as a civil rights bill. But, in a larger sense, most of the program I am recommending is a civil rights program. Its object is to open the city of hope to all people of all races.

Because all Americans just must have the right to vote. And we are going to give them that right.

All Americans must have the privileges of citizenship regardless of race. And they are going to have those privileges of citizenship regardless of race.

But I would like to caution you and remind you that to exercise these privileges takes much more than just legal right. It requires a trained mind and a healthy body. It requires a decent home, and the chance to find a job, and the opportunity to escape from the clutches of poverty.

Of course, people cannot contribute to the Nation if they are never taught to read or write, if their bodies are stunted from hunger, if their sickness goes untended, if their life is spent in hopeless poverty just drawing a welfare check.

So we want to open the gates to opportunity. But we are also going to give all our people, black and white, the help that they need to walk through those gates.

READING 17.2

The Media Revolution—Television

Looking back on the twentieth century, the daily lives of all peoples everywhere have been dramatically affected by two revolutions: transportation and communications. The readings in Part 1 of this book described the pioneering role of the Wright brothers in the development of airplanes and of Henry Ford in the automobile industry. Travel by both plane and car is now an integral part of the daily lives of many. In the media revolution, there was first the radio, or wireless, which uses electromagnetic waves to transmit and receive signals without wires. The radio set, common in most American homes before World War II, brought the sound of music and news to millions and government leaders—for example President Roosevelt through his fireside chats (review Reading 9.1) and the people to close contact. Radios are still a part of our daily lives. Television transmitted and recovered on a screen moving visual images and accompanying sounds. Invented before World War II, TV became increasingly available after 1945. As prices of TVs, first in black-and-white, then in color, became ever cheaper and therefore more affordable, they, too, became commonplace.

The impact of television is difficult to exaggerate. With satellites transmitting images around the world instantaneously, almost every household in the United States and much of the rest of the world can see and hear news from anywhere as it is being made. TV has also played a key role in revolutionizing politics, making the likeness of politicians immediately recognizable to their constituents and, in the process, helping those who appear telegenic and hurting others less apt at manipulating this medium. TV has also brought advertising, entertainment, sports, and culture from around the world to all homes, affecting lives and social mores, changing patterns of entertainment, and cutting into the readership of books, magazines, and newspapers. Thus, the impact of TV on politics, entertainment, education, and the stimulation of consumption (review Reading 14.2) cannot be exaggerated.

The United States led the way in the development of the television industry. David Brinkley began his distinguished career as a reporter after World War II. When he retired in 1997, he was the doyen among TV news reporters and commentators. Brinkley's book entitled *11 Presidents, 4 Wars, 22 Political Conventions, 1 Moon Landing, 3 Assassinations, 2,000 Weeks of News and Other Stuff on Television and 18 Years of Growing Up in North Carolina* (1995) details some of his experiences, told in his inimitable way. Excerpts from this book on early television coverage of political conventions and other news follow.

In 1948 television made its first appearance at a political convention. The two parties did not know what to make of the new medium, and we did not know what to make of a convention, since none of our crew at NBC had ever covered one. It appeared mainly to be a crowd of middle-aged white men aimlessly milling around in a huge hall, talking, smoking cigars and shaking hands, and occasionally pushing through the crowds to get out to cadge free drinks from a bar operated by the Association of American Railroads,

Brinkley, David. *11 Presidents, 4 Wars, 22 Political Conventions, 1 Moon Landing, 3 Assassinations, 2,000 Weeks of News and Other Stuff on Television and 18 Years of Growing Up in North Carolina.* New York: Alfred A. Knopf, 1995, pp. 80–81, 92–93, 96, 106–7, 141–42.

and after a stop at the men's room to return to the convention floor only to find that the speaker who had been so boring he drove them out of the hall in the first place was still on the rostrum and still talking. The television picture in 1948 was available only in a small area of the East Coast, and even there it could be seen only in the tiny number of households owning television sets. Nevertheless, NBC sent cameras to Philadelphia, only a few since at that time it only had a few. John Cameron Swayze, whose knowledge of politics was limited, went with them to explain the proceedings to what little audience there was. He and the cameras arrived to find a less than effusive welcome. The Republicans would allow only one camera in the convention hall and said NBC must install it in a cubicle high up among the rafters. There would be nothing up there but Swayze and a few pigeons. So many steps had to be climbed to get up to the camera booth that many Republicans, when invited up to be interviewed, squinted up into the half-dark spaces just under the roof and declined to make the long climb. Since the party leaders were not young athletes most of them were never seen or heard from.

In view of this, in view of the convention camera's being physically inaccessible, and the television picture's being seen only in a small area of the East Coast and nowhere else, and Dewey's being nominated once more and going on to lose the fifth election in a row to still another Democrat, both the Republicans and television might as well have stayed home.

The next month, the Democrats met in the same Philadelphia hall, with Swayze and television still up in the rafters, but the party had more serious problems than television reporters and pigeons. The southern states were furious that race and civil rights were coming to be an irresistible political force, more and more difficult to ignore as they had ignored them for years. The convention was near to revolt, the southerners feeling like strangers in their own land, and there was even talk of a third-party candidate who would be more amenable on questions of race. . . .

By 1952 when the Republicans and Democrats both held their conventions in Chicago, television was growing into a political force too big to ignore and too important to send up to the rafters with the pigeons. About 17 million homes had TV sets now, and the conventions were seen in sixty-four cities in thirty-eight states. This was before there were satellites, and we still used coaxial cables installed by the telephone company to carry our programs into most but not all of the United States. As yet only one cable ran all the way to California, and the three networks had to share it, with NBC, CBS and ABC all sending the same picture to the West Coast. While there was only one cable to carry the picture, there were plenty of wires in use since early radio days to carry sound and speech. The three networks had to share the one video cable, but each could send its own narration. Since no network was willing to carry the voices or names of reporters other than those of its own staff members, what was sent to California was the same picture with three separate narrations, each going only to the affiliated stations of one of the three networks. . . .

. . . But the pool was still interesting because its director, Bob Doyle of NBC, had an eye for engaging, amusing detail. During the dull spots when nothing was happening, and there were many of these, Doyle had his cameras roam around to find such close-ups as a portly state chairman asleep in his chair, a delegate splattering his necktie with mustard dripping off his hot dog, others reading the papers and ignoring the speeches.

The mail told us the audience loved it. But the politicians did not, and in the next day's session each delegate found a printed notice on his chair warning that "you might be on television without knowing it. Please consider how you will look to viewers across the country and behave accordingly." . . .

Since this was the first convention I had ever attended or even seen, I didn't and couldn't do much. I did NBC's narration to the West Coast, talking over whatever picture popped up on the pool feed, never knowing what was coming next nor for how long. We did not yet know much about how to cover a huge, sprawling political event, but we did learn this: if you are to talk over a television picture, you must talk about what is in the picture. Anything else is confusing to the viewers, as if a newspaper printed a picture of a home-run hitter sliding into the plate and under the picture a caption telling something about the gross national product. . . .

. . . After the years of war and radio's often brilliant news from the fronts, nobody could seriously consider television without news. Over time, with the cold war, fears of nuclear war, the murder of a president, the landing on the moon and a thousand other events seen on television and in time in full color, the afternoon papers died one by one, and there was no more news on the front steps. Now it was inside the house on the TV screen and nowhere else. The evening news had moved to television. With a few exceptions—not many—radio turned itself into an entertainment medium offering rock music for adolescents while the Benny Goodmans and Tommy Dorseys packed up their saxophones and trombones and went away. . . .

. . . In the early days of television, the rules were tight and explicit. For example, I was not allowed to say the word "rape" on the air. A rape had to be called a criminal assault, a code word then widely understood. I was not permitted to say the word "abortion" on the air. It had to be called an "illegal operation." As everyone is aware, since Kennedy's time, the sixties, there has been a more or less dramatic change in the unspoken, unwritten rules or habits in public communication, helped along by various court rulings. Look at movies insisting on at least one bedroom scene with nudity, even when it serves no dramatic purpose but is put in only to avoid a G rating. It seems Hollywood fears that a G rating means to the public that the movie is about cute children, kittens and puppies. Look at the supermarket tabloids, at the array of sex magazines on the newsstands. None of this was true in Kennedy's time. It would all be made public if he were to become president now. It simply was that a communications device, television, with a circulation so massive and so indiscriminate, going everywhere at home and abroad, was reluctant to join in the trend toward sexual candor and openness, restrained by its own intrinsic massiveness and its managers' fears of giving offense, fears of losing their new and valuable broadcast licenses. What finally ushered in the new licentiousness were the rulings of the Supreme Court of the United States saying pornography was speech, and under the Constitution speech must be free.

READING 17.3

Dictators and Revolutionaries in Latin America

After World War II, as before, dictators and strongmen ruled in many Latin American countries. In Argentina, army colonel Juan Peron was elected president in 1946 and reelected in 1951. Peron was a political adventurer who wooed and won the loyalty of Argentina's urban poor. He organized urban workers into unions and gave them pay bonuses and pensions. He was ably assisted by his ambitious wife, Eva (Evita) Duarte Peron, who had been a popular radio star before their marriage. Until his ouster in 1955 (she had died in 1952), the Perons exemplified personalist rule, which had been prevalent in Latin American politics. Both were charismatic personalities—he for his macho image and magnetic speaking style, she for her beauty and couture clothes. They won widespread support because he nationalized industries and launched expensive social programs that favored workers, while she administered extensive social welfare organizations and campaigned for and won suffrage for women. Both Perons, but especially Eva, enjoyed enormous public adulation, even after they died. Reading 17.3A is from Juan Peron's presidential addresses, in which he explains the meaning of Peronism and the ideology of the Peronist party, which he headed.

In 1959, Fidel Castro came to power in Cuba, thereby establishing a Marxist beachhead in Latin America. With opponents either jailed or exiled and with economic, military, and political support from the Soviet Union and other communist bloc countries, Castro's government instituted wide-ranging social and economic reforms. Like Peron in Argentina, Castro nationalized industries. However, he went further than Peron in seizing landed estates that belonged to rich Cubans and foreign companies, which he formed into large national corporations similar to state farms in the Soviet Union. Castro also promised to export revolution throughout Latin America, and he sent guerrilla warfare experts, the most famous being Ernesto Che Guevara, to several countries in the region to incite and organize revolution.

Born into a well-to-do family in Argentina and trained as a medical doctor, Guevara joined Castro's cause and served in his government. Between November 1966 and his capture and execution in October 1967, he led a guerrilla movement in Bolivia. The Bolivian peasants, however, did not rise to join him, and most of his small band were hunted down and killed by the Bolivian army with the aid of the United States. Reading 17.3B is from the unfinished memoirs by Inti Peredo, one of five revolutionaries who escaped the dragnet that killed Guevara. While writing his account, Peredo was caught and executed by Bolivian forces in 1969. It recounts the last days of Guevara's guerrilla campaign.

Although Peronism and Marxism have lost much appeal in Latin America in recent decades, they remain relevant. In 1997, the Peronist party controlled the elected legislature in Argentina, while Castro's Communist party continued to rule Cuba. However, both have extensively modified their original platforms. Interestingly, several decades after their deaths, both Eva Peron and Che Guevara remain cult heroes. She being the subject of a recent musical and movie called *Evita*.

Eva Peron. Juan and Eva Peron were the charismatic first couple of Argentina. Besides heading several important government organizations, Eva also represented Argentina on tours abroad. Reproduced from the Collection of the Library of Congress.

READING 17.3A: JUAN PERON ON PERONISM

In Congress a few days ago, some of our legislators have asked what Peronism is. Peronism is humanism in action; Peronism is a new political doctrine, which rejects all the ills of the politics of previous times; in the social sphere it is a theory which establishes a little equality among men, which grants them similar opportunities and assures them of a future so that in this land there may be no one who lacks what he needs for a living, even though it may be necessary that those who are wildly squandering what they possess may be deprived of the right to do so, for the benefit of those who have nothing at all; in the economic sphere its aim is that every Argentine should pull his weight for the Argentines and that economic policy which maintained that this was a permanent and perfect school of capitalist exploitation should be replaced by a doctrine of social economy under which the distribution of our wealth, which we force the earth to yield up to us and which furthermore we are elaborating, may be shared out fairly among all those who have contributed by their efforts to amass it.

That is Peronism. And Peronism is not learned, nor just talked about: one feels it or else disagrees. Peronism is a question of the heart rather than of the head. Fortunately I am not one of those Presidents who live a life apart, but on the contrary I live among my people, just as I have always lived; so that I share all the ups and downs, all their successes and all their disappointments with my working class people. I feel an intimate

Peron, Juan Domingo. *Peronist Doctrine.* Buenos Aires: The Peronist Party, 1952.

satisfaction when I see a workman who is well dressed or taking his family to the the-
atre. I feel just as satisfied as I would feel if I were that workman myself. That is Peronism. (from a speech made in 1948)

I have never been of the opinion that in this world there should be groups of men
against other groups, nations against nations and much less can I admit that men should
be enemies because they profess a different religion. How could it be admitted, how
could it be explained that anti-semitism should exist in Argentina? In Argentina there
should not be more than one single class of men: men who work together for the welfare of the nation, without any discrimination whatever. They are good Argentines, no
matter what their origin, their race or their religion may be, if they work every day for
the greatness of the Nation, and they are bad Argentines, no matter what they say or how
much they shout, if they are not laying a new stone every day towards the construction
of the building of the happiness and grandeur of our Nation.

That is the only discrimination which Argentina should make among its inhabitants:
those who are doing constructive work and those who are not; those who are benefac-
tors to the country and those who are not. For this reason in this freest land of the free,
as long as I am President of the Republic, no one will be persecuted by anyone else.
(from a speech made in 1950)

READING 17.3B: CHE GUEVARA'S FAILED BOLIVIAN UPRISING

This was the situation as we came to October 8.

The previous evening marked eleven months since Che had gone into the mountains
of Bolivia. Up to that point the balance sheet was not particularly unfavorable for us. The
army had dealt us only one serious blow, at La Higuera, which on the other hand was accidental. Everything else had been positive on balance. Despite our small numbers, we
had captured almost a hundred soldiers, including high-ranking officers; we had put a
large number of enemy troops out of commission; and we had captured various weapons
and a lot of ammunition.

We now faced a new tactical phase, where it was absolutely necessary to break out of
the encirclement in order to reach a new zone of operations. There we would have been
able to engage the enemy under conditions set by us, while at the same time making contact with the city, an important question in this period, in order to reinforce our column.

Anyone who reads Che's diary will realize that at no time can one detect desperation
or lack of faith, despite the many anguished moments we had passed through. (It should
be kept in mind that the diary contains only notations for Che's personal use, primarily
reflecting negative aspects, with the aim of analyzing these and later correcting them.)
That is why, in reviewing eleven months of operations, Che summed up his thoughts by
saying that the time had passed "without complications, bucolically."

The early morning of October 8 was cold. Those of us with wool ponchos put them
on. Our hike was slow because Chino walked badly at night, and because Moro's illness

Walters, Mary-Alice. *The Bolivian Diary of Ernesto Che Guevara.* New York: Pathfinder, 1994,
pp. 384–97, 401–4.

was getting worse. At 2:00 a.m. we stopped to rest, resuming our hike at 4:00. We were 17 silent figures, camouflaged in darkness, walking through a narrow canyon called the Yuro ravine.

At dawn a beautiful sun broke out over the horizon, enabling us to carefully scan the terrain. We were looking for a hillcrest we could take to the San Lorenzo river. Extreme security measures were taken, particularly because the gorge and the hill were semibar-ren, with very low bushes, making it almost impossible to hide.

Che then decided to send out three pairs of scouts: one along the hill to the right, made up of Benigno and Pacho; another along the hill to the left, made up of Urbano and an-other comrade; and the last one to the area in front of us, assigned to Aniceto and Darío. Benigno and Pacho soon returned with news that left no doubt as to the situation: soldiers were closing off the pass. The problem was to know whether they had detected us or not.

What were the alternatives left to us?

We could not turn back, since the path we had taken, very unprotected, would make us easy targets for the soldiers. Nor could we go forward, since this would mean walk-ing straight into the position occupied by the soldiers. Che made the only decision pos-sible at that moment. He gave the order to hide in a small lateral canyon, and organized the taking of positions. It was approximately 8:30 a.m. The 17 of us were positioned at the center and at both sides of the canyon, waiting.

The great dilemma faced by Che, and all of us, was to know whether the army had discovered our presence, or whether this was simply a tactical maneuver within the broader encirclement they had been putting in place for several days.

Che made a rapid analysis. If the soldiers attacked between 10:00 a.m. and 1:00 p.m., we would be at a profound disadvantage, and our prospects would be minimal, since it would be very difficult to resist for a prolonged period of time. If they attacked between 1:00 and 3:00 p.m., our prospects for neutralizing them were better. If the battle occurred from 3:00 p.m. on, the advantage would be ours, since night would soon be falling, and night is comrade and ally to the guerrilla.

At approximately 11:00 a.m., I went to replace Benigno at his position, but he did not climb down and instead remained there spread out on the ground, since the wound in his shoulder had become infected and was very painful. Benigno, Darío, and I would remain there from then on. On the other side of the ravine were Pombo and Urbano, and in the center was Che with the rest of the combatants.

At approximately 1:30 p.m., Che sent Ñato and Aniceto to relieve Pombo and Ur-bano. To cross over to their position, we had to cross a clearing that the enemy's posi-tion overlooked. The first to try it was Aniceto, but he was killed by a bullet.

The battle had begun. Our exit was closed off. The soldiers shouted, "We got one! We got one!"

From the same narrow gorge, in a position occupied by soldiers, one could hear the regular rattle of machine guns, which appeared to cover the path we had come through the night before.

The group I was in was positioned directly facing one section of the army, at an equal height, which enabled us to observe their movements without being seen. We therefore fired only when fired upon, to not give ourselves away. The army, for its part, believed that all our firing was coming from down below, i.e., from Che's position. . . .

We put on our knapsacks and headed quickly to the contact point. Along the way we found food supplies thrown on the ground, including flour. This troubled us deeply, because Che never permitted anyone to throw food on the ground. When it was necessary to do so, it would be carefully hidden. Farther ahead I found Che's plate, completely trampled. I recognized it immediately, because it was a wide bowl made of aluminum with unique characteristics. I picked it up and stored it in my knapsack.

We found no one at the meeting place, although we recognized footprints from Che's sandals, which left a different mark than the others, making it easy to identify. But these tracks disappeared farther ahead. . . .

How did we survive the encirclements placed around us after the battle at the Yuro ravine, against forces vastly superior in both numbers and weapons? . . .

We were in poor physical condition. We had eaten little and had exerted great efforts during the previous days. In addition, the great tension we had been under also left its mark on us.

We lightened our load once again. Ñato, who carried all the medical supplies, buried them, since these would be of no use to us in the future. The metal box that had been used previously for sterilization was turned into a cooking pot. The flour soup we prepared after so many days of privation served only to "fool our insides," but did not restore our strength.

In the early morning hours of October 12, we began walking in the direction of one part of the circle. At 3:00 a.m. we crossed the road to La Higuera at the Abra del Picacho, just as we had done earlier with Che. It was completely silent all around. When it got light we were at the other side of the pass. We came upon a hut and decided to go ask its inhabitants for the exact location, reorient ourselves, try to stock up on food supplies, and continue on. We looked for the peasants but found no one. Remaining in the hut was too dangerous, so we decided it would be better to hide ourselves in the bushes surrounding the house.

Two totally opposite events marked the day. A boy about twelve years old, very alert, identified our exact location for us. He pointed out the direction of the river, offered us a pot to cook in, and began to milk a cow for us. Unfortunately, a peasant passing by saw us and ran off toward the pass to denounce us to the soldiers, large numbers of whom were concentrated there as part of the strategic encirclement around our dwindling column. Owing to our physical weakness, we were unable to catch up with him. And because he was a peasant, we did not want to shoot him. . . .

Some peasants began to circle around the area, and the army began to surround it. At approximately 4:30 p.m. on October 12, a tight circle of soldiers was moving in on the "island." This was their best opportunity to eliminate us, but the final word had not been spoken.

The six of us resolved to group ourselves in the highest part of the small wood, and to respond to enemy fire only when we were sure of hitting the mark. The soldiers opened fire, insulting us and calling on us to surrender. We kept our silence, aware of their movements. . . .

As Pombo had foreseen, the firing stopped when night fell. But to our misfortune, there appeared a beautiful moon, showering its light on every corner. To try to leave under such circumstances was too risky.

We remained vigilant. A terrible chill had fallen and went right through one's clothing down to the bone. We shivered as we watched the sky, waiting for the moon to be obscured.

At 3:00 a.m., clouds came down over the entire area. This was the moment we had been waiting for with impatience. We crawled slowly. To our surprise, the soldiers had pulled back a bit. Apparently the four losses they suffered during the afternoon drove them to take precautions. Soon we were close to enemy positions. The soldiers were posted five meters apart from each other. The weather and the wait had affected them as well.

We continued advancing until suddenly one of the soldiers, instead of firing, shouted, "Halt! Who goes there?"

That was our salvation. We threw ourselves at one of the trenches, killed a few of the soldiers, and crouched together there. An intense exchange of fire broke out on all sides, lasting approximately 15 minutes or longer. When it ended, we began to leave. The army's encirclement had been broken.

DISCUSSION QUESTION

Describe the different methods that Peron and Guevara used to gain power. How did their methods for making reforms differ from those used in the United States?

CHAPTER EIGHTEEN

Asia Since World War II

A new balance of power emerged in East Asia at the end of World War II. Japan, which had dominated Asia since the early twentieth century, lay in ruins and was under foreign occupation for the first time in its history. Between 1945 and 1952, the United States occupation authorities set out to transform Japan from a military-dominated, imperialist nation to a peaceful and open parliamentary democracy. Although many of the reforms, including the language in some of them, were imposed by the United States, there were many Japanese who had been silenced by the militarist regime that supported them. These epoch-making reforms broke the mold that had made Japan hated and reviled by its World War II victims and set the pattern that Japan follows today. The occupation succeeded because of good will on both sides. The first reading in this chapter is from the *Memoirs* of Japan's foremost early postwar leader, Shigeru Yoshida. As prime minister in the immediate postwar era, he played a pivotal role in working with the Americans to rebuild Japan. The years ending in 1955 have, as a result, been dubbed the "Yoshida decade." This reading describes the writing of a new constitution to provide the framework for the new Japan. Democratic and prosperous, Japan became a model for other Asian nations seeking progress and democracy.

After a century of humiliation by imperialist nations, China emerged as one of the victorious great powers. But China, too, was devastated, after an eight-year war fought on its soil. Its agony would continue as civil war between the Nationalist government and the Chinese Communist party resumed almost as soon as World War II ended. By 1949, the communists had won.

The People's Republic of China, led by Mao Zedong, transformed China in ways similar to the Soviet Union after World War I. The communist government first instituted land reforms that eliminated landlords and divided farmlands among the peasants. Then it collectivized the land and forced all peasants into collectives and communes, where they were ordered to do what the central planners wanted, with no room for personal or economic initiatives. Wielding total power, the Communist party controlled people's lives and attempted to mold their thoughts. The second reading was written by Wei Jingsheng, China's most famous human rights fighter. Brought up an ardent communist, he turned against the party when as a teenage Red Guard he saw the dire poverty and suffering that communism had caused and perpetuated. His experiences led him to believe that only democracy could check the tyranny of the Communist party. For daring to ask the Communist party for democratic reform, Wei has spent most of his adult life in labor camps. Here he describes what he has seen.

The quest for democracy and equality for women has been a worldwide phenomenon throughout the twentieth century. Both ideals were new to Asia. Though much progress was made in women's rights, many progressive laws remained to be implemented. India led much of Asia in the women's movement. Indian women were the first in Asia to be granted the right to vote, and many women rose to prominence in India and elsewhere on the subcontinent. However, the majority of the women of the region remained poor, rural, and oppressed, ignorant of their rights or powerless to claim them. Reading 18.3 has two selections. The first is by a lawyer who details some of the problems that she and other professional women have had to contend with. Many of the problems that handicapped middle-class Indian professional women were shared by their counterparts throughout the world. The second selection is from an interview of poor, rural Indian women; their experiences, too, are similar to those of other poor working-class women, especially in underdeveloped parts of the world.

READING 18.1

The New Japan

Resoundingly defeated, Japan surrendered unconditionally on August 14, 1945, ending World War II. For the next seven years, it was occupied by United States military forces (although the occupation was nominally supervised by a thirteen-nation Allied Commission). General Douglas MacArthur, Supreme Commander for the Allied Powers (SCAP), orchestrated the remaking of postwar Japan.

Expecting a harsh and vindictive occupation similar to the way they had dealt with their defeated enemies, the Japanese found the Americans benevolent and constructive. As a result, most Japanese cooperated with the occupation authorities in remaking Japan. The many revolutionary changes made during the occupation so transformed the country that they were called the "second opening" of Japan, comparable in importance to the first opening by the United States in 1853 (review Reading 2.3).

SCAP's most important reform was the enactment of a new constitution in 1947. It renounced war, emancipated women, and made Japan into a democratic, parliamentary state led by a prime minister, who headed the majority party in the lower chamber of the bicameral legislature. To ease the dramatic transition, the emperor was retained but was stripped of his former "divine" and sovereign power and was changed to a symbol of the state and the people. Although the catalyst for the fundamental changes came from the outside, the constitution has been retained with no major demands for revisions, indicating that the majority of the Japanese people supported its provisions.

Shigeru Yoshida was a diplomat who had opposed the policies that had culminated in World War II. With the purging of the leading politicians who had been involved in Japan's aggressions, Yoshida was chosen to be prime minister in 1946–1947, and again between 1949 and 1955. He was the reluctant instrument of some of the reforms mandated by SCAP during his first term in office; later, he led Japan's rehabilitation, the beginning of its economic prosperity, and its recovery of sovereignty. This reading quotes from the part of his *Memoirs* that deals with the American role in the writing of the new constitution.

We did not find much to propose to the Occupation authorities, for the zeal of the men and women of the Occupation took care of practically everything, so that it was sufficient (and rather more than sufficient) for us to take the directives as they were issued one after another, and to strive to assert ourselves, as the Government, whenever they seemed to err on the side of impracticability. The impetus came from the Occupation; for the final form that was given that impetus, we at least did what we could to realise what seemed best, according to our views at that time.

The revision of the Constitution was perhaps the most important single reform undertaken after the termination of the Pacific war. . . . Dr. Matsumoto [cabinet minister in charge of rewriting the constitution] explained that, since a great deal of alteration was bound to be demanded from all sides once the draft was made public, it was prudent to introduce as little change in the original draft as possible. This draft was forwarded to General MacArthur's headquarters in February 1946. . . .

Yoshida, Shigeru. *The Yoshida Memoirs: The Story of Japan in Crisis.* Cambridge, MA: The Riverside Press, 1962, pp. 129, 132–40.

Possibly prompted by the fact that this draft was widely reported in the Japanese press, General MacArthur instructed General Courtney Whitney to prepare a draft Constitution in the shortest possible time. The Occupation authorities must have thought that, since our draft did not differ very conspicuously from the old Meiji Constitution, the only course was to prepare another, incorporating their own ideas, and show it to us as an example of the kind of thing they wanted. The work of drafting the G H Q [General Headquarters] version took one week.

On 13 February, officials of G H Q came to see us by appointment, at the official residence of the Foreign Minister. There were present, on the Japanese side, myself as Foreign Minister. . . . General Whitney informed me that G H Q was not satisfied with the Japanese draft of the revised Constitution, and that he had brought with him a model draft, blueprinted within G H Q, and that he wanted us to turn out a version based upon this draft as soon as possible. He then handed us several copies of the draft and went on to say that it would meet with the approval both of the United States Government and the Far Eastern Commission; that General MacArthur had given much thought to the question of the position of the Emperor, which could best be safeguarded by revising our Constitution along lines laid down in the model version drafted by G H Q; and that if this was not done, G H Q could not answer for whatever might happen to the Emperor. He added that this was not an order, but that G H Q desired most earnestly that the Japanese Government should forward to General MacArthur's headquarters as soon as possible a draft Constitution incorporating the basic principles and form of the G H Q model version.

After this statement, the G H Q officials went for a walk in the garden in order to give us time to look over the draft thus presented to us. Dr. Matsumoto began reading it with great attention, and I too had a look. The document began with the words 'We, the Japanese people', indicating that it was the people who were framing the Constitution and not the Emperor. And it was stated in Chapter I that the Emperor was 'the symbol of the State'. Also, in this original draft, the Diet was to be composed of one Chamber only. After they returned from the Garden, Dr. Matsumoto asked the G H Q officials some questions, and then informed them that we would read over the contents of the draft carefully and give our considered opinion later. General Whitney and his companions then left.

As indicated by the few words already quoted, the G H Q draft was of a revolutionary nature. The Government was not prepared to frame a new Constitution based upon such a model and started negotiations with G H Q to see if there was not some means of coming to a compromise. General MacArthur's headquarters remained adamant, however, regarding the basic principles of revision. . . .

Baron Shidehara accordingly paid a visit to General MacArthur on 21 February to ascertain the Supreme Commander's own views concerning the question of revision. From the account of the interview given by the Prime Minister at a Cabinet meeting held the next day, it seems that the General had stated that the welfare of Japan was foremost in his mind and that, particularly since he had met the Emperor, it had been one of his primary concerns to safeguard the position of the Throne . . . and that the two main points to be stressed in the draft were the definition of the Emperor as the symbol of the State and the renunciation-of-war clause. . . . Matsumoto accordingly set to work to frame a Constitution based on the G H Q model with the assistance of the Councillor of the Bureau of Legislation. But it then appeared that G H Q wanted this task finished in about the same time that had been needed to produce their model version, and a completed Japanese draft was accordingly submitted to G H Q on 4 March, without an English translation, which there was no time to prepare. The new Japanese version was then gone over in the Government Section of General MacArthur's headquarters by American and Japanese experts, the work taking all night and the best part of 5 March. The Cabinet met on the morning of the 5th and Dr. Matsumoto gave his report of what had taken place the previous day. The final draft of the new Constitution, as finally approved by G H Q, reached us in batches while the cabinet was meeting and we discussed it point by point. . . .

The question why G H Q was in such haste to complete steps for the revision of the Constitution remains unanswered. To my thinking, one of the main reasons for this was a sincere desire on the part of General MacArthur to make secure the position of the Throne. . . . The fact remains, however, that there was a good deal of the American spirit of enterprise in the undertaking of such a fundamental piece of reform as revision of the Constitution within two months of Japan's defeat; as for wishing to see that reform realised in so short a period as half a year or a year, one can only put it down to that impulsiveness common to military people of all countries. We should remember that there were all these factors at work at that time, as a result of which, as well as others, the Japanese Constitution was revised in the way it was.

Thus it came to pass that on 6 March 1946 a summary of the draft of the proposed revised Constitution was published. In actual fact, what was proposed was not anything in the nature of a revision of the Meiji Constitution but the substitution of a completely new

Japanese Emperor Hirohito paid a precedent-shattering visit to General MacArthur at the U.S. Embassy in Tokyo, September 1945. UPI/Corbis-Bettmann

Constitution for the old, or, as was stated in the Imperial rescript issued for the occasion, 'a fundamental revision.' . . .

In my first reply to questions in the House, I stated that we had all come to regard the Meiji Constitution as an immutable set of laws to be accorded all the respect that was due through the ages, but that the spirit of that basic law had, unfortunately, become distorted with the passage of time, leading to the national calamity with which the nation was faced. I added that, from the point of view of the Potsdam Declaration, the Constitution as it then stood was found to be inadequate for the government of the country. I further said that, in order to enable Japan to preserve its traditional system of government and the happiness and well-being of its people despite the disaster that had befallen us, it was necessary to remove the misunderstanding then current among other nations of the world that the Japanese national structure in its traditional form represented a menace to world peace; and that, in order to achieve that aim, it was most important that we should frame the new Constitution along the lines of democracy and pacifism. . . .

. . . Concerning the renunciation of war, I pointed out that the right of self-defence was not specifically denied in the draft of the new Constitution, but that since both the right of belligerency and the maintenance of all forms of war potential were renounced in Clause 9 of the new Constitution as drafted, it followed that war as a means of self-defence was also renounced. This provision, I indicated, was desirable because self-defence had been the excuse advanced by both sides in most wars waged in recent years, while Japan had come to be widely regarded as a militaristic nation, liable to embark upon a war of retaliation the moment the country had recovered sufficiently from the losses of the Pacific conflict. The renunciation of war, even in self-defence, was therefore a necessary step in order to rectify this wrong impression, held by other nations, of our aims and intentions.

READING 18.2

China's Champion for Democracy

Wei Jingsheng (b. 1950) is the son of committed communist parents. He lived comfortably in Beijing and attended schools with other privileged children. As a teenager, he became a fanatical Red Guard during the Cultural Revolution begun by Mao Zedong in 1966. Mao used the Red Guards to oust his opponents in the party and government; the reign of terror caused by the Red Guards cost China ten years of destructive chaos. Travelling to the country on a "fact-finding" tour, Wei became aware for the first time of the sufferings of millions under communist rule, about the earlier Mao-made famine during the Great Leap Forward (1959–1960, when Mao forced peasants into communes), and about labor camps. As a soldier between 1969 and 1973, Wei guarded state granaries against hungry mobs. During the Cultural Revolution, both his parents were sent to labor reform camps, where his mother died of cancer for lack of medical treatment.

After Mao's death in 1976, his successor, Deng Xiaoping, sought to pull China out of its communist-imposed economic disaster by reforms known as the "Four

Modernizations"—of agriculture, industry, science and technology, and defense. Wei
wrote an article entitled "The Fifth Modernization: Democracy" and posted it on the
Democracy Wall, a forum for airing opinions Deng briefly allowed in Beijing in
1978. It was an instant sensation; however, because Deng had no intention of allowing political reforms to accompany his economic ones, the article made Wei an enemy of the communist regime. He was arrested; given a show trial, which convicted
him for "counter-revolution"; and sentenced to fifteen years of hard labor, served
mostly in solitary confinement. He was released under strict conditions in 1993, just
short of serving his full term. He was rearrested in 1994 and charged with treason for
his writings on the regime's abuses of human rights, such as the suppression of the
people of Tibet, and sentenced to fourteen years in prison. Wei was suddenly released
in 1997, probably the result of international pressure on Beijing, and was exiled to
the United States. He has been a prominent nominee for the Nobel Prize for Peace
and is the recipient of the Olov Palme Award and the European Parliament's
Sakharov Prize for Freedom of Thought.

I reached my father's ancestral village just as the personality cult of Mao Zedong and
movements like "cleansing the class ranks" were going strong. In the wake of the expanding class struggle, many who had once stood firmly on the side of Mao Zedong and
the Communist Party also fell victim to class struggle and purges. I began to wonder
whether class struggle was really supposed to be taken so seriously. Of course I still
agreed that former landlords and rich peasants should not hold any special place in the
economy after the revolution. But I also felt that ordinary workers and peasants had no
special right or need to oppress them either. According to Marxism, "class is a function
of economic status," so doesn't that mean that former rich peasants and ordinary workers and peasants were now all members of the same class? As for the cadres, who held
real power and economic and political positions far superior to those of the workers and
peasants, shouldn't they also be considered a class unto themselves? These two classes
were commonly perceived to be as incompatible as fire and water. I was always aware
of this, but was only able to clarify it for myself after using methods of Marxist class
analysis to think about it on a theoretical level.

   I felt as if I had suddenly awakened from a long dream, but everyone around me
was still plunged in darkness. I began to feel that all my previous views and political
notions were no longer reliable and needed to be completely rethought and reexam-
ined. I made use of the quiet of the village to immerse myself in the classic texts of
Marx, Engels, Lenin, and Stalin. Marx and Engels inspired the most trust in me, for I
felt that their work was far more scientific than that of the others. I liked only one of
Lenin's works, however—*The State and Revolution,* particularly the part on proletarian democracy. . . .

   During my stay in the village, the aftermath of the Great Leap Forward and the Communist Wind left a deep impression on me. From the moment I arrived, I frequently
heard the peasants discussing the Great Leap Forward in terms of a "doomsday" period
and noticed that they could barely hide their feeling of being lucky to have survived. I

Wei, Jingsheng. *The Courage to Stand Alone.* New York: Penguin USA, 1997, pp. 245–48.

soon developed a great interest in this topic and would often question them for more details. Gradually I began to realize that there was nothing at all "natural" about the period known as the "three years of natural disaster," for it was actually caused by misguided policies. The peasants recalled how, during the Communist Wind from 1959 to 1960, rice was left to rot in the fields because the peasants were too weak from hunger to harvest it. Many starved to death watching the ripe rice grains blow in the fields, as not a single person was able to go out to harvest in some fields. Once, on the way to a neighboring village with a relative, we passed a deserted village with houses that were no more than roofless mud walls. I figured this village had been merged with another during the Great Leap Forward and asked my relative why the walls hadn't been knocked down to make room for fields. He replied, "These are people's homes. How could they be torn down without their consent?" I had seen clearly that there were no roofs on these houses and didn't believe that anyone was living in them. My relative went on, "Of course there isn't anyone living in them now; the entire village starved to death during the Communist Wind. No one has returned since, so their fields were divided up among the neighboring production teams. People used to think that somebody might return, so they didn't tear down their homes. But it's been years now. I doubt anybody is ever coming back."

Just as the two of us passed by the village, the bright sunlight shone on the green weeds growing through the cracks in the mud walls, making a chilling contrast with the neat rice paddies surrounding it. Later, at a gathering in a friend's home, I heard stories of how villagers had exchanged babies as food. I felt like I could practically see, hovering up from the weeds in the cracks of those mud walls, the pained expressions of parents chewing the flesh of children they had exchanged with their own babies. Were the children happily catching butterflies in the fields nearby reincarnations of those children who had been eaten? I felt sorry for them, and even sorrier for their parents. Who had made them do this? Who had made them swallow, along with the tears and misery of other parents, the human flesh that they had never imagined tasting?

By now I could make out the face of the executioner quite clearly. He was a man of the kind that appears, as the saying goes, only "once every few centuries worldwide, and once in several millennia in China"; he was Mao Zedong. It was Mao and his followers who had used their most evil systems and policies to force those parents, starved beyond reason, to give up their own flesh and blood to feed others in exchange for flesh to feed themselves. It was Mao Zedong, who in order to make up for his crime of smothering democracy and carrying out the Great Leap Forward, had driven millions of dazed peasants to take up their hoes to strike down their neighbors and eat the flesh of people just like themselves to save their own lives. They were not the executioners; Mao Zedong and his followers were. Only then did I understand where Peng Dehuai had found the strength to attack the Mao-led Party Central Committee. Only then did I understand why the peasants so bitterly hated "communism" and why they couldn't comprehend why Liu Shaoqi's policy of calling for more private plots and enterprises and fixed output quotas had been overturned. It was because never again did they want to be forced to give up their own flesh and blood for others to devour or to lose all reason and kill their neighbors for food; it was because they wanted to go on living. This was a much stronger reason than any "ism."

It might seem that to call Mao Zedong an executioner was, under the circumstances, a crazy or at best foolhardy act. But I came to this conclusion very naturally and un-pressured because all that I had witnessed with my own eyes had shown me that this was the case. There was no other explanation. What I couldn't understand, however, was how people went on enthusiastically hailing this executioner, even pledging their lives to pro-tect him. After all, weren't the soldiers and police ranks filled with the sons and broth-ers of peasants, workers, and others?

During the more than a year I spent in the countryside, I saw for myself how Mao's theory of "class struggle" was actually played out in real life; and when I went on to do a stint in the army, I saw once again how the theory of class struggle had seeped into every corner of life. Mao Zedong had used class struggle to divide the people into *imag-inary* interest groups, rendering them incapable of distinguishing their true interests and inciting them to murder one another for goals that, in fact, were detrimental to their own interests. It was precisely through this technique that he manipulated the millions he had oppressed and fooled into supporting him. It was precisely for this reason that an exe-cutioner was able to masquerade as the leader of the people.

READING 18.3

Indian Women at Work

Although enormous changes have occurred for women worldwide during the twenti-eth century, nowhere have they been as dramatic as in India. The reforms started in the nineteenth century, when the British rulers of the subcontinent introduced laws to im-prove the status of Indian women. Modern Western schools gave Indian girls their first formal education. While Indian women and men have on the one hand fought for raising the status and rights of women of the subcontinent, the weight of conservative traditions and religious teachings that favored male dominance have continued to keep women in subservience.

Indian women gained the same voting rights as men soon after World War I, and women subsequently rose to prominence in many fields. Sarojini Naidu became the first woman provincial governor in the 1940s, and in 1964 Indira Gandhi was elected the first woman prime minister in the world. Under the Indian constitution and legal codes, women have enjoyed equality with men and protection against violence and exploitation. However, as in any part of the world, especially in traditional societies throughout much of Asia, it would be a fallacy to believe that enacting a law com-pletely solves the problem it intended to redress. Much depends on access to the law, who administers it, and how.

Generally speaking, urban, middle-class women in India have been conscious of their rights and status, and they have been organized and ready to defend them against injustices. Unfortunately, a clear boundary has separated the educated, urban, and middle-class Indian women from their poor, uneducated, and mostly rural sisters.

Reading 18.3A is from a paper presented before a Seminar on Problems and Con-cerns of Women, organized by the United Lawyer's Association and cosponsored by the Legal Service Clinic for Women and Children, held on February 8, 1986, at New Delhi, India. It is titled "Problems of Working Women," by a lawyer named Seita Vaidalingam. Her paper mainly concerns the problems faced by urban professional women in India. While some of the issues she mentions are uniquely Indian, others are shared by women in like situations in Western countries. Reading 18.3B is from an interview with female agricultural workers in a village in central India in 1975. This and other interviews of Indian women led to the United Women's Liberation Conference held in Puna, India. While it describes the hardships faced by poor women in India—and, by inference, elsewhere—these sufferings are also part of the burden of poverty and illiteracy shared equally by poor Indian men and women. Thus, it symbolizes the suffering and indignity shared by poor people everywhere.

READING 18.3A: PROBLEMS FACING PROFESSIONAL WOMEN

The Indian Constitution assures and seeks to ensure equality for all its citizens irrespective of sex. It also propounds the concept that men and women are equal in the eyes of the law. The Supreme Court has laid down the rule of equal pay for equal work. Despite all these assurances from the highest quarters, women face problems all along the line even if they happen to be working women.

At the outset, I must confess that I am no feminist. I am just a professional lawyer and, of course, a woman. I treat everybody as persons primarily and not as men or women. . . .

While financial wherewithal is necessary for every human being to develop self-esteem and live with dignity, the way to it for women is fraught with ills, problems and even greater exploitation simply because they work. In other words, according to me, working women are subject to more exploitative problems and pressures than their non-working sisters. Finding a suitable occupation is the first problem. Invoking her right and wish to do so proceeds it and of course fighting for the right amount of education to secure a decent job tops it all. After having completed her education when a woman steps into the field of her chosen vocation she soon learns that people's attitudes to working women are not quite encouraging or correct. We tend to be skeptical of women's staying capacity and the usual remark is that, "She'll be there only for a short while she's on a transitory course to marriage and therefore why take her seriously or pay her adequately". This kind of attitude can spoil a woman's chances at all levels and particularly in the field of self employment. With a job come other problematic situations—late hours and having to cope with all kinds of people at work especially men. Late hours necessarily mean having to be prepared for unsafe situations while returning home. . . . The home situation is also not always particularly conducive to the working woman. A woman's job gets low priority and the household chores and social obligations that await her tend to be distracting. At this stage if a woman works the main accent seems to be

Kal, B.K. ed. *Problems and Concerns of Indian Women Ins.* New Delhi: ABC Publishing House, 1987, pp. 60–64.

on her earnings—they are either expected to be used towards household expenses or for collecting a dowry for a further marriage mainly comprising jewellery and clothes. Whereas young men who have just started to work tend to utilise their money either towards getting a vehicle or equipping an office—both items of expenditure calculated to make them go further in their chosen field. . . .

The instances of discrimination are numerous. If a woman works and the marriage breaks for no fault of hers, her earnings are taken into account and she may be denied alimony even if she cannot maintain the same standard of living as she did when she was married on her salary. In India most investments are made in the husband's name and as there is as yet no concept of community property—namely joint property—if a marriage fails the wife may be left with nothing to call her own even if she has been working and augmenting the family income.

Once a working woman marries as she eventually does and indeed must more problems are in the offing. A change of residence may prove fatal to her present job. If she goes into a joint family, then the expectations of that family will definitely tell on her working life. The demands of married life also take their toll. The onerous burden of household chores, child raising and the mental and physical pressures of a job are not for the faint hearted. Indian men are not entirely the house husband kind. And are not quite used to the working women although they like the extra money. . . .

This according to me is double exploitation at its extreme worst because in such a situation the woman concerned is subjected to all the harassment a housewife is subjected to plus the strain of holding a job with not even the right to control her finances. This is contradictory with the people who maintain that working gives a woman financial independence and the right to control money. . . .

The single working woman face an accommodation problem if working in a city where their families do not live. One has heard and read in the newspapers of the unfavourable and unsafe conditions prevailing in hostels which in any case are not enough to meet the need. . . .

Children constitute yet another problem for the working woman. The leave she compulsorily has to take during the days of confinement, delivery and post-delivery may prove a set-back in her career and besides in most cases maternity leave and benefits are hopelessly inadequate. Domestic help to look after the children is becoming more and more scarce and creches are a far from satisfactory solution. The Joint Family system has its own inbuilt tensions. A working woman may well find that what she has to spend on transport, child care and other increased expenses because of her job may not be worth the job in terms of monetary return. . . .

A decade and a half ago, an Indian woman who was well educated was a rarity—one who worked even more so. I do not remember any of my friends' mothers working. My own mother has never done a day's work despite having secured a Medical Education from the Madras Medical College. . . . Times have changed—so many women work now—some like me out of choice, many more out of sheer necessity—many of my friends are successful lawyers, doctors, engineers and heads of business organisations. In our position it appears that if a woman works it's roses all the way—the world outside sees the facade, the statistics and applauds and shouts "Vive la femme," in that moment of glory, the stress and strain, both mental and physical—but when the curtain comes down—the problems remain.

READING 18.3B: PROBLEMS FACING FEMALE FARM LABORERS

. . . [W]e [the interviewers] begin concretely: what time do you get up in the morning and what do you do? And it doesn't take them long to get over whatever hesitancy or shyness in speaking may be there. One woman, Kaminibai, a strong, independent-looking woman of indefinable middle age, emerges as the main speaker.

What is their work day like? They get up at 5 a.m., get water from the well, collect cow-pats for fuel, cook, clean the floor, take their baths, wash clothes and then go to the fields at 8 or 10 a.m. They work until 6 p.m.—on the days when they can get work—and then return for cooking and household duties until they finally go to sleep at 9 or 10 p.m. Sixteen hours of work a day—we add it up together—and for this the landowners pay them 1¼ to 1½ rupees.

'What do men get?'

'Two and a half rupees for light work, three for heavier work.'

What is the difference in work? Kaminibai tells me: men's work is ploughing, cutting ears of corn, collecting the crop, carrying it away, collecting leftovers for cattle. Women's work is winnowing grain from chaff, weeding, picking cotton and removing the seeds, sowing. This is the normal division of labour in India; it only has to be added that women generally apply fertilizer where this is used and do the work of rice-transplanting in rice areas.

'What do you eat?'

'*Bhakri—jawari bhakri* or *lal bhakri.*' This means a coarse, tortilla-like bread made of millet and sometimes of American *milo* (sorghum) which is often imported and sold or given to the poor.

'And vegetables?'

'Vegetables—what shall we tell you?' says Kaminibai. 'If we have vegetables we can have spices but no salt, or salt but no spices, such is our poverty! There is no work. Some collect twigs, some collect wood and sell it, or use it for fuel. What can we do? We are poor . . . .'

They complain of the lack of work. Sometimes they get it, sometimes not, about two or three days of work a week. If they don't get work, they often just lie around and try to sleep because there is no food and they have no strength to do more. They can't eat, they say; all have become beggars these days because prices keep rising while wages remain stagnant. . . .

'But is there male supremacy?' I ask. . . .

'Yes, there is male supremacy. Still, during the days of government relief work during the famine, they got equal pay. But in the work they do in the fields, men get more daily wages and they get less, and the reason for that is that men's work is heavier, more toilsome. Women's work is different. . . . '

'[Women] have to do *double* work!' (And again an English word!) 'We have to do the housework and when the housework is finished we have to do the field work and when the field work is finished we have to take care of the children, we have to do all the work! Suppose someone is thinking like this, some reader-and-writer, let him sit down and

Omvedt, Gail. *We Will Smash This Prison.* London: Zed Press, 1980, pp. 13, 15.

write an account: what sort of work has to be done, what sort of work the men do, what work we do. I am ready to tell you! What do men do? They get up, they take a bath, they eat some bread and go to the fields. But understand what their duty is: they only do the work that is allotted to them in the fields. They only do one sort of work.

DISCUSSION QUESTION

How were the governments of Japan and China different after World War II? How much equality did Indian women enjoy?

NINETEEN

The Struggle for Political and Economic Independence in Africa

The drive for independence in Asia and Africa accelerated after World War II. For many nations, such as Libya, Morocco, and Tunisia in North Africa and Nigeria and Ghana in West Africa, independence was achieved with relatively little violence. In other nations, such as Algeria in North Africa, and in most of southern Africa, the struggles for independence were protracted and often bloody.

From the 1950s to 1980s, the newly independent, mostly poor agricultural nations in Africa, Asia, and the Western Hemisphere were known as the Third World. While the Third World existed more as an ideological concept than as a real union of diverse nations, the terminology helped to distinguish the unique goals and problems of these new nations from those of the so-called First World, the rich Western, capitalist nations led by the United States, and from those of the Second World, the largely communist bloc led by the Soviet Union. Frantz Fanon (1925–1961), a French-educated psychiatrist from the island of Martinique, was a major figure in articulating the ideological dynamics of the Third World. Fanon analyzed the process of decolonization, whereby peoples formerly dominated by Western imperial powers gained their independence. His writings influenced an entire generation of revolutionary leaders and students. Reading 19.1A is from Fanon's *The Wretched of the Earth,* in which he discusses the "politics of violence" and its importance in liberation struggles. In Reading 19.1B, a young nationalist describes how the Mau Mau and Jomo Kenyatta organized Kenyans in their struggle for independence. This reading provides a continuation of the historical narrative by Kenyatta in Chapter 11.

With independence, African nations faced daunting problems of political and economic development. In Reading 19.2A, Julius Nyerere, president of Tanzania from 1964 to 1985, urged his people and others to become self-reliant through education. Nyerere argued that only through self-reliance could poor Third World nations hope to develop economically and to avoid domination by the richer and more powerful superpowers.

The last reading in this chapter (19.2B) is from the autobiography of Nelson Mandela, the long-time leader of the African National Congress in South Africa and that nation's first elected black president. In his aptly titled autobiography, *Long Walk to Freedom,* Mandela recounts his long struggle against the white apartheid regime, which enforced a strict system of racial segregation and denied 22 million black Africans and 3 million Asians and people of mixed racial origin any participation in the political system of the nation. For his opposition to the apartheid regime, Mandela spent over two decades in prison. After the apartheid system was dismantled, Mandela was elected president of South Africa in 1994. Contrary to the dire predictions of many, freedom for all South Africans came with relatively little violence. The wise guidance of Mandela and others in the ANC, coupled with a willingness to negotiate changes by at least some within the white establishment, was largely responsible for the generally peaceful transition. In the following reading, Mandela movingly describes his feelings on the day of his presidential inauguration and his realization that the achievement of independence was just another step along the road to national development and democracy.

READING 19.1

The Fight for Independence

The following two readings focus on independence struggles in Africa during the 1950s. The first, from Frantz Fanon's *The Wretched of the Earth,* provides a theoretical analysis on the use of violence by liberation movements. The second is a firsthand account of how nationalist movements—in this instance, in Kenya—attracted the support of Third World peoples, particularly the youth.

From 1954 to 1962, the Algerians fought a bloody war of liberation against French colonialism. The French fought tenaciously to keep their Algerian colony, which they viewed as an integral part of France. More than a million Algerians and thousands of French citizens were killed in the war that in many ways paralleled the long war between the North Vietnamese and the United States. Ultimately, both France and the United States were forced to withdraw and Algeria and Vietnam gained independence. As a psychiatrist, Fanon was sent to practice in a French hospital in Algeria during the war. Shocked and angered by the war's viciousness and its impact on both the colonizer and the colonized, Fanon became openly sympathetic to the Algerian cause. After the French government expelled Fanon from Algeria, he joined the Algerian National Liberation Front (FLN) in exile in neighboring Tunisia and began writing for its official journal. In *The Wretched of the Earth,* Fanon details the interrelated problems of race and class in the impact of colonialism and in the armed struggles to defeat the colonial powers.

Fanon was convinced that the peoples living under imperial political, economic, and often military domination by Western nations would be forced to resort to violence in order to secure their independence. As previously noted, Fanon's works had an enormous impact and provided the underpinnings for many independence movements. However, Fanon did not live to see the end of colonialism; he died from cancer in 1961, before most African nations achieved independence.

In the second reading, a young Kenyan student, Karari Njama, recounts how he was galvanized into political activity during a 1952 rally led by Jomo Kenyatta. The account vividly describes the emotional and intellectual impact of nationalist songs and speeches; it also emphasizes that some Kenyans opposed the more violent tactics of the Mau Mau, who organized militant attacks against the British colonists, beginning in 1948. Although Kenyatta denounced the Mau Mau, the British held him accountable for its violence and sentenced him to seven years' hard labor in 1953. Even after his release, Kenyatta was kept under surveillance; however, the British finally reversed their colonial policy toward Kenya, and it received full independence in 1963. Kenyatta became the first president of the republic in 1964, a position he held until his death in 1978.

READING 19.1A: FRANTZ FANON: SPOKESPERSON FOR THE THIRD WORLD

National liberation, national renaissance, the restoration of nationhood to the people, commonwealth: whatever may be the headings used or the new formulas introduced, decolonization is always a violent phenomenon. At whatever level we study it—relationships

Fanon, Frantz. *The Wretched of the Earth.* Trans. Constance Farrington. New York: Grove Press, Inc., 1963, pp. 35–39.

between individuals, new names for sports clubs, the human admixture at cocktail parties, in the police, on the directing boards of national or private banks—decolonization is quite simply the replacing of a certain "species" of men by another "species" of men. Without any period of transition, there is a total, complete, and absolute substitution. It is true that we could equally well stress the rise of a new nation, the setting up of a new state, its diplomatic relations, and its economic and political trends. But we have precisely chosen to speak of that kind of *tabula rasa* [clean slate] which characterizes at the outset all decolonization. Its unusual importance is that it constitutes, from the very first day, the minimum demands of the colonized. To tell the truth, the proof of success lies in a whole social structure being changed from the bottom up. The extraordinary importance of this change is that it is willed, called for, demanded. The need for this change exists in its crude state, impetuous and compelling, in the consciousness and in the lives of the men and women who are colonized. But the possibility of this change is equally experienced in the form of a terrifying future in the consciousness of another "species" of men and women: the colonizers.

Decolonization, which sets out to change the order of the world, is, obviously, a program of complete disorder. But it cannot come as a result of magical practices, nor of a natural shock, nor of a friendly understanding. Decolonization, as we know, is a historical process: that is to say that it cannot be understood, it cannot become intelligible nor clear to itself except in the exact measure that we can discern the movements which give it historical form and content. Decolonization is the meeting of two forces, opposed to each other by their very nature, which in fact owe their originality to that sort of substantification which results from and is nourished by the situation in the colonies. Their first encounter was marked by violence and their existence together—that is to say the exploitation of the native by the settler—was carried on by dint of a great array of bayonets and cannons. The settler and the native are old acquaintances. In fact, the settler is right when he speaks of knowing "them" well. For it is the settler who has brought the native into existence and who perpetuates his existence. The settler owes the fact of his very existence, that is to say, his property, to the colonial system.

Decolonization never takes place unnoticed, for it influences individuals and modifies them fundamentally. It transforms spectators crushed with their inessentiality into privileged actors, with the grandiose glare of history's floodlights upon them. It brings a natural rhythm into existence, introduced by new men, and with it a new language and a new humanity. Decolonization is the veritable creation of new men. But this creation owes nothing of its legitimacy to any supernatural power; the "thing" which has been colonized becomes man during the same process by which it frees itself.

In decolonization, there is therefore the need of a complete calling in question of the colonial situation. If we wish to describe it precisely, we might find it in the well-known words: "The last shall be first and the first last." Decolonization is the putting into practice of this sentence. That is why, if we try to describe it, all decolonization is successful.

The naked truth of decolonization evokes for us the searing bullets and bloodstained knives which emanate from it. For if the last shall be first, this will only come to pass after a murderous and decisive struggle between the two protagonists. That affirmed intention to place the last at the head of things, and to make them climb at a pace (too quickly, some say) the well-known steps which characterize an organized society, can only triumph if we use all means to turn the scale, including, of course, that of violence.

You do not turn any society, however primitive it may be, upside down with such a program if you have not decided from the very beginning, that is to say from the actual formulation of that program, to overcome all the obstacles that you will come across in so doing. The native who decides to put the program into practice, and to become its moving force, is ready for violence at all times. From birth it is clear to him that this narrow world, strewn with prohibitions, can only be called in question by absolute violence.

The colonial world is a world divided into compartments. It is probably unnecessary to recall the existence of native quarters and European quarters, of schools for natives and schools for Europeans; in the same way we need not recall apartheid [state-instituted policy of racial segregation] in South Africa. Yet, if we examine closely this system of compartments, we will at least be able to reveal the lines of force it implies. This approach to the colonial world, its ordering and its geographical layout will allow us to mark out the lines on which a decolonized society will be reorganized.

The colonial world is a world cut in two. The dividing line, the frontiers are shown by barracks and police stations. In the colonies it is the policeman and the soldier who are the official, instituted go-betweens, the spokesmen of the settler and his rule of oppression. In capitalist societies the educational system, whether lay or clerical, the structure of moral reflexes handed down from father to son, the exemplary honesty of workers who are given a medal after fifty years of good and loyal service, and the affection which springs from harmonious relations and good behavior—all these aesthetic expressions of respect for the established order serve to create around the exploited person an atmosphere of submission and of inhibition which lightens the task of policing considerably. In the capitalist countries a multitude of moral teachers, counselors and "bewilderers" separate the exploited from those in power. In the colonial countries, on the contrary, the policeman and the soldier, by their immediate presence and their frequent and direct action maintain contact with the native and advise him by means of rifle butts and napalm not to budge. It is obvious here that the agents of government speak the language of pure force. The intermediary does not lighten the oppression, nor seek to hide the domination; he shows them up and puts them into practice with the clear conscience of an upholder of the peace; yet he is the bringer of violence into the home and into the mind of the native.

The zone where the natives live is not complementary to the zone inhabited by the settlers. The two zones are opposed, but not in the service of a higher unity. Obedient to the rules of pure Aristotelian logic, they both follow the principle of reciprocal exclusivity. No conciliation is possible, for of the two terms, one is superfluous. The settlers' town is a strongly built town, all made of stone and steel. It is a brightly lit town; the streets are covered with asphalt, and the garbage cans swallow all the leavings, unseen, unknown and hardly thought about. The settler's feet are never visible, except perhaps in the sea; but there you're never close enough to see them. His feet are protected by strong shoes although the streets of his town are clean and even, with no holes or stones. The settler's town is a well-fed town, an easygoing town; its belly is always full of good things. The settlers' town is a town of white people, of foreigners. . . .

This world divided into compartments.

READING 19.1B: THE KENYAN INDEPENDENCE MOVEMENT

It was 26 July 1952 and I sat in the Nyeri Showgrounds packed in with a crowd of over 30,000 people. The Kenya African Union [KAU] was holding a rally and it was presided over by Jomo Kenyatta. He talked first of LAND. In the Kikuyu [a major ethnic group in the Kenyan highlands, where many British colonists settled on land taken from Kikuyu farmers] country, nearly half of the people are landless and have an earnest desire to acquire land so that they can have something to live on. Kenyatta pointed out that there was a lot of land lying idly in the country and only the wild game enjoy that, while Africans are starving of hunger. The White Highland, he went on, together with the forest reserves which were under the Government control, were taken from the Africans unjustly. This forced me to turn my eyes toward the Aberdare Forest. I could clearly see Karari's Hill, almost in the middle of the Aberdare Forest. The hill that bears my grandfather's name and whom I am named after. Surely that is my land by inheritance and only the wild game which grandfather used to trap enjoy that very fertile land. This reminds me of my youth life in a Boer's farm in the White Highland, but I felt that I must attend to what Jomo Kenyatta would say next. . . .

The other point that Jomo Kenyatta stressed during the meeting was African FREEDOM. He raised the KAU flag to symbolize African Government. He said Kenya must be freed from colonial exploitation. Africans must be given freedom of speech, freedom of movement, freedom of worship and freedom of press. Explaining this to the people, he said that with the exception of freedom of worship, the other freedoms are severely limited with respect to the Africans. Freedom of movement: many Africans have been prosecuted for trespass on European land or for entering a town outside his own district. I personally faced a resident magistrate, the D.C. at Nanyuki, in December 1949 charged under trespass on a European farm. Without a fine, he sentenced me to three months imprisonment. He refused to my paying money for the sentence.

I was struck by its [the flag's] red colour in the middle of black and green, which signified blood. An hour passed without any description of the KAU flag. Most of the time I was pondering how and when we shall officially hoist that National flag to signify the Kenya African freedom. I recalled Kenyatta's words in 1947 at a KAU rally on the same ground. 'The freedom tree can only grow when you pour blood on it, but not water. I shall firmly hold the lion's jaws so that it will not bite you. Will you bear its claws?" He was replied with a great applause of admittance.

When Kenyatta returned on the platform for the third time, after a few other speakers, he explained the flag. He said, 'Black is to show that this is for black people. Red is to show that the blood of an African is the same colour as the blood of a European, and green is to show that when we were given this country by God it was green, fertile and good but now you see the green is below the red and is suppressed.' (Tremendous applause!) I tried to figure out his real meaning. What was meant by green being 'suppressed' and below the red? Special Branch agents were at the meeting recording all the speeches so Kenyatta couldn't speak his mind directly. What he said must mean that our fertile lands (green) could only be regained by the blood (red) of the African (black).

Barnett, Donald L., and Karari Njama. *Mau Mau from Within: Autobiography and Analysis of Kenya's Peasant Revolt*. London: MacGibbon & Kee, 1966, pp. 73–78.

That was it! The black was separated from the green by red; the African could only get to his land through blood.

'You also see on the flag a shield, a spear and an arrow,' he went on. 'This means that we should remember our forefathers who used these weapons to guard this land for us. The "U" is placed over the shield and indicates that the shield will guard the Union against all evils. . . .'

This flashed to me a few new songs that were sung before the opening of the meeting:

Gikuyu and Mumbi, what do you think?
You were robbed of your land, you didn't sell it

Chorus: Kenyatta leads, Koinange at the rear and Mbiyu on the
      flank
      Each a good shepherd of the masses
      We have been demanding the return of African lands
      And will never give up

Dedan Mugo, friend of the Blacks, was deported because of his
      struggle for the Africans . . . (I remembered Dedan Mugo to
      having been convicted for administering a Mau Mau oath in
      Kiambu in April 1950.)

The other song I remembered said:

My people, we have to think whether or not this land of ours
Left to us long ago by Iregi, will ever be returned

Chorus: God blessed this land of ours, we Kikuyu
        And said we should never abandon it

My people, Waiyaki died leaving us this curse:
'Never sell or give up this land of ours,' and
See how freely we have given it up!

Those of you who have been arrested and detained or imprisoned
In your struggle for freedom, don't despair!
Give up your tears and sorrows, for God will help you

The Europeans are but guests and they will leave this land of ours
Where then will you, the traitors, go when the Kikuyu rise up?

'Yes, this is a call for the return and defence of land,' I thought, 'and what about freedom. . . .'

Jomo appealled to unity, saying if we united completely tomorrow, our independence would come tomorrow. The four freedoms spoken of by Kenyatta could be practiced under the colonial rule. But for sure he did not mean this when he raised the KAU flag. He meant African self-government, which is often termed as freedom by the Africans. Most of the people are still illiterate or with very little education and cannot figure out by themselves the sort of self-government we all want. All the old people always think of freedom as the old lives they had prior to the coming of the European—and they go on teaching the young ones that the past would become our future freedom, while many ignorant young people interpret the freedom as casting down all the present laws with a replacement of liberty to do what he personally wishes. The trouble is that the leaders up to this present moment have failed to construe to the minds of the public the self-government Kenya is longing for.

I also noted that the meeting did not want to listen to anything about Mau Mau. When Ebrahim, the African Assistant District Officer, asked Jomo Kenyatta in the meeting what he was going to do to stop Mau Mau, he was forced to sit down by discouraging barracking [jeering]. The same thing happened to chief Nderi when he referred to 'night activities'.

When Kenyatta returned to the platform, he talked to the people about the African EDUCATION, saying that it was at a very low level and maintaining that the Government should develop it in a way they were not doing. He also said that European children were getting eight times more money than the African children from the Government agencies. The Africans did not realize how much money the European community pays in tax and felt that their own money paid in Poll Taxes went to educate European children, while at the same time, Government is hindering African education with its Beecher Report.

As a teacher, I understood what was meant by Beecher's Ten Year Plan and also understood the parents' thoughts. The plan would result in most students having to leave the school after Standard 4, and gave no chance for further education except for a very small percentage. The elementary schools were so many compared to the top primaries that the vast majority of students would be forced to leave school after only four years of education. This, it was felt, was very detrimental to African children. Beecher's Ten Year Plan suggested that out of every 100 who entered school, 75% would have to leave after four years of education. Of those that continued, 75% would have to quit after two more years of education. This meant that less than 10% of all children who entered school each year would get a chance to sit for the Kenya African Preliminary Examination, the lowest exam for which Government issues a certificate. The Beecher Report was thus very detrimental to African education. Most Africans thought that the intention of the plan was to get these African children to go to work on the settlers' coffee or pyrethrum plantations after four or so years of schooling. This created a certain amount of bitterness toward Rev. Beecher and his plan and to make it worse, the man was a missionary whose ideas were already rejected by the Kisa [Kikuyu Independent Schools Association] due to their earlier difficulties with the missions. Beecher, being the leader of the East African churches, was felt to be once again trying to bring the independent schools under his control. Government supported the Beecher Report and passed legislation in 1951 to the effect that it would be experimented with over a ten year period. This demonstrated to the African—particularly those Kikuyu attached to Kisa or KKES [Kikuyu Karing'a Education Society]—that the whole aim of the Government and the missionaries was to bring the independent schools once again under the control of the missionaries. At the same time, the plan would prevent the spread of education and guarantee an ever growing amount of cheap labour for the settlers.

The fourth point that Jomo Kenyatta talked of was the African WAGES. He said that Europeans were using the Africans as cheap labourers, as tools who were not really to be considered human beings. Treatment was bad on the European farms and they were given extremely low wages, poor houses, no education and couldn't even clothe themselves. When he talked of the skilled labourers, he said that the Africans who did exactly the same job as a European or an Asian would get less than a fifth of their wage. He demanded that colour-bar be abolished, since it existed everywhere in public services and operated to oppress the African. This being very true, there could be no argument or hesitation from the crowd in accepting it.

Taking into account the five points covered by Jomo Kenyatta, i.e., land, freedom, education, wages and colour-bar, all of them discriminated the African on a racial basis and rested on nothing but the white man's selfishness. People felt that the white community was extremely selfish, completely disregarding the African, and hindering the Africans. They didn't want the African to rise in standard; all they wanted was to retain a cheap source of labour.

Though the speakers at the meeting were supposed to denounce the evil secret society which was spreading rapidly through Kikuyuland and had earned for itself the unheard-of name, Mau Mau, the latter organization was given considerable publicity because most of the organizers of the meeting were Mau Mau leaders and most of the crowd, Mau Mau members. They were given the opportunity to circulate Mau Mau propaganda songs when both coming and leaving the meeting.

As I was pushing my bicycle uphill toward Muthuaini School where I was teaching, I enjoyed many Mau Mau songs which were sung by the crowd as they left the meeting. Here are a few verses from different songs:

If you are asked What? And you What?
Whether you are of Gikuyu?
I will raise both my hands and say:
'I am of Gikuyu'

The white community are foreigners
This land they must quit
And where will you go, their sympathizers
When all the Kikuyu will gather?

Chorus: This land of ours Kikuyu
                God blessed it for us
                And he said we will never leave it

The House of Mumbi, we are very many
We are in every place
The time is flying and never retreats
Our cry is for education
We want our children to learn
Now when there is time

[Another] song was Marari—a warriors song instigating the singers to fight.

From the songs, one could learn that Gikuyu and Mumbi was referring to a new society and not to the Kikuyu tribe to which we all belonged.

READING 19.2

Problems Facing Independent African Nations

In the following readings, 19.2A and 19.2B, two African leaders write about their involvement in nationalist struggles and address their nations' postindependence problems. Julius Nyerere (b. 1922), the author of the first reading, was educated in Tanganyika and at Edinburgh University in Scotland. A teacher by profession, Nyerere
was instrumental in organizing the Tanganyika African National Union in 1954 and
was elected president when independence was granted by the British in 1962. After
Tanganyika and Zanzibar unified, Nyerere became the president of Tanzania in 1964.
Although he attempted to steer a neutral course in the Cold War, he supported the creation of a socialist economy in Tanzania. In the following account, Nyerere stresses
the centrality of the rural sector in Tanzania—and in most African nations—and the
importance of self-reliance. He also believed that education was essential to foster a
society that stressed equality and cooperation.

Under Nyerere, Tanzania made strides in the fields of education and health care.
According to possibly inflated government statistics, a state-financed campaign raised
adult literacy from 33 percent in 1967 to 90.4 percent in 1986. However, the state-run
economy failed to improve living standards for most Tanzanians. By the 1990s, political leaders in Tanzania and other African nations had reluctantly admitted that many
of the state-controlled economic policies had been abysmal failures. Although Nyerere
retired from the presidency in 1985, he remained a major power in the dominant political party, which moved, in spite of his opposition, to restructure the economy along
capitalist lines. As in other nations, this process proved to be a long and arduous one.
Thus, in 1993, over 70 percent of the Tanzanian labor force remained in the agricultural sector, which accounted for 61 percent of the gross domestic product (GDP), and
Tanzania remained one of the world's poorest nations.

The last reading in this chapter is by Nelson Mandela (b. 1918), president of South
Africa. The son of a Thembu chief, Mandela was a lawyer by profession but as a
young man joined the African National Congress (ANC), the major political party opposing the apartheid regime of the white minority in South Africa. After the ANC was
outlawed in 1961, Mandela went into hiding but was captured and jailed in 1962. He
was then tried under the "Suppression of Communism Act"; found guilty; and, along

with a number of other ANC members, sentenced to life imprisonment. Mandela spent the next twenty-seven years in prison, much of it in hard labor or solitary confinement. He refers to that time as "the dark years."

In 1990, a new South African government under F.W. deKlerk freed Mandela and dismantled many of the apartheid laws; however, Mandela and the ANC continued to demand full political rights for the black majority in South Africa. In 1993, Mandela and deKlerk both received Nobel Prizes for their work toward a peaceful settlement in South Africa. After protracted negotiations and some violence, a new constitution was drafted, and the first all-race elections were held in 1994. The ANC won a resounding victory, and Mandela became the first president elected by South Africans of all races. The reading recounts Mandela's emotions and thoughts on the day of his inauguration. He remembers and gives credit to the many opponents of apartheid, some of whom gave their lives in order to attain political rights.

The extreme poverty and high unemployment among the black majority posed daunting problems to the new administration. Mandela responded by returning at least some land to black owners and by encouraging foreign investment and economic aid. While investigative committees were formed to address the wrongs and criminal acts that occurred under the apartheid regime, the ANC and other South African parties also sought to foster national reconciliation rather than recriminations. Mandela's commitment to human rights and democracy have earned him the respect and admiration of people around the world.

READING 19.2A: JULIUS K. NYERERE ON EDUCATION AND SELF-RELIANCE

Only when we are clear about the kind of society we are trying to build can we design our educational service to serve our goals. But this is not now a problem in Tanzania. Although we do not claim to have drawn up a blueprint of the future, the values and objectives of our society have been stated many times. We have said that we want to create a socialist society which is based on three principles: equality and respect for human dignity; sharing of the resources which are produced by our efforts; work by everyone and exploitation by none. We have said on many occasions that our objective is greater African unity, and that we shall work for this objective while in the meantime defending the absolute integrity and sovereignty of the United Republic [Tanzania]. Most often of all, our government and people have stressed the equality of all citizens, and our determination that economic, political, and social policies shall be deliberately designed to make a reality of that equality in all spheres of life. We are, in other words, committed to a socialist future and one in which the people will themselves determine the policies pursued by a government which is responsible to them.

It is obvious, however, that if we are to make progress towards these goals, we in Tanzania must accept the realities of our present position, internally and externally, and then work to change these realities into something more in accord with our desires. And the truth is that our United Republic has at present a poor, undeveloped, and agricultural

Nyerere, Julius K. *Education for Self-Reliance.* Dar es Salaam: Government Printer, 1967, in Wilfred Cartey and Martin Kilson, Eds., *The Africa Reader: Independent Africa.* New York: Random House, 1970, pp. 237–39.

economy. We have very little capital to invest in big factories or modern machines; we are short of people with skill and experience. What we do have is land in abundance and people who are willing to work hard for their own improvement. It is the use of these latter resources which will decide whether we reach our total goals or not. If we use these resources in a spirit of self-reliance as the basis for development, then we shall make progress slowly but surely. And it will then be real progress, affecting the lives of the masses, not just having spectacular showpieces in the towns while the rest of the people of Tanzania live in their present poverty.

Pursuing this path means that Tanzania will continue to have a predominantly rural economy for a long time to come. And as it is in the rural areas that people live and work, so it is in the rural areas that life must be improved. This is not to say that we shall have no industries and factories in the near future. We have some now and they will continue to expand. But it would be grossly unrealistic to imagine that in the near future more than a small proportion of our people will live in towns and work in modern industrial enterprises. It is therefore the villages which must be made into places where people live a good life; it is in the rural areas that people must be able to find their material well-being and their satisfactions.

This improvement in village life will not, however, come automatically. It will come only if we pursue a deliberate policy of using the resources we have—our manpower and our land—to the best advantage. This means people working hard, intelligently, and to-gether; in other words, working in cooperation. Our people in the rural areas, as well as their government, must organize themselves cooperatively and work for themselves through working for the community of which they are members. Our village life, as well as our state organization, must be based on the principles of socialism and that equality in work and return which is part of it.

This is what our educational system has to encourage. It has to foster the social goals of living together, and working together, for the common good. It has to prepare our young people to play a dynamic and constructive part in the development of a society in which all members share fairly in the good or bad fortune of the group, and in which progress is measured in terms of human well-being, not prestige buildings, cars, or other such things, whether privately or publicly owned. Our education must therefore incul-cate a sense of commitment to the total community, and help the pupils to accept the val-ues appropriate to our kind of future, not those appropriate to our colonial past.

This means that the educational system of Tanzania must emphasize cooperative en-deavor, not individual advancement; it must stress concepts of equality and the respon-sibility to give service which goes with any special ability, whether it be in carpentry, in animal husbandry, or in academic pursuits. And, in particular, our education must coun-teract the temptation to intellectual arrogance; for this leads to the well-educated de-spising those whose abilities are nonacademic or who have no special abilities but are just human beings. Such arrogance has no place in a society of equal citizens.

It is, however, not only in relation to social values that our educational system has a task to do. It must also prepare young people for the work they will be called upon to do in the society which exists in Tanzania—a rural society where improvement will depend largely upon the efforts of the people in agriculture and in village development.

READING 19.2B: NELSON MANDELA'S "LONG WALK TO FREEDOM"

On the day of the inauguration, I was overwhelmed with a sense of history. In the first decade of the twentieth century, a few years after the bitter Anglo-Boer War [1899–1902] and before my own birth, the white-skinned peoples of South Africa patched up their differences and erected a system of racial domination against the dark-skinned peoples of their own land. The structure they created formed the basis of one of the harshest, most inhuman societies the world has ever known. Now, in the last decade of the twentieth century, and my own eighth decade as a man, that system had been overturned forever and replaced by one that recognized the rights and freedoms of all peoples regardless of the color of their skin.

That day had come about through the unimaginable sacrifices of thousands of my people, people whose suffering and courage can never be counted or repaid. I felt that day, as I have on so many other days, that I was simply the sum of all those African patriots who had gone before me. That long and noble line ended and now began again with me. I was pained that I was not able to thank them and that they were not able to see what their sacrifices had wrought.

The policy of apartheid created a deep and lasting wound in my country and my people. All of us will spend many years, if not generations, recovering from that profound hurt. But the decades of oppression and brutality had another, unintended effect, and that was that it produced the Oliver Tambos, the Walter Sisulus, the Chief Luthulis, the Yusuf Dadoos, the Bram Fischers, the Robert Sobukwes of our time—men of such extraordinary courage, wisdom, and generosity that their like may never be known again. Perhaps it requires such depth of oppression to create such heights of character. My country is rich in the minerals and gems that lie beneath its soil, but I have always known that its greatest wealth is its people, finer and truer than the purest diamonds.

It is from these comrades in the struggle that I learned the meaning of courage. Time and again, I have seen men and women risk and give their lives for an idea. I have seen men stand up to attacks and torture without breaking, showing a strength and resiliency that defies the imagination. I learned that courage was not the absence of fear, but the triumph over it. I felt fear myself more times than I can remember, but I hid it behind a mask of boldness. The brave man is not he who does not feel afraid, but he who conquers that fear.

I never lost hope that this great transformation would occur. Not only because of the great heroes I have already cited, but because of the courage of the ordinary men and women of my country. I always knew that deep down in every human heart, there is mercy and generosity. No one is born hating another person because of the color of his skin, or his background, or his religion. People must learn to hate, and if they can learn to hate, they can be taught to love, for love comes more naturally to the human heart than its opposite. Even in the grimmest times in prison, when my comrades and I were pushed to our limits, I would see a glimmer of humanity in one of the guards, perhaps just for a

Mandela, Nelson. *Long Walk to Freedom.* Boston: Little, Brown and Company, 1994, pp. 541–44.

Here, Nelson Mandela is being sworn in as the president of South Africa in 1994; Mandela was the first South African president to be elected by all South African citizens after the collapse of the apartheid system, which had denied political rights to the 80 percent black population. Reuters/Peter Andrews/Archive Photos.

second, but it was enough to reassure me and keep me going. Man's goodness is a flame that can be hidden but never extinguished.

We took up the struggle with our eyes wide open, under no illusion that the path would be an easy one. As a young man, when I joined the African National Congress, I saw the price my comrades paid for their beliefs, and it was high. For myself, I have never regretted my commitment to the struggle, and I was always prepared to face the hardships that affected me personally. But my family paid a terrible price, perhaps too dear a price for my commitment.

In life, every man has twin obligations—obligations to his family, to his parents, to his wife and children; and he has an obligation to his people, his community, his country. In a civil and humane society, each man is able to fulfill those obligations according to his own inclinations and abilities. But in a country like South Africa, it was almost impossible for a man of my birth and color to fulfill both of those obligations. In South Africa, a man of color who attempted to live as a human being was punished and isolated. In South Africa, a man who tried to fulfill his duty to his people was inevitably ripped from his family and his home and was forced to live a life apart, a twilight existence of secrecy and rebellion. I did not in the beginning choose to place my people above my family, but in attempting to serve my people, I found that I was prevented from fulfilling my obligations as a son, a brother, a father, and a husband.

In that way, my commitment to my people, to the millions of South Africans I would never know or meet, was at the expense of the people I knew best and loved most. It was as simple and yet as incomprehensible as the moment a small child asks her father, "Why can you not be with us?" And the father must utter the terrible words: "There are other children like you, a great many of them . . ." and then one's voice trails off.

I was not born with a hunger to be free. I was born free—free in every way that I could know. Free to run in the fields near my mother's hut, free to swim in the clear stream that ran through my village, free to roast mealies under the stars and ride the broad backs of slow-moving bulls. As long as I obeyed my father and abided by the customs of my tribe, I was not troubled by the laws of man or God.

It was only when I began to learn that my boyhood freedom was an illusion, when I discovered as a young man that my freedom had already been taken from me, that I began to hunger for it. At first, as a student, I wanted freedom only for myself, the transitory freedoms of being able to stay out at night, read what I pleased, and go where I chose. Later, as a young man in Johannesburg, I yearned for the basic and honorable freedoms of achieving my potential, of earning my keep, of marrying and having a family—the freedom not to be obstructed in a lawful life.

But then I slowly saw that not only was I not free, but my brothers and sisters were not free. I saw that it was not just my freedom that was curtailed, but the freedom of everyone who looked like I did. That is when I joined the African National Congress, and that is when the hunger for my own freedom became the greater hunger for the freedom of my people. It was this desire for the freedom of my people to live their lives with dignity and self-respect that animated my life, that transformed a frightened young man into a bold one, that drove a law-abiding attorney to become a criminal, that turned a family-loving husband into a man without a home, that forced a life-loving man to live like a monk. I am no more virtuous or self-sacrificing than the next man, but I found that I could not even enjoy the poor and limited freedoms I was allowed when I knew my people were not free. Freedom is indivisible; the chains on any one of my people were the chains on all of them, the chains on all of my people were the chains on me.

It was during those long and lonely years that my hunger for the freedom of my own people became a hunger for the freedom of all people, white and black. I knew as well as I knew anything that the oppressor must be liberated just as surely as the oppressed. A man who takes away another man's freedom is a prisoner of hatred, he is locked behind the bars of prejudice and narrow-mindedness. I am not truly free if I am taking away someone else's freedom, just as surely as I am not free when my freedom is taken from me. The oppressed and the oppressor alike are robbed of their humanity.

When I walked out of prison, that was my mission, to liberate the oppressed and the oppressor both. Some say that has now been achieved. But I know that that is not the case. The truth is that we are not yet free; we have merely achieved the freedom to be free, the right not to be oppressed. We have not taken the final step of our journey, but the first step on a longer and even more difficult road. For to be free is not merely to cast off one's chains, but to live in a way that respects and enhances the freedom of others. The true test of our devotion to freedom is just beginning.

I have walked that long road to freedom. I have tried not to falter; I have made missteps along the way. But I have discovered the secret that after climbing a great hill, one only finds that there are many more hills to climb. I have taken a moment here to rest, to steal a view of the glorious vista that surrounds me, to look back on the distance I have come. But I can rest only for a moment, for with freedom comes responsibilities, and I dare not linger, for my long walk is not yet ended.

DISCUSSION QUESTION

Compare and contrast the various methods and goals of African independence movements and their leaders in the decades after World War II.

CHAPTER TWENTY

Change and Conflict in the Middle East

The Middle East remained a "hot spot" throughout the Cold War. With its strategic location and vast petroleum reserves, the region was important to both the Soviet Union and the United States. Although the peoples in the area had long expressed their hostility to outside domination (see Chapter 11), the two superpowers competed for influence and control over the region. These conflicting forces contributed to ongoing political instability and eventually led to a series of revolutions aimed at ousting foreign domination and establishing truly independent governments. In the Middle East and elsewhere, many such nationalist-based revolutions were led by military officers.

The 1952 revolution in Egypt typified the revolts against the existing order and served as a model for subsequent upheavals in nations as diverse as Iraq, Yemen, and Libya. In 1952, a group of military officers led by Gamal Abdul Nasser (1918–1970) overthrew the corrupt monarchy of King Faruk. The grievances and aims of the so-called Free Officers are enunciated in the reading by Khaled Mohi El Din, one of the key participants in the movement. By championing the cause of anti-imperialism and secular Arab nationalism, Nasser became the most charismatic and popular leader, not only in Egypt but throughout the Arab world. He was a brilliant public speaker in colloquial Arabic, and a measure of his oratorical powers can be seen in his rousing speech (Reading 20.1B) on the main objectives of Arab nationalism he gave in Damascus, Syria, in 1961.

The Arab-Israeli conflict was the other main source of contention in the region. The antagonism between the Zionists, who wished to establish a Jewish state, Israel, and the Palestinians, who wished to establish an Arab state, Palestine, in the same territory led to prolonged violence and a series of wars. The Zionists were supported first by the British (see Chapter 11) and then by the United States. The Palestinians were supported by the other Arab nations, who viewed Israel as a Western imperialist state planted in the middle of the Arab world. The Arab-Israeli-Palestinian conflict has proven to be one of the most intractable of the twentieth century.

The first reading on the conflict is by Golda Meir, one of the founders and later prime minister of the state of Israel. In this excerpt, Meir recounts her excitement on May 14, 1948, the day that the independent state of Israel was declared, against what seemed to be almost insurmountable odds. Although thrilled at the fulfillment of the Zionist dream, Meir also expressed her concern about the future. The Palestinian and Arab opposition to Israel led to the first Arab-Israeli war in 1948. Although Israel would win the 1948 war and subsequent ones (1956, 1967, 1973, 1982), often extending its territorial holdings as a result, none of the military victories led to an overall peace settlement.

The realization of the Zionist dream came at the expense of the Palestinians, who lost their homeland and who, in many cases, became refugees in neighboring Arab states. The Palestinians continued to seek self-determination and, after diplomacy, negotiations, and political maneuvering failed, some turned to violence to achieve their national aspirations. After decades of spiraling violence, mutual recriminations, and refusals to negotiate publicly, the Israeli government and Palestine Liberation Organization (PLO) signed the Oslo agreements in 1993, which seemed to pave the way for the establishment of Palestinian autonomy.

In Reading 20.2B on the Arab-Israeli conflict, Hanan Ashrawi, a Palestinian nationalist and spokesperson for the Palestinian cause, writes about her reactions to the agreement, which was sponsored by the United States. President Clinton, PLO Chairman Yasir Arafat, and Israeli Prime Minister Yitzhak Rabin and Labor leader Shimon Peres signed the agreement amid much fanfare on the White House lawn in Washington. Like Meir almost fifty years earlier, Ashrawi was pleased to see at least a small portion of her people's dream fulfilled, yet she remained exceedingly pessimistic that full Palestinian independence could be achieved unless Israel was willing to implement the agreement's terms and trade "land for peace." She was also deeply concerned over allegations of human rights abuses, corruption, and nepotism by the PLO and its leader, Yasir Arafat.

Ashrawi's fears were well founded. Some Palestinian groups, particularly Hamas, a Palestinian Islamist movement seeking the establishment of a state based on Islam, and segments of the Israeli population that were vehemently opposed to giving back even one inch of territory condemned the agreements. Hamas resorted to terrorist bombing attacks within Israel, while Israeli settlers in Gaza and the West Bank attacked Palestinians. The cycle of violence culminated when an Israeli assassinated Prime Minister Rabin in 1995. Rabin's assassin hoped that by killing the prime minister he could stop the peace process. With the subsequent election of a more hardline Israeli government under Benyamin Netanyahu, the peace process slowed to a mere crawl, and peace between Israelis and Palestinians remained more elusive than ever.

READING 20.1

Nasser and Arab Nationalism

The first reading is from Khaled Mohi El Din's memoirs on the Egyptian revolution in 1952. In his memoirs, Mohi El Din reproduced the written proposal of objectives he presented to a meeting of the Free Officers prior to the revolution. He wrote of the fight against British imperialism and the means to combat it. In addition, Mohi El Din listed precise programs, including the building of a strong army, neutrality in any future war, and the need to avoid intangling foreign treaties. Nasser and other Free Officers were not enthusiastic about the program, not because they opposed its objectives, but because they feared that the publication of such a document would impel the British to take direct hostile action against them. Mohi El Din admits that Nasser's analysis was probably correct and the program was never publicly released; however, as the second reading indicates, large portions of it would be incorporated by Nasser and other Arab nationalists in their subsequent proclamations.

Reading 20.1B is an excerpt from a speech Nasser delivered in 1961 while visiting Syria. In 1958, Syria had joined into a formal union, The United Arab Republic (UAR), with Egypt. Initially, the union was wildly popular in Syria and was supported by public opinion throughout the Arab world. At the same time, more conservative Arab regimes, such as the monarchies in Jordan and Iraq, were threatened by mass demonstrations in favor of union with Egypt and in support of Nasser. Although the monarchy in Jordan survived with assistance from Great Britain, the Iraqi monarchy was overthrown in a bloody revolution in 1958.

In the following speech, Nasser calls for nonalignment in the Cold War, resistance against foreign exploitation, and support for other Third World struggles in Africa and Asia. He also speaks against Israel and its alliance with Western powers. Shortly after this speech, the Syrians, many of whom had chafed under Egypt's dominant role in the union, withdrew from the UAR. Although the union of the Arab world remained the goal of many, its realization in actual political terms proved elusive, and the region remained divided by conflicting political forces and the Arab-Israeli conflict.

READING 20.1A: NASSER AND ARAB NATIONALISM: THE EGYPTIAN REVOLUTION OF 1952

. . . I immediately presented the proposal and in a voice overcome by tense emotion I read the draft aloud:

Objectives of the Free Officers

First: Eliminating colonialism and its treacherous supporters in the Nile Valley.

(a) In reality, imperialism is the economic exploitation by a foreign country of the resources and people of another nation. This is achieved through foreign companies and capital that loot raw materials and exploit the colonized people. It may be accompanied by military occupation, as in the case of Egypt, or may not involve military occupation, as in the case of Iran, where foreign companies are looting its oil for their private interest.

Mohi El Din, Khaled. *Memories of a Revolution: Egypt 1952.* Cairo: The American University in Cairo Press, in Arabic 1992, English 1995, pp. 57–60.

Egypt is mainly under British colonialism. However, it is also subject to colonialism by other countries which are plundering its resources, such as France in the form of the Suez Canal company, Belgium in the form of the Tram and Heliopolis companies, and America in the form of the Pepsi Cola and Coca Cola companies, the artificial silk industry, and others.

(b) Why do we fight imperialism?

1. Because imperialism is the underlying cause of the country's tragedy and backwardness, economically and financially, as well as in the fields of education, health, and the army.

2. Because imperialism has impeded our industrial progress, destroyed our existing industry to eliminate competition with its own industries, and turned Egypt into a purely agricultural country that still applies the primitive farming methods of the pharaohs.

3. Because imperialism has destroyed the Egyptian army and prevented its development. In the days of Muhammad 'Ali, we had a 100,000-man-strong army, a fleet that ranked third in the Mediterranean, and huge arsenals and military factories. Now we have nothing. There is no hope of building a strong army except by eliminating imperialism.

4. Because foreign imperialism seeks to drag us into a third world war, which it shall fight for its own interests, sacrificing the lives of Egyptian soldiers, after losing its large colonies in India, Burma, and other places that provided the necessary manpower.

(c) How are we ruled by imperialism? Imperialism does not rule us directly by means of British viceroys or high commissioners as in the underdeveloped countries in Central Africa. We are ruled indirectly by means of treacherous Egyptians, whose interests are bound to imperialism by means of bribery, special privileges, appointments on company boards, huge bonuses, titles and foreign decorations, and awards. These are the coterie of the Palace and the various parties that come to power, as well as the corrupt press which explicitly or implicitly defends imperialism. We must eliminate all these traitors to purge the land.

(d) How do we fight imperialism and its supporters?

1. By refusing to have any kind of relationship with any imperialist country, such as joint-defense pacts or other similar conspiracies.

2. By maintaining neutrality in any future war. The armed forces must have a say in the matter. Consequently, the army should be reorganized and re-equipped so as to be capable of defending the country. The army must realize that it is part of the people and that it will have no status except in a strong, independent, and free country.

3. By ensuring civil liberties to all people so that they can play an effective role in the battle against imperialism.

4. By assisting in the establishment of a national front, from among all people and loyal anti-imperialist national organizations, as well as confronting non-nationalistic bodies.

Second: The formation of a strong national army is based on the following:

1. Establishing a new command comprising efficient young officers.

2. Retraining and reorganization of the armed forces on sound bases.

3. Comprehensive training of non-commissioned officers (NCOs) and providing the opportunity for promotion to officer rank to those who excel in their work.

4. Ensuring an appropriate standard of living for officers and men.

5. Promoting national awareness among the officers and men.

Egypt does not have any hostile intentions, but we must be able to repel any form of aggression, be it political, economic, or military.

My colleagues in the Command Committee listened to my impassioned reading with apparently little interest or concern. It was obvious they were not very eager to issue such a document. Nasser was the least enthusiastic of them all, saying that the program was good but such a proclamation would focus attention on us and muster hostile forces against us. He was very far-sighted and said candidly, "Such a document could prompt the British to intervene, claiming that it is against their interests. This also applies to the Americans."

Nasser considered at length some of the terms which expressed nationalism and patriotism in leftist terminology. In fact neither he nor the rest of the colleagues paused very long before these terms and phrases. It can be said that they did not realize their significance or perhaps they did not wish to attach great importance to them. However, the phrase that attracted Nasser's attention most was "American imperialism," to which he objected, saying, "The people only know British imperialism. Why should we confuse them by talking about the Americans?" When I explained that British imperialism was collapsing and that the real danger now lay in American imperialism, he said, "But this is a phrase used by the communists only." I said, "Many of the national liberation movements in the world now use this phrase."

Aside from this limited debate, none of the others had much to say about the document. I spoke passionately about the importance of a program that would rally the officers and convince our members that we were a movement with defined objectives around which all could unite. The others, however, remained unenthusiastic. Then Nasser, as usual, came up with a satisfactory solution, saying, "If you wish to inform our members, we could circulate this paper among them to read and then to be returned to your safekeeping. But there is no need to have it printed and distributed." I accepted this compromise.

This paper, "Objectives of the Free Officers," written in my own hand, became almost inseparable from me and my wife. It would be given to a group of officers and then returned for safekeeping to either me or my wife. I even slept with it under my pillow. Neither of us ever lost sight of it until the outbreak of the revolution, when I handed it over to Nasser.

READING 20.1B: NASSER SPEAKS ON ARAB NATIONALISM

During these festivities which our United Arab Republic is celebrating three years after the Merger [of Egypt and Syria] which you achieved with your will and determination, I feel as I meet you today that our Revolution will forge ahead in accordance with your will, determination and resolve.

President Gamal Abdel-Nasser's Speeches and Press-Interviews: January–December 1961. Cairo: Egyptian Government Press, 1961, pp. 14–16.

This Merger was but a revolution which you were resolved and determined to achieve. Three years after the great Arab Revolution we feel confident and reassured. We thank God for making us feel stronger every day. Every time I meet you I feel stronger and notice that our unity has become firmer. I also feel that your hopes are greater, that our Revolution, with God's help, will always emerge victorious and our Arab Nationalism, for which we have struggled so hard, will always triumph.

This sweeping political and social Revolution, which you have determined to make a reflection of your will, derives strength from you. In fact, the strength of your Revolution emanates from your strength.

The unity you have achieved is a political and social revolution aiming at the abolition of internal and external political, economic and social exploitation.

Non-Alignment

This is why, when we decided upon an independent policy, we declared that it would be a policy of non-alignment. Our Revolution advocated complete independence and liberty, putting an end to the regime of agents and stooges of imperialism, and calling for the achievement of complete Arab unity arising from the heart of the Arab nation. It also advocated political and social liberty for every Arab country and every Arab individual.

In advocating Arab Nationalism and Arab Unity, we know our aims and our path. The revolution for liberty, means the eradication of Imperialism and its stooges. The social revolution means the eradication of monopoly, domination of capital, feudalism and exploitation.

This, Brethren, is our Revolution and this is our path. Every time I meet you I feel we are leading our Revolution from victory unto victory, thus making it stronger and stronger. . . .

Main Objectives

Brethren, the objectives of your great revolution are independence, freedom, the extermination of Imperialism and Zionism, and the stooges of Imperialism. It also aims at ending political exploitation and sectarianism. Thus we will be able to establish a national unity between all sons of this nation. This unity will protect the homeland and enable the people to realise their objectives.

Without national unity, we can never face Imperialism or Zionism. We all know how Imperialism and Zionism conspired against us, and we therefore have declared our determination to establish a national unity and remove partisanship and sectarian differences.

The imperialists often used partisanship to cause dissension amongst us, to weaken and dominate us and to place us within their spheres of influence.

We have resisted political exploitation, for it implied detestable opportunism which would impede the realisation of the aims of the Arab nation, which we are determined to achieve. When we declared that we would put an end to Imperialism and imperialist stooges, we also made known our determination to consolidate the unity of the people and to work to achieve the objectives of the Arab Nation.

We Remember

We remember how the free people everywhere rose to support us and we feel that the support of the free people in Africa and Asia enabled us to triumph in the battle of the Suez Canal. . . . Thus we can see that the cause of freedom is one and the same everywhere. The triumph of freedom anywhere is a triumph for our freedom and a consolidation of our independence and our strength. Therefore we cannot renounce our principles and our objectives. When we call for freedom, principles and ideals we know that we must support all those who strive for freedom and independence, as well as those who struggle to throw off the yoke of Imperialism and its agents.

READING 20.2

Israeli and Palestinian Independence

The independence of the State of Israel was proclaimed by David Ben-Gurion, its first prime minister, on May 14, 1948. In her autobiography, *My Life,* Golda Meir (1898–1978) recounted her long commitment to the establishment of a Jewish state and her political career. In Reading 20.2A, Meir, an ardent member of the Labor Party and supporter of Ben-Gurion, remembers her reactions to the creation of Israel. Meir's family had immigrated to the United States from Russia early in the twentieth century, and she had moved to Palestine, then under the British mandate, in 1921. Golda Meir was elected prime minister of Israel in 1969. She acted in that capacity until, following the 1973 war, she resigned in 1974, to be succeeded by General Yitzhak Rabin. Rabin was voted in and out of successive governments but was again prime minister in 1993 when the Oslo agreements were signed with the Palestinians. As previously noted, he was assassinated by an Israeli fanatic who opposed the agreements with the Palestinians.

Reading 20.2B is from *This Side of Peace,* Hanan Ashrawi's memoir on her involvement with the Palestinian national struggle. American educated with a Ph.D. in literature, Hanan Ashrawi was a professor at Birzeit University on the West Bank during the decades of Israeli occupation from 1967. She was a firsthand witness to Palestinian struggles under occupation and to their opposition to Israeli rule. Like most Palestinians, she supported the PLO as the sole legitimate representative of the Palestinians. During protracted negotiations among Israelis, Palestinians, and others during the 1990s, she became a well-known spokesperson for the Palestinians in the Western media. In the following excerpt, Ashrawi describes her reactions to the Oslo agreements and her fears for the future. She also compares the extremely limited gains of the Palestinians with the celebrations surrounding the institution of full suffrage for all the people in South Africa (see Chapter 21). Ashrawi continues to be an outspoken champion of Palestinian human rights and a critic of abuses by both Israelis and Palestinians.

READING 20.2A: GOLDA MEIR REMEMBERS ISRAEL'S INDEPENDENCE DAY

So it was on that bright note that the final decision was made. On Friday, May 14, 1948 (the fifth of Iyar, 5708, according to the Hebrew calendar); the Jewish state would come into being, its population numbering 650,000, its chance of surviving its birth depending on whether or not the *yishuv* could possibly meet the assault of five regular Arab armies actively aided by Palestine's 1,000,000 Arabs.

According to the original plan, I was to return to Jerusalem on Thursday and remain there for the duration. Needless to say, I very much wanted to stay in Tel Aviv, at least for long enough to attend the proclamation ceremony—the time and place of which were being kept secret (except for the 200-odd invitees) until about an hour before the event. All day Wednesday I hoped against hope that Ben-Gurion would relent, but he was adamant. "You must go back to Jerusalem," he said. So on Thursday, May 13, I was back in that little Piper Cub again. The pilot's orders were to take me to Jerusalem and return to Tel Aviv at once with Yitzhak Gruenbaum, who was to be the minister of interior in the provisional government. But as soon as we got past the coastal plain and reached the Judean Hills, the engine began to act up in the most alarming way. I was sitting next to the pilot (those tiny planes, which we affectionately called Primuses, boasted only two seats), and I could see that even he was very nervous. The engine began to sound as though it were about to break away from the plane altogether, and I wasn't really surprised when the pilot said, apologetically, "I'm awfully sorry, but I don't think I can clear the hills. I'll have to go back." He turned the plane around; but the engine went on making dreadful sounds, and I noticed that the pilot was looking around below. I didn't say a word, yet after a while the engine picked up a bit and he asked me, "Do you know what is happening?"

"Yes," I replied.

"I was looking," he said, "for the most likely Arab village where we could land." This was on May 13, mind you. Then he added, "But now I think I can put down in Ben Shemen." At that point the engine improved a bit more. "No," he said, "I think we can make it back to Tel Aviv."

So I was able to attend the ceremony after all, and poor Yitzhak Gruenbaum had to stay in Jerusalem and couldn't sign the Declaration of Independence until after the first cease-fire.

On the morning of May 14, I participated in a meeting of the People's Council at which we were to decide on the name of the state and on the final formulation of the declaration. The name was less of a problem than the declaration because there was a last-minute argument about the inclusion of a reference to God. Actually the issue had been brought up the day before. The very last sentence, as finally submitted to the small subcommittee charged with producing the final version of the proclamation, began with the words "With trust in the Rock of Israel, we set our hands in witness to this Proclamation. . . ." Ben-Gurion had hoped that the phrase "Rock of Israel" was sufficiently ambiguous to satisfy those Jews for whom it was inconceivable that the document which established the Jewish state should not contain any reference to God,

Meir, Golda. *My Life*. New York: Dell Publishing, 1975, pp. 213–18.

Golda Meir served as prime minister of Israel from 1969 to 1974. A lifelong Zionist and supporter of the Israeli Labor party, Meir emigrated to Palestine from the United States in 1921; she worked tirelessly for the creation of Israel in 1948. Archive Photos

as well as those who were certain to object strenuously to even the least hint of clericalism in the proclamation.

But the compromise was not so easily accepted. The spokesman of the religious parties, Rabbi Fishman-Maimon, demanded that the reference to God be unequivocal and said that he would approve of the "Rock of Israel" only if the words "and its Redeemer" were added, while Aaron Zisling of the left wing of the Labor Party was just as determined in the opposite direction. "I cannot sign a document referring in any way to a God in whom I do not believe," he said. It took Ben-Gurion most of the morning to persuade Maimon and Zisling that the meaning of the "Rock of Israel" was actually twofold: While it signified "God" for a great many Jews, perhaps for most, it could also be considered a symbolic and secular reference to the "strength of the Jewish people." In the end Maimon agreed that the word "Redeemer" should be left out of the text, though, funnily enough, the first English-language translation of the proclamation, released for publication abroad that day, contained no reference at all to the "Rock of Israel" since the military censor had struck out the entire last paragraph as a security precaution because it mentioned the time and place of the ceremony.

The argument itself, however, although it was perhaps not exactly what one would have expected a prime minister-designate to be spending his time on only a few hours before proclaiming the independence of a new state—particularly one threatened by immediate invasion—was far from being just an argument about terminology. We were all deeply aware of the fact that the proclamation not only spelled the formal end to 2,000

years of Jewish homelessness, but also gave expression to the most fundamental principles of the State of Israel. For this reason, each and every word mattered greatly. . . .

At about 2 P.M. I went back to my hotel on the seashore, washed my hair and
changed into my best black dress. Then I sat down for a few minutes, partly to catch
my breath, partly to think—for the first time in the past two or three days—about the
children. . . .

I was so lost in my thoughts about the children that I can remember being momen-
tarily surprised when the phone rang in my room and I was told that a car was waiting
to take me to the museum. It had been decided to hold the ceremony at the Tel Aviv museum on Rothschild Boulevard, not because it was such an imposing building (which it
wasn't), but because it was small enough to be easily guarded. One of the oldest buildings in Tel Aviv, it had originally belonged to the city's first mayor, who had willed it to
the citizens of Tel Aviv for use as an art museum. The grand total of about $200 had been
allocated for decorating it suitably for the ceremony; the floors had been scrubbed, the
nude paintings on the walls modestly draped, the windows blacked out in case of an air
raid and a large picture of Theodor Herzl hung behind the table at which the thirteen
members of the provisional government were to sit. Although supposedly only the 200-
odd people who had been invited to participate knew the details, a large crowd was already waiting outside the museum by the time I arrived there.

A few minutes later, at exactly 4 P.M., the ceremony began. Ben-Gurion, wearing a
dark suit and tie, stood up and rapped a gavel. According to the plan, this was to be the
signal for the orchestra, tucked away in a second floor gallery, to play "Hatikvah." But
something went wrong, and there was no music. Spontaneously, we rose to our feet and
sang our national anthem. Then Ben-Gurion cleared his throat and said quietly, "I shall
now read the Scroll of Independence." It took him only a quarter of an hour to read the
entire proclamation. He read it slowly and very clearly, and I remember his voice changing and rising a little as he came to the eleventh paragraph:

> Accordingly we, the members of the National Council, representing the Jewish people in the
> Land of Israel and the Zionist movement, have assembled on the day of the termination of the
> British mandate for Palestine, and, by virtue of our natural and historic right and of the reso-
> lution of the General Assembly of the United Nations, do hereby proclaim the establishment
> of a Jewish state in the Land of Israel—the State of Israel.

The State of Israel! My eyes filled with tears, and my hands shook. We had done it.
We had brought the Jewish state into existence—and I, Golda Mabovitch Meyerson, had
lived to see the day. Whatever happened now, whatever price any of us would have to
pay for it, we had recreated the Jewish national home. The long exile was over. From
this day on we would no longer live on sufferance in the land of our forefathers. Now
we were a nation like other nations, master—for the first time in twenty centuries—of
our own destiny. The dream had come true—too late to save those who had perished in
the Holocaust, but not too late for the generations to come. Almost exactly fifty years
ago, at the close of the First Zionist Congress in Basel, Theodor Herzl had written in his
diary: "At Basel, I founded the Jewish state. If I were to say this today, I would be greeted
with laughter. In five years perhaps, and certainly in fifty, everyone will see it." And so
it had come to pass.

READING 20.2B: HANAN ASHRAWI
ON PALESTINIAN INDEPENDENCE

The ceremony started at 11:07. The spectacle on the White House lawn was a huge success. As for me, I knew that the hard part had just started. This whole event was a signal, a passage. The crossing out of "delegation" and writing in of "PLO" had ushered in a whole new phase. Whether Arafat and Rabin got something more than their green T-shirts from the White House ceremony still remained to be seen. So would the passage from Tunis to Washington. A transition of tremendous magnitude was taking place, and I would have to choose a few stations along the way.

With the amendment of the text on the White House lawn, we had come full cycle. The actual denouement was yet to come as we now had to look within. That famous handshake between a reluctant Rabin and an eager Arafat represented to us more of a challenge than a reconciliation, a beginning rather than an end. Both leaders would henceforth be held directly accountable and responsible by their own people. Their future would hang on the success or failure of the tremendous tasks they had undertaken with that loaded handshake. Peace with our historical enemy was not possible unless we proved capable of forging peace among ourselves and with ourselves. The minefield that lay ahead was not only across the border but on our own terrain, and that was the more difficult course to steer. Could we generate the language of our future to shape and express an inner harmony, or would we revert to the rhetoric of strife and self-deception? For years, I had urged Faisal never to use the first-person singular pronoun in political discourse, for ours was a collective mission. For years, I had tried to transform our reality from an adjective to a noun, from Palestinian to Palestine, and to introduce into global discourse the use of the term "people" as a recognition of our humanity in conjunction with our land of Palestine as a contemporary reality instead of a geographical abstraction. Had we succeeded in substituting the PLO for Palestine as our historical noun, and had we accepted the dismemberment of our land along with the fragmentation of our concept of peoplehood? If the PLO, in the fullness of its recognition, could pass the test of wholeness, then it could carry us through to the future. If it could pull together all the different threads of this tormented people's narrative, then it would be capable of weaving an image of our destiny. It had placed itself squarely at the crossroads of external recognition and internal validation, precisely where our past and future would meet and merge to shape our collective memory for the future or would clash and be wrenched apart in sorrow and fury. . . .

The first steps of implementation were delayed, and then moved forward only in fits and starts. All eyes were turned toward Gaza and Jericho, looking toward the crossing points for the first signs of the promised Palestinian police. A journalist from the *New York Times* told me she had never seen people approach independence with such a sense of gloom and foreboding. I compared the celebration of democracy in South Africa with our lot: "I find it sad that while Mandela is triumphant in ending apartheid and claiming his people's inheritance, we are legalizing apartheid in Palestine by this agreement and entering a diminished phase of nation building with sorrow and reluctance. The fact that

Ashrawi, Hanan. *This Side of Peace: A Personal Account.* New York: Simon & Schuster, 1995, pp. 271–72, 292–93, 302–3.

our first sign of independence is the arrival of the police force encapsulates the irony." Mandela had told us not to forget them when we had our state, and now it was our turn to tell our gentle and dignified friend not to forget us in his triumph.

The people, confused, were still shocked. All the traditional factions had faced and failed their historical test and were now called upon to rethink their platforms and structures in light of the agreement. The opposition who sought to sabotage and destroy the agreement had to come to grips with the fact that they had no alternative to offer and that reality was being shaped before their very eyes where their slogans could no longer prevail or apply. Those who wanted to stand by the sidelines and bide their time also knew that they could be abandoned by history, and that a total collapse would destroy them as well. The failure of the PLO would bring the Islamic opposition to the forefront as the strongest alternative, not the left-wing opposition. A crisis of the soul held the intellectuals in its grip, and cries for a new national consensus were being heard with increasing frequency. . . .

Already the offices of the Commission for Citizens' Rights in Jerusalem were receiving a flood of cases and complaints. The test we were all facing was the most difficult of all, for we had come full circle to begin our internal quest. Would he, would we, pass the ultimate test of *amanah* with our people? Abu Ammar, with his military and political authorities, was launching a new phase of the quest for statehood from the confines of Gaza-Jericho. Other Palestinians, including myself, had launched the quest for nationhood and democracy through institutions of civil society. A Palestinian Genesis had begun, launched from the chaos and pain of a past almost beyond time.

Here, Palestinian children in a refugee camp in the Gaza Strip flash the victory/peace sign, signifying their aspirations for self-determination and the creation of an independent Palestinian state. Janice Terry

My personal narrative is also unfolding. Often when I find the pain of self-inflicted wounds unbearable, as on my inspection of interrogation cells where Palestinians used violence on other Palestinians, or when I investigate cases of dark deals concluded in secret, I am reminded of the words of an Old English poem, "Deor." As the poet catalogues a series of past disasters, whether with the comitatus or of personal import, he repeats at the end of each stanza a formula of consolation for the present misfortune: "All that passed, so may this." Our catalogue of disasters from a past almost beyond time is long, but it passed. So may this.

My pledge to unfolding time is Amal and Zeina, Emile and our garden. From there I drive to Jerusalem every day where I take upon myself the pain of a people still in a state of emergence, still longing for *amanah* and peace, both from the world outside and from their reality within. Thus, once again, we recount an ancient narrative but with a new beginning. Once more we shall undertake a confrontation with history, unrepentant and untamed, but armed with the knowledge of our own sorrow and in possession of the full potential of a joy yet to come.

DISCUSSION QUESTION

What were the sources of conflict in the Middle East, and what solutions have been suggested to resolve them over the past fifty years?

TWENTY-ONE

After the Cold War: The Birth of a New Era

The end of the Cold War promised to herald in a new world. Democratically elected governments came to power in most eastern European nations and the former Soviet republics. In many parts of Asia and Africa, people demonstrated against old, entrenched dictatorships. Many anticipated that the collapse of the Soviet Union would end the arms race and result in a "peace dividend," with money previously spent on armaments going toward housing, education, health care, and social service programs. Many also hoped that steps toward privatization and away from state-controlled economies would pave the way for increased efficiency and production, leading to economic prosperity.

Although sweeping changes occurred, particularly in eastern Europe, old problems remained and new ones emerged. The hoped for "peace dividend" did not materialize. Although military spending in Russia decreased considerably, many nations, including the United States, continued to spend huge sums on their militaries. Further, the dismantling of state-run economies in former communist countries removed the social "safety net" of welfare programs many had come to depend upon; thus, while a few prospered, the living standards of many others, particularly the elderly and families with children, dropped precipitously. Governmental and economic changes also contributed to a revival of old ethnic rivalries and xenophobia. For example, Bosnia in the Balkans and Rwanda in Africa both experienced horrific wars and "ethnic cleansing."

The readings in this chapter address the challenges and dangers of this new era. The first two highlight the ongoing struggles for human rights and equality. Struggles for racial, ethnic, religious, and gender equality have been waged around the world throughout much of the twentieth century. Readings 2.2, 14.1, 18.3A, and 18.3B all highlighted various aspects of the fight for gender equality, beginning with the suffragists' movement for political rights at the beginning of the century and moving to the advocacy of equal pay for equal work and improved conditions for women and families by international organizations toward the end of the century. Over the past thirty years, conferences on women have been held in venues around the globe. These conferences, and similar ones on environmental and economic issues, represent the globalization of vital social issues.

The first reading in this chapter (21.1A) details the program affirmed by participants at the Fourth World Conference on Women held in Beijing in 1995. Although the legal and political rights of women in much of the world have improved since the time of the suffragist movement, major inequalities remain. The second reading (21.1B), an oral history by an Amerindian feminist, provides a human face to the problems encountered by millions around the world.

The last two readings address the vital issue of nationalism and its many different facets. Nationalism has been one of the major and most enduring trends of the twentieth century. In the last two readings (21.2A and 21.2B), Wole Soyinka of Nigeria and Vaclav Havel of the Czech Republic discuss the problems of nationalism and democracy. Both Soyinka and Havel are noted writers and political activists, and their discourses are infused with passion and perceptivity. Because of his merciless criticism of the dictatorship in Nigeria, Soyinka, holder of a Nobel Prize for Literature, has been forced to live in exile. Similarly, Havel was persecuted by the communist regime in Czechoslovakia for publishing plays that criticized the government. After the collapse of Soviet control over eastern Europe, Havel was elected president of Czechoslovakia, but even his enormous personal reputation was not enough to prevent Slovakia from breaking away from the union in 1993 and forming a separate state, in yet another demonstration of ethnic hostilities. Within a historical context, Soyinka and Havel realistically assess the future of their respective nations as the century draws to a close. They both also deal with the nature of the state and political systems, thereby providing further thought on a subject touched on earlier in this volume, especially in Chapter 6.

READING 21.1

The Struggle for Gender Equality

In 1995, thousands of women from around the world met in Beijing, China, to discuss issues of importance to women, children, and families. This Fourth World Conference on Women agreed on a lengthy program to address women's concerns. Portions of that program are included in this reading. Among other concerns, the conference urged the cessation of discrimination against women and called for improved health care, education, and legislation protecting women. Many of these problems affect those in wealthy, northern nations (Europe, Japan, United States), as well as those in poor, southern nations (e.g., Africa, South America, and parts of Asia). Because conference participants recognized the particular problems faced by women in the latter nations, they emphasized the need for "sustainable development" that would provide meaningful social and economic improvements, not merely increase the availability of consumer goods or profit the wealthy few.

In the second reading, Laura Waterman Wittstock from the Seneca nation recounts her personal history. As an Amerindian from a poor family, Wittstock has faced a myriad of problems throughout her life, including discrimination as both a woman and an Amerindian. As a recognized community activist, she attended the 1975 International Women's Conference in Mexico; in the following excerpt, she describes what that conference meant to her. Wittstock goes on to address the problems of discrimination in the society at large, but she also honestly confronts the internal divisions within her own community. Her story is reflective of many minorities and of women throughout the world.

READING 21.1A: WORLD CONFERENCE ON WOMEN

1 We, the Governments participating in the Fourth World Conference on Women,

2 Gathered here in Beijing in September 1995, the year of the fiftieth anniversary of the founding of the United Nations, ...

We reaffirm our commitment to:

8 The equal rights and inherent human dignity of women and men and other purposes and principles enshrined in the Charter of the United Nations, to the Universal Declaration of Human Rights and other international human rights instruments, in particular the Convention on the Elimination of All Forms of Discrimination against Women and the Convention on the Rights of the Child, as well as the Declaration on the Elimination of Violence against Women and the Declaration on the Right to Development;

9 Ensure the full implementation of the human rights of women and of the girl child as an inalienable, integral and indivisible part of all human rights and fundamental freedoms; . . . .

Beijing Declaration, September 1995, originally disseminated by the United Nations Department for Policy Coordination and Sustainable Development (DPCSD) in *Women's Studies Quarterly* 1996: 1 & 2, pp. 154–57.

We are convinced that:

13 Women's empowerment and their full participation on the basis of equality in all spheres of society, including participation in the decision-making process and access to power, are fundamental for the achievement of equality, development and peace;

14 Women's rights are human rights;

15 Equal rights, opportunities and access to resources, equal sharing of responsibilities for the family by men and women, and a harmonious partnership between them are critical to their well-being and that of their families as well as to the consolidation of democracy;

16 Eradication of poverty based on sustained economic growth, social development, environmental protection and social justice requires the involvement of women in economic and social development, equal opportunities and the full and equal participation of women and men as agents and beneficiaries of people-centered sustainable development;

17 The explicit recognition and reaffirmation of the right of all women to control all aspects of their health, in particular their own fertility, is basic to their empowerment;

18 Local, national, regional and global peace is attainable and is inextricably linked with the advancement of women, who are a fundamental force for leadership, conflict resolution and the promotion of lasting peace at all levels; . . . .

We are determined to:

22 Intensify efforts and actions to achieve the goals of the Nairobi Forward-looking Strategies for the Advancement of Women by the end of this century;

23 Ensure the full enjoyment by women and the girl child of all human rights and fundamental freedoms and take effective action against violations of these rights and freedoms;

24 Take all necessary measures to eliminate all forms of discrimination against women and the girl child and remove all obstacles to gender equality and the advancement and empowerment of women;

25 Encourage men to participate fully in all actions towards equality;

26 Promote women's economic independence, including employment, and eradicate the persistent and increasing burden of poverty on women by addressing the structural causes of poverty through changes in economic structures, ensuring equal access for all women, including those in rural areas, as vital development agents, to productive resources, opportunities and public services;

27 Promote people-centered sustainable development, including sustained economic growth, through the provision of basic education, lifelong education, literacy and training, and primary health care for girls and women;

28 Take positive steps to ensure peace for the advancement of women and, recognizing the leading role that women have played in the peace movement, work actively towards general and complete disarmament under strict and effective international control, and support negotiations on the conclusion, without delay, of a universal and multilaterally and effectively verifiable comprehensive nuclear-test-ban treaty which contributes to nuclear disarmament and the prevention of the proliferation of nuclear weapons in all its aspects;

29 Prevent and eliminate all forms of violence against women and girls;

30 Ensure equal access to and equal treatment of women and men in education and health care and enhance women's sexual and reproductive health as well as education;

31 Promote and protect all human rights of women and girls;

32 Intensify efforts to ensure equal enjoyment of all human rights and fundamental freedoms for all women and girls who face multiple barriers to their empowerment and advancement because of such factors as their race, age, language, ethnicity, culture, religion, or disability, or because they are indigenous people;

33 Ensure respect for international law, including humanitarian law, in order to protect women and girls in particular;

34 Develop the fullest potential of girls and women of all ages, ensure their full and equal participation in building a better world for all and enhance their role in the development process.

READING 21.1B: AN AMERINDIAN WOMAN'S STORY

I come from the Seneca nation, which is part of the Iroquois Confederacy, and which is matrilineal still today. You gain your identity not from your father, but from your mother. So I had an unfair advantage over lots of other women, of never having to shed the father domination.

My mother was my role model. At the age of 63, she founded the San Francisco American Indian Center. This was during the relocation period when Indians were being seduced into cities with promises of jobs and training. They were beginning to die in those cities, and families wanted the bodies sent home, but there was no money. So my mother formed a women's sewing group, and they did what they knew how to do. They made beautiful things out of cloth and yarn, then sold them and paid to send the bodies back.

I first identified as a feminist in 1975. I had done an article called "Little White Dove"* about the groupie women who follow male Indian leaders around. Some of them actually were Indians, sad to say, chasing after these men. And a few years earlier, I had been asked to review the draft of *Our Bodies, Ourselves.*** I felt really privileged to do that. I instantly recognized it as an important work. But I didn't really see the potential of women until I attended the International Women's Year conference in Mexico City in 1975.

One thing that hit me right between the eyes was, these women from other countries, women of color, thought that Indians had it soft. They didn't separate Indians from the "ugly Americans." We were considered pets of the "ugly Americans" because we lived in the fat country. And there we were in Mexico City, where there are Indian beggars on the street, Indian people starving.

---

*A reference to a country-western song in which ill-fated Indian lovers drown trying to reach one another.
**By the Boston Women's Health Book Collective (1973).

"Laura Waterman Wittstock," Bonnie Watkins and Nina Rothchild. *In the Company of Women: Voices from the Women's Movement.* St. Paul: Minnesota Historical Society Press, 1996, pp. 15–18.

Then I realized that many of these women were high officials in their countries. I was more or less a peasant, and these women were more or less the elite. For them to be talking about Indians in that way, I realized it was a political statement. The northern European women were very educated, they had written numerous books. They were extremely rude, extremely arrogant. Even in those early days, in 1975, the stratification of women was apparent.

But our major themes were very much in agreement: the more "civilization" that occurred, the more the deterioration of women. In earlier times, almost everywhere, the marketplace had been a place for women. But with industrialization, men were taught to drive the big trucks, men were taught agribusiness, and the women were subjugated. Women were made into the childbearers, the beasts of burden, and the prostitutes.

There were 10,000 women at that conference! And despite all the tensions, I recognized the tremendous potential. There actually was a great deal of accommodation that took place, a lot of eagerness to understand one another. In terms of an awakening, I realized then that you have to seek out ways to work with other women. It's not going to come naturally or easily. But the potential is there.

One practical thing that came out of that conference for me was, I never again had a secretary. All that stuff has nothing to do with efficient work. It's everything to do with prejudice and the willingness to enslave others. Unfortunately, as women took over men's roles they also took over men's prejudices, class distinctions like not typing and pretending not to know how to use a copier.

Thirteen years later, in April 1988, I went to the pro-choice rally in Washington, D.C. A million people walking is an intoxicating, rejuvenating experience. I saw all kinds of women there—Indian women, Black women, Asian women, Hispanics, European-Americans. It made me realize that the pro-choice issue isn't only about a woman's right to choose. It's about women being allowed to be human, fighting the power of the elite to call the shots. At times I felt like we were almost angels, transcending the veil of control. Then at other times, I felt we were lab rats—thinking that we have something to express, but that nothing will really change.

We have got to do something about the racial question. Right now, the discussions I've been in, some women are saying, "I didn't cause your pain. I wasn't there when Columbus stepped on the first Indian's neck." On the other hand, women of color need to say what they need to say and they have to be heard. I think there's right on both sides.

There are plenty of women of color who are conservative, who would not share my views at all. But simply by virtue of having color we are manipulated by people in power. They say, "Oh look, we've got women of color and they think thus!" So the rest of us stand outside the window looking in.

The leadership of the national women's organizations has got to change color. They can't play the game of getting a few who have the skin color required, but whose philosophy is so close to that of the leadership that it's indistinguishable. They have got to get people up there who don't agree with them. I don't mean on choice. I mean on strategy.

I've also seen diversity within the European-American culture that isn't getting heard: rural women, older women, farm women. Poor women, those that are on welfare, those that have to struggle with issues like single parenting. Think about welfare people who have to spend hours in their day just maintaining their poverty, standing in line for this, filling out that, answering to the various authorities about your children, and so on. Being poor is a time-consuming job, and getting women in poverty involved in decision-making is very tough.

Some of my views have been considered too radical for native people, which is understandable. Native culture is conservative, that's one of the ironies we have to deal with. You don't have a society that has been around for a hundred thousand years without it being conservative. And when something like feminism comes along, it has negative connotations to a people who are used to a thousand years not being a very long time.

The whole idea of individuals over groups is the idea of the dominant culture. In native communities, it's group over individual. So feminism is seen as a betrayal. But it's only a problem, it isn't an impossible barrier. It's a problem of, How do you work in the context of groups to advance women?

There's also what I call the cowboy mentality or the playboy mentality. That is, native groups have readily accepted, without knowing it, the male domination which comes from the external culture. Now we have to understand and restore that balance of men and women, because it is out of whack.

For example, there's the treatment of lesbians in native culture. In the old days, homosexuals of both genders were celebrated throughout the native cultures. There's almost no record anywhere of them being persecuted in any way. But now they are outcasts in the community. It's bad enough to be a woman and be assertive, but to be a lesbian. . . . So that's part of the playboy mentality that has turned Indian culture on its head. People that were once considered to have unusual abilities, once cherished by the group, are now being ostracized.

Feminism is very unpopular. To look through the eyes of women is considered abnormal. So in addition to being a minority as a female of color, to be a feminist is another way to be a minority. That's a burden that many women of color don't want to take on. Understandably. It's bad enough as things are, why make it worse?

READING 21.2

Nationalism, Politics, and Human Rights

The final readings in this collection are by two major figures in contemporary literature who are also vitally involved in the political lives of their respective nations. The first excerpt is from *The Open Sore of a Continent: A Personal Narrative of the Nigerian Crisis* by Nigerian writer Wole Soyinka. The book arose out of a series of lectures in which Soyinka offered a scathing critique of political life in Nigeria. When open elections were held in Nigeria in 1993, hopes were high for a return to democratic government after decades of corruption and mismanagement under military rule. However, when a civilian, Basorun M.K.O. Abiola, won, the military simply hijacked the elections, and a professional soldier, Sani Abacha, took power. Abacha then arrested Abiola and other opponents. Some were tortured; others, such as the political activist Ken Saro-Wiwa, were executed. Using Nigeria as an example, Soyinka condemns all dictators.

Soyinka also addresses one of the basic questions of the twentieth century: "What is a nation?" Soyinka's analysis ranges from Bosnia, to South Africa, to Pakistan, to Ireland. In the process, he makes a number of pertinent observations about the emergence of nations over the course of the century. At the same time, he poses difficult questions regarding the future of many nations that have come under increasing pressure from such global forces as multinational corporations; international financial institutions, including the World Bank and International Monetary Fund; and environmental concerns that transcend national boundaries.

Vaclav Havel, the president of the Czech Republic, raises many of the same issues in his highly personal *Summer Meditations.* In the portion excerpted here, Havel discusses the importance of politics and morality, two concepts many would view as mutually exclusive. Havel argues that democracies seeking to uphold human rights must be both moral and civil. Like Soyinka, he realizes that recent history has demonstrated the fragility of democratic governments and the protection of human rights. However, Havel, like many others around the globe, remains cautiously optimistic about the future.

READING 21.2A: THE CRISIS OF NATIONALISM IN THE POST–COLD WAR WORLD

I am obliged to concede that the overall tenor of my remarks could be easily construed as a requiem for what we know as the nation of Nigeria, so let me caution at the beginning that this is not my intention. The chain of political crises in Nigeria is, however, tied, recognizably, to the goal of evolving into a nation, and it is therefore unavoidable that we examine, in the light of such perennial crises, just how valid are the definitions of nationhood in the first place, and whose definitions these are, both in the conception and in the physical manifestation of the concept itself. This prompts a re-examination, at the very least, of the process of nationhood itself and its fortunes in contemporary experience. . . .

Whatever outlandish or original solutions do suggest themselves, we are thrown back on one question. It has become lately insistent, and not merely for our continent but in the global search for stability within what passes for national boundaries, and, indeed, for ensuring civilized relationships and security in daily transactions between neighbors. That question is: *When is a nation?* The question could be phrased in several other ways: For instance, what price a nation? Half a million lives lost in brutish termination, within the cheap span of a mere month, and for no discernable purpose but vengeance, a vengeance that is also opportunistic, since it harbors the undeclared goal of creating a Rwandan "nation" of pure Hutu [an African ethnic group] breed? What mores define a nation? Or indeed, what yardsticks? What does the claim "I belong to this nation" mean to the individual, and when did it begin to mean anything? For instance, to the Ewe [ethnic group] split between Ghana and Togo? Or the Albanians within the former Yugoslavian borders? These are unavoidable details of the terms in which I have posed the question, a

Soyinka, Wole. *The Open Sore of a Continent: A Personal Narrative of the Nigerian Crisis.* New York: Oxford University Press, 1996, pp. 18–25 passim.

version that is meant to be summative. When, and this is what is demanded, when are all the conditions present that make a nation? Can they be upheld by objective tests? Or is a nation simply a condition of the collective mind? Or will? A coerced state, the objective manifestation of an individual will? A passive, unquestioned habit of cohabitation? Or a rigorous conclusion that derives from history?

We must not even shy away from the possibility that a nation is a mere sentimental concept, unfounded in any practical advantages for its occupants. Or that the only hard fact that confers the status of nationhood on any human collectivity is its right to issue passports. We could simplify the issue and restrict ourselves to contemporary times, employing the club membership of the United Nations; when that organization chooses to admit you into its fold, does that unequivocally confer on you the status of nationhood? But what then of apartheid South Africa; did it cease to be a nation when it was expelled from the United Nations? The Boers would have a word or two to contribute in that context, guaranteed to be irreconcilable with the position of the oppressed black majority. Nationhood then may prove itself to be more complicated than the actualized sovereignty of any human grouping, not necessarily homogenous, for when, as in that last example, a distinctive minority exercises state power, controls national assets including choice lands that exclude but are contested by the majority, we find that we cannot totally evade the subjective actuality of nation being. An apt description of such actualities would be that of two human torsos in uneasy cohabitation within the same shirt. Even when such a phenomenon appears to be an "act of nature," as in Siamese twins, we know that the corrective ingenuity of the surgeon is often summoned as the arbiter of such a "natural" abnormality. What then shall we say of seeming abnormalities that are the product of human disingenousness, of adventurism? That they are immutable once fashioned into nation being or addressed as such? . . .

Even geographical coherence, within any arbitrarily elected measure of contemporaneity, does not appear to offer any certitudes. First there was India, and it included present-day Pakistan, uncomfortably sliced in half by what remained of India after Pakistan went its independent way. Before splitting up in turn into present-day Pakistan and Bangladesh, Pakistan, despite being thrust apart by the landmass of India, appeared to consider herself and be accepted by others as one nation—East and West Pakistan. For that duration at least, the factor of geographical separation did not noticeably vitiate the claims of a single national entity. Fortunately we need not journey from the African continent to find our examples: Various unions have attempted to redefine their nation being on that landmass—the Ghana-Guinea-Mali Union, the even shorter-lived United Arab Republic of Libya and Egypt, or the more recently abrogated semi-union between Senegal and Gambia.

Nation making from the top (what I earlier referred to as the objective manifestation of the will of one individual or a handful of individuals) never does, however, appear to have much staying power: witness the sanguinary face-off between North and South Yemen in recent times. Plebiscites—genuine plebiscites, that is—appear to stand a better chance. We had an instructive experience of it in our history when a slice of eastern Nigeria decided to go with Cameroon. That section is still very much part of the Cameroon, whatever second thoughts the population might have had, periodically, about that decision. Today, however, I suspect that one serious look at the condition of the Nigerian nation would persuade them that they were indeed wise and fortunate to have sought their fortune elsewhere. . . .

The lesson we are obliged to extract from the contrast outlined between nation stitching from the top and its evolution from the base—that is, the latter as an expression of the will or habit and usage of peoples, even if imperfectly educed—is that the latter might provide us one of the clues to our central question, When is a nation? Could one of the conditions in resolving this sometimes emotive issue be the articulated or demonstrable decision by the polity that actually makes up the nation? I propose that we keep this possibility in mind as we go forward, which imposes on us a readiness to consider that invocation of the absence of such a stamp of accord throws any nation claim back into question, if only on the theoretical level. Whether we prefer to wait for the lurking Rwandas on the continent to materialize in the absence of such an accord is another matter altogether; until the explosion, we are at liberty to continue to take the European imperial will as the final arbiter in such matters of death and destruction. If we choose to confront reality, however, then I do suggest that many nations on the African continent are only in a state of limbo, that they exist in a halfway space of purgatory until, by mundane processes or through dramatic events, their citizens are enabled to raise the nation reality to a higher level, then even higher still, until it attains a status of irreversibility— either as paradise or hell.

There are of course many ways of arriving at a just answer to our basic question; indeed, a nation accord is not one that necessarily comes about by any formal or structured process, such as a plebiscite. A political entity that, for an appreciable period, has saluted a common flag, adopted a common anthem, a motto, or a common pledge for ceremonial or instructional occasions, a polity that uniformly loses its collective sense of proportion when its football team goes to battle, fights a war or two as one entity, flaunts a common passport, and pools and distributes its economic resources by some form of consensus, even where such a system of distribution is periodically challenged—I repeat, one that has, for an appreciable length of time, managed its affairs within the context of these unifying virtues or irrationalities—such an entity may indeed be deemed a nation by obvious status quo. Its categorization as such is contested neither from within nor without, and this of course is true of most nations that we refer to as such today. No one questions the nation status of France, Sweden, Japan, Ghana, Zambia, or Portugal. When we take the question to Portugal's Iberian neighbor, Spain, we are held up by the violent veto of the Basque separatist movement, which continues to insist that the nation that we are conditioned to regard as one Spain is, for them, two nations—the Basque and the rest! Six decades of repression and/or blandishments in the name of unity have done nothing to mellow the Basque nationalist quest. Even Catalonia, whose language and culture were viciously repressed under General Francisco Franco, has only grudgingly, in recent times, accepted a less extreme relationship to mother Spain. Its language has, however, been resurrected, its literature flourishes in the once forbidden Catalan, just as any occasion is used to stress its distinct culture and nation origin.

As we seek to widen our examples, we find even more aggravating complications. Morocco, for instance: Is Morocco a nation? A decade or two ago, such a question would have sounded preposterous but since that nation made a grab for former Spanish Sahara, we now have to question where precisely lies the nation of Morocco. Clearly it cannot be that geographical space that includes the Saharouis region, contested by Polisario. And Turkey? The Kurds, with increasing militancy, question the nation space of that country. Indeed, the Kurds have inserted fissures in the nation claims not only of Turkey but of Iraq and Iran, just like the Armenians in the new nation-states of the former Soviet Union. This matter is far more serious, far more profoundly relevant to our quest. Not only do the Kurds battle for autonomous or semi-autonomous existence within these countries, they have gone back in their own history and reproclaimed themselves a nation. They demand that the world redress the historically acknowledged pogrom of their people and the erasure of their nation actuality from the map of the world. The Kurds perceive themselves already as a nation, even as the Palestinians have done for decades as they move closer to the actualization of a nation dream too long deferred.

We are entering, it must be apparent by now, the possibility—not of a discovery—but of the recovery of a certain historical truth: that nation status has never been an absolute or a constant, that it has ever followed the politics of conflict, interest, alliances, power, and even accident. We know how the Middle East oil states came to be, a fact that was not missed by Saddam Hussein when he embarked on his misadventure and claimed Kuwait as an integral province of Iraq. The Yemens, Saudi Arabia, Qatar, Jordan, et cetera: Are these truly nations? Or, put the question another way: Could it also be claimed that they were always nations, albeit by another name, defined by another concept that was first ridiculed, then rehabilitated—with some emendations, of course, under European imperialism? If you reexamine the various properties that we have listed as being germane to the definition of a state (and I use that word loosely) we may find that the so-called tribal kingdoms or clan principalities that were later supplanted by European imperialist arrangements do indeed qualify for nation status. Even to the extent of securing recognition for their passports, or letters of authority that amounted to passports, for what is a passport anyway but a request that ease of passage and protection be offered to the bearer, at the behest of some authority under whose suzerainty the bearer of that document belongs?

The erstwhile Union of Soviet Socialist Republics, under its Communist structure, played a most fascinating game with its nationalities. Within the United Nations, these various entities—Georgia, Russia, Uzbekistan, Siberia, and so forth—existed and were recognized as individual nations, an arrangement that awarded the Soviet Union a few more votes than, shall we say, the United States of America, which presented a single national front despite her fifty states. Within the Soviet Union, however, we do know that during the monolithic reigns of Lenin and Stalin "the natives were restless." Ruthless as was the repression of nationalist claims, concessions had to be made from time to time to such stirrings, especially in the matter of culture and language. . . .

On our part, it is sufficient to state—not even to explain but simply to declare—our preference for continuing as one nation. And we must ground such a preference in self-interest, the common denominator, the common tangibly identifiable factor that governs the many choices that are agreed upon by society. We can then proceed to map out a strategy for removing all obstacles toward the realization of that common goal, the choice of remaining one, that we have acknowledged as the least problematic structure for guaranteeing our various areas of self-interest. But we must also not neglect to decide the precise nature of the *problématique:* That is, are we trying to keep Nigeria a nation? Or are we trying to make it one? The difference is crucial. It outlines the magnitude of the task and qualifies the methodology to be adopted. It returns us again and again to our commencing question:

When *is* a nation?

READING 21.2B: BUILDING DEMOCRACY IN THE POST–COLD WAR ERA

The return of freedom to a society that was morally unhinged has produced something it clearly had to produce, and something we therefore might have expected, but which has turned out to be far more serious than anyone could have predicted: an enormous and dazzling explosion of every imaginable human vice. A wide range of questionable or at least morally ambiguous human tendencies, subtly encouraged over the years and, at the same time, subtly pressed to serve the daily operation of the totalitarian system, have suddenly been liberated, as it were, from their straitjacket and given freedom at last. The authoritarian regime imposed a certain order—if that is the right expression for it— on these vices (and in doing so "legitimized" them, in a sense). This order has now been shattered, but a new order that would limit rather than exploit these vices, an order based on freely accepted responsibility to and for the whole of society, has not yet been built— nor could it have been, for such an order takes years to develop and cultivate.

Thus we are witnesses to a bizarre state of affairs: society has freed itself, true, but in some ways it behaves worse than when it was in chains. Criminality has grown rapidly, and the familiar sewage that in times of historical reversal always wells up from the nether regions of the collective psyche has overflowed into the mass media, especially the gutter press. But there are other, more serious and dangerous symptoms: hatred among nationalities, suspicion, racism, even signs of Fascism; politicking, an unrestrained, unheeding struggle for purely particular interests, unadulterated ambition, fanaticism of every conceivable kind, new and unprecedented varieties of robbery, the rise of different mafias; and a prevailing lack of tolerance, understanding, taste, moderation, and reason. There is a new attraction to ideologies, too—as if Marxism had left behind it a great, disturbing void that had to be filled at any cost. . . .

Demagogy is rife, and even something as important as the natural longing of a people for autonomy is exploited in power plays, as rivals compete in lying to the public. Many members of the party elite, the so-called *nomenklatura* [Communist party bureaucrats] who, until very recently, were faking concern about social justice and the working class, have cast aside their masks and, almost overnight, openly become speculators and thieves. Many a once-feared Communist is now an unscrupulous capitalist, shamelessly and unequivocally laughing in the face of the same worker whose interests he once allegedly defended.

Citizens are becoming more and more disgusted with all this, and their disgust is understandably directed against the democratic government they themselves elected.

Havel, Vaclav. *Summer Meditations.* Trans. Paul Wilson. New York: Alfred A. Knopf, 1992, pp. 1–3, 18–19.

Vaclav Havel (center) and Alexander Dubcek (left), two noted Czechoslovakian nationalists, celebrated the end of Soviet domination over eastern Europe in 1989. Havel, a well-known author and dissident, was elected president of Czechoslovakia, but he was unable to prevent the division of the country along ethnic lines into Slovakia and the Czech republic. Reuters/Petar Kujundizc/Archive Photos.

Making the most of this situation, some characters with suspicious backgrounds have been gaining popular favour with ideas such as, for instance, the need to throw the entire government into the Vltava River.

And yet, if a handful of friends and I were able to bang our heads against the wall for years by speaking the truth about Communist totalitarianism while surrounded by an ocean of apathy, there is no reason why I shouldn't go on banging my head against the wall by speaking *ad nauseam,* despite the condescending smiles, about responsibility and morality in the face of our present social marasmus. There is no reason to think that this struggle is a lost cause. The only lost cause is one we give up on before we enter the struggle. . . .

I do not see, however, why a democratic state, armed with a legislature and the power to draw up a budget, cannot strive for a certain fairness in, for example, pension policies or tax policies, or support to the unemployed, or salaries to public employees, or assistance to the elderly living alone, people who have health problems, or those who, for various reasons, find themselves at the bottom of society. Every civilized state attempts, in different ways and with different degrees of success, to come up with reasonable policies in these areas, and not even the most ardent supporters of the market economy have anything against it in principle. In the end, then, it is a conflict not of beliefs, but rather of terminology.

I am repeating these basic, self-evident, and rather general facts for the sake of completeness and order. But I would like to say more about other aspects of the state that may be somewhat less obvious and are certainly much less talked about, but are no less important—because they qualify and make possible everything that is considered self-evident.

I am convinced that we will never build a democratic state based on rule of law if we do not at the same time build a state that is—regardless of how unscientific this may sound to the ears of a political scientist—humane, moral, intellectual and spiritual, and cultural. The best laws and the best-conceived democratic mechanisms will not in themselves guarantee legality or freedom or human rights—anything, in short, for which they were intended—if they are not underpinned by certain human and social values. What good, for instance, would a law be if no one respected it, no one defended it, and no one tried responsibly to follow it? It would be nothing but a scrap of paper. What use would elections be in which the voter's only choice was between a greater and a lesser scoundrel? What use would a wide variety of political parties be if not one of them had the general interest of society at heart?

No state—that is, no constitutional, legal, and political system—is anything in and of itself, outside historical time and social space. It is not the clever technical invention of a team of experts, like a computer or a telephone. Every state, on the contrary, grows out of specific intellectual, spiritual, and cultural traditions that breathe substance into it and give it meaning.

So we are back to the same point: without commonly shared and widely entrenched moral values and obligations, neither the law, nor democratic government, nor even the market economy will function properly. They are all marvellous products of the human spirit, mechanisms that can, in turn, serve the spirit magnificently—assuming that the human spirit wants these mechanisms to serve it, respects them, believes in them, guarantees them, understands their meaning, and is willing, if necessary, to fight for them or make sacrifices for them. . . .

In the somewhat chaotic provisional activity around the technical aspects of building the state, it will do us no harm occasionally to remind ourselves of the meaning of the state, which is, and must remain, truly human—which means it must be intellectual, spiritual, and moral.

DISCUSSION QUESTION

Using the readings as a basis, discuss what problems and challenges face societies as this century draws to a close.